D1389251

RUPERT HART-DAVIS
Man of Letters

PHILIP ZIEGLER

RUPERT HART-DAVIS
Man of Letters

Chatto & Windus
LONDON

Published by Chatto & Windus 2004

2 4 6 8 10 9 7 5 3 1

Copyright © Philip Ziegler 2004

Philip Ziegler has asserted his right under the Copyright, Designs
and Patents Act 1988 to be identified as the author of this work

First published in Great Britain in 2004 by
Chatto & Windus
Random House, 20 Vauxhall Bridge Road,
London SW1V 2SA

Random House Australia (Pty) Limited
20 Alfred Street, Milsons Point, Sydney,
New South Wales 2061, Australia

Random House New Zealand Limited
18 Poland Road, Glenfield,
Auckland 10, New Zealand

Random House (Pty) Limited
Endulini, 5A Jubilee Road, Parktown 2193, South Africa

The Random House Group Limited Reg. 954009
www.randomhouse.co.uk

A CIP catalogue record for this book
is available from the British Library

ISBN 0 7011 7320 3

Papers used by Random House are natural
recyclable products made from wood grown in sustainable forests;
the manufacturing processes conform to the environmental
regulations of the country of origin

Typeset by Deltatype Ltd, Birkenhead, Merseyside
Printed in Great Britain by
Clays Ltd, St Ives plc

Contents

	List of Illustrations	vii
	Acknowledgments	ix
	Table of Comparative Values	xi
Chapter One	Birth of a Bookman	1
Chapter Two	Shades of Eton	16
Chapter Three	Balliol Man	31
Chapter Four	*Per Ardua*	43
Chapter Five	Two Moons	57
Chapter Six	Tyro Publisher	71
Chapter Seven	Jonathan Cape's	88
Chapter Eight	Soldier of the King	104
Chapter Nine	Part-time Publisher	117
Chapter Ten	A Firm is Born	130
Chapter Eleven	Ruth	144
Chapter Twelve	Shipwreck	160
Chapter Thirteen	Back to Heinemann's	180
Chapter Fourteen	False Dawn	200
Chapter Fifteen	A New Life	213
Chapter Sixteen	Triumph and Tragedy	225
Chapter Seventeen	Life Renewed	241
Chapter Eighteen	Halfway to Heaven	263
Chapter Nineteen	Dying Fall	280
	Books written or edited by Rupert Hart-Davis	296
	Note on Manuscript Sources	297
	Notes	299
	Index	321

List of Illustrations

1a Richard Hart-Davis
1b Sibbie Hart-Davis and Gervase Beckett

2   Sibbie with her children

3a Rupert drawn by Augustus John
3b Deirdre Hart-Davis in 1920
3c Rupert with his mother

4   Rupert in *King Henry V*

5a Celia Johnson
5b Peggy Ashcroft
5c Peggy and Rupert

6a Edward Garnett
6b Jamie Hamilton
6c Jonathan Cape

7a Rupert and Edmund Blunden
7b Watching cricket

8   Rupert and Comfort on their honeymoon

9   Rupert and Duff Hart-Davis

10 Hugh Walpole, Comfort and Rupert

11a Guardsman recruit
11b Adjutant
11c The family reunited

12a Rupert, Ruth Simon and Leon Edel
12b Osbert Lancaster's Christmas card of 36 Soho Square

12c Richard Garnett

13   Ruth Simon

14a Rupert and June in 1968
14b Rupert, Boyk Severs and Joyce Grenfell

15a Kisdon Lodge
15b The Old Rectory, Marske

16a The seventieth birthday party
16b Rupert in his study

Acknowledgments

Rupert Hart-Davis's elder son, Duff, suggested that I should write this biography and to him therefore must go the first acknowledgment. He and Rupert's widow June not merely provided a mass of indispensable manuscript material but were endlessly helpful and encouraging through the years taken by the writing of this book.

Rupert's other children, Bridget Silsoe and Adam Hart-Davis, were equally co-operative, as were his nieces, Susan Balfour, Annabel Rathbone and Lucy Bland. His cousin John Julius Norwich kindly gave me access to the diaries of his father, Duff Cooper, and to the correspondence between Rupert and Duff and Diana Cooper.

Richard Garnett, with his unrivalled knowledge of the affairs of Rupert Hart-Davis Ltd, gave me invaluable help and showed both generosity and much patience. The three articles that he wrote on the subject for the *Book Collector* provided a bible for my work on that part of Rupert's life. He has compounded his kindness, as has another former member of Rupert's staff, James Chesterman, by reading this book in typescript.

I am most grateful to all those who have showed me papers or spared the time to talk or offer advice. I must beg the forgiveness of anyone whom I have failed to mention but I owe much to: Verily Anderson; Joan Astley; The Right Rev. Jonathan Bailey; Nicolas Barker; Professor John Bayley; the late Sir Martyn Beckett; John Bell; Viscountess Boyd of Merton; Paul Chipchase; Hon. Mrs Annabel Chisholm; Lady Mary Clive; Robert Cross; Laura Duguid; Viscount Eccles; Owen Dudley Edwards; Lord Egremont; Lucy Fleming; the late Diana Gamble; Jane Gardam; Victoria Glendinning; Jill Goodman; Hon. Mrs Kate Grimond; John Gross; Janie Hampton; Lavinia Hankinson; Lady Selina Hastings; Lady Hodgkin; Merlin Holland; Michael Holroyd; Diana Viscountess Hood; Jacqueline Hone; Roger Hudson; David Hughes;

Lady Susan Hussey; Lord Hutchinson of Lullington; Anne Kindersley; Richard Kingzett; Brendan Lehane; Andrew Linklater; Magnus Link-later; Ernest and Joy Mehew; Brian Miller; John and Virginia Murray; Rita Pinnekamp-Pooley; the late Violet Powell; George Ramsden; Professor Andrew Roberts; Christopher Sinclair-Stevenson; Peter Stuart-Heaton; Harry Townshend; Guido Waldman; the late Edward Young.

Those who work in libraries are almost universally both helpful and omniscient. I acknowledge with many thanks Dr John Jones, Dean and Archivist of Balliol College, Oxford; Clare Brown of the Special Collections in the Bodleian Library; Megan Humphries of the University Library at Bristol; Kathleen Cann of the Cambridge University Library; Louise King of the Churchill Archives Centre at Churchill College, Cambridge; Andrew Gray of the University Library in Durham; Margaret Weare of the Ellen Terry Memorial Museum; Dr Rosalind Moad of King's College Library, Cambridge; Karen Davies, Archivist of Lucy Cavendish College, Cambridge; Malcolm Davis of the Brotherton Library at Leeds University; Dr Stella Butler of the John Rylands Library at the University of Manchester; Michael Bott of the University of Reading Library; Dr Iain Brown of the National Library of Scotland; Lesley Price of the Archives Division of SOAS Library; Dorothy Sheridan of the University of Sussex Library; Stuart Ó Seanóir of Trinity College Library, Dublin, and Arwel Jones of the National Library of Wales.

In the United States I received much help from Lori Curtis of the McFarlin Library of the University of Tulsa and Tara Wenger of the Harry Ransom Humanities Research Center at the University of Texas at Austin. My stay in America was made immeasurably more agreeable by the kindness of my friends Professor Philip Bobbitt, Professor Roger and Dagmar Louis, Jim and Sese McElwain, and Harry and Joan Seay.

Since he has, alas, elected most prematurely to retire, this is the last time that I will have cause to thank my agent, Michael Shaw. I would be distraught if I thought the same was likely to happen to my editor, Penelope Hoare, whose creative skills and eye for detail have been of inestimable value to me over the last years.

To my wife, as always, the greatest debt is owed.

Table of Comparative Values

The pound sterling was decimalised in 1969; previously it had been divided into 20 shillings (20s.) and 240 pence (240d.). A shilling, which comprised 12 pence, was written 1/–; one and a half shillings would have appeared as 1/6d. The main units in the old currency, with their equivalents in new pence, were:

1 farthing ($\frac{1}{4}d$.)	just over 0.1 of a new penny
1 halfpenny ($\frac{1}{2}d$.)	just over 0.2 of a new penny
1 penny (1d.)	just over 0.4 of a new penny
Sixpence (6d.)	$2\frac{1}{2}$ new pence
1 shilling (1/–)	5 new pence
Half a crown (2/6d.)	$12\frac{1}{2}$ new pence (a crown had been worth five shillings, hence the name)

Comparisons between the purchasing powers of the pound at different periods are notoriously misleading and calculations are further complicated by the fact that the period between the two world wars was one of deflation, the pound in 1939 buying significantly more than it had in 1918. As a rough and ready guide, however, one would not be too grossly misled if one assumed that between 1918 and 1939 the pound bought approximately 25 times what it would today. By the end of the war the figure was nearer 20. Between 1945 and 1965 it was halved in value and dramatic inflation continued until 1980, when the pace slackened and the pound drifted down by an average 5 per cent or so per annum to its present level.

Chapter One

Birth of a Bookman

Rupert Hart-Davis hated his father and was in love with his mother; circumstances no doubt reassuringly familiar to the psychologist but calculated to inspire caution in even the most intrepid of biographers.

In the first volume of his memoirs[*] Rupert devoted eleven pages to his mother's family while dismissing his father's antecedents in a few lines. Sybil Hart-Davis's ancestors were certainly more extravagant. Her mother, Lady Agnes Duff, was descended from King William IV out of his long, fruitful but unconsecrated relationship with the actress Mrs Jordan. Lady Agnes, when eighteen, eloped with the raffish Viscount Dupplin and then compounded her iniquities by running away a second time with Herbert Flower, a man of many qualities but a younger son and accordingly impecunious. Divorce from Dupplin quickly followed, and when Flower died at the age of twenty-seven he left his young wife short of money and ostracised by a disapproving society. From this plight she was rescued by Alfred Cooper, a distinguished surgeon who specialised in sexual diseases. He enjoyed a fashionable practice in London and the news that 'Cooper's clap-trap' had been spotted outside some great house would give rise to much ribald speculation in the clubs. Sybil (Sibbie) was the second surviving child of this marriage; her younger brother Duff was born three years later.

Compared with all this, the Hart-Davises were a humdrum lot. The Davises were small squires in Monmouthshire, one of whom in the early eighteenth century married a rich Miss Hart. This access of fortune brought a double-barrelled name and, in due course, a seat in Parliament. The family flourished briefly but Vaughan Hart-Davis, also a Member of Parliament, squandered most of the money and his son throve only to the extent of becoming a major in the Royal Engineers.

[*] *The Arms of Time*, London, 1979.

He was a kindly, patient, talented man who painted and carved with some skill but lacked more worldly ambitions. His patience was needed, for his wife suffered from acute digestive problems, survived on a diet of patent medicines and charcoal biscuits and got her own back on all around her by displays of peevish disaffection. Their son Richard, who was to marry Sibbie Cooper, inherited some at least of his mother's rancorous disposition, though without her excuse of ill health.

Richard Hart-Davis was a stockbroker with the firm of Panmure Gordon. He enjoyed making money and was reasonably good at it, ending up as senior partner; but his true passion was music. As a young man he trained in Leipzig with a view to becoming a professional pianist; he would never have achieved greatness and soon abandoned music as a career but he continued to play at a high amateur level. His tastes were circumscribed – he believed that the age of serious composition ended with Beethoven – but he got immense pleasure from performing and listening to music throughout his life. There his artistic interests ended: he never looked at a picture, rarely read a book, by preference would spend his evenings drinking and playing cards in his club. What most people remembered about him was his violent temper. His brother-in-law Duff Cooper recalled how when they went to 'a quite good farce' whilst together in Paris, Richard for some reason took against it 'and swore all the time'.[1] Once he lost control when a train ran an hour and a half late because of the fog and showed his indignation by smashing the glass over the map on the carriage wall.[2] He was 'full of hatred of everything', remarked Duff,[3] and self-pity spiced with resentment of anyone who was more fortunate than he was seems to have been his habitual state of mind. Yet in spite of this Duff liked him and enjoyed his company. So did many others. Susan Tweedsmuir for one thought him charming, 'so easy to talk to and so amusing and light-hearted'.[4] He sometimes showed a dry and self-deprecating humour. During a lunch at Panmure Gordon's the bell of a nearby church began to toll. 'I wonder who that's for,' said Richard. 'It can't be me, or my secretary would have told me.'

According to Rupert, his parents met at a house-party. Sibbie Cooper was only just seventeen. Richard Hart-Davis seduced her, and then discovered to his mild consternation that what for him had been an entertaining diversion, for her was a grand passion. Sibbie, romantic, impetuous and alarmingly ignorant of the facts of life, took it for granted that her encounter must lead to pregnancy – which, in the event, it did not – and that the next step must be marriage – a possibility which had not occurred to Richard but which he accepted with reasonably good grace. A certain amount of parental opposition was quickly overcome and the couple married on 19 January 1904.

The full extent of their incompatibility quickly became evident. Music was about the only form of art in which Sibbie took no interest. Intellectually she was turbulent, bursting with inchoate ambitions, restlessly seeking short cuts to wisdom and learning. She was forever adopting new fields of study: philosophy, classical Greek, theology, a translation of the Abbé Dimnet's new book on the Brontë sisters. Her eager intelligence led her quickly through the foothills of each new intellectual mountain range, yet time and again she faltered when the going got rougher and success had to be more hardly earned. 'I want to be more profound,' she wrote in her diary. It was an aspiration that was never fulfilled. Always her stamina betrayed her. She went to hear W. B. Yeats lecture with Bernard Shaw in the chair. She knew that the occasion must be a momentous one, but somehow attention faltered – 'If one could absolutely concentrate one's thoughts on one thing for even a few minutes . . .' she commented wistfully. She couldn't even keep her diary for more than a few weeks or sometimes only days at a time, 'which is after all somewhat symbolical of myself – hard and fast rules made and never kept'. Time and again she made new resolutions, time and again she failed to observe them and bitterly reproached herself for her frailty: 'Child, girl, woman grow ashamed! *What* a wasted day! Idle morning, nothing read, thought, understood. This must not continue a moment longer.'[5]

To Richard her aims seemed futile and her activities frivolous. He could not see the point of her intellectual quests. Why could she not concentrate on things that mattered, like providing a suitable home to which he could invite important friends or working the drawing-rooms 'of London in the interests of social advancement? He never wholly lost an irritated affection for his wife, but once the first charm had worn off he realised that each of them had made a disastrous mistake. Sibbie must have been a maddening wife for a striving businessman: casual, irreverent, inconsequential.

To those who saw her less frequently or felt more sympathy for her aspirations, she was irresistible. 'There is absolutely nothing in the world I can do the least bit well,' she admitted, 'yet what is rather pathetic, is that I always in the back of my mind think I am rather a splendid person.'[6] Many people shared her view. 'She was exquisite, dreamy and generous,' wrote the Irish man of letters and eccentric

Shane Leslie, 'busy thinking little acts of practical phantasy to please and (of course) amuse her friends.' Nor was it only her multitude of male admirers who praised her; to Nancy Cunard she was 'My Liberator', the woman who more than anybody else had made her realise her potential as an individual. At first Nancy was impressed mainly by the panache, the style; then: 'I discovered the courage and spirit and all the sterling quality of her as well.'[7]

The newly married couple settled into a substantial house in a cul-de-sac at the bottom of Victoria Road in Kensington, an area now much sought after but then decidedly dowdy. They quickly discovered new grounds for feeling they were ill-suited to each other. Richard was well paid but not a rich man: Sibbie thought him cheese-paring and obsessed by money; he felt her to be a monster of extravagance. He expected her to keep accounts and explain the use made of every penny; she had no idea how her money had gone, and cared less. Money was there to be spent; if it was not there then it should be spent just the same; something would turn up to save the day. The unpunctuality, the untidiness, the ability to lose every ticket and misplace every address had to begin with seemed charming to Richard but became maddening when the first ardour faded. If Sibbie had indeed been pregnant before they married, or if she had managed to conceive a child within a few months of their wedding, it is possible that things might have gone differently. For some reason, however, this did not happen; and soon sexually they began to lose enthusiasm for each other. Always inclined to insomnia, Sibbie insisted on sleeping in a separate room; Richard, who soon reverted to old habits and took a string of mistresses, was happy to let her do so; the couple drifted apart.

Warm-hearted, impetuous, outstandingly attractive; it was inevitable that Sibbie should seek consolation outside her marriage. What was perhaps less inevitable was that she should have sought it in so many quarters. 'How many lovers can Mummy have had in 1906–1908?' Rupert asked his sister Deirdre despairingly, when considering the problem of his paternity. 'Any number, I suppose . . .'[8] Duff Cooper, Sibbie's brother, once asked her, after a bibulous lunch, who had fathered her children. She replied, with alarming frankness, that she had often wondered herself; there were several possible candidates. The one putative parent whom she does not seem even to have considered was her own husband. Presumably she had good grounds for ruling him out. External evidence supports her. Both physically and temperamentally

Richard and Rupert Hart-Davis were far apart: the first was dark and of medium height, the second fair and very tall; the first loved money and despised literature, the second attached little importance to riches but lived for books; the first valued music above all other pleasures, the second enjoyed a good tune when he heard it but neither had nor professed to have any serious interest in the subject.

Sibbie herself contended that the most likely father was Lionel Bulteel; Rupert met him once but dismissed the possibility on the grounds that he was even smaller than Richard Hart-Davis. The father whom Rupert himself favoured was Gervase Beckett, a cultivated Yorkshire banker whose love of reading and devotion to cricket seemed to make him a plausible candidate for the role. Beckett, Rupert found, 'was gay and amusing in company, but liked to get away from it all – a trait which has always been strong in my own nature'.[9] The clinching proof, in Rupert's eyes, came in 1961 when he was having a drink in the Garrick Club. Gervase Beckett's son, Martyn – whom Rupert had at that time never met – came into the room, saw Rupert in silhouette against the window, and exclaimed, 'By God, that's my father!' Physical likenesses are tricky things from which to establish a blood relationship. Martyn Beckett many years later admitted that he had not been quite as struck by the resemblance as Rupert's account of the event suggested but had felt that it would be churlish to contest the issue.[10] It is equally true that photographs of Richard Hart-Davis's sister, Madge Crum, make her look strikingly like her nephew.[11] The point will never be finally resolved and anyway was not one which seriously preoccupied Rupert. He never doubted his paternity until he was middle-aged and then saw the question as being one for entertaining speculation rather than anguish. What is certain is that Richard Hart-Davis, whatever his private suspicions, never in any way suggested openly that he believed his children not to be his own. To the outside world, Rupert was, and remained, his son.[*]

Rupert was born in Victoria Road at 6.15 a.m. on Wednesday 28 August 1907; his mother was still less than twenty-one years old. In not much over a year she was pregnant again. In spite of its six bedrooms the house in Victoria Road did not seem sufficiently spacious for parents who took it for granted that they would employ a nanny and nursery maid, a cook and butler, a housemaid and a lady's maid. They migrated

[*] And Rupert referred to himself as such; an example I have followed in this book.

across the park to Stanhope Street in Lancaster Gate, where they were to stay until the outbreak of the First World War. Sibbie's second child, Deirdre, was born there on 5 July 1909. Rupert had grown used to monopolising his mother's attention during his first two years – a task made more easy by her patent indifference to her husband – and resented the intrusion of this upstart. The next fifteen years were dominated by a largely unconscious competition between the two children for the greater share of their mother's affection.

Deirdre was a beautiful child who became a beautiful woman and quickly showed that she possessed her mother's charm, vivacity and intellectual curiosity. Though acclaimed as débutante of her year, she was not a beauty by classical standards; 'it is her eyes that lift her to heights of loveliness,' wrote a society journalist: 'they are the most exquisite violet, rarest of colours'.[12] Less charitably, some forty years later, Joyce Grenfell paid tribute to 'those beautiful lidded eyes that gaze dreamily into space,' but added: 'The problem is that she's a bit of a bore. She has a loud cackling laugh and when she starts talking it's like a torrent.'[13] Not many men would have endorsed that verdict; a great many fell in love with Deirdre and more than the usual number married her. As was true of her mother, her restless inconsequentiality could sometimes infuriate but her high spirits and sense of fun almost always repaired the damage. In extreme old age Rupert tried to encapsulate his feelings for her in 'a love letter, a feeble attempt to tell you how uninterruptedly I have loved you for about 87 years. I was two years old when you were born, and I loved you from the first moment as a lovely little sister, first as a toy and then as a companion.'

He overstated his initial affection; as small children the two were not particularly close and mildly resented each other's existence. When he went to boarding school, Rupert went on to tell his sister, 'I was rather jealous of you because you were always with our beloved mother.' Deirdre for her part was jealous of Rupert because 'I was the eldest, the favourite, the boy.'[14] Their relationship was not poisoned by this rivalry but was certainly impaired by it. She suspected, and with some reason, that her mother was slightly bored by her company and thought her preoccupation with her innumerable pets both juvenile and tedious. Deirdre accepted that Rupert was more intelligent and better educated but resented the way he exploited his advantage: 'Rupert was always asking me general knowledge questions to show up my ignorance, which was easy enough to do . . . We quarrelled a lot in the holidays in a silly, nagging way.'[15] She was left with a sense of inferiority and, still worse, of exclusion from an alliance between mother and son which was intense and totally absorbing. From birth, wrote Rupert of his mother, 'I became, and ever remained, the still centre of her somewhat unstable universe; she was certainly the whole extent of mine.'[16] To the casual observer Sibbie must have seemed much like any other upper-class English parent: taking long holidays away from her children; leaving their education to others; dealing with them only through a mesh of nannies and nursery maids. In fact she was fond of her daughter in a detached sort of way but obsessed by her son, lavishing on him the attentions of a passionate nature, the love of a woman who could find no satisfaction in her marriage and not enough in the frequent affairs with which she tried to fill her life.

'Blue eyes, fair hair, very jolly and good,' was the first description of Rupert in the baby book in which Sibbie recorded her son's progress. He was baptised when five weeks old – 'Baby was *so* good all the time'; his weight was noted at monthly intervals – he seems to have been a substantial child; he cut his first tooth at the proper time and without undue irritation for either him or his parents. The enthusiasm for the baby book waned; the spaces reserved for recording the first step and the first articulate word were left blank. But Sibbie's diary shows that her feelings for Rupert remained unabated. When he was three she took him for the first time to the zoo. Rupert, she wrote, was delighted by all he saw and never stopped talking, 'but I must stop thinking of him or else I shall be obliged to rush upstairs and kiss him which would wake him up and make great trouble'. Later in the same year he was a page at the wedding of Richard Hart-Davis's sister: 'wondrous good in white satin and buckle shoes', noted his doting mother. No doubt he relished the attention paid him and the chance to wear such outlandish garb; all his life he enjoyed dressing up, and, whatever role he was called on to play, would adopt the appropriate uniform with enthusiasm and panache.

After Sibbie's death Rupert's old nanny reminded him how she breast-fed her son at a time when this was relatively unusual and would break away from whatever dinner party she was attending to come home at feeding time: 'Nothing was too much trouble to give her son a good start in life.'[17] But she paid tribute also to Rupert's father: 'He too loved you both. No matter who was in the drawing room at night he always had to be told when you were ready for bed so that he could hear you lisp your evening prayer.' Richard Hart-Davis is almost entirely excluded from his son's memories of childhood; if he is referred to at all it is as an aloof curmudgeon who was rarely at home and whose absence enhanced the harmony of domestic life. No doubt there is some truth in this, but Rupert was viewing his parents' marriage very much through the eyes of his mother. Other sources suggest that Richard was genuinely fond of children and was generally well liked by them; he seems to have done his best to be a good father and was at least as attentive as most men of his class and generation. But the atmosphere in Stanhope Street was at the best cool, at the worst fiercely acrimonious; Rupert was painfully conscious of the fact that his mother was unhappy and that his father was in some way responsible; inevitably he took Sibbie's side.

The First World War, which meant that Richard was commissioned in the Royal Fusiliers and was rarely at home, did something to ease the tensions within the family but nothing to bring Sibbie and her husband closer together. She and her children spent an itinerant war, sometimes staying with relations in different parts of the country, sometimes camping out in hotels or boarding houses. Money was always short and providing Rupert and Deirdre with suitable food, clothing and accommodation was a constant worry, but Sibbie did not allow such preoccupations to distract her from her retinue of lovers (an elastic term which did not necessarily imply anything very strenuous in the way of physical relationship). For a time Augustus John played a large part in her life; he certainly encouraged her to drink too much and it would have been unlike him to make do with a platonic friendship but there is no evidence that anything very passionate or enduring was involved. Duff Cooper was once lunching at the Savoy when John came in with Sibbie. 'They both looked dirty, drunken and decadent beyond words,' he noted severely in his diary. 'I was ashamed of her.'[18] Wyndham Lewis, the artist and writer, was another of her admirers from the more rarefied reaches of Bohemia. Sibbie wrote to him after an ecstatic evening: 'Darling, how happy we were – Roses, roses all the way . . . You were so perfect all the time.' Perfection did not endure; within a few months she was denouncing him as 'a fiend . . . sent from Hell's lower intestine to plague me'.[19]

The most serious and long-lasting of her lovers was Sidney Herbert, a dashing and eminently good-natured Conservative Member of Parliament who was five years her junior. This was the only one of her affairs which seriously threatened her marriage. To the dismay of Duff Cooper, a close friend of Herbert's but preoccupied above all with averting a scandal in the family, Sibbie insisted on telling her husband what was going on. Richard responded with dignity and some generosity: 'I only wish with all my heart that you were married to someone who would be a better husband to you and make you happier.' He offered a separation but pointed out that this would make necessary some decisions about the custody of the children: 'The most normal thing would be of course for me to have Rupert and you Weedy [Deirdre] – but I feel sure you would never consent to that.'[20] He was right. Sibbie had never contemplated the possibility of losing control of the children or considered the implications of the break-up of her marriage. She was flung into a frenzy of indecision. She sought a reconciliation with her husband, regretted it as soon as it was achieved, renounced Sidney Herbert, promptly reclaimed him, then announced that she was leaving her lover for ever. She took refuge in Duff's rooms, drank a bottle of brandy and made a singularly ineffective attempt to stab herself with a small jack-knife. Duff, who disliked any sort of messiness and felt that love affairs should be properly regulated and not allowed to disturb the even tenor of society, became disenchanted with his sister. 'She has a strange paralysing effect on me,' he wrote, 'making me bored and uncomfortable,' and then again, 'she was so on my nerves that it became an obsession.' He never ceased to love her and to support her loyally, but there were moments at which he would have wished her anywhere but in his life.[21]

In the end the marriage was patched up, though it gave little satisfaction to either party. 'Richard vile and sullen,' wrote Nancy Cunard after dining with the Hart-Davises. 'What an appalling life there.'[22] 'Daddy very morose and gloomy,' reported Rupert after another such occasion.[23] Duff wrote hopefully that the reconciliation was proving a miraculous success and that Sibbie was 'quite happy now and fond of him', but he deluded himself. Both parents did their best to make sure that the poisoned atmosphere at home did not affect the children; but their best never had any hope of being good enough. 'There was always this black cloud hanging over us of her unhappiness and her hopelessly bad relationship with Dick,'[24] Deirdre remembered. Rupert was still more intimately involved and found the pressure almost unendurable. His passionate commitment to his mother ensured that he made no attempt to see his father's point of view but in every case cast him as the villain and Sibbie as the innocent victim. He found it increasingly difficult even to be moderately polite to Richard. Sibbie found herself in the invidious and slightly absurd position of trying to keep the peace between the two. 'Darlingest,' Sibbie wrote to Rupert, 'I could not sleep last night . . . I felt worried and unhappy about you.' Richard was indignant because Rupert had failed to write to thank him for a gift of money; 'He thought I spoil you so, and that your manners have got so bad of late – ungenerous and careless. He is afraid that you do not care for him.'[25] His fears were fully justified. On this occasion Rupert accepted the rebuke and wrote an apologetic letter but the contrition was only half-hearted and often was not shown at all. 'Long before I had heard of Oedipus,' Rupert wrote many years later, 'I would gladly have murdered my father and married my mother.'[26] Neither course of action proved practicable, but even as a child of seven or eight he brooded over his father's insensitivity and dreamed of a family life from which he had been miraculously removed.

Rupert survived remarkably well a childhood that might have embittered him for life. His resentment of his father did not spill over into his feelings for other people, nor did his absorption with his mother prevent him forming strong bonds elsewhere. He was warm-hearted and friendly. Duff Cooper lunched with Sibbie in 1917 and noted with disapproval that Rupert was 'a tiresome, spoilt little boy', but this was the last word of criticism he ever launched against his nephew. Only a few months later Rupert was judged to be 'a nice little boy',[27] and this was an opinion that was never to be revised. For Duff, Rupert was not merely personable and well mannered but had the all-important attribute of loving books. 'Rupert is just like his Uncle Duff,' Diana Cooper was to observe approvingly. 'Put him in a comfortable chair with a good book and he's no trouble.'[28] Let the chair be uncomfortable or even let there be no chair at all and the result would have been little different. Duff encouraged him by offering a pound if he would learn to recite Macaulay's 'Horatius' (a generous bribe for a boy of eleven or twelve, worth some £25 at current prices*); he accepted the challenge with relish and in the next six years learnt more than a hundred poems by heart. His early reading was not notably sophisticated; like any self-respecting ten year old of the period he devoured the *Gem* and the *Magnet* and any adventure story that came along, but he rapidly reached the conclusion that reading was neither a pastime nor a duty but a necessity of life; one read, as one breathed or ate, because otherwise existence would become impossible.

Voracious readers are rarely successful schoolboys, if to be successful

---

*See page xi for a Table of Comparative Values.

as a schoolboy is to be popular and renowned among one's contemporaries. Rupert was too easy-going, too amiable, physically too large, to be an appropriate target for the bullies, but equally he was not cut out to be a hero. He went to his first boarding school when still only nine years old. Seal House at Selsey-on-Sea, run by two spinster sisters, was hardly a threatening environment, but he found the sudden exile from home and the separation from his mother acutely painful. 'Took little Rupert to school, felt very sad when I got back after leaving him,' noted Sibbie.[29] It is probable that little Rupert felt at least as sad. He maintained a decorously stiff upper lip while at school but broke down when reunited with his mother, disrupting a smart weekend party by throwing himself hysterically into her arms. He never forgot the pains of leaving home. Many years later he was lunching with the actor Eric Portman in the restaurant at Waterloo Station. It was the beginning of term and the concourse was full of little boys creeping like snails unwillingly to school. 'My heart went out to them in sympathy,' Rupert wrote in his diary. 'I can remember so well the real agony of it.'[30]

Seal House was only a preparation for the serious business of schooling. After a year there he went on to Stanmore, a preparatory school which sent most of its boys to nearby Harrow. Stanmore occupied a large but unpretentious eighteenth-century stately home, since demolished, in what was then relatively open country but is now Middlesex suburbia. In good times it was a well-run and thriving establishment but in 1917 most of the younger masters were away at the war or already dead, their replacements sometimes excellent but more often well past their prime. The food was appalling, even by the standards of war-time diet. Twice a week, Rupert dolefully recorded, the boys were confronted by 'a tepid, orange-coloured mess of curried lentils'.[31] Rupert, already tall for his age and growing fast, found what was on offer inadequate for his needs; his mother supplemented it with 'two sections of honey and pots of strawberry, raspberry, gooseberry and blackcurrant jam'. Within a few weeks the plea went out for more. Even with such support, however, his health was never strong: he suffered from all the traditional childhood ailments but usually in an aggravated form. Since each time he began to recover his mother removed him from school for a week's convalescence at Brighton, his career at Stanmore was subject to frequent interruptions.

It was there, though, that he learnt to love cricket. He was never more than a competent player at village level but the intricacies of the game; the beauty of the surroundings in which it was often played; its

history, rituals and literature: all delighted him. It proved to be a
solitary exception in a life that otherwise inclined towards the sedentary.
'I loathe football, it is much too rough for me,' he told his mother;
tennis was more nearly tolerable but he abandoned it with some relief
when more interesting pursuits were on offer; golf, which his father
sometimes prevailed on him to play, bored and enraged him. He was
prepared to walk, though as a boy and young man this was more
probably done as a means of getting from one point to another than as a
form of exercise; he enjoyed bathing in the sea; rugger had its interest as
a spectator sport: but none of these – even cricket – could compare with
the satisfaction of sitting down with a good book. In his first term at
Stanmore he read *The Thirty-Nine Steps*; by the time he left he had
progressed to *Barnaby Rudge*. Among his holiday tasks were *The Jungle
Books*, *The Talisman* and *Ivanhoe*. The need to read a book and then to
pass a test on it has poisoned the pleasure that innumerable boys and
girls would otherwise have found in reading; it is a mark of his literary
stamina that Rupert took them in his stride and conceived an affection
for Kipling and Scott that never wavered throughout his life. Kipling
was a genius, he pronounced some fifty years later,[32] while he was still
re-reading Scott, with some judicious skipping, within a few months of
his death.

'Very good,' the headmaster appended dutifully to every report that
covered Rupert's four years at Stanmore, with occasional perfunctory
regrets that he had been so much absent through illness. 'Very good'
was in fact over-enthusiastic as a description of Rupert's first few terms;
he was a slow developer and was rarely placed among the leaders of his
class. Generally he did well at English and less well at Latin. 'He might
possibly show rather more "grit",' remarked one classics master, who
evidently felt his performance verged on the dilettante. Once he earned
the comment: 'A most promising mathematician' – an accolade
unexpected in that this arcane science was to baffle him throughout his
career. The praise was not repeated. In 1920 and 1921, when his time at
Stanmore was nearing its end, he came into his own. His judgment of
people and books became more nuanced and assured. 'A person called
Miss Bacon' lectured to the school about her adventures in balloons and
airships. 'It wasn't *extraordinarily* good,' Rupert reported, 'but not bad.'
He consistently came first or at least near the top in every subject and
finished his career in glory: 'Is making a capital Head Boy,' wrote the
headmaster. 'I shall miss him very much.' With success came greater
enjoyment: Rupert was homesick and lonely for his first few terms,

cautiously acquiescent in the period that followed, positively enjoying life in his final year. He made one close friend during his time at Stanmore: Wyndham Ketton-Cremer, the future squire of the great north Norfolk house of Felbrigg and as much a man of letters in the making as Rupert was himself. Ketton-Cremer went off with him to Eton; most of the other boys were destined for other schools – usually Harrow – and were lost to him for ever. An exception was Esmond Warner, son of Sir Pelham, one of England's most celebrated cricketing panjandrums, and himself to become prominent on London's literary scene. Neither common interests nor the bond of the old school tie proved sufficient to create a friendship. When Warner died in 1982 Rupert wrote uncharitably that he was 'relieved to know that there is no chance of running into him again in this world – or, pray Heaven, in the next. He was a horrid little boy at Stanmore and remained horrid to the end.'[33]

By now his family had installed itself in Halcot, a substantial Queen Anne house with later additions which stood in a hundred acres of woods, paddocks and gardens near the village of Bexley in Kent. Today it has been demolished to clear a path for a motorway and even in 1920 it was perilously close to urban life. 'There were two fields,' Deirdre recollected, 'and in the second one, if you sat in a certain spot, you couldn't see the gasworks and could pretend you were in deep countryside. The wood was beautiful until you came to the far side, where there were tramlines and the worrying thought of perhaps meeting one of the tramps or suchlike who left unattractive signs of having come in to relieve themselves.'[34]

When Rupert and Deirdre first visited Halcot it still belonged to Richard Hart-Davis's parents, with Richard's grandmother lingering on in an upstairs room, communicating only through a long black tube shaped like an elephant's trunk. Since every remark had to be bellowed into this device at least three times before there was any chance of it being heard, conversation was exhausting and the children visited their great-grandmother as rarely as possible. But in spite of this hazard they loved the house and rejoiced whenever it was time to go there. Even before the old Hart-Davises sold Halcot to their son, it had been the first real home that Rupert and Deirdre had known and to them it meant stability. Deirdre made it home too to a menagerie of dogs, rabbits, guinea pigs, mice, bantams and above all pigeons, which she bred successfully and sold by advertisements in the local paper. Rupert felt that to keep pets was in some way childish while to trade in them was to lose caste. He deplored Deirdre's somewhat unscrupulous business methods and was outraged when she sold as 'a beautiful young pair' a pigeon and its grandmother. This was dishonest, he protested. So, indeed, it was; his reluctance to indulge in insincere hyperbole survived his youth and in time became something of a handicap in his publishing career.

The servants were almost as numerous as Deirdre's pets: a cook, a footman, a lady's maid, an undermaid and a lugubrious butler called Blackler who eventually gave notice because he could put up no longer with the way Richard shouted at him. 'I've been with some irritable gentlemen in my time,' Blackler told Sibbie, 'but Mr Hart-Davis has got me beat.'[35] The house was said to be haunted. Richard told Duff in confidence that he believed Sibbie to be the medium responsible for the apparitions; she was always wandering in the garden and sometimes he thought he saw other people looking out of her eyes. 'When I heard this I wondered whether Richard was losing his sanity,' wrote Duff Cooper in his diary.[36] Rupert sometimes wondered the same thing, but more because of his father's uncontrollable temper than his transcendental fancies. He contrived to steer well clear of Richard during the school holidays, usually taking refuge in the library, a room which he felt confident his father would rarely visit. He began to catalogue the books and in so doing grew to appreciate the excitement of a first edition and the pleasure of possessing a complete set of an author's works. It was during these tranquil hours that he laid the foundations of his life as a compulsive book collector.

Sibbie had no such consolation. She was bored at Halcot and felt cut off, not only from her lovers but from everything that made life worthwhile. Only when Rupert was home for the holidays did she find country life tolerable. She bewailed her condition in letters to her son: 'I do wish I could get myself into better spirits. This sort of heavy depression is so dreadful and I can't shake it off much . . . Oh, if only we could get rid of Halcot.' 'You *are* beautiful *and* brilliant,' Rupert stoutly reassured her, 'and you are certainly adored by all and sundry. Your health will soon be right as right, when I take charge of you. It's no earthly use worrying about Halcot. I do love you so.'[37]

By the time he wrote this letter he had moved on from Stanmore to Eton. The headmaster of his preparatory school had decided that he was not scholarship material and that he should not subject himself to a test which he would almost certainly fail. Probably this was a mistake. Rupert was not much of a classicist, which would have disqualified him for one of the top scholarships, but he wrote well, had a retentive memory and quick wits and might well have scraped in among the lower places. If he had done so he would have gone to College, the part of the school reserved for scholars, where he would have mixed with boys who were intellectually more ambitious than their contemporaries in the average Oppidan house. It might have changed the pattern of his development. As it was he took remove, the highest level at which a new boy could enter. He left Stanmore in some triumph, as so often spending the last few days in the sanatorium where his mother found him 'looking very tall and white'. 'I wish him every success and happiness,' wrote the headmaster in his final report. 'He ought to do well.'[38]

Chapter Two

Shades of Eton

The traditional Etonian – a fantastical creature found more often in the mind of the cliché-ridden journalist than in the suburbs of Slough but still not wholly without a resemblance to the real thing – is a relaxed and languid figure. He disdains obvious effort, conceals ambition, and relies on charm and social connections to fill whatever gap there may be between his abilities and his pretensions. He provided a role model to which Rupert found it all too easy to conform. Rupert was relaxed almost to a fault, priding himself on his ability to put out of his mind any problem that did not call for immediate solution. He was, of course, not so free from worry as he sought to appear, but the carapace of calm was very thick. Some ten years later, in his sister's house, he spent an hour or two with an eminent psychologist who afterwards observed that Rupert was the least neurotic man he had ever met. 'I've always considered it the most complimentary remark that was ever made about me,' wrote Rupert proudly.[1] Ambition, in the sense of an urge to do better than others, meant little to him; he liked to do well but neither longed to be placed ahead of X and Y nor felt chagrin if X and Y finished ahead of him. He worked hard when the mood took him, but because he was interested in the subject rather than to get good marks; the affectation of idleness came easily to him because, in most or at least many fields of activity, he was, if not idle, then at least singularly lacking in energy. Many years later his wife reproached their ten-year-old son Adam with lolling around in the house when he could have been doing something vigorous outside. 'I'm a sitting-down sort of person, like Dad,' Adam explained.[2]

Charm, that most dangerous of qualities which has both smoothed and blighted the careers of generations of Etonians, was prominent in Rupert's make-up. His, however, was not the spurious charm that can be turned on or off at will, but was based on a real warmth, an interest in other people and a readiness to see the best in them. He was a pleasure to be with. Nancy Cunard found it easy to get on with him when he was a boy because of his 'niceness, good-manners, charm and lack of timidity'.[3] All these were attributes that marked him as much in later years as when he was a schoolboy.

Sibbie took Rupert to visit his Uncle Duff on the day he first went to Eton. 'He seemed to be taking the prospect very calmly,' Duff wrote in his diary. 'We gave them a good lunch.'[4] Rupert remembered the good lunch – asparagus and strawberries: without being greedy he enjoyed his food and usually recorded the details of any meal that pleased him – but was less calm than his uncle supposed. A week earlier it had seemed that the coal strike might delay the start of the Eton half;* he was elated by the prospect of more time at home and correspondingly cast down when the efforts of the miners failed to avert nemesis. Duff gave him an edition of Horace and assured him that his time at Eton would prove to be the happiest of his life; Rupert accepted the book with due gratitude but was sceptical about the prophecy. Later that afternoon they took tea with Osbert Sitwell, who gave him ten shillings and told him that he had been miserable at Eton and that Rupert almost certainly would be the same. Rupert accepted the money with still greater gratitude and thought that Sitwell was much more likely to be right than his Uncle Duff.

In the train on the way to Eton Sibbie braced herself to give her son a few of the facts of life at public school. The older boys, she warned Rupert, starved of female company, sometimes fancied themselves in love with girlish-looking younger boys. 'This is a bad thing, and you must have nothing to do with it,'[5] she enjoined him. Rupert was mildly surprised to hear that boys behaved in such a way but thought no more about it. Perhaps because he was himself far from girlish-looking he was never troubled by the importunities of his seniors; nor, either then or later, did he have any such inclinations himself. The fact that other people had different tastes caused him no concern. For most of his life he numbered homosexuals among his closest friends and the two writers to whom he devoted a great part of his working life – Hugh Walpole and Oscar Wilde – were firmly of that persuasion. 'I realise all the gradations and variations,' he told Alan Lascelles with some pride.[6]

---

* Always called a 'half' though it was patently a third of the academic or about a sixth of the calendar year.

Probably he overstated his expertise; but he certainly viewed homosexuality with benevolent curiosity and felt no inclination to condemn it.

His housemaster was E. L. Churchill – nicknamed 'Jelly' for reasons that were no doubt apparent at the time but are now long forgotten. Churchill was a disciplinarian but a kindly one, a man who could be relied on to be absolutely fair and let every boy have his hearing. He was a shrewd judge of character and within a few weeks had identified one of his new pupil's most marked characteristics. He found Rupert diligently copying out the essay which had to be written every weekend and was known as Sunday Questions:

> The first copy was very good and neat, but did not satisfy his own standard of perfection. Personally, though I am beakish* enough to admire Rupert greatly for the spirit that moves him to take all this trouble, I believe that this meticulous care about external form is a waste of time. Of course if he is only to waste this time in some less laudable way, he had better go on doing this sort of thing. But if he will use the time thus spent at present to read some of the more fascinating things about Greek or Roman affairs – or English History or Literature, anything good on any subject in the world – he will to my mind be doing himself far more good.[7]

Probably Rupert was read or allowed to see this report. If so, he did not take it to heart. A 'meticulous care about external form' was apparent throughout his life. When he in due course became a publisher it manifested itself in the high quality of the editing and production of the books he published. As such it was a most desirable attribute, but when it became an obsession, when presentation was emphasised to the point at which it made it more difficult, even impossible, to produce a saleable object, then it became a liability. If Rupert had heeded his housemaster's advice, he might not have been a better publisher but he would have been far more likely to make a success commercially.

Rupert quite enjoyed his first half at Eton, settled down in his house and seemed to have made a promising start, but the health which had let him down so often at Stanmore now disastrously betrayed him. Within a few days of his return after the summer holidays he was struck down with agonising abdominal pains. Dr Attlee, the school doctor, examined him, announced that nothing was the matter and passed him fit to play football.[8] Rupert appealed to his mother. The pain was no better, he

* 'beak' is Etonian slang for a schoolmaster.

reported: 'I'm longing to see you on Tuesday. Please bring my Bible and umbrella.' Suitably equipped, Sibbie stormed down to Eton and told the housemaster that she did not accept the doctor's verdict and proposed to remove her son to London for a proper examination. Churchill no doubt felt that she was just another fussy mother, but she considered herself justified when the surgeon decided that it would be best to remove Rupert's appendix. This was duly done but to no avail: the appendix proved perfectly healthy and the pains continued. Then followed a second opinion, which detected an internal abscess. It was drained and the wound sewn up, but still the pains continued. By now Rupert was wafer thin and his life was clearly in danger. Yet a third operation was undertaken and another abscess found and drained; this time the wound was left open with two pieces of rubber tubing protruding which had to be painfully removed and sterilised every day. It was more than three months after the original diagnosis before Rupert was on the mend.

Meanwhile Sibbie suffered almost as much as her son. She 'is in a very tiresome overwrought state and drinking a good deal,' Duff recorded unsympathetically. 'It is a bore having her in the house. I wish I didn't dislike her so.'[9] She sustained some sort of breakdown and retreated to the nursing home where Rupert was confined, occupying a nearby room and driving nurses and doctors to distraction. Only when her son was clearly out of danger did she begin to recover. Duff called on Rupert in mid-November and thought him 'wonderfully well. He is so nice and so nice-looking. Sybil was there – looking awful and quite mad.'[10] 'Wonderfully well' was an over-statement; the worst of the crisis was over but it was to be several years before Rupert was fully fit. In the year before his illness and still more rapidly during his time in the nursing home, his height increased by $7\frac{1}{2}$ inches; meanwhile he put on less than a stone in weight. He outgrew his strength, fell prey to any bug that might be around, frequently ran a high temperature and from October to May was rarely free of a heavy cold. Sibbie, her moral ascendancy established by the school doctor's failure to detect Rupert's abscesses, harried the luckless Churchill to allow her son exemption from anything potentially damaging to his health. Football and Early School – a particularly unpleasant pre-breakfast class – were two of her chosen targets. 'It's all right about the football,' Rupert reported, 'but no word has been said about Early School. You might talk it over with Churchill. I'm sure he'll do what you want, he likes you so.' Evidently she did what her son expected of her. A week later came the triumphant message: 'It's all right about Early School after all!!! You are a clever little creature. Bless you, my sweet.'[11]

Churchill liked Rupert and believed that he had real potential, but Sibbie's constant importunities taxed his patience. By the end of 1922 he was near despair. Rupert, he pointed out, had effectively only been in full work for six weeks out of the last fifteen months:

> Do the doctors hold out any hope that he will be fit for school in the proper sense this next year? If not, is it worth the expense of keeping him here? Looked at from the business point of view, he is a big expense to you, a considerable loss to me, and no earthly use, that I can see, to himself . . . my present idea is that I shall never get him properly at work and playing his games here – and that it is a waste keeping his name down.[12]

Possibly this broadside affected Sibbie's thinking and thus led her to give her son rather less encouragement to consider himself an invalid; possibly it coincided with what would anyway have been an upturn in Rupert's health. Nineteen twenty-three was a much better year, and though he continued to suffer from heavy colds he managed to play a much larger part in school life. 'He is a most delightful boy,' wrote Churchill after the Lent half, 'never repining after all his bad luck, and when in school doing his level best to make up for the time he has lost.' When Sibbie contemplated sending Rupert to the South of France for the winter – a proposal which her son enthusiastically supported – Churchill urged her not to do so. There were new inoculations which would protect the boy against the perils of influenza, colds were neither here nor there, Rupert was already making up the ground he had lost through illness, a few more months would see him abreast of all but the cleverest of his contemporaries.[13] He won the day, and by the end of the year Rupert was for the first time poised to make a real start as a practising and fully-fledged Etonian.

For this happy conclusion Sibbie deserved much credit. She believed that Rupert would have died but for her intervention and it is perfectly possible that she was right. Her love and unwavering support were indispensable during the darkest period. But there was a high price to pay. Rupert had become obsessively addicted to her love and required constant reassurance that her feelings for him were unabated. To take a typical week in October 1922: on Sunday, 'feeling very stiff and wretched', he wrote a long letter to his mother bewailing his lot and pleading with her to visit him. On Monday he received two letters from her and 'spoke to darling Mins on telephone. Very cheered up.' Tuesday: 'Again spoke to sweet little Mins. Think it will be all right. *Mins v sweet.*' Wednesday and Thursday he had to make do with letters; and the deprivation cost him dear so that by Friday he was 'feeling miserable and very coldy. Thank goodness going to see Mins soon.' Saturday was worse still: 'Feeling absolutely wretched and moping v much. How I wish Mins were here. She will be very soon!!!!!!' And on Sunday she duly was, and the cycle renewed itself over another week. There were few days that half on which he did not send and receive a letter, telephone calls were made two or three times a week, most weekends Sibbie managed to squeeze in a visit to Eton on Saturday or Sunday.

Rupert's dependence on his mother was extravagant but in the circumstances hardly unexpected; more dangerous was Sibbie's dependence on her son. When Rupert left the nursing home after his operations, his housemaster wrote to congratulate him. 'I hope your mother is getting all right again,' he added. 'I expect her recovery will depend a good deal on the pace at which you get well. I know that half her illness was due to the trouble she was in at your having such a wretched time.'[14] The letter was kindly meant, but it can hardly have helped Rupert to be told that he was to some extent responsible for his mother's plight. She for her part never hesitated to unload her woes on her all-too-receptive son. She wrote to thank him for 'two lovely letters. I do love them so: they are my one joy these days, for I must admit quite privately to you that my spirits are far from good . . . Forgive this gloomy letter. After all, you and I must pour out our troubles to each other, and then we get better.'[15] It does not seem unduly heartless to observe that a mother must *not* pour out her troubles to a sensitive and vulnerable boy of just sixteen. It was an unfair burden to thrust upon him. Sibbie was herself distraught and in no state to behave with rational moderation. It is still a fact that more was demanded from her son than it was fair or reasonable to ask.

'All my life is centred upon you and your success is mine,' Sibbie wrote from a hotel at Windsor after spending the day with her son. 'I shall and do miss you horribly, but I think of all our time apart as a sort of preparation to make me more able and fit to be your Mother, to learn things and get nicer and more useful for you.'[16] Re-reading this letter more than fifty years later Rupert told Deirdre that it reduced him to tears: 'It's more like a woman writing to her lover than a mother writing to her son. Most boys, perhaps, would have felt overwhelmed by so much, as it were, responsibility, but to me it seemed perfectly natural, for that's how things were.'[17] That was how things were, perhaps: but they were not for that reason natural.

His mother compounded his problems by trying to take him with her in her quest for fulfilment within the Roman Catholic Church. She became a Catholic on a sudden impulse while on a visit to Paris and adopted her new faith with the frenzied commitment that marked all her enthusiasms. 'Daddy is not wholly pleased about it, I fear,' she told Rupert, 'but perhaps he will come round in time.'[18] Rupert for his part was delighted. 'I think it is an excellent thing,' he told her, 'especially as it is such a comfort to you, and I am sure you did right.'[19] But he viewed her action as being a form of therapy rather than an act of faith. He himself, if not a committed unbeliever, gave little thought to religious matters and was disinclined to involve himself in any sort of spiritual adventure. The preaching of the Provost of Eton, Montague James, was generally held to be of outstanding quality, and won over many boys to, at least temporary, religious enthusiasm, but Rupert remained cool. 'I think his ghost stories are better than his sermons,' he told his mother.[20] When Sibbie urged him to follow her example, making repeated visits to the Brompton Oratory to pray for his conversion, he remained politely non-committal. 'Darling, I am not a complete heathen as you seem to think,' he told her, 'but it seems to me that everyone should have full time to make up his mind.' Under pressure he conceded: 'I think it more than probable that I shall become a Catholic sooner or later,' but further than that he would not go.[21] Possibly he did seriously consider following her; more probably he remembered the speed with which in the past Sibbie's passions had flared up and then fizzled out and reckoned that if he played for time she would move on to fresh pursuits. 'This was the only time I disregarded her wishes,' he noted in his memoirs.[22]

'A stifling connection with his mother; an uncomfortable paternity, parents mutually at odds, poorish health . . . It is a fairly ominous picture,' was Anthony Powell's summary of Rupert's school days.[23] The remarkable thing is that Rupert throve despite it all; indeed he sometimes profited by his liabilities. A long period as an invalid offers wonderful opportunities to any boy or girl with a propensity to be bookish. Rupert was encouraged by his housemaster to indulge his cravings. 'When you are getting fitter you must let me know if you want any of my big books,' Churchill wrote. 'It might be a good way of passing the time while you may not run about.'[24] It is uncertain whether by 'big' he referred to physical dimensions or intellectual stature; it anyway mattered little to Rupert, who was notably eclectic in his tastes. His reading lists show that both in quantity and variety he was ready to tackle material at which most boys of his age would have baulked. At the age of fifteen he dismissed his Holiday Task, Boswell's *Journal of a Tour to the Hebrides*, as 'that dreary book' but was 'deep in *Anna Karenina*' and the poems of Oscar Wilde. He dipped into Carlyle's *Historical Sketches*. 'I rather like his style,' he concluded, though, perhaps fortunately, he felt no wish to imitate it. For the first time he began seriously to apply himself to drama. About *King Lear* he observed: 'Comment is useless, but in my opinion it does not rank with *Hamlet*.' The judgment was not conspicuously profound or sophisticated but it showed a welcome readiness to confront the Himalayas of literature without being wholly over-awed by them. He enjoyed and read most of Bernard Shaw, thought Barrie had 'great charm and easy style', and of *The Rivals* remarked: 'Mrs Malaprop is very, very funny – otherwise I thought it *very, very* dull.' He was cautious of work that smelt too much of an alien culture. He found the plays of Eugene O'Neill 'all rather sordid' and dismissed *Desire Under the Elms* as unequivocally 'bad'.

He was suspicious – as he was to be all his life – of anything that smacked of chic modernity. Aldous Huxley's *Antic Hay* he considered a 'very cheap rotten book', though he regretfully added that he found it 'rather readable all the same'. Flecker, on the other hand, appealed strongly to him; he found *Hassan* 'Quite delicious. Like it more and more, there are some quite lovely lines in it.' When he was particularly struck by the work of someone who was still alive he did not keep his enthusiasm to himself or to his friends but formed the habit of writing to the author. The earliest surviving of what were to be several thousand of such fan letters was written after he bought and read Maurice Baring's most celebrated novel, *C*. Rupert enjoyed it greatly and at once wrote to Baring to tell him so. The response was patently sincere. 'Your letter gave me untold delight,' Baring replied. 'It is a great thing to get praise from the young. The most precious and rare of all presents. However underveerd. Forgive my typing. It means well.'[25]

When he particularly enjoyed a book he almost at once re-read it, and some old favourites he revisited twenty or thirty times in the course of his life. In 1926 he got especial pleasure from Lytton Strachey's *Queen*

Victoria – 'a marvellous book: enjoyed it more than ever second time'. Of *Le Cid* he sententiously observed '*Corneille peint les hommes, tels qu'ils devraient être. Mais oui, c'est ça.*' But he took unabashed pleasure in good bad books: the unpretentious thriller or swashbuckling adventure that took little account of style or characterisation but told an exciting story well. E. Phillips Oppenheim was an author to whom he remained faithful all his life. Edgar Wallace's *The Four Just Men* he described as: 'Thrilling, one of the best detective stories read lately.' But he could not wholly suspend his critical judgment; about a later book by Wallace he remarked: 'I certainly enjoyed it. It is a great pity he can't write.'

In 1927 his taste markedly matured. He remained faithful to old favourites but between two novels by Phillips Oppenheim came André Gide's *La Symphonie Pastorale* – 'A beautiful little book. Perhaps the end is a trifle abrupt, but I am all for short books' – and *Tess of the D'Urbervilles* – 'A very great book – the work of a master-stylist, so simple and beautiful'. With *Chamber Music* he ventured into the more accessible regions of James Joyce; some of the poems, he wrote, 'have a lovely delicacy – most in fact – a curious character' – the last words, presumably, relating to the author rather than his works.

By the time that he left Eton he was, by any standard, remarkably well read, and his excellent memory ensured that most of his reading did not slip away into an inchoate miasma but remained clear and accessible in his mind. At Eton too, in the second-hand bookshops that then abounded, he began to accumulate the massive library which he developed throughout his life and which was the most precious of his possessions. Early purchases were modest – an Oppenheim thriller, a novel by Rider Haggard, a good edition of Keats's poems – but soon he was buying a book or two a week and his room at Halcot rapidly filled up with his acquisitions. His mother applauded his activities; his father deplored extravagance of any kind but did not pay much attention to Rupert's doings and was barely aware of the library that was forming under his roof. While Sibbie visited Eton almost every week, Richard Hart-Davis barely went once a half. 'Daddy came down 12.02. Sat on Upper Club and watched 2nd XI match. Tea Rowlands, strawberry messes and iced coffee. Great fun,' Rupert duly recorded in his diary.[26] Great fun it may have been, but though he welcomed the advent of his father it was his mother's company for which he pined.

By now those masters who had gone away to the war and yet survived it had come back to teaching, and the staff at Eton had returned to the standards that it complacently – and not without some reason – assumed to be the highest in the world. Rupert was less impressed. In 1924 he was up to Gurney Lubbock. 'Lubbock isn't at all bad,' he told Sibbie. 'He thinks that he is all that a cultivated man ought to be.' Rupert, who thought that he was all that a cultivated boy ought to be, was suspicious of these pretensions. Initially he had been quite impressed, then he decided that his teacher was at best 'quite a harmless man', finally he concluded that he was getting 'more boring every day'.[27] 'Satan' Ford seemed even more inadequate. He had a reputation for being a ferocious disciplinarian, but while he terrorised the smaller boys his knowledge of French and German, which he was supposed to teach, was notably limited. When Rupert encountered him as a specialist he soon realised that Ford was little, if at all, more proficient than his pupils. A tacit deal was done: if Ford would leave the boys in peace they would do nothing to expose his limitations. The results were surprisingly satisfactory – if Rupert's memory a quarter of a century after the event is to be trusted. 'We spent two carefree years and ended up winning the top three language prizes – thus making his name as a tutor.'[28]

Only one teacher really made a mark on Rupert. George Lyttelton, then in his mid-thirties and not yet a housemaster, was a man of wit, exuberance and humanity. He would impress small boys by tearing a hard-bound Latin grammar in two with his bare hands, while awing the more sophisticated by his encyclopaedic knowledge of English literature. It was the greatest fun to be taught by him. Rupert caught his attention when he was able to cap Lyttelton's quotation from Meredith's *Love in the Valley* and, still more impressive, to refer knowledgeably to another version of the same poem. Many hundreds of boys passed through Lyttelton's life and the two men did not meet again for more than thirty years but the relationship finally matured into something of great significance to both of them.

By the time Rupert was up to George Lyttelton he was entering his final year and the worst of his time at Eton was long behind him. His final impressions of the school were happy ones. He never came anywhere near achieving heroic status. The only way to do that at Eton between the two world wars was to excel at games, and Rupert was no athlete. He played cricket assiduously and with pleasure but no marked success. His affection for the game was sometimes sorely tested: 'Very badly hit on the arm'; 'hit full toss by a ball on the chest. Hurt awfully,' were typical diary entries that suggested a difficult time at the wicket.

Once he made thirty-eight not out but that was a solitary triumph; his average was only eleven and the final entry read: 'M'tutors all out for 26, beaten by nine wickets. Made o. Oh dear! Oh dear!' And cricket was his best game. Football he continued to dislike, and his incompetence matched his disaffection. When he was in the nursing home Churchill once assured him that the Lower Boy team was much the poorer for his absence: 'Your weight and strength is badly needed in the bully.'[29] Rupert was unpersuaded, as he was when his Uncle Duff told him that he should learn how to box. In his last year he scraped into the house football team but the 'scug cap', ignominious livery of those who had failed to win their colours in any sport, remained his lot throughout his career at Eton. But though the sporting hero was admired, those who conspicuously failed to shine at games were not for that reason pilloried or treated as inadequate. Eton as a school was remarkably tolerant and boys were encouraged to develop their talents in their own way. Far from being despised or pitied, Rupert was respected and well liked. In due course he was elected to the Library, the elite group who ruled the house, occupied a common room of modest comfort, and were allowed to employ Lower Boys as 'fags' to run errands and do odd jobs. 'All the fags look upon me as a harmless imbecile and roar with laughter at anything and everything I say,' he told his mother. 'Slightly trying!'[30] In fact he did not find it trying at all; he knew they liked him and was delighted if they found his jokes irresistibly amusing.

Though he got on perfectly well with the other boys in his house he made no particular friends among them. The only one whom he kept up with in later life was David Smith, scion of the great retailing firm and, as a bookseller, a figure of some significance in Rupert's career. Smith asked him to stay at his home for the Henley Regatta – an experience which the non-rowing Rupert found intimidating – and then again to visit him for a week or two in the summer holidays. He told his mother about this invitation, which he would have liked to accept. According to his version of her letter as it appeared in his memoirs she replied that 'I should miss you very much but I mustn't be selfish and make you into too much of a recluse'. The original of the letter has been destroyed but according to somebody who read it, Rupert quoted only a much modified version. What Sibbie actually wrote was a cry of indignant pain, protesting that she could not bear it if he deserted her. 'I have absolutely no intention whatsoever of going to stay with David,' Rupert replied. 'Did you really think I was going to leave you, darling?'[31] The sacrifice in this case was not great, but he found himself wondering what would happen when he grew older and the path of his life led him ever further away from his mother.

In the first two or three years of an Etonian's time at school his acquaintanceship is largely confined to the boys who happen to be boarding in the same house. As he grows more senior, however, he can look around him and draw his friends from a wider pool. Rupert was quick to do so. Basil Ava, the future Marquess of Dufferin and Ava, who was to die in the Burmese campaign of 1945, was one of the first of his new friends. Through him Rupert met 'a fellow called Lees-Milne (very nice)'.[32] The very nice James Lees-Milne was to remain close to Rupert for the rest of his life. Lees-Milne wrote in his memoirs that his passionate wish while at Eton had been that he might be the son of a divorced Earl with a house in Belgrave Square, a fleet of Rolls-Royces with footmen on the box and a private aeroplane. Instead he found that his natural grouping was with 'a number of friends with whom I spent blissful summer afternoons, idly floating on the river and discussing the merits of Thackeray and Meredith, Shelley and Swinburne'.[33]

The literary discussions would have been very much to Rupert's taste but he would probably have been too busily employed on the cricket field to leave much time for idle floating. In a world polarised between aesthetes and hearties he belonged to neither camp but was at home in either. On the whole, and increasingly, he found that he had more in common with the aesthetes, but he was never ill at ease in the company of those who preferred games or country sports. In some people this might have suggested an uneasy disinclination to stand out, a chameleon-like ability to share the pleasures and prejudices of those around them. Rupert felt no such urge. In any society he remained imperturbably himself. His self-confidence and indifference to the perilous pleasures of introspective self-examination meant that he took things and people as they came. He struck no kind of attitude because he was satisfied with himself as he was and felt no need to impose any different vision of himself on the rest of the world. His tastes and habits were his own affair; he was neither ashamed nor particularly proud of them and asked no more than that people should accept him for what he was while he did as much for them.

Certainly his closest friend had little use for languid discussions of Shelley while floating on the river. Peter Fleming, member of a rich and powerful banking family, was intelligent and well read but also restless, adventurous and frenetically energetic. He and Rupert viewed each other with mild perplexity and a keen appreciation of each other's qualities; they shared a sense of humour and the unstated, even unrecognised, yet deeply held conviction that as men, and still more as Etonians, they were superior members of the human race. At any time over the next fifty years Rupert would have said that Peter Fleming was his closest and dearest friend.

They first got to know each other in the Symposium Club, a body which Fleming had set up, at first to read plays, then, more ambitiously, to put them on. The authorities took some persuading, but Fleming was nothing if not persistent and George Lyttelton volunteered to supervise the venture and direct whatever play was picked. Rupert was delighted to join in: he had a fine speaking voice, enjoyed reading aloud and was never reluctant to make a spectacle of himself. 'Gave a conjuring entertainment to the servants. Quite a success,' he had written in his diary when thirteen years old,[34] and he felt sure that his talents as an entertainer would translate to the stage. Bernard Shaw's *Androcles and the Lion* was the first choice of the Symposium Club. Rupert was cast as Ferrovius, the muscular Christian, a part which Shaw wrote for laughs but Rupert played as straight drama. The result seems to have been reasonably effective: the *Eton College Chronicle* reported that Hart-Davis, 'with a face of brilliant red, gave a real impression of the fierce fighter with his lust for battle . . . Perhaps his serious acting did more than anything else to make the play interesting as well as amusing.'[35]

Encouraged by this success, Rupert was eager to have a bigger part in the next play. It was Shaw again, this time *The Devil's Disciple*, and Rupert played Anderson, the minister. 'I love the feeling of speaking to a room full of people,' Rupert noted after the first performance.[36] A London critic who wrote a brief notice for *The Times* complained that the performers were too self-conscious: 'only R. C. Hart-Davis as the parson and R. P. Fleming as Dick Dudgeon showed much ease of manner', but George Lyttelton, who reviewed the play in the *Chronicle*, said that Rupert was misfitted 'both with his part and with his make-up'. 'Hart-Davis struggled nobly,' Lyttelton concluded in a back-handed compliment, 'but – well, could Forbes-Robertson play Falstaff?'[37] In Rupert's eyes the experience had been, if not totally triumphant, then at least enjoyable. He acquired a taste for acting which was not to be extinguished for several years.

Some of his more austere teachers felt that these theatrical forays were distracting him from the serious business of scholarship: 'He must not allow his dramatic leanings to impair the quality of his work,' wrote his Modern Tutor, severely.[38] Jelly Churchill might have agreed, but he had now retired, to be replaced by E. W. Powell. As well as being a distinguished oarsman Powell loved the stage and actually directed the performance of *The Devil's Disciple*. 'I like him very much indeed,' Powell wrote of Rupert, 'and I feel sure that his influence in the house is entirely beneficial. Anything that he takes up he takes up with his whole heart: a good example to others and a pleasure to me. I do hate the half-hearted.'[39] His last few months at Eton Rupert devoted whole-heartedly to the pursuit of pleasure; they were passed in a haze of sunshine, cider and conversation. Academically he did well, though perhaps not quite as well as might have been expected; his Modern Tutor relented so far as to say that any such shortfall arose because 'he has been comparatively fit and enjoying life during his last Half here. I would not have it otherwise.'

A year or so before, Rupert had told his mother that Churchill had 'found a scholarship of sorts at Balliol that I might do in December: I think it sounds fairly easy.'[40] He duly took the examination but discovered that it was not as easy as all that; he did well enough to be offered a place but not to win a scholarship. Given the amount of teaching he had missed, anything else would have been surprising. Churchill had never thought it likely and Powell wrote that it was not really to be expected, 'but it must nonetheless have been a bitter disappointment to one of his nature'.

This suggests some misunderstanding of Rupert's character. He would have liked to have won a scholarship, if only to please his mother, but his failure to do so cost him no sleepless nights. There is no hint of 'bitter disappointment' in his letters or diary; though the fact that Peter Fleming had won a scholarship to Christ Church may mildly have piqued him. Oxford seemed a natural next step after Eton, and though he had no particular reason to favour Balliol before any other college, he had heard well of it from Churchill and expected to enjoy himself during his stay there.

Meanwhile there were a few months of holiday. At Cap d'Antibes he met a 'slim young man' sunbathing on a raft anchored off shore; he turned out to be the budding critic and reviewer Raymond Mortimer, and the source both of much useful information about Balliol and of literary gossip. This was much to Rupert's taste and offered an agreeable foretaste of the life he intended to make his own. Back in London he refused to be drawn into the social orbit which his mother felt should be his natural scene. 'I don't want to be rude or anything of that sort,' he protested, 'but I should like to make it quite clear, once and for all, that I don't want or intend to go to the Smiths' dance, because firstly I hate dancing, second I don't know or want to know any of the people there, and thirdly I don't see why I shouldn't go on cataloguing books all my life. Anatole France and Charles Lamb did little else.'[41] Sibbie would have liked to think of her son shining in the ballrooms of Mayfair, but she could hardly complain if he chose to take his pleasures in more cloistered paths. She had, after all, pointed the way herself. One day, a few months before, she and Rupert had driven in a taxi through Berkeley Square, conducting one of their many inconclusive discussions about his future. 'I know,' she suddenly announced. 'You'd better be a man of letters.'[42]

Chapter Three

Balliol Man

The five years after he left Eton were the most miserable of Rupert's life. He had little reason to expect this in the summer of 1926. His mother was very obviously not a happy woman but she seemed in no way desperate; rather better, in fact, than she had been over the previous years. His relationship with his father was cool but far from hostile; they did not enjoy each other's company but conducted themselves with reasonable propriety whenever circumstances brought them together. He had no great hopes of Oxford but expected that he would enjoy it; he saw it as an extension of his public school with rather greater comfort and independence and more interesting work. Some friends would be moving on with him from Eton and he had no doubt that he would quickly be making many more.

His acceptance by Balliol had not been so much a matter of course as he had rather loftily assumed. The Tutor for Admissions, M. R. Ridley, told Jelly Churchill: 'his English Literature was pretty hopeless. I think our taking him must be conditional on him arranging with the English Literature Tutor to do some regular course of work.'[1] Given the trajectory of Rupert's career, it was a surprising weakness for the examiners to pick out. The explanation seems to have been that Rupert had read omnivorously but with little system; a few masters like George Lyttelton had urged him on to literary adventures but there had been almost nothing in the way of formal teaching. Then as now, many university dons distrusted enthusiasm; they were not particularly impressed by the width of a pupil's reading but anxious that it should be in a clearly defined direction. Rupert struck them as naïve and undisciplined. He was accepted not because of his examination results but thanks to the glowing reference which his housemaster had provided:

Rupert Hart-Davis is all right! He has the best brains of any boy I have met for a long time, but he does not know much for one of his capacity as unluckily since 1921 or 1922 he has spent half the time trying very hard to die and the other half recovering. [Churchill listed his various misfortunes, after which] it was too late for him to catch up on his competitors in Classics; but for his illness he would have got a scholarship in that line . . . He is a very charming fellow, never gives any one a moment's trouble and is very much liked by all the boys, and at the same time much respected.[2]

Churchill was well regarded in Balliol and his good opinion of Rupert swung the day. In his letter thanking the Tutor for Admissions he accepted that he must bear the responsibility if things subsequently went wrong and concluded: 'I do not feel much fear as to the result. As an individual I know you cannot help liking him. His brains are beyond doubt excellent and will improve if only he can contrive to get stronger. He is one of the boys about whom it is easy to feel quite confident.'[3]

Balliol in 1926 was not the intellectual power-house it had been before the First World War but was still one of Oxford's leading colleges. Its Master, A. D. Lindsay, was a radical who believed passionately in a classless society and was determined to take his college along that road. He made some headway but at the price of alienating his more conservative colleagues and earning Balliol some derision among the smarter colleges. To the Christ Church of Sebastian Flyte or the Scone of Alistair Digby-Vaine-Trumpington[*], Balliol was the haunt of niggers and Scotsmen. Being at a college that was socially looked down on would have been of little concern to Rupert if it had not been that his closest friend was at Christ Church. Peter Fleming had nothing in common with Sebastian Flyte but there was a trace of Digby-Vaine-Trumpington in his make-up. Rupert looked at Balliol through his eyes and saw something that was architecturally inelegant and socially dowdy. Fleming was the first man from another college to visit Rupert's rooms; he was offensive about the furnishings and refused to go into the windowless and unlit lavatory on the grounds that he was sure there was a black man using it already. It was there that they first experimented with the expensive pipes they had bought at Fribourg and Treyer in the High; Fleming acquitted himself with dignity, Rupert was violently sick and – black man or not – had to make use of the unlit lavatory.[4]

---

[*] figuring respectively in Evelyn Waugh's *Brideshead Revisited* and *Decline and Fall*

Things might have gone better if he had made friends in his own college but, though he was delighted to re-encounter his old ally from Stanmore, Wyndham Ketton-Cremer, and a handful of fellow Etonians came on with him, he made little effort to widen his acquaintance. When he came up to take the scholarship examination he had remarked disdainfully, 'I have never seen so many awful-looking people as there were doing the paper – revolting.'[5] Now the awful-looking people were all around him. Nor did the dons seem much better: Rupert respected Lindsay and liked Ridley but the others seemed either unapproachable or distasteful. Balliol's most prominent personality was the egregious toady and manipulator 'Sligger' Urquhart – Rupert later described him as 'a purring old doctored tom-cat . . . ! I've never seen a more completely homosexual man.'[6] Instead of mixing with his fellow Balliol men, he took refuge in Fleming's rooms in Christ Church where they listened to jazz on a portable wind-up gramophone. This silly exclusiveness would undoubtedly have worn off in time but in his first term and under considerable emotional pressure, Rupert was in no mood to experiment or take new initiatives.

Nor did he find the work congenial. In his first week he was required to write an essay either on proportional representation or on Carlyle's curious philosophical extravaganza *Sartor Resartus*. These subjects might have seemed sufficiently varied to accommodate most tastes, but Rupert would have none of it. 'The first I didn't (and still don't) fully understand,' he told George Lyttelton many years later, 'and the second looked to me unreadable, so with the utmost pusillanimity I went sick.'[7] He could hardly continue to go sick whenever an essay was required but his tutor could neither command his respect nor interest him in his work, and he got by with a minimal amount of study.

Other aspects of university life seemed little more agreeable. Oxford in the mid-1920s was not nearly so politicised as it would be ten years later but many undergraduates, particularly in Balliol, took the issues seriously and seized any opportunity to trumpet their views in public. Some years before, Iris Tree had tried to persuade Sibbie to indoctrinate her son. 'I hope you are bringing up Rupert as an anarchist,' she wrote. 'Begin now to show Rupert the red shirt idea, fill him with desire to become the great anti-capitalist and so forth. Seriously, I think it is the only thing worth doing in these times.'[8] Red shirt, black shirt, they would have been much the same to Sibbie, who eschewed politics and made not the slightest effort to follow her friend's advice. It would have made no great difference if she had. Though

Rupert gradually drifted into a dyed-in-the-wool conservatism, he never
showed the slightest interest in politics and viewed its practitioners with
suspicion and even dislike. Aged nineteen he had no vote and would
have been unlikely to cast it if he had. His earnest and predominantly
left-wing contemporaries at Balliol urged him to take up the workers'
cause; he was too good-natured to rebuff them rudely but he viewed
their approaches with baffled boredom. Baldwin was not a prime
minister likely to inspire his loyalties but the rest seemed even worse. It
was the year that *Mein Kampf* was first published, but even the most
politically prescient of undergraduates would hardly have seen that this
was the moment to take a stand. Rupert closed his eyes to politics and
got on with his life.

That life did not encompass much outside the British Isles. Rupert
knew little if anything about the travails of the Weimar Republic or the
growing power of Mussolini, but nor did he feel any burning wish to
visit the wonders of the Louvre or the Uffizi. 'I should hate to go up the
Nile,' he told Deirdre much later, 'all mud and crocodiles and dishonest
Wogs'.[9] For Rupert, as for many other Englishmen, Wogs began at
Calais: they had done so when he was at Balliol and would continue to
do so until any travel was beyond him. He would not have maintained
that they were all of them dishonest but the balance of probability
suggested that they well might be and, what was worse, hardly any of
them spoke decent English. Throughout his life he went on few
holidays outside Britain and they were almost always undertaken on
somebody else's initiative; he would, provided they were well translated,
read foreign books with interest, but he saw no good reason to seek out
their authors on their native heath.

Good-looking, intelligent, conversable and enjoying company, he
would inevitably have become a figure of some prominence on Oxford's
social scene. He had, however, neither the money nor the inclination to
parade himself on a grander stage. Deirdre recorded his horror when he
attended a smart weekend party in the country and was asked by the
footman 'if he had brought his guns or whether he would prefer to
ride'.[10] Having no guns and disliking horses, he quickly decided this was
no place for him. He felt more at home with the Morrells at Garsington;
he thought Philip Morrell 'a randy old bore, always chasing the
housemaids round the house',[11] but Lady Ottoline amused and
intrigued him and he enjoyed the glamorous and sometimes unpredict-
able company. One lifelong friend whom he met there for the first time
was David Cecil. When Cecil died Rupert recalled their first encounter

and the pleasure their friendship had given him. 'As far as literature was concerned he was a life-enhancer,' he wrote, 'for he made one want to read what he thought was good.'[12] Rupert never doubted that this was what literary criticism should be about. He found himself less and less in fashion – a development that disturbed him little – but he never ceased to believe that books were there to be enjoyed and that to increase that enjoyment was a worthy goal.

It was at Oxford that he finally succumbed to another life-time addiction. He had done his first acrostic early in 1924 and the following year completed his first crossword puzzle. He took to the pursuit with delight; at the peak of his powers he was regularly finishing *The Times* crossword in ten minutes or less, and extended his attention in due course to the *New Statesman*, the *Spectator*, the *Observer*, the *Listener* and the *Sunday Times*. Particularly irritating to lesser mortals was his habit of solving a puzzle in his head, while scribbling in only a few letters or even leaving it blank. In the course of his long life he must have spent many thousands of hours on this innocent but time-consuming diversion; his more assiduous colleagues sometimes wondered whether the time and effort might not more appropriately have been devoted to something relevant to his daily work.

Such pastimes were enjoyable but not to be taken too seriously; the theatre was another matter. A week rarely passed without his attending the Playhouse Theatre, where a repertory company worked in a tin hut on the Banbury Road. Standards were high and the repertoire ambitious; there Rupert saw his first plays by Ibsen, Strindberg, Chekhov, Synge. Whilst at Eton he had read almost all Shakespeare's plays; in London he had seen several of them; now his eyes were opened to more modern drama. He joined the Oxford University Dramatic Society, the OUDS, where the Russian director Theodore Komisarjevsky was preparing a production of *King Lear*, and was promised a small part when the play opened the following term. At the audition he met another hopeful, John Betjeman, who became another lasting friend. Betjeman landed the part of the Fool but was later dismissed for idleness at rehearsals; Rupert, if lucky, might have been given Kent or Gloucester, and would certainly have applied himself to the role with admirable conscientiousness. If he had remained at Oxford he would have devoted much of his time to acting. Possibly this would have appeased an appetite which, as it was, remained unabated; more probably it would merely have convinced him that this was where his future lay.

*

It was not to be, however. His first term at Oxford had been marred by
the dramatically worsening condition of his mother. Quite what was
wrong with her, the doctors were unable to decide; there were no very
obvious physical symptoms, she just seemed to lose the will to live.
Rupert's move to Oxford, which must have seemed to her to herald the
ending of the relationship most important in her life, undoubtedly
contributed, but she was almost forty years old – a landmark she
dreaded – her teeth had been causing her much pain and she was always
prone to depression in the autumn. In mid-October she was consigned
to a nursing home. Her doctor decided that she needed a complete rest;
he felt he could not bar her husband from seeing her but ruled out visits
by Rupert, claiming that Sibbie would find them emotionally too
disturbing. Rupert later reproached himself with not having defied this
embargo but at the time he felt some relief that he was absolved from
the need to pay frequent and painful visits to London. He did make
periodic efforts to pierce the barrier set up by the doctors. 'I was so
sorry not to see you yesterday,' he wrote after one abortive visit, 'but I
am sure it was better for you to rest.' 'I was so dreadfully disappointed
at not seeing you,' Sibbie responded, 'it was horrid. However, let's be
wise and good and then perhaps we shall soon be allowed to meet.' The
weeks passed and they were never wise and good enough: 'Darlingest,
how I long to see you. Do come soon, *do*,' Sibbie wrote on 9 November,
and then a few days later, 'sometimes I feel quite sick with longing for a
sight of your sweet face'.[13] The feeling that he had betrayed his mother
when her need was greatest haunted Rupert in later life. 'I should have
known that it would have done her good to see me (perhaps it wouldn't
– we shall never know). Anyhow, I didn't go for weeks . . . It's all too
easy to be wise long after the event, but ever since I have had varying
nightmares, in most of which she has been ill for *years* and I have failed
to visit her.'[14]

Belatedly, Sibbie's doctor concluded that he was unable to help his
patient and called in the eminent alienist, Sir Maurice Craig. She was
removed to a nursing home in Hampstead, put in the charge of a
leading neurologist and at first seemed to be improving. Her favourite
nurse, Patsy Geoghegan, told Rupert how much his mother had been
loved in the nursing home and how great her pleasure had been
whenever she heard from him: 'The countless times she sent me
downstairs to see if there was a letter from you, and when I brought her
one, how she would slip it under the clothes and hold it next to her

heart to keep the pleasure of opening it as long as she possibly could. I don't think you will ever know how much she loved you.'[15]

He knew only too well, and knew too how much *he* loved *her*. At the beginning of December the doctors changed their tactics and Rupert was allowed to visit his mother. He was horrified by her physical deterioration but told himself, and her, that all would now go better. 'You were so sweet and good,' he wrote bravely. 'If all goes well I shall come and see you on Tuesday, perhaps on Thursday, Saturday and then every day. I will read and recite to you, take you out for drives and soon home. You are bound to get well if you see me all the time, and as long as we are together everything is all right. Remember that.'[16] Though he could hardly bring himself to admit it, secretly he knew that everything would never be all right; his mother was dying slowly before his eyes.

He felt terribly alone. Richard Hart-Davis was genuinely distressed by his wife's condition – 'I can assure you that no one could have shown more devotion, or have made greater efforts to save his wife,' the neurologist told him[17] – but he was incapable of sharing his feelings with his son. Rupert's friends were anxious to help but had no idea how to set about it. Peter Fleming wrote him a letter of unrelenting facetiousness concluding with a few words that betrayed his sympathy: 'I hope your mother is better, I only wish I could do something about the bloody situation.'[18] Deirdre, who had been in Paris for several months but came home for Christmas, was more than anybody else able to share his anguish, but he knew that compared with him, even she meant little to his mother. He was Sibbie's only support and he could do nothing to save her.

Her last days were far from peaceful. Terrified of the sleep that she knew would bring her fearsome nightmares, she fought the drugs that might have stabilised her condition. Phases of near-normality would be followed by hours in which she heard strange voices or suffered harrowing delusions. One dreadful afternoon she convinced herself that Rupert was an enemy intent on harming her, abused him and pelted him with anything on which she could lay her hands. She died in the early evening of 3 January 1927. That morning Duff Cooper had come up from the country to visit what he realised was likely to be her death bed. He was dismayed to find her shrunken and wizened like an old woman. 'The sight of the two children sitting one each side of the bed where they had been all night, holding her hands and Rupert whispering to her and kissing her all the time, was heartbreaking. I have never seen anything so lovely as his devotion.'[19]

Almost always a mourner's immediate reaction to the end of a long drawn-out death is one of relief that it is over. Then the real pain begins. 'It was as if the whole fabric of our world had collapsed,' Deirdre told her daughter many years later. 'There had always been a kind of magic feeling about her; in our hour of need, nothing, literally nothing, would prevent her getting to us . . . It therefore seemed utterly impossible that she would disappear from our lives completely. We were stunned and shattered and it seemed an intolerable burden having to continue with daily life. I remember how I resented having to continue doing small everyday things like cleaning my teeth. It all seemed so utterly pointless.'[20] Rupert tried to cope with the situation by carrying around with him in a bag a copy of *Pilgrim's Progress* from which he would chant aloud on every possible occasion. It was a characteristically bookish response to a tragedy which others might have sought to mitigate by talking to their family or friends. The only other thing in the bag was a huge bottle of liquid sleeping draught. This eventually lost its cork and saturated Bunyan; but, as Rupert told George Lyttelton, 'he had done his saving work by then'.[21]

Richard Hart-Davis, devoured by remorse at having so evidently failed to save his wife, had recourse to spiritualists to try to get in touch with her. Rupert was sceptical about the efficacy of such a venture but saw no harm in it. 'Let him do it if it gives him any comfort,' was his response. Duff found Rupert 'terribly broken with misery but very simple and unaffected about it as people who are really unhappy usually are'.[22] Duff was at one time fearful lest his nephew's great grief might derange him[23] but though Rupert was stunned and inconsolable he never lost his grasp on reality. Nancy Cunard wrote him a letter which he greatly valued and accepted as the truth:

I know how unhappy you are, darling – there is nothing to say about it, but somehow, I suppose, everything – even the most terrible – becomes bearable . . . I've never been over-burdened with hope or the belief that life was happy – it has bits, times, that can be wonderful (they'll come to you) and that makes it worthwhile. She used to think that too, I believe, and I know how *absolutely* she would want you to be as little unhappy as possible and to feel, no matter how blindly at the moment, that there will be things in life that *will* make you happier . . . I know she would hate to see you brood, and being with people and forcing yourself to do things will in no way lessen your love of her.[24]

But though he saw the force in Nancy's argument, he found it almost impossible to follow her advice. The only person in whose company he took any pleasure was his sister Deirdre and she returned to Paris a few weeks after their mother died. They wrote to each other almost every day: 'They're full of love,' Rupert told Deirdre when he re-read her letters many years later, 'for then I was the only person left for you to love.'[25] He forced himself to go to the theatre, to attend the occasional party, but found no joy in any occupation. Constantly he reproached himself with not having been sufficiently nice to his mother while she was alive: he knew that this was something felt by many people who had lost a loved one, knew too that there was no substance in the self-accusation, but was no more free from guilt as a result. For him, almost the most painful time came when his mother began to slip into the background of his mind. Every moment in which he did not think about her seemed to him a fresh betrayal. If he found pleasure in a book or the company of friends he would at once reproach himself in the conviction that he had no right to do so. Little by little he found that he was 'beginning to forget about her – even what she looked like – and it made me very unhappy'.[26]

In such a mood, it was hardly likely that he would find Oxford congenial, even tolerable. Duff Cooper told him that he should immerse himself in university life. He thought that it was essential Rupert should get away from London and interminable conversations with other people who had known his mother. Oxford would provide the distractions needed to restore him to full life. Reluctantly Rupert acquiesced and returned to Balliol, but without much hope and with less enthusiasm. He gave it a few weeks and then concluded he was getting nowhere. He went to see the Master of Balliol and told him he wanted to go down: he could see only two reasons for being at Oxford, he said, to work hard or to enjoy oneself. He lacked the application to do the first and the heart to do the second: better call it off. Lindsay was probably not too distressed to see the last of a student about whom there had been uncertainty from the start and who had conspicuously failed to fit in. 'What will you do instead?' he asked. Rupert had scarcely considered the question; now he remembered the pleasure he had found in acting while at Eton and more or less at random replied that he thought he would go on the stage. 'Oh,' said Lindsay doubtfully. 'You

won't find many Old Balliol men there.'[27] The point was incontrovert-
ible but in Rupert's present mood was calculated more to encourage
than to deter.

Duff Cooper and Maurice Baring came to see him shortly after he
had made up his mind. They were sceptical about Rupert's proposed
career. 'You might move to Cambridge,' suggested Baring. 'I tried
both.'[28] Rupert found the idea less than appealing. He left Oxford with
little regret. Ridley, who had put such faith in him, was almost the only
person he felt he had let down. He wrote to him remorsefully. 'Don't be
a silly old ass,' Ridley replied. 'The Master explained the whole thing to
me, and though I am very sorry on personal and other grounds that you
won't be back again, I think you are probably quite right. The only
thing that is much worthwhile in this wicked world is either preparing
for or being in a job that you really care about, and if the preparation
period is all the time against the grain, or the wrong kind of preparation,
it is often a waste of time. The best of luck to you in your progress
towards being a star, *per ardua* I don't doubt.'[29]

Richard Hart-Davis was not unreasonably put out when he heard of
Rupert's sudden decision to abandon his education, the more so since it
was presented to him as a *fait accompli*. His indignation grew when he
discovered that his son did not propose to follow him into Panmure
Gordon as a stockbroker but instead was envisaging a career as
indecorous and uncertain as the stage. Eventually he proposed a
compromise: no final decision would be taken for a few months while
Rupert went to the Continent to improve his French and German; if
after that he was still bent on acting, then Richard would acquiesce. No
doubt he hoped that the interval would give his son time to reflect and
to see the advantages of a stable and prosperous career. He deluded
himself. Rupert was not passionately committed to the theatre but he
knew that nothing would induce him to become a stockbroker. He
decided to defer further argument until his return and went off to
Fontainebleau with tolerably good grace to serve his term in exile.

There was another reason for Richard to want his son out of London.
Before going back to Oxford Rupert had spent two or three weeks with
the Meynell family near Pulborough in Sussex. The poet Alice Meynell
had died five years before, but her aged husband Victor and their
descendants lived on in a pleasant, rambling country house. Rupert felt
entirely at home there, was fond of all of them and, most particularly,
quickly fell in love with the twenty-seven-year-old Anne Brindley, who

was helping look after Victor Meynell but was treated very much as part of the family. To be in love was a natural state for Rupert – 'I need a lover,' he told Deirdre. 'I desperately need to be needed as well as loved.'[30] For nineteen years his mother had supplied the need, now he was bereft. Almost anyone who was available and remotely suitable might have filled the gap; though Anne was eight years the elder she was attractive, warm-hearted and passionately interested in literature. The Meynells, who sympathised with Rupert in his desolate loneliness, encouraged the romance. Before he returned home, the couple were informally engaged and making plans to set up together in a second-hand bookshop.

Richard was once more outraged. His son, with no means and no profession, was far too young to marry, particularly when the girl in question was a penniless orphan much older than her fiancé. Rupert stuck to his guns, but while absence did nothing to convince him that he would be happy as a stockbroker it also failed in its more traditional role of making the heart grow fonder. By the time he met Anne again he had realised that he had been looking on her not as a wife but as a substitute mother. He liked her no less, but he did not love her. With genuine shame and regret, he broke the news to her. She must have been a woman of exceptional generosity and sweetness of nature. She had prepared for him a volume of love poetry which she had written out and charmingly decorated herself. In it is still her last letter.

We must be friends and I want you to write or come and tell me that this is so. Our world is harsh enough and full of stings enough, without my adding to them, and I think that I should be leaving you only a sting for memory . . . if I left you to think that you had given me only sorrow. You see, you gave me instead something infinitely perfect, not only for then but for ever. Dearest, after all, we shall be going back only to the beginning. If you mistook your capacity for love you mustn't think you mistook everything. I allow you lost love, my sweet, but not lost sympathy, lost truth, lost pleasure in companionship . . . I don't want you to regret anything, ever.[31]

Rupert had a remarkable facility for retaining the affection of women who had once loved him and whom he had loved. He never met Anne Brindley again but fifty years later he sent her a copy of his first volume of autobiography, *The Arms of Time*. When she died her son wrote to say how touched she had been by the gift. She had often spoken about her relationship with Rupert, though never with regret, still less bitterness: 'She really suffered at the break-up of your engagement, but in her heart of hearts felt it was the right thing, though her admiration for you never diminished.'[32]

The way was clear to begin a new life. The worst scars caused by Sibbie's death were beginning to heal. Rupert took up residence in a comfortable flat carved out of the large new house which his father had bought in Hans Place, close to Harrods. Grudgingly his father produced the £40 necessary for him to be enrolled as a student at the Old Vic. An audition was held – farcical, since there were almost no other male students applying for a place – and passed successfully. In August 1927 Rupert became an actor.

Chapter Four

Per Ardua

There was never much chance that Rupert would achieve success in the theatre. 'I hear you want to go on the stage and that you are six foot four!' wrote Augustus John. 'A certain incongruity here perhaps.'[1] Other actors have overcome the handicap of being exceptionally tall but Rupert lacked the versatility, the flexibility, the capacity for recklessness, to make an actor. He could declaim handsomely, move well, radiate forceful dignity, but he could neither allow a part to impose itself on him nor impose himself upon a part. He would be competent, someone who could be relied on not to make a fool of himself and to perform any role with intelligence and integrity, but he would never be touched, even fleetingly, by the breath of greatness.

At one time he played with the idea of trying the cinema. He had an interview with the representative of a film company and with encouragement might have taken it further. No encouragement followed but in August 1928 he got together with a group of friends to make a movie. Since by then he had had some experience on the London stage and considered himself a professional he was allowed to play the fisherman hero who saved from drowning the heroine – played by his then girlfriend Lady Prudence Pelham – and was later discovered to be the son and heir of the murdered squire – played by Lord Gage. This snobbish extravaganza won some attention in the society journals but otherwise was esteemed only by those who took part in it and their immediate friends. Rupert himself thought it 'really not bad', but added that he had suffered 'a nasty disillusionment as to my own face and figure'.[2] It did not give him a taste for the medium. One of the few evenings he spent with his father included a visit to Charlie Chaplin's latest film, *The Circus*. He found it very amusing but 'I infinitely prefer any play to any but a super film.'[3]

The stage was where he was resolved to shine. The Old Vic, at which

Rupert presented himself in August 1927, was the creation of Lilian Baylis, who had transformed it from a philanthropic temperance institution into the nearest thing London had to a people's theatre. During the First World War it had become associated above all with the plays of Shakespeare and earned the reputation of employing first-rate actors and actresses at second- or even third-rate salaries. Miss Baylis was perpetually in financial difficulties and kept the theatre going by a combination of faith, fervour and unscrupulous exploitation of everyone associated with her rickety enterprise. One of her fund-raising devices was to extract a fee from 'apprentices' and then use them, without payment, as stage hands and bit-part actors. They learned a lot while so employed, but little systematic attempt was made to train them. Few of them resented this treatment: people who worked at the Old Vic imitated Miss Baylis, mocked her, sometimes feared her, but almost always revered her. Some thought her 'too careful about money, a prude about morals, ill-educated, conceited, a fanatical egotist'. Others found her 'affectionate, humorous, faithful', even a saint. Both were right.[4] She saw herself as a warrior and a crusader. Once she told Sybil Thorndike how much she admired Joan of Arc for being able to face generals, kings and bishops and make them do what she wanted. 'It's difficult enough with the Vic,' she said, 'but thinking of Joan is a help to me.'[5]

Rupert loved the atmosphere of the Old Vic: the energy, the excitement, the hard work and expertise that lay under the superficially chaotic surface. Its audiences, he wrote, 'are large, vastly enthusiastic, wholly indiscriminating, highly prejudiced against novelty in any shape or form and (quite rightly) entirely unswayed by newspaper criticism'.[6] Though he would have considered himself more discriminating than the average member of the Old Vic audience, he would have admitted to being, if not prejudiced against, then at least suspicious of novelty. His personal taste inclined toward the unadventurous. He thought R. C. Sherriff's *Outward Bound* 'one of the very best plays of modern years' and thoroughly enjoyed A. A. Milne's *The Fourth Wall* – 'Milne is an excellent and witty craftsman,' he wrote approvingly. Ibsen's *Ghosts*, on the other hand, he thought 'not a good play' (though, to be fair to him, he saw only a rehearsal of what was anyway a not very distinguished production).[7] He attached great importance, perhaps exaggerated importance, to good craftsmanship. Yet on the whole his judgment was sound. He knew well, and loved, all the monuments of the classical repertoire, recognised and responded eagerly to great acting, and could spot potential in what some felt to be unlikely quarters. He went to see Jerome Kern's enormously successful operetta *Show Boat* and enjoyed it greatly. But, he asked, 'why not give Paul Robeson – a unique and magnificent man – something to do? He sings his one song perfectly. I should like to see him play Othello.'[8]

Rupert's arrival at the Old Vic coincided with the building's closure for badly needed renovation. The company migrated to the Lyric, Hammersmith. 'I should imagine it's foul having to trail out there,' wrote a friend sympathetically, clearly feeling Hammersmith to be the Ultima Thule, far beyond the limits set for civilised theatre-goers.[9] Luckily the Old Vic audience proved more intrepid and the first production in its temporary home, *The Taming of the Shrew*, played to full houses. Rupert was allowed to walk on in various guises but was given no word to utter. The stars were Sybil Thorndike and her husband Lewis Casson; Rupert admired them extravagantly but was far too lowly to do more than gaze respectfully at them from afar. He enormously enjoyed the mixture of people who staffed the theatre and acted in the plays. Up to then his circle of acquaintances had been confined almost entirely to Etonians and their relations; he in no way now turned against them but was delighted to find that there was a world elsewhere into which he could venture and where he would be accepted.

His closest friend was Charlie Marford, the self-educated son of an East End baker who had worked at the Old Vic for three years playing minor parts and painting scenery. 'He was one of the most intelligent and witty people I have known, and his company was always a delight,' wrote Rupert.[10] Marford took Rupert's theatrical education in hand, taught him how to use greasepaint and equipped him with a repertoire of theatrical anecdotes which were to serve him well throughout his life. They kept in touch until Marford died, long after the Second World War, and several hundred of his letters survive: gossipy, idiosyncratic, and laced with a pungent slang that makes them vividly readable if at times obscure. Rupert's other ally in the company was Eric Portman, already well established in his career and playing juvenile leads. Portman was homosexual, which put him somewhat at a loss when Lilian Baylis one day asked him whether he was pure. After some hesitation he assured her that he was. She was relieved: 'I'm all for everybody having their proper mate in life, but I don't like it going on in the wings.'[11] She would have found Portman's mate most improper but he was too wise to exhibit him in the theatre, or indeed anywhere where he might come to Miss Baylis's attention. The first lines Rupert spoke on the London stage were in *The Merchant of Venice*, in which he played Portia's servant, Stephano. Stephano has no lines specifically assigned to him but is allowed to share a few trivialities with his fellow servant, Balthazar. Nobody mentioned Rupert by name in the reviews but the *Observer* struck him a glancing blow. The servants who stood by while the Princes of Morocco and Aragon were undergoing their ordeal, it complained, 'manifested no interest whatever in proceedings that mightily involved the welfare and happiness of their mistress'. Rupert, no doubt, would have retorted that displays of emotion would ill become a manservant on duty in a noble household. Certainly his friend Harman Grisewood, then just beginning the career that was to take him almost to the top of the BBC, saw nothing amiss in the performance, though he made the forgivable mistake of confusing the two servants. 'I saw you the other night in the colossal role of Balthazar in that great Shakespearian blunder *The Merchant of Venice*,' he wrote. 'When are they going to let you play a good part, or have they and have I missed it?'[12]

In March he was despatched with Charlie Marford and two or three other disposable actors from the Old Vic staff to put on a concert party in a leper colony in Essex. They acted scenes from Shakespeare; sang songs; Marford drew sketches of donkeys which, when turned upside down, proved to be caricatures of Lloyd George; Rupert read Oscar Wilde's story *The Happy Prince*. 'It was all most exhausting and strangely moving,' Rupert remembered, 'all those doomed and mutilated people apparently so simply delighted.'[13] In his diary that night he recorded that he felt boundless compassion for the victims of leprosy. 'I say "boundless" but actually it is closely bounded by selfishness. Going there has made me ashamed of myself for ever complaining. I should be for ever rejoicing.'[14]

Another similarly altruistic but less inspiring occasion was the London County Council's Schoolchildren's Matinée, on which occasion seventeen hundred bored and rebellious children were packed into the gigantic auditorium. They were treated to a performance of *The Merchant of Venice*. Most of the senior actors had discovered some compelling reason why they could not be there so Rupert was allowed to play the not particularly appealing but still relatively substantial part of Gratiano. The previous year the hubbub had been so appalling that the management had protested and on this occasion the children had been threatened with capital punishment if they made a sound. The resultant hush was so striking that Charlie Marford crept into the dress circle to see if the audience had slipped out under cover of darkness. He found a small boy battering his neighbour's head against the brass rail in front of him, occasionally pausing to put his finger to his lips and whisper 'Sh!' before resuming the assault. The audience left its mark even if it did not make itself heard: 'The effect of two hours of Shakespeare,' Rupert told Deirdre, 'was to make the children pee in their seats and the cleaners had a nasty job next day.'[15]

The Old Vic returned to its proper home in February 1928. *School for Scandal* was the opening production; Rupert was given the trivial role of Careless but also understudied Eric Portman, who was playing Charles Surface. The word 'understudy' carried little significance in the Old Vic; rehearsals for understudies were a luxury in which Miss Baylis did not indulge. When Portman went down with jaundice, and Rupert was told he must take over the part the following day, he was therefore partly aghast, partly enraptured. 'I don't know it properly. God help me!' he wrote in his diary. Luckily Careless was much of the time on stage with Surface so he already had a working knowledge of his lines. He stumbled through the first performance and managed the second with much greater confidence: 'I think a slight triumph – got through well enough. Balliol Holloway is to play the part from Monday. However I have tomorrow night. Am feeling a nervous wreck.' That performance too passed off well: 'Feeling rather triumphant. A lovely audience – everything went very well. How I wish I was playing the part next week too!' It was not to be, however, and he did not even have the satisfaction of finding his replacement incompetent. Holloway turned out to be 'a delightful man with great personal charm' as well as an experienced and skilful actor.[16] The *Old Vic Magazine* duly reported that Rupert had 'very pluckily' stood in for Portman, though still only a student. 'Comedy of this mannered type,' it observed, 'needs a tremendous amount of rehearsal', and the understudies had been given only the most scanty run through for their parts. The comment suggests that Rupert's performance was far from highly polished, but the conclusion was: 'Fate has been unusually kind to understudies this season and they have taken their chances with both hands.' He may not have acquitted himself quite as triumphantly as he imagined, but certainly there had been no disgrace.[17]

It is likely that a young actor, barely in the foothills of his career, will view the mountains ahead of him from a somewhat solipsistic point of view. When Rupert was told that he would be appearing in *Hamlet* he did not reflect how privileged he was to act in what he believed to be the greatest play ever written but grumbled: 'Really, Guildenstern is a tiresome part.' Then the company did *King Lear* – 'Am playing Burgundy. "Waterish" and all too short,' he gloomily observed.[18] *Lear* was the last play he did with the Old Vic. 'Thank goodness I have finished with the place,' he wrote, yet he knew that it had served him well and that he had learned a lot. It had given him credentials too; managers knew that anyone who had worked under Miss Baylis and survived to tell the tale must be employable if not necessarily a future star. 'I have made full use of it,' he concluded, when he reflected on his experience to date. 'I'm so glad the Old Vic is proving such good value,' Peter Fleming had written a few months before: 'You were right to go down, though I wish you hadn't.'[19] Rupert was glad he had, and faced the future with some confidence.

He was to have need of it. Theatrical life is never easy, least of all for a beginner, and if Rupert had not lived rent-free in a comfortable flat and enjoyed an allowance from his father he would have found it difficult to survive the next few months. The only job that he was offered was with the Stage Society, a group which had done much pioneering work with Shaw, Ibsen and Chekhov and which, because of its private status, was able to escape the censorship of the Lord Chamberlain. It was highly esteemed but apt to put on productions too obscure or impenetrable for the public taste. Rupert was involved in *Paul among the Jews*, a translation from the German of an interminable and almost entirely action-free play by the Austrian Paul Werfel. The critics thought little of it: it was 'among the duller of recent Stage Society productions,' wrote Hubert Griffith, 'and those who regularly attend the Stage Society's plays of the last couple of seasons will know that is a distinction not easily earned or equalled.' Rupert enjoyed it none the less: it gave him his first outing on the West End stage, it enabled him to say in later years that he had acted with Laurence Olivier, and best of all, it gained him two guineas for the two performances, the first money that he had earned in his new career.

It was by no means the last. In June he was summoned by Nigel Playfair, one of London's grandest actor-managers, proprietor of the Lyric, Hammersmith, and recently knighted for services to drama. 'Can it be a job? To sleep, highly excited,' Rupert wrote in his diary. It was a job, though only a small one, a walk-on part in Goldsmith's *She Stoops to Conquer*. Rupert was relieved to be employed but disappointed by the role offered him: he liked the atmosphere of the Lyric theatre but, having got a taste of the West End, felt that he was once more being exiled to the suburbs. 'Excellent house and first-rate notices,' he recorded after the first night, and then, with some gloom, 'Fear it will run for months.'[20] It did, and within a few weeks Rupert was offered modest promotion: his pay was increased from £4 to £6 a week and he was allowed to understudy one of the principal characters. Peter Fleming was playing with the idea of following his friend on to the stage – to the dismay of his snobbish and ambitious mother. He rejoiced in Rupert's success. 'It really is marvellous,' he wrote, 'and will be a great help in arguments about the stage at Castle Fleming.'[21] Rupert was less enthusiastic: the actor he was understudying stayed obstinately healthy, time moved on and he seemed to be getting nowhere. When *She Stoops to Conquer* finally closed his main sensation was one of relief: 'Personally thankful it's over, though the salary is A1.'[22]

The relief was the greater because Playfair offered him a small but decidedly more substantial part in his next production, Sheridan's *The Critic*. The £6 salary was to continue. 'Marvellous notices . . . Hopes of a longer run,' Rupert recorded after the first night. But the uncertainty of life in the theatre was soon brought home to him. In November 1928 King George V fell ill and his life was feared for. The risk for London's theatres was quickly apparent. 'If only the King doesn't die it should do well,' Rupert wrote of the new production. 'Fear the King is dying,' was the next day's entry in his diary. On 3 December: 'Walked to Buckingham Palace to see the latest bulletin. Slightly better'; by 6 December 'The King is recovering!' then four days later, 'The King is worse again. Our play is doing badly. My cold is awful.' On 13 December all was going well: 'My cold is better. So is the King. Things are looking up!' But it was a false dawn. The King's recovery continued, the play's did not. On 28 December came the sad entry, 'No *Critic* this week or for ever.' The royal illness cannot alone be blamed for the failure of what would anyway have been a somewhat uncertain enterprise, but it did not help and it left Rupert wondering whether there might not have been something to say for stockbroking after all.

'So ends 1928,' Rupert reflected in his diary. 'On the whole a goodish year, I suppose: a car, a salary, a larger library, a new overcoat – and so for 1929.' The salary by theatrical standards was respectable but was well under £10,000 a year at current values and certainly not enough to pay for car, larger library or new overcoat. Still less would it have paid for the two weeks which he now proceeded to spend in Monte Carlo, losing modestly in the casino and visiting bookshops. 'Drove into Italy,' he noted on 11 January. 'My first visit. Rather thrilled. Delicious lunch at San Remo Casino. Bought Tauchnitz edition of *The Brook Kerith*.'

He was beginning to accept that his theatrical career was unlikely to take him far. He was not yet ready to give up, however. For a few months he had to content himself with brief appearances in one-off productions in art theatres, then Playfair offered him a place in a three-week tour of *She Stoops to Conquer*. He would play Hastings, not a plum part but more considerable than anything he had been entrusted with at Hammersmith. The first stop was at Cambridge. 'Started badly but improved,' Rupert wrote of the performance. 'Lousy personally, and tired out.' His fatigue was unsurprising given that on the way down in his motor car he had 'biffed into a man in Watford', been stopped by the police in Bedford for disregarding a traffic signal and set the car on fire by forgetting to fill it up with water.

Later performances went better and by the time the tour reached its final stage at Oxford he was reasonably confident. Many of his contemporaries were still up at the university and he could be sure of a friendly audience. 'The Old Vic has improved you enormously,' wrote Peter Fleming. 'I was really impressed.'[23] But the tone of the critics on the whole was one of slightly condescending commiseration on his unworthy role: 'difficult and rather ungracious', the *Oxford Magazine* called the part of Hastings, while to the *Cherwell* it was 'awkward and subordinate'. It was generally felt that he had done his best with poor materials but not everyone even agreed on this: 'Mr Rupert Hart-Davis was rather gauche,' read one unwelcome comment. It was not the triumphant return for which he had hoped.

Almost as galling as his failure to win important roles or serious attention from the critics was the interest taken in his career by society newspapers and gossip columnists. Deirdre was coming out in London and was acclaimed as one of the most striking débutantes of the year; Rupert found himself referred to as her brother, 'good-looking, witty and a collector of first editions' certainly, but only incidentally a 'promising young actor'. The cast of *The Taming of the Shrew*, the *Daily Chronicle* assured its readers, included 'a young actor who can claim cousinship once removed with two members of the royal family'. First nights were no longer such glamorous affairs as they had used to be, the *Chronicle* reported regretfully, but Lady Diana Cooper would probably be attending because 'her nephew, Mr Rupert Hart-Davis, is in the cast'.[24] Better be ignored altogether, Rupert felt, than celebrated for the wrong reasons.

By the summer of 1929 he had made up his mind that the stage was not for him. He made one last appearance in an amateur production of a play by Rostand and then renounced acting for ever. 'Thank God I no longer have any ties with that intolerable profession the Theatre!' he exclaimed twenty years later. Yet he did not regret the years that he had spent as an actor. It had been a far more enjoyable and interesting way of passing the time than he would have found at Oxford; he had learnt as much – more indeed – of relevance to his future life; he had met a range of people who he would never have dreamed existed if he had stayed at university. And he could claim that he had acted with Gielgud and Olivier, Lewis Casson, Sybil Thorndike and Peggy Ashcroft. These luminaries would not necessarily have noticed that they had been acting with him, but it was still something to have rubbed shoulders with the great. 'Brief, almost mute and wholly inglorious,' Rupert described his theatrical career.[25] The adjectives were not entirely inappropriate but the experiment had still been worthwhile. He would have been sorry if he had not tried and felt no shame that he had failed.

The theatre had anyhow never absorbed all his energies; it spilt over into his private life but by no means took it over. A grand but not untypical supper party at his flat at Hans Place included Nigel Playfair, Bea Lillie, Jack Buchanan, Marie Ney, Angela Baddeley, Richard Goulden, Glen Byam Shaw – a rich galaxy for so humble a performer to have assembled – but another evening it might have consisted of bookish friends discussing poetry, or more mondaine visitors from the world of his sister Deirdre. When he was not acting – a situation which occurred much more often than he would have wished – he was as likely as not to be at a 'bloody dance in Westbourne Terrace. Jews and sweet champagne',* or his sister's decidedly grander coming-out ball with a dinner for thirty-six given by Philip Sassoon and the Prince of Wales present at the dance that followed. 'Didn't hate it half as much as I expected,' was his comment.[26] He went to many dances on the grounds

---

*The diary entry about the Westbourne Terrace dance is of interest as being one of the very few instances that Rupert made an even mildly disparaging remark about Jews. A casual and largely meaningless anti-Semitism was at that time endemic among the British upper and middle classes but Rupert was almost entirely free of it and would have considered the fact that somebody was Jewish to be, if anything, a point in his or her favour.

that to do so was a convenient way of meeting women, catching up with old friends and getting a free dinner, but he did so with small expectation of enjoyment. He disliked dancing and found little to talk about with most of his fellow guests. 'I shudder to remember the agonies I went through,' he told Deirdre many years later. 'How I used to hide, and the daughter of the house, sent down to round up recalcitrants, forced me into the arms of some huge dumb girl who could find no other partner. Night after bloody night the masquerade continued.'[27]

He found Deirdre's dance tolerable partly at least because he took Jean Forbes-Robertson as his partner. Jean was the daughter of one of London's most eminent actors and was herself on the threshold of a successful career. She 'was more like a spirit than a mortal', Rupert wrote of her, 'with her unearthly beauty and individual approach to every role'.[28] She was a year or two older than Rupert and more experienced, both sexually and theatrically; she was never particularly close to him but he admired her and greatly enjoyed her company. It was with her, at the Greyhound Ball at the end of 1928, that he met 'James Hamilton. A publisher'. Hamilton had been christened James, was at that time generally known as Jimmy, changed his name by deed poll to Hamish and for the most of his life was called by everyone Jamie. He was seven years older than Rupert and was already well established as London manager of the American publisher Harper Brothers. In a short time he would found his own eponymous company, a concern which flourished until it was taken over by the Thomson Organisation in 1965. He was an Olympic oarsman, a pastime which Rupert found unaccountable, and regarded books more as a source of profit than a subject for leisurely discussion. The two men, therefore, did not seem particularly compatible but in fact Rupert was amused by and respected Hamilton and circumstances drew them together.

The antithesis of Jamie Hamilton, in that he asked nothing better than to talk endlessly about books, was Rupert's friend from Eton, James Lees-Milne. Lees-Milne was mildly admiring of Rupert's prowess on the stage but took no great interest in it. Whenever an opportunity arose, however, he would escape from the dreary world of commerce in which his father was seeking to sequester him and visit Rupert in his flat in Hans Place. The large sitting-room, he wrote, 'made a tremendous impression on me. It was the most civilised room I had ever entered. The walls were lined from floor to ceiling with books that had been read, the spines of their immaculate jackets flickering in the golden light of a deep coal fire. The air of well-being and culture was something beyond my wildest dreams of attainment.'[29] Rupert, he said, 'looked like a big Airedale puppy, affectionate, boisterous and intensely extrovert'. By themselves, or with other like-minded friends, they endlessly discussed the books they were reading or were about to read. Rupert was always lending him books, urging him to try some new author, inveighing against another. 'I can never forget what you did for me,' Lees-Milne wrote many years later. 'Without being aware of it you civilised me. It was a slow process perhaps and it took me years to realise what you had done for me.'[30] To those who knew him only in later life, the idea of an *uncivilised* Lees-Milne must seem fantastical; if Rupert indeed was responsible for such a change he did his job extraordinarily well.

His own reading remained omnivorous. More than at any other time in his life he ventured into modernism and was open to new impressions. He read and admired Eliot's 'Prufrock,' and then embarked on *Ulysses*. 'An amazing work,' he wrote of the latter in his diary. 'Went to bed intoxicated with literature,' and then a few days later, 'read more of *Ulysses*. A terrific work.' He quoted with approval Lucas di Penna saying that books were to him 'the light of the heart, the mirror of the body, the myrrh-pot of eloquence', yet they were also dear old friends to be revisited. Above all, they were sources of pleasure. They did not need to be complicated or demanding to win his esteem; it was enough that he enjoyed them. The day after he read 'Prufrock' he took up Sapper's Bulldog Drummond extravaganza *The Female of the Species*. 'Couldn't put it down. All his worst faults but admirably entertaining.' The day after that it was Ronald Firbank's *Prancing Nigger*: 'A delicious book – precious and stilted but beautifully chiselled.' A man who could read Eliot, Sapper and Firbank within a week and relish them all might perhaps be called indiscriminating but could certainly not be accused of elitism or literary snobbishness. Rupert *was* discriminating, in the sense that he recognised and appreciated quality in almost any genre, but he was markedly eclectic in his reading and never shrank from championing authors whom literary pundits deemed lowbrow or unfashionable. Nor did he pay much heed to the fulminations of the moralists. He read Radclyffe Hall's novel about lesbianism, *The Well of Loneliness*, and enjoyed it more than any book he had read for years. A few days later it was banned by the Home Secretary. 'England, my England,' was Rupert's wondering comment.[31]

Though Peter Fleming was still at Oxford, he and Rupert kept in close touch. 'Oxford without you is trying to a degree, even more so than with you,' Fleming wrote to his friend,[32] but in fact he was having a highly successful and, on the whole, enjoyable time. One of his responsibilities was to edit the undergraduate weekly, *Isis*. He decided to revive a series of 'London Letters', written by former Oxford undergraduates and giving a lively if not always reliable account of society and culture in the capital. Rupert, he felt, would be an ideal contributor. The offer was accepted with alacrity. Re-reading his articles many years later Rupert found them 'touching and amusing'.[33] They were also, it must be admitted, verbose, pretentious and heavy-handed. He strained too energetically for effect and dragged in the *bon mot* whether or not it was relevant or appropriate. Of the Old Vic audience, he wrote, '*As You Like It* is as they find it', Paul Nash's trees were 'as different from Corot's trees as hell from a hot cross bun'; Charles Darway bore 'as much resemblance to Sydney Carton as Wigan to Waikiki'. But these were a young man's faults; they did not conceal the fact that he had a wide range of interests, considerable knowledge, and the capacity to think with originality about what he saw and read. The letters were never dull and often said something of value about their subjects.

His life in London was made far more enjoyable by the acquisition of a car, a Morris two-seater. Whether his fellow Londoners shared his pleasure is another matter. Apart from the man in Watford whom he had biffed into on the way to Cambridge, he knocked down an old man in Hammersmith and reversed into a pedestrian near his home in Knightsbridge; in Richmond there was 'an-all-but-fatal-skid' and in Grosvenor Square he ran into another car and sprained his companion's ankle. Throughout his life he viewed all machinery with suspicion and resentment; usually his dislike was reciprocated. During his tyro years as a driver his cars were constantly breaking down, catching on fire or ending up in ditches. Few long journeys were completed without a catalogue of unspecified 'slight contretemps' or 'various vicissitudes'. Those who allowed him to drive them must have been exceptionally loving, trusting or anxious to have a lift. Yet there were many such valiant souls. It was above all as an aid to wooing that he found his car of value and he put it to such purposes with impressive frequency. From the age of nineteen, when he first met Anne Brindley, Rupert was almost continually in love; usually with one person at a time, sometimes with two or more. 'Things, or rather everything that I thought settled is swept away,' he announced portentously in his diary at the end of

February 1928 – a reference, presumably, to the ending of his affair with Anne. He had decided that 'the only way to keep sane (anyhow at my age) is to live solely for the present – look back by all means on past happiness – but the future – may the stars be kind'.

The stars, on the whole, played their part pretty well. Life, for any susceptible and romantic young man, is filled with vicissitudes, some of which are likely to be painful. Rupert had a fair share of such episodes. 'Went to bed full of loneliness and self-pity,'[34] was a typical diary entry. In this case it was provoked by the fact that for the moment there was no woman significantly involved in his life but far more often the cause for such plaints lay in some setback in his current love affair. He took each new relationship with great seriousness. 'If I had been a person who could flit from flower to flower,' he wrote with mingled pride and regret, 'that might have provided a solution, but I am not: sex to me is indissolubly linked with love.'[35] The claim was justified, but he might have added that love came easily and at frequent intervals. Cupid, in the case of Rupert, seems to have used not so much a bow and arrow as a shotgun.

Anne Brindley had hardly left the scene before he was involved with Marjorie MacIntyre, a Scottish girl who was a student at RADA. She was 'vibrantly pretty' wrote the biographer of her future husband, 'a vivacious and attractive young woman', who had never done much more than flirt with the idea of being an actress.[36] Playing the truth game with a group of friends Rupert found himself forced to admit that he was in love with Marjorie. But was he really, he at once asked himself: 'What am I really thinking at the moment? Wishing I was rich and famous – who doesn't? Feeling rather cynical about life and love – a phase all pass through? Vaguely in love with several people – chiefly with Mac? I can't resist people whom I know to be in love with me – vanity, all is vanity! She is a sweet girl and, unlike most of the women I like, younger than me. I don't want to marry her, I just like being with her at the moment. My God! What selfish brutes men are!'[37] In fact it does not seem that Marjorie felt any more passionately committed to Rupert than he to her. Certainly they never went to bed with each other – though that was unsurprising given the conventions of the time. Many years later she said to him: 'It's a shame that we were never lovers, isn't it?' Rupert agreed that it was – 'alas, too late by now'.[38]

Probably the affair would have amicably petered out; before it did, however, Marjorie's brother died, aged only twenty-seven, and she felt bound to return to Scotland to console her parents. Rupert saw her off to Edinburgh: 'She was very loving and sweet and I shall miss her a lot.'[39] A few years later she married the Scottish writer Eric Linklater, and re-entered Rupert's life as the wife of a close friend. They remained fond of each other all their lives. Inevitably her disappearance from London made Rupert reflect on what he had lost. There were more evenings of 'loneliness and self-pity', but not too many or too lonely. There was far too much going on in his life to allow of much repining.

His diaries are bewildering in their catalogue of women to whom he was at one time attracted. There was Yolande: 'a lovely girl, large and gay and beautiful'; there was Iris: 'She is a perfect companion – adaptable to a degree, beautiful, intelligent, natural. I love her very much'; there was Kitty: 'too nice for words. Sympathetic and so intelligent'; most of all, there was Prue. Prudence Pelham was the daughter of the Earl of Chichester. She scored heavily over her competitors by not being in love with Rupert, or at least concealing it if she was. One evening she would spare Rupert several hours of intimate conversation, the next she would be remote, even chilly. He danced with her at the Burnhams' ball. She 'was looking too divine but was very distant and unsympathetic. Home about 2.30, miserable, almost weeping, loathing myself, dreading tomorrow, wishing I was dead. Iris loves me and I don't care for her. I worship Prue and she doesn't care for me. Oh dear! Oh dear!'[40] To read such entries is to make one thank God one does not have to be young again.

The pangs were real but they were not deeply felt. Soon all these fleeting fancies would be forgotten.

> You meaner beauties of the night,
>   That poorly satisfy our eyes,
> More by your number than your light;
>   You common people of the skies,
>   What are you when the moon shall rise?

The problem for Rupert was that there were two moons.

Chapter Five

Two Moons

Rupert first saw Celia Johnson on 27 January 1929 at a party on stage at the Lyric, Hammersmith. She was then in the early stages of a career which turned her into an iconic figure; the quintessence of vulnerable yet indomitable British womanhood, loving not wisely but too well but always in the last analysis putting duty and family first. With Noël Coward in *In Which We Serve*, still more with Trevor Howard in *Brief Encounter*, her wistful beauty, her radiant decency, won a nation's heart. She was tall and slender, and though her retroussé nose and huge spaniel eyes did not accord with the strict tenets of classical beauty, they combined with her charm and genuine good nature to make her irresistible to a young man like Rupert who was ever anxious to fall in love. She was just twenty-one: her middle-class background and education at St Paul's Girls' School made her feel slightly ill at ease in the more relaxed and raffish ambience of the theatre and she recognised in Rupert a respectability and restraint which made her feel secure.

Temperamentally she was far removed from the heroines whose parts she played. She loved certainly, but always wisely; duty and family did indeed matter to her but only in moderation – on the whole she preferred bridge. She found it difficult to commit herself totally to anyone or anything; grand passion was not within her range, the physical side of sex she found a shade unseemly. She met Rupert's impetuous ardour with an amused affection that at times enraged, at times enchanted him.

Their relationship was at its height during the spring of 1929. Under-employed, sometimes even unemployed, Rupert was happy to ferry Celia around: to an audition, to a hairdresser, from her home to the theatre and back again. She lived in Richmond, and he grew to know every detail of the road that led there. Exaltation alternated with black gloom. One night he took her to a dance at the Savoy: 'Worship Celia.

Took her home 4.30 am. Fear she doesn't care much for me. Cried aloud coming home in the car. To bed unhappy.' 'It's loving that matters, not being loved,' he told himself, but he didn't really believe it. A few days later things were going better. He took her for a drive in the country: 'Looked at pigs and woods. Drove home happy as a king . . . thanked God on my knees for Celia and today.' To read his diary one would think that a passionate love affair was raging. Entries were marked with one, two or three crosses, presumably to indicate different degrees of intimacy. The visit to the pigs and woods was prefaced with an X; 'a very happy day, she was divine' was worth two Xs; 'She kissed me goodbye in the car' carried a maximum three.[1] Yet a chaste embrace in the car was the worst or best of it. 'I was a pitifully young 21 and, as you can see, besotted,' he wrote in explanation to Celia Johnson's biographer. '"Divine", "happy day", etc meant that I had been rewarded by a sisterly kiss on the cheek. I repeatedly asked her to marry me, but she (very sensibly) brushed all such suggestions aside.'[2]

    It might have gone on in this way for months – with Rupert constantly repelled yet never finally rebuffed – if an actress had not been needed to play opposite him in the touring version of She Stoops to Conquer. He asked for the part to be given to Celia but was told she was too tall; instead 'a good young actress called Peggy Ashcroft' was taken on. Rupert met her and decided he liked her; he went to see her perform at the Everyman Theatre in Hampstead and realised that she was a great actress in the making; by the time they set out for Cambridge on the first leg of the tour he was well on the way to falling in love.

    Peggy came from the same sort of background as Celia, comfortably and unpretentiously middle class, a little more exotic in origins because her mother was part Danish and part German Jewish. Her father had been killed during the war, her mother had died in 1926, leaving her an orphan and very conscious of the fact. She was more advanced in her career than Celia, having trained at the Central School of Speech and Drama and made a small but noteworthy name for herself outside the West End, but both women were near the bottom of a ladder that was long and vertiginously steep. In character, however, they were strikingly different. Peter Hall referred to Peggy's 'extreme passion and extreme sexuality';[3] if Celia was extreme in anything it was in her moderation. Peggy 'was like quicksilver,' said Harold Pinter, 'and her moods were like quicksilver'.[4] It was soon clear to Rupert that any relationship with her would be a tempestuous roller-coaster.

    What particularly drew Rupert to Peggy was that her enthusiasm for poetry was equal to his own. 'Drove to a beautiful field beyond Godstow, lay under a tree and read aloud "The Scholar Gypsy",' is an entry from Rupert's diary when the tour reached its final stage at Oxford.[5] A few days before they had been reading Donne, another day it was Kipling; when they were separated they would learn poems by heart so that they could recite them when they met again. John Gielgud remarked derisively that they would walk through the fields together, holding hands but without the slightest idea what they were supposed to do next. No wonder, he concluded, that the relationship did not last.[6] In those first halcyon weeks, however, it seemed to both of them that life could hold no more. At the end of May Rupert wrote triumphantly that he had talked to Peggy till three in the morning: 'We love each other.'

His only difficulty was that, while he had fallen in love with Peggy, he had not yet contrived to fall out of love with Celia. When he told her about his new attachment he was disconcerted to find that the news upset her deeply: 'She burst into floods of tears, said she had always loved me and became almost hysterical.'[7] Rupert, who was due on stage in half an hour, met the immediate crisis by persuading Peter Fleming to take Celia in hand and look after her for the rest of the day. But what would happen then? He could not help being flattered by and a little grateful for Celia's avowal of love. If she had been so positive a little earlier, would he ever have looked at Peggy? 'Torture – agonising, despairing indecision,' he wrote in his diary. As he put it many years later, he was fast approaching the state of Macheath in *The Beggar's Opera*: 'How happy could I be with either. / Were t'other dear charmer away.' Throughout June he dithered. He went on seeing Celia regularly, but though he made his doubts obvious he could not bring himself finally to end the affair. 'Serious talk, took her home. Feeling wretched,' he wrote in his diary on 23 June, and then the following day: 'Drove C home. More or less said goodbye. Very very sad and hurting myself like hell. Poor darling.' But it was still only 'more or less'; in Celia's eyes at least the last goodbye had not been said.

Peggy meanwhile, out of London on a provincial tour, felt on stronger grounds than Celia but was still far from confident. On 12 June she suggested to Rupert that they should test their love by letting a fortnight pass without exchanging any letters. 'I suffer from what I like to call a passionate soul,' she wrote, 'and I must love with it, and now I do understand God and strength and feel at rest – all because of you.' No doubt everyone would say they were very young to be thinking of marriage, Peggy went on, 'and so we are. But let's be young and hope we'll never get old.'[8] The period of silence did nothing to abate their ardour; on 26 June they met at a house near Hindhead – 'a day in Heaven,' Peggy described it – and found that they were more resolved than ever not to let themselves be separated.[9] Peggy celebrated their reunion with a lyrical effusion of immense length and fervour:

> Rupert! Rupert! Rupert! How shall I ever stop writing to you tonight? Oh my darling I need you so . . . All day I live on the thought of you, it gets intenser and intenser till each blade of grass I pass on the road shouts your name and I cannot bear the smell of the wet grass and worst of all the May. Oh my darling, everything is lovelier because of you and all day I have been in a queer tension of exhilaration, but tonight it has snapped and I feel I am pouring out my spirit into nothingness since you are not here to receive it
>
> [There was uncertainty behind the exultation] Dearest, am I very weak or am I only human? It was awful of me, but when you told me about your seeing Celia and how happy she was I could not help a pang. I wanted to call out to you, oh *please* don't look in just the way you do with me, is it the same to have her in your arms and must you kiss her in just our way? Darling, forgive me, I *had* to tell you this for you must not think me too noble . . . It is only that I wonder is Celia's or mine the fool's paradise?[10]

Rupert was almost sure that it was Celia's but he was still not prepared finally to commit himself. In the middle of July he took off on a European holiday with Peter Fleming, promising that he would definitely have made up his mind by the time he returned. It is a remarkable tribute to his charms that two beautiful, much sought-after and, in the case of Peggy Ashcroft particularly, high-spirited women, should have put up with such treatment. There is no reason to think that they even contemplated revolt. Peggy's patience, however, did sometimes run thin. On the envelope of one particularly loving letter she scrawled as an afterthought: 'Dear Rupert, you are a great oaf and a foul procrastinator and vacillator. Damn you!'[11] No doubt Rupert took the message to heart but it in no way changed his attitude.

The holiday with Fleming took them through Spain and France to Corsica. Rupert was determined not to enjoy himself, or at least to give that impression to Peggy in his frequent letters. In Bordeaux there was a heatwave; the bank was closed so they were almost destitute; worst of all, there were no letters waiting at the post office: 'I nearly cried . . .

Our tempers grew irritable and more irritable.' Fleming was far more hardy than his companion and liked to alternate stays in luxury hotels with nights on some barren hillside. Once they were woken by a thunderstorm and the wind knocked over a bottle of Evian water which soaked Rupert's pillow: 'Oh darling, I do hate sleeping out. Don't make me do much of it, please.' Spain was even worse. Neither of them spoke more than a few words of the language and Rupert found the inhabitants 'truculent, idle, dirty and stupid – moreover the filth of the villages passes belief'. He considered fleeing back to France but reflected that to do so would be to lose any chance of receiving Peggy's letters, gritted his teeth and carried on. Corsica, when they finally got there, proved worst of all. The people were 'flagrantly dishonest and speak no known language'; the only two Corsicans of any repute were Napoleon and Christopher Columbus, both of whom, Rupert felt, had a great deal to answer for. When at last they found a comfortable hotel Fleming insisted on leaving it to drive twenty miles over bumpy roads in searing heat to picnic in the mountains – 'some people can't keep still; or is it just that I'm the world's laziest chap?'

He wrote to Peggy almost every day, the grumbles punctuated by passages of ardent passion. He listed all the things he loved her for, concluding: 'I love, adore and worship you for everything you say, think, and do – past, present and future.' The past could look after itself. Peggy's present was at that moment concentrated on the first night in Blackpool of an adaptation of Lion Feuchtwanger's best-selling novel, *Jew Süss*. If the production was well received it would move on to London. It was to establish Peggy as a coming star but as the first night approached she knew only that it was the most important part she had yet played. The prospect filled her with enraptured terror. Rupert refused to wish her luck: 'You don't need any – you've got genius, my pet, and all the love of a lanky, unemployed, beach-combing youth – not that that's much good.' The future for Peggy still contained the uneasy wraith of Celia Johnson. Rupert was by now clear in his own mind the affair was over, but still he hesitated and could not bring himself to apply the *coup de grâce*. He was in France, on the point of returning to England, before he finally screwed himself up to send Celia what he told Peggy was 'a rather horrid little letter. I hated doing it, but it's a weight off my mind. We shall soon have no more ghosts to lay – please.'[12]

Celia Johnson received the letter in Blackpool, where she was also on tour. For five minutes she could not bring herself to open it: 'You see, I

knew, and I wanted to keep my hopes till the last minute, after which I
cried and cried and cried and the landlady was most concerned . . . I
think she thinks I'm homesick but I'm not, I'm you sick.' Her reply was
generously poignant:

> What can I say? Really there's only one thing I've any right to say which
> is 'Be very happy' – and oh Rupert my darling do believe me when I say
> that underneath everything I'm glad you are. I couldn't bear it when you
> looked so miserable and worried and I can think of you as gay and
> making absurd little jokes. Do you remember saying the night you went
> that I hadn't lost you for ever? I knew when you said it that I had but
> I've refused to believe it and I've just been living through the days till
> you came back. Oh Rupert, I can't believe *now* that I'll never tell you all
> the little things I've saved up for you and I don't think I'll ever get out of
> the habit [of thinking], whenever anything amusing, or attractive or
> pathetic happens – 'I must tell Rupert that'.[13]

Peggy was acting in Glasgow when Rupert got back (as he had
already discovered, emotional entanglements with people on the stage
involved many painful separations and expeditions to unlovely parts of
the British Isles). He was by nature something of a dandy but now he
spruced himself up with especial care, bought a new shirt and tie, had
his nails done at Harrods, then went to Hill's 'and had everything
known to modern science done to my hair, cut and oiled and washed
and massaged with electricity – all very refreshing but unfortunately it
now reeks of scent!'[14] Thus equipped, it was off to the north, with a
brief visit to Felbrigg on the way, where he stayed with his old friend
Wyndham Ketton-Cremer and allowed the smell of the scent to die
down. If he had any lingering doubts that he had made the right
decision they were quickly dispelled when he got to Glasgow. The
reunion was idyllic, and tearing himself away from her after four days
proved almost unbearable. He wept as he drove south – 'silly really, I
know, but I couldn't help it'. For the first time, he told Peggy, he felt
that he understood what Browning had meant in 'The Ring and the
Book' when he had written:

> Oh lyric love, half angel and half bird
> And all a wonder and a wild desire.

It was exactly what he now felt. 'I wonder and wonder at your limitless
perfection – and worship you madly and utterly and always – every

minute in Glasgow was pure and utter joy – and you, my angel, you are love and joy and beauty and peace and heaven and my silly, sweet, beautiful, snuggly, nice-smelling little girl.'[15] When the tour reached Manchester, Rupert was there again to cheer on his beloved. Alistair Cooke, whose 'Letter from America' was to educate and entertain the British listener for more than fifty years, was the young supporting actor deputed to catch Peggy when she plunged from the window to her death. 'It was very nice breaking her fall,' he remembered. 'She was twenty-one years old, not beautiful but very sexy.' Eventually Cooke plucked up his courage and asked her to tea. 'Oh, I'd love to,' she said, 'but my fiancé is coming up to see me so I'm afraid it won't be possible.'[16] At least Cooke was allowed to meet the lucky man. The two became firm friends and in time Rupert was to be Cooke's publisher.

'Fiancé' was a term used more *de facto* than *de jure*. It was still a few weeks before they were formally engaged. While in Spain Rupert had received an invitation to the wedding of Jean Forbes-Robertson and Jamie Hamilton, which was to be celebrated with much pomp in London. He knew they would have preferred a marriage in a register office but had been bullied by Lady Forbes-Robertson into make it a society event. He would go, he told Peggy, but only to satisfy himself 'how much nicer Gretna Green will be'.[17] As it turned out, Hamilton asked him to be the principal usher, so he could hardly have refused without causing grave offence. The ceremony reinforced all his doubts. 'What a barbaric, foul, obscene, unnecessary habit,' he wrote spleneti-cally, 'all those old people gloating and the people themselves miserable. What we will do is find a tiny country church that we really like and then arrange it without anybody knowing . . . I don't know about you, but *I* can't wait two years, please, please.'[18]

Peggy had no intention of waiting two years; even two months seemed too long. There was no Lady Forbes-Robertson on either side to insist on a fatuous ceremony; by mid-October plans were made and their friends were being told. Most of them were suitably enthusiastic. 'It'll not only be tremendous and lovely fun, but a very sound scheme into the bargain,' wrote Peter Fleming. 'I think she is sweet and I'm quite positive you'll be wildly happy.'[19] But some of those who knew Peggy best had their doubts. The engagement was a mistake, Fabia Drake believed: 'She is such an infant and so very keen and ambitious that she will find it hard to run everything at once. Still, she is an orphan . . . so I suspect she feels rather alone in the world and wants to have a background.'[20]

She was only half right. Peggy was passionately, romantically in love. A background was low on her list of priorities, as was financial security. Rupert had by now taken the first steps towards a job in publishing but even if it worked out she knew that he would never be rich. Nor was her career as an actress well enough established to guarantee a substantial income. Richard Hart-Davis had just come back from Le Touquet where he had lost a small fortune at the tables. 'What a fool the man is,' Rupert wrote contemptuously. 'I promise you we won't lose any that way. He seemed quite pleased about my job and said I must be prepared always to be poor. I agreed with an arch-hypocritical smile.'[21] The hypocrisy presumably related to the fact that he had not yet broken it to his father that he planned to marry a penniless actress. When Richard got the news he was predictably indignant and insisted that no help could be expected from him. Peggy was undiscomfited. In the radiant light of first love poverty seemed positively attractive. She urged her fiancé towards frugality. 'Every debt you pay will be like killing a dragon,' she assured him. 'And, oh, I'll try and save too and everything, everything is going to be lovely. I feel it is – in spite of your father and perhaps we *are* being too pessimistic about that. But he seems the *only* cloud, and I just don't feel that it's a false one because then things would be too good to be true.'[22]

Rupert and Peggy were married on 23 December in St Saviour's, Walton Place, a stone's throw from the Hart-Davis family home in Hans Place. 'I intend to continue with my work on the stage,' Peggy had told the *Evening Standard* when the engagement was announced. The *Daily Mirror* announced that the happy couple had found an original way of spending their honeymoon. Her marriage had not been allowed to interfere with her acting: 'She has not been away for a single performance since the wedding.' Both statements were patently correct and Rupert would have seen no harm in them. Together, however, they demonstrated vividly the pattern of Peggy's priorities. They presaged the shipwreck of the marriage.[23]

Their views of married life were fundamentally different. Rupert wanted a Darby and Joan relationship, a wife who – metaphorically at least – would put his slippers out for him in the evening; keep house for him; nurse him in sickness; take an interest in his work; share his enthusiasms; love, honour and, in the last resort, obey. Peggy was an intensely ambitious actress who would allow nothing to deflect her from her climb to greatness; once the novelty had worn off – and it wore off pretty quickly – she had no use for domesticity. Rupert was at heart monogamous: he had wavered briefly between Celia and Peggy but almost always he loved one woman at a time. Peggy found any exclusive relationship stultifying and confining. 'I feel I am an unmarriageable person,' she later confessed. 'You are essentially faithful and I the reverse. At least, I am not unfaithful in that I cease to love, but in that I feel I can love so much and so many.'[24] In the long run they could never have stayed married to their mutual contentment.

In the short run it was sex on which the marriage foundered. They were young and terrifyingly innocent when they fell in love; both were virgins, Peggy avowedly regretting it, Rupert taking it for granted. 'My love for Peggy,' he told George Lyttelton thirty years later, was 'chiefly an intellectual and spiritual passion, tied up with poetry and music, drama, youth and spring. Basically it wasn't a physical passion at all.'[25] This tidies things up a little too conveniently. The physical passion was there, though burning less strongly in Rupert than in Peggy. What was lacking was the ability to fulfil it. It is too easy to imagine how the tragedy developed: Rupert clumsy, frightened, not really sure what was expected of him; Peggy too inexperienced to help. Failure would beget failure, each fresh disaster seeming more humiliating and distressing than the last. What should have been a supreme pleasure would have become a fearsome and ever more distasteful challenge. Rupert would have been left with a sense of ignominious failure, Peggy with a resentful feeling that she was being rejected and deprived of something to which she was entitled. At first neither realised how important it was going to be, yet within the first few weeks of marriage the relationship was doomed.

For a time they brushed the problem under the carpet, pretended to believe that all was well, that Rupert was worried about his work and that a holiday together would set everything right. Finally, Peggy's patience – never her strongest quality – was exhausted. 'You see, my dear one,' she told him, 'our relationship is lovely but it is *not* fundamentally a marriage relationship. And between men and women sex is *the most fundamental* and necessary thing, the deepest relationship. There are exceptions, you may be one. But I think you are thwarted and wretched through lack of it and I do want you so to have everything . . . I loved you so much that I did not think very much about the physical side when we married – I took it for granted.' An irritation became a festering agony: 'For both of us it seemed far too important a factor in our relationship and gradually the unappeased monster was crushing all that is good between us.'[26]

The sadness was that in many ways they complemented each other admirably and got great pleasure from each other's company. They went to Arnold Haskell's fancy dress party as Romeo and Juliet and that, though less star-crossed, was how their friends imagined them. 'They were together only for a fortnight,' James Lees-Milne wrote much later in his diary.[27] In fact it was more like two years, though in the last six months or so the marriage was wearing painfully thin. Early in January 1930 they moved into a flat close to Piccadilly Circus: one large sitting- and dining-room giving on to the street; a tiny bedroom, bathroom and kitchen at the back. It was not the most salubrious of buildings – the flat below them was used by prostitutes while beneath that was a hairdressing salon which they suspected of being a centre for the white-slave traffic – but it was close to the theatres and offered plenty of scope for the entertainment of their friends. This they did on a lavish scale; far beyond anything their exiguous joint incomes could support. Their visitors' book was a name-dropper's delight and as such was proudly annexed by Rupert to the second volume of memoirs.* Among those who clambered up the shabby stairs to the fourth floor of 213 Piccadilly were John Gielgud, Laurence Olivier and Ralph Richardson, Paul Robeson, Ann Todd, Ian and Peter Fleming, Graham Greene, A. P. Herbert, Aldous Huxley, Duff and Diana Cooper and a bevy of lesser celebrities who would have warmed the heart of any social climber. Neither Rupert nor Peggy were social climbers: these were their friends; that they were famous too was a source of pleasure to their hosts but not a reason for inviting them.

On Sundays, or over the weekend if Peggy was not acting, they would drive out to visit friends who lived within striking distance of London. Once they went to stay with the enormously successful and prolific author Edgar Wallace at his Thames-side palace near Bourne End. They were allowed to sit and watch as he dictated his latest novel into his dictaphone. It was being serialised in the *Daily Express* and Wallace knew that the newspaper had used almost everything he had written. He started hesitantly, since he was working on two or three other projects at the same time and had forgotten the characters' names, but soon he was in the groove. Twenty-four hours later, Rupert was returning to London in Wallace's yellow Rolls-Royce with cylinders containing seven thousand words of the latest masterpiece.

When they went to stay at Dartington Hall, where the Elmhirsts were

---

* *The Power of Chance*, London, 1991, p182.

just about to open a school run on radically libertarian lines, they took with them the black singer and actor Paul Robeson. On the hall table they found a roneoed sheet listing points of interest. The first item was 'Mr and Mrs Hart-Davis and Mr Paul Robeson have arrived and will leave on Monday,' the second, 'The recuperative power of the soya bean is now established.' This curious combination reduced them to hysterical laughter and Robeson actually rolled on the floor in his delight. 'The vision of this gigantic Negro helpless with laughter on the floor of the great fourteenth-century hall will remain with me always,' wrote Rupert in his memoirs.[28]

Robeson was at that time playing Othello to Peggy's Desdemona, a production which was memorable and would have been memorably great if Robeson's magnificent voice and bearing had been matched by his ability to handle Shakespearian verse. He became a close friend of the Hart-Davises and was one of the few people to address Rupert as 'Rupe'; they took him to dinner with Jamie and Jean Hamilton, where he insisted on trying out the very expensive new sculling machine that Jamie had just acquired. It shattered under his massive frame. There can be no doubt that Peggy grew attached to him. 'It is not known exactly when she and Robeson became lovers,' states Peggy Ashcroft's biographer baldly.[29] It is not as certain as all that. Peggy was fiercely resentful of the racial prejudice which Robeson from time to time confronted, and was swayed by his powerful, almost over-powering personality. The hours on stage with him possessed a vivid reality of their own. 'How could one not fall in love in such a situation with such a man?' she asked long afterwards.[30] But this does not prove, or even strongly suggest that they were lovers. Rupert always maintained stoutly that they were not; and he had few illusions about his wife's behaviour. And yet perhaps he had doubts. As he wrote in his memoirs, 'simulated love-making on the stage often turns to the real thing off-stage',[31] and Peggy would not have been the first Desdemona to succumb to her Othello.

What is certain is that she had a protracted and torrid relationship with the novelist and playwright J. B. Priestley. Both physically and professionally Priestley was a powerful figure; a notorious womaniser but one who had the capacity to convince any woman – and no doubt for a time himself – that she was the only person who had ever mattered in his life. He became obsessed by Peggy Ashcroft, who acted in one of his less successful plays; she was in some ways repelled by him, but also fascinated and attracted. His wife, Jane, driven almost to the point of suicide by his repeated infidelities, telephoned Rupert to appeal for his support. Rupert assured her that he knew all about the liaison and that there was nothing in it about which she need worry. When they met, however, Rupert admitted that the affair was causing him great unhappiness. He confronted Peggy, Jane reproached her husband, there were quarrels, promises that the relationship was over, reunions, fresh recriminations; the summer and autumn of 1931 passed in an emotional turmoil that left at least two of the people involved close to despair.[32] Finally in November Peggy announced that she was going to break with Priestley: 'I may not even see him again, for I know he will feel bitterly.'[33] He did feel bitterly, and she did see him again, but the affair was spluttering out and never resumed in its full ardour.

The fact that she was no longer Priestley's mistress did not mean that in any real sense Peggy had returned to being Rupert's wife. 'I am going to live by myself and work very hard and just take what comes . . . And, darling, remember I am always I – Peggy, even if I am not Rupert's wife – for Peggy is real and your wife wasn't.' Rupert did not understand, she wrote, perhaps never would understand 'that human people cannot and must not depend on another person for their reason for existence'. The best kind of love was free, it 'must feel no terrible weight of responsibility'.

One reason for the disintegration of the marriage was that there had always been three people in it. At first Peggy thought that she could happily co-exist with the shadow of her husband's mother. 'Darling, why is it that when you talk about your Mother I always want to cry?' she had asked him before they became engaged. 'I feel I love her too – do you mind my saying that? Will you tell me things about her sometimes so that I can try and be like her?'[34] Far from minding her saying that, it was what above all he wished to hear. 'I'll tell you *all* about her, please. I love you to love her and I know she loves you. And you're so like her in things you say and do.'[35] But Peggy Ashcroft as mother-substitute was an unconvincing figure; even Rupert could not quite bring himself to believe in it. She made desultory efforts to play the role. In March 1930 he had been ill and was packed off to Brighton to convalesce. 'You looked so pathetic in the train,' Peggy wrote. 'I very nearly cried – poor little baby left in the puff puff without its mummy.' But already she was beginning to see the memory of Sibbie as a threat to their relationship. She blamed her for what she felt to be Rupert's unhealthy hankering for an exclusive and mutually dependent relationship: 'You see, your first and strongest love was for your mother, and part of a maternal relationship is the desire to be depended on – in a stronger degree than in any other relationship.'[36]

She never overtly blamed Sibbie for the failure of their marriage but she must have felt that Rupert's mother should bear part of the responsibility. Even if their marriage had worked in bed it would not have satisfied them both for ever, but it would have lasted considerably longer. As it was, the last entry in the visitors' book for 213 Piccadilly was for 16 September 1931; some time in the next few weeks Rupert went off to work in the morning knowing that he would find Peggy gone when he came back. 'I can see her now, sobbing in her dressing gown at the top of the stairs, and I was weeping too.' Years later, in Terence Rattigan's *The Deep Blue Sea*, she was required to stand at the top of a flight of stairs, weeping hysterically and calling 'Don't leave me! Don't leave me!' 'Art was brilliantly imitating nature,' Rupert told Deirdre.[37] There was a touch of mockery in the comment, but Peggy's grief was unfeigned; her affection for Rupert was deep and lasted all her life. As for Rupert, he felt not merely irreparable loss but also a sense of failure. It was a crushing blow to his self-confidence and must have left him wondering whether he would ever be able to sustain a full relationship with a woman. He slammed the door of his flat in Piccadilly and fled to Ireland, to take refuge with the family of the painter William Nicholson, and with his old theatrical friend Charlie Marford. His friends were as supportive as he would let them be. Jamie Hamilton's marriage was also under stress, for reasons very similar to Rupert's, so he was especially well placed to understand if not to give comfort. 'Your insight and sympathy are really wonderful,' Rupert wrote to him from Dublin, 'whereas my dear father . . . keeps on writing to me to "be brave and come back and face things", which irritates me a good deal. The first few days here were hell but I am getting calmer and less nervy every moment. I don't know how long I shall stay here. Maybe only a week or two, if I can fix up a few visits in the country. Anything but London for a bit.'[38] Other friends wrote to give news of Peggy. He had seen her the previous night, Harman Grisewood told him. 'She seems very well. Interested in the election.' What were the politics in Ireland? he wondered. 'Tell me about it, but above all about you, Rupert, my dear, are you well, how uncomfortable are you, are you seeing people a lot, are they amusing you at all?'[39]

Staying as he was with Charlie Marford or the Nicholsons, he could hardly have avoided seeing people and being amused by them. He even managed to convince himself that he was in love with 'a beautiful little

Irish colleen with black hair and blue eyes' called Betty Chancellor.[40] But his heart was not in it. Peggy had left him, but she proved curiously reluctant to make the rupture final. He wrote to her regularly: 'Your letters sound so utterly wretched and you try so bravely to hide it a bit,' Peggy replied to him. 'You must write as you feel, darling.' She even seemed to be hinting that they might try again: 'Oh, darling, it is so difficult. I just can't imagine what's going to make me make up my mind. But I will soon.' She heard that Rupert was playing with the idea of going to New York to take up a job with the American publishers Doubleday's. 'I am awfully pleased as I feel that it is so much the best thing for you.' She encouraged him to have an affair with someone whom he found physically attractive: 'If you wanted to tell me I should understand, but if not it needn't matter.'[41] She for her part would follow her inclinations and, if he liked, keep him posted on her progress. Rupert possibly hoped that the idea that he might go to New York would panic her into trying to reclaim him before it was too late. There is no record of any serious negotiations with Doubleday's and he was at that time violently antipathetic to anything American. 'I despise the whole bloody nation,' he stormed a few months later, when confronted by a particularly unwholesome manuscript. If he had hoped to make her change her mind, Peggy's enthusiastic endorsement of the idea must have sorely disappointed him. He returned to London early in 1932 more or less reconciled to the fact that his marriage was over and would never be resumed.

Chapter Six

Tyro Publisher

Rupert's first eighteen months of publishing were spent against a background of his disintegrating marriage. It was not a period on which he looked back with pleasure. Yet it all began so hopefully. When he got back from his holiday with Peter Fleming he had found a message from Jamie Hamilton saying that there was news about a possible job. Excitedly he rang back and was told that Charley Evans, the Managing Director of the publishing house of Heinemann's, was looking for a promising young man who could be trained for a responsible job. A lunch was fixed for the following day at the Garrick Club, that favourite watering place of barristers, publishers, authors, actors and other members of the entertainment industry. Hamilton was already a member, Rupert was to join it eighteen months later. Rupert took it for granted that the job was his for the asking. Moreover, he told Peggy, 'Mr Evans may apparently die or retire at any moment, the other chap isn't much good, so who knows but that I may not control the whole place. Jimmy says there's never been such a chance.'[1]

These airy castles were slightly tarnished the following day, when it became clear that Rupert's starting salary would be only £2 a week – not generous even by the standards of the day – rising to £4 a week after a year if he proved worthy of his hire. In spite of this, the post was much sought after, with forty people or more said to be in the running. The lunch went well. Rupert liked Evans – 'charming: small, bald, active, might be an American but thank God isn't' – and Evans evidently reciprocated the good opinion for the following day Rupert was told the job was his. The obvious thing to do, he told Peggy, was to understudy Evans and make himself indispensable; then, when the moment came, he would be well placed to take over the vacant chair.[2] In the excitement of the moment such vainglory can be forgiven, but he was to look back wryly on his expectations in years to come.

Jamie Hamilton had been quite right when he said that the job was one to strive for. In a publishing scene dominated by medium-sized independent houses, Heinemann's were one of the larger and more successful. Their eponymous founder, William Heinemann, had specialised in foreign literature. He was particularly celebrated for employing Constance Garnett to translate Turgenev and Dostoevsky, but his list of English novelists was little less impressive: John Galsworthy, George Moore, Somerset Maugham, H. G. Wells, were all names which were critically esteemed if not revered and earned both author and publisher a great deal of money. At William Heinemann's death the firm had been bought by the American publisher Double-day's, so a new element had been added to the already potent brew. A lot of capital was also brought in; one of the first things Doubleday's did was to commission a grand new building near Kingswood in Surrey where printing, binding and all the administration could be based. It was there that Rupert began work as an editor; frustratingly from the point of view of his ambitions, since Charley Evans, the man he was planning to understudy and then supplant, only came to Kingswood for board meetings and spent most of his time in the Queen Anne house in Great Russell Street where the firm formally had its headquarters.

It is easy to see why Evans had thought Rupert suitable for the job. He was impressively well read, with a commanding grasp of the English classics and a better than working knowledge of the continental giants. If William Heinemann had still been alive he might have been surprised that Rupert had never read a word of Proust, even though most of Scott Moncrieff's translations were available by the early 1930s, and was unaware of such monuments of modern European literature as Kafka's *The Trial* or Svevo's *The Confessions of Zeno*. Heinemann had been dead more than ten years, however, and the firm had moved into less rarefied pastures. Rupert had some curious literary prejudices – he found Jane Austen 'finicky and boring' and dismissed Bernard Shaw with a tetchy 'always so bloody pleased with himself, and thinks his own jokes so funny. I am sure he is over-rated' – but in general he was a sound judge of the sort of upper-middlebrow fiction which was the staple of Heinemann's list. When the weekly journal *Time and Tide* had a poll among its readers to establish Britain's most popular writers, Rupert named twenty-two out of the top forty. He reproached himself with not having taken sufficient account of popular taste but in fact his selections reflected exactly the mix that Heinemann's had exploited so success-fully.[3] He had high standards but a common touch; he enjoyed and admired D. H. Lawrence, particularly the short stories, but the English novel which had given him the greatest pleasure from the two or three years before he became a publisher had been Mary Webb's *Precious Bane*. He loved thrillers and detective stories; by now his collection of the works of E. Phillips Oppenheim numbered ninety. A year or two later he disposed of it on the grounds that it was childish, then regretted his decision, started again and accumulated a hundred and fifty of Oppenheim's titles.

A publisher employing a tyro editor might be mildly interested in his views on James Joyce or his knowledge of the plays of Webster, but he would be more concerned with his ability to spell and construct a sentence that would be both comprehensible and agreeable to read. Rupert had a good ear for prose, a more than adequate grasp of grammar and a penchant for tinkering with other people's writings. He was a born editor and could safely be entrusted with the work of any author; even if it was not to his taste, his judgment of its merits would be sensible and his ideas for its improvement to the point. In time he became increasingly reluctant to work on texts that seemed to him to have no literary merit but in his early days at Heinemann's he derived some pleasure from making the best of the most unpromising materials. When the work of a friend was involved – and a high proportion of the authors with whom he worked became his friends – he set about it with particular relish. When much later he worked on a book by Peter Fleming he congratulated himself that he had removed the words 'It would seem' at least twenty-five times. Probably he had removed 'of course' even more frequently. Nearly always he was right to do so.[*] 'I dare say that all this trouble is quite unnecessary,' he told George Lyttelton, 'since few realise or notice what has been done, but I hate to publish sloppy writing if it can be improved.'[4] He showed every sign of being conscientious and hard-working; Evans must have congratulated himself that he had found a potentially valuable recruit.

But he promised too to be an asset in other ways. He was personable, friendly, a good talker and – more important when authors are involved – a good listener. He was a useful presence at an office party. Within a few weeks of his arrival he found himself at a Columbus Day party in honour of one of Heinemann's most important authors. 'All very excited,' he wrote in his diary. 'Party lasted from 9.30 to 2. Hardly sat

[*] He removed more than fifty 'of courses' from my biography of Diana Cooper. I reinstated three.

down. Played butler in the hall, circulated drinks, was photographed, talked to many people . . . The waiters got quite blotto and refused to leave. Utterly exhausted by bedtime.'5 'Priestley in wonderful form and very nice to Peg,' he added, a comment which must have caused him a slight grimace when he re-read his diary nearly sixty years later.

He already had a wide circle of acquaintances and intended to make it wider; a senior publisher relies on younger members of his staff to keep in touch with the up-and-coming writer, and Rupert, not yet twenty-five, was obviously well qualified to do so. But he was as much at home in the literary *beau monde*. On one day in June 1931 he lunched at the *Spectator*, went on to spend an hour and a half with J. B. Priestley in Hampstead, took tea with Charles Morgan, then went on to Virginia and Leonard Woolf for three hours' conversation with them, Vanessa Bell, Duncan Grant, John Lehmann and 'that affected and insufferable cow, Christabel McLaren'.6 He was asked to play badminton with H. G. Wells and his mistress, Moura Budberg: 'She was very good at badminton, hitting like a horse. HG was good and tricky, not above cheating if he could get away with it: he liked to win. I was hopelessly bad, but I suppose just good enough to make up their four.'7

He was not perfect. He did not take kindly to instructions, still less reprimands from those whom he felt were not qualified to deliver them. He could irritate his contemporaries by his air of effortless superiority. If he disliked someone he found it hard to conceal the fact. By the time he joined Heinemann's Cyril Connolly was already a reviewer of some influence. Most publishers found it desirable to propitiate him. Rupert put him down at dinner when he was pontificating about the absence of any first-rate poetry outside France since the middle of the nineteenth century. 'Have you read Meredith's "Modern Love"?' demanded Rupert. Connolly confessed that he had not. 'Then you've no business to make such pronouncements.'8 The two men were mutually antipathetic, though one suspects that the feud was much more significant to Rupert than it was to Connolly. Rupert found it difficult to be even formally polite to the critic when they met at literary gatherings. He was a 'horrible man,' he told Deirdre, 'dishonest financially and intellectually, a cadger, a snob and a sponger ugh!'9 He never got over his aversion; when after Connolly's death he received an appeal to help the widow and children he rejected it: Connolly had been a parasite all his life, 'and the process is still going on'.

But all in all he knew that he gave good value for his paltry pay. The fact that the financial reward was so inadequate did not concern him overmuch provided he could feel that he was establishing his position in the company. In the first few months, however, while he was learning the job at Kingswood, he had little chance to impress those who would decide his future. So far as it went, the work was pleasant enough. Every morning he would drive down with Arnold Haskell, another young editor who would soon abandon publishing for a distinguished career as a writer about ballet and director of the Royal Ballet School. Isolated in the country, with the directors visiting only once a week, the atmosphere in the rooms where the editors worked was pleasantly relaxed, with much undergraduate debate about issues of love, life and death and riotous steeplechases around the office furniture.[10] Rupert liked to claim subsequently that he had been employed as an office boy. The future editor of the *Bookseller* indignantly refuted this boast. It was he who had occupied that position; Rupert's role, he insisted, had been less onerous but slightly grander.[11]

In fact Rupert's principal task was to read the scores of novels, many of them unsolicited and almost all of them unpublishable, which descended on Heinemann's every week. It was, for the most part, an unrewarding if instructive task. Almost his only success came when the man responsible for handing out manuscripts to the readers asked if anyone could stand the novels of Mary Webb. Rupert admitted that he actually enjoyed them. He was at once passed an enormously long typescript which seemed to be more or less in the style of that then immensely popular novelist, now remembered mainly for the cruel parody of her work in Stella Gibbons's *Cold Comfort Farm*. Rather to his surprise he thought it excellent and strongly recommended it for publication. Beatrice Tunstall's *The Shiny Night* is now even less read than the works of her more eminent inspirer, but re-reading it in 1990 Rupert was relieved to find that he still thought his judgment sound.[12] Another typescript of some promise was sent in by a then unheard-of young writer, Louis MacNeice. Rupert wrote him an encouraging letter and urged him to revise his book radically; MacNeice thanked him for 'smiling on my novel' but did not think major changes would be possible. He tried another novel, which he then sent to Rupert. By that time Rupert had left Heinemann's but he thought it good enough to pass to his former employers and offer to edit it if they took it on. Instead they rejected it and it ended up with Putnam's. Both Heinemann's and Rupert can claim to have been right; the book got generally benevolent reviews but sold poorly and was soon forgotten. MacNeice himself went on to achieve eminence as a poet.[13]

Disillusionment set in when Rupert was moved to London: to
understudy Evans, as he still optimistically saw it; to act as general
dog's-body in his employer's view. It was a tribute to Rupert's air of
self-confident authority that the outside world often seemed ready to
take him at his own valuation. He mixed without embarrassment in a
literary milieu not usually open to junior editors. People assumed that
he possessed powers far more wide-ranging than he did. Nancy Cunard,
once she had established that he was a publisher rather than a
bookseller, offered to send him suitable items for him to launch on the
world;[14] an undergraduate acquaintance who had just published a first
novel urged him to 'use your influence to have the book advertised in
next week's *Observer* and *Sunday Times* in as large letters as is decently
possible'.[15] Evans had no such illusions about his young editor's
importance. Rupert saw and spoke to Lawrence of Arabia when he came
into the office – 'He was much smaller than I imagined, dressed in RAF
uniform, very jolly and engaging to speak to. An alive and rather lined
face'[16] – but casual acquaintanceship with the great was not the same as
doing business with them and he could not delude himself that he was
likely to be admitted to the inner conclaves of Heinemann's.

He had his minor victories. He was impressed by the poems of
Romilly John and secured the backing of Maurice Baring and Edmund
Blunden. At first he got nowhere. 'Evans still does not want to publish
Romilly's poems, curse him,' he wrote indignantly; but then, a week
later, 'We are definitely going to publish Romilly's poems! Hurrah!'[17]
But this was an exception; generally, it seemed to him, his opinion was
treated with scant respect. He was particularly put out when his uncle,
Duff Cooper, sent him the typescript of the new biography of
Talleyrand which he had just completed. Rupert was enthusiastic about
it and passed it to Evans, who said he was too busy to read it; he then
tried it on Evans's deputy, A. S. Frere, who decided that it was no good
at all. In the end it was published by Cape's and proved outstandingly
successful.

He was realistic enough to know that this was the sort of thing that
happened to young editors in every house. What he found harder to
forgive was that Evans was slow to encourage and grudging of praise.
When Rupert arrived the morning after the Columbus Day party, at
which he had slaved until 2 a.m., Evans merely complained that he was
late. If he did something bad he was reprimanded; if good he was
ignored. Evans was absurdly jealous of his position, and resentful if
anyone seemed to be encroaching on his territory. Rupert was not alone

in finding him hard to work with; Arnold Gyde, senior of the Kingswood editors, thought him 'a bald and bespectacled little fright, with twitching hands and eyes – suspicious, bankrupt of any kindly thoughts, and supremely anxious that nobody should get any credit for anything'.[18] But Evans had his champions. Arnold Haskell for one – perhaps because he was much less concerned than Rupert to get on in publishing – thought well of his Managing Director. He found Evans sympathetic and intelligent, a man whom 'I learned to love and respect'.[19]

By the spring of 1931 it was becoming clear to Rupert that his dreams of succeeding Evans were no more than fantasy; he was going nowhere. Once more he appealed to Jamie Hamilton and once more Hamilton responded; he arranged a lunch for Rupert to meet Wren Howard of Jonathan Cape's. The two men got on well; there was no immediate vacancy at Cape's but there would be openings in the future. Rupert felt sufficiently encouraged to tell Evans that he wanted to leave. Upset at the thought of losing a promising youngster, Evans at once became all charm; Rupert was getting on extremely well, he said, he had the ball at his feet, he would be mad to kick it all away. Rupert was unmoved. He did not believe that his position would change in any serious respect and Evans said nothing to convince him that he was wrong. On 11 June 1931 he wrote with some satisfaction in his diary: 'Cleared up, finished, and said goodbye at Heinemann's without, I am glad to say, the slightest qualms.'

It was one of the few reasons for satisfaction in that disastrous summer and autumn. In the first months after he left Heinemann's he was above all preoccupied by the state of his marriage. In theory he was negotiating with Cape's about his future role, in fact he had retired hurt, stunned by his misery and his humiliation. 'I hope you are not depressed about a job,' Peter Fleming wrote to him from Port Arthur. 'If you haven't got one already, you soon will. Don't imagine for a moment that you are the sort of stone the discerning will leave unturned eventually.'[20] Rupert accepted that his friend was probably right but found little comfort in the thought; he could not bring himself to return to London and settle down to the serious business of earning a living. It was almost the end of 1931 before he began to try to clinch a deal with Cape's, and then his plans were diverted into a fresh direction.

It was J. B. Priestley – with whom Rupert had remained on remarkably good terms in spite of the author's relationship with Peggy –

who was responsible for the new departure. Priestley was one of the five judges of the Book Society who each month selected a 'Book Society Choice' for the benefit of their members, and listed half a dozen or so other books which they felt worthy of recommendation. The Society had been the brainchild of Arnold Bennett, had started in 1929, and was run by a highly capable writer and editor, Alan Bott. Bott wanted a young assistant to take on most of the donkey work and Priestley, who considered himself *primus inter pares* among the judges, pressed the claim of his former mistress's husband.

Rupert was at first uncertain but whatever doubts he harboured were largely disposed of by a letter which he received from the young novelist, Graham Greene. Greene had become a friend when Rupert met him to discuss a biography of the poet and satirist the Earl of Rochester, which was to be published by Heinemann's.* 'Graham is very unattractive but I like something about him,' he noted in his diary.[21] Now Greene wrote to him, cautiously feeling out the ground: 'I want to approach you, on padded feet, with whiskers tentatively advanced, ready to retreat at the first sign. If for some reason you decide not to apply for or if, more unaccountably, you fail to get appointed by the Book Society, could you at once let me know and I shall try for the job? Though there is no reason to suppose that I should have any better luck than you.'[22] Nothing makes one want a thing more than the discovery that someone else is anxious to obtain it. Rupert consulted Cape's, who said that they would be delighted if he would spend a year or so with the Book Society; they had no immediate need for his services and the experience he would gain could only make him a more useful publisher. The job was his.

Priestley told him what he must expect. The other judges were the novelists Hugh Walpole and Clemence Dane; the poet and novelist Sylvia Lynd; and the President of Magdalen College, Oxford, George Gordon. The Selection Committee met once a month in Hugh Walpole's flat overlooking Green Park in Piccadilly. Walpole, Priestley warned Rupert, wanted to choose every book; he himself wanted to choose no book; Sylvia Lynd wanted to choose books by people with whom she had had dinner; Gordon never had time to read any of the books; 'As for Clemence Dane, she takes a pre-Caxton view of books and the sight of print on the page excites her to madness.'[23] The assessment proved more or less accurate. Rupert had scarcely joined the

---

* *Lord Rochester's Monkey* eventually appeared in 1974.

Book Society, however, before Priestley had left the panel, to be replaced by the poet Edmund Blunden. The change affected the balance of the committee; Rupert found that it now fell to him to curb the enthusiasm of the judges and to persuade them not that one particular book should be chosen but that only one deserved the honour.

Edmund Blunden, the new judge, was to be one of his closest friends for more than forty years. Rupert had first encountered his work three years before and had at once become an ardent admirer: 'nobility and serenity and, above all, England' he found in Blunden's poetry.[24] Robert Graves wrote of him as 'a cross between Julius Caesar and a bird', and Rupert found the description apt: 'His tiny frame, his shyness, his quick darting eyes and gestures, had all the grace and agility of a wren, while his noble nose suggested the *gravitas* of a Roman emperor.'[25] Blunden was no less enthusiastic. Rupert Hart-Davis, he told Siegfried Sassoon, 'is a great discovery to my mind, he has much brightened my old age [Blunden was thirty-seven years at the time of writing] and I am sure you would like him at once'. When he later met George Orwell Blunden described him as 'an Etonian worthy to rank with Rupert – and that as you know is an eulogy indeed'.[26] When Rupert published his biography of Hugh Walpole he wrote to Blunden to acknowledge his debt:

> When we first met, twenty years ago, I was extremely young, unsure of myself and (however great my outward show of *savoir faire*) diffident. You immediately accepted me as a contemporary and a literary and intellectual equal. This fiction you have exquisitely maintained ever since, and it was largely the desire to live up to, and justify, your wild confidence in me that gave me the self-confidence and strength of purpose to tackle this book. For I have always admired, revered and loved you . . . So now you know![27]

Clemence Dane too became a friend. She was a generous-hearted woman, lavish in figure and in enthusiasms, who was much mocked by the intelligentsia. Osbert Sitwell called her 'The Great Dane' and told a gullible Swiss lady that he had written her plays and novels under a pseudonym; she was generally no better than competent but in the underrated and largely forgotten *Broome Stages* she wrote one of the few successful novels about theatrical life. As a judge she had the disadvantage of nurturing a strong streak of prudishness. When Rupert tentatively advanced the claims for selection of an autobiographical work by Eric Muspratt, in which the author touched lightly on a brush with the homosexual world in Venice, Clemence Dane wrote sternly: 'I think it *impossible*. I don't think it fair to thrust on our readers a book which deals, however dispassionately with forms of sexual difficulty which would normally not come the way of the average reader.'[28] But it was Hugh Walpole who was most to affect Rupert's life. Walpole was an enormously successful novelist and a figure of some power on the literary scene; he was discreetly homosexual and notably generous to other writers. He knew that the avant-garde considered him impossibly middlebrow and old-fashioned, but took comfort in the scale of his earnings and the fact that Henry James and Virginia Woolf counted him as a friend and corresponded with him regularly. Blunden described him as being 'magnificent in bowler hat and massive overcoat, rather like Mr Pickwick in countenance'.[29] Rupert warmed to him immediately and was soon numbered among his closest confidantes. In time Rupert was to become Walpole's biographer, literary executor and inheritor of a large proportion of his earnings.

'I'm terribly excited and glad to hear about the new job,' Peggy Ashcroft wrote enthusiastically. 'I *knew* you were going to be successful and now you actually are being so. It's lovely.'[30] It was a modest success, but better than what had gone before. Rupert knew that he was valued by the Society and that his views were taken seriously by the judges. Indeed, his influence over them was considerable. Graham Greene's new novel, *Stamboul Train*, was a possible Book Society Choice. Early in August 1932 Rupert went to have a drink with Greene in the country. 'Under the influence of sun and parsnip wine,' reported Greene, he promised to do what he could to advance the novel's prospects. In fact not much parsnip wine was needed; Rupert had a high opinion of both book and author and would have pushed it in any case.[31] Walpole and Lynd shared his view; Blunden, as a close friend of Greene, felt bound to play a minor role in the discussion; Clemence Dane was on balance against it; George Gordon strongly opposed the choice: 'It is a failure in my opinion, and its feeble unpleasantness doesn't make the failure any better.'[32] Not being a judge himself, Rupert had to be careful not to intervene too obviously, but he was already developing the skills that were to make him a master when it came to managing a committee. He contrived so to steer things that *Stamboul Train* was chosen in spite of the opposition of two of the judges. He would probably have had less success if J. B. Priestley had still been on the panel, for Priestley reviewed the novel harshly and complained that he had been libelled in Greene's portrayal of one of the characters. The Book Club selection ensured that Greene's sales shot up from one or two thousand to twenty thousand and the grateful author presented Rupert with the corrected typescript. George Gordon shared the last laugh, however: a large number of copies were returned by members of the Society. 'Are none of your members pure in heart?' asked one outraged lady reader, while a second commented: 'This may be like life, but if it is I don't want to read it.'[33]

One of the less attractive features of the new job was the obligation to produce a monthly journal for the members. 'Over all hangs the black threat of the *Book Society News*,' Rupert told Blunden. 'I wonder whether any single member opens the bloody thing?'[34] He knew that they did, and though its compilation might have been a chore, it meant that he had to deal with a multitude of contributors who would be useful contacts in later life. Among the authors whom he persuaded, or at least tried to persuade to write for him were Somerset Maugham, Walter de la Mare, Harold Nicolson, E. M. Forster, Charles Morgan, Compton Mackenzie, Havelock Ellis – the list could be interminable. 'You are very sweet, and no wonder all the girls adore you,' wrote Maugham, in recognition of some unspecified favour.[35] 'Sweet' was not an adjective that could have been applied to Maugham himself but he was still the sort of acquaintance that any publisher would value. Cape's had been quite right when they had calculated that Rupert would be of greater value to them after he had served his time with the Book Society.

Though he knew publishing suited him far better than life on the stage, Rupert did not feel that he was irrevocably committed. From time to time overtures were made to him from other fields. Some time before he went to the Book Society it was suggested that he should join the *Spectator*, to shadow the then literary editor, his friend Derek Verschoyle, and to contribute to other sections of the paper. 'Asked if I would like to write most of the *Spectator*,' he commented laconically in his diary. 'Quite certain I couldn't, but Peter could.'[36] Peter Fleming took up the offer and featured largely in the *Spectator*'s columns for the rest of his life.

But this was not the only reason Fleming had to be grateful to Rupert. When the final breach came with Celia Johnson, Fleming had been deputed to look after her and make sure that she did not repine too much. He took his duties seriously, so much so that by the early summer of 1932 he and Celia were informally engaged. He then set off on one of his interminable journeys, this time to Brazil, leaving Rupert in his turn to succour the unfortunate Celia. Rupert, whose own marriage was by now close to shipwreck, accepted the duty willingly – more willingly, perhaps, than Fleming would have anticipated. 'A sickly apathy of moping is creeping over me,' Rupert told Celia. 'I should like to get splendidly drunk and make love to someone in blank verse – you, if you felt like it, which of course you wouldn't . . . Come back soon and I will tell you how nice you look and you will be thinking of Peter and I shall feel obscenely self-pitiful . . . *Au revoir*, my beautiful nebulous pekingese.'[37] The fact that Celia kept this letter suggests she was in no way offended by it, but if she had any inclination to take up the veiled invitation she certainly repressed it.

She might have been less reticent if she had known that her wandering fiancé was meanwhile airing his doubts to Rupert. 'Will you write to me, at length and honestly, about Celia as often as you can,' he asked. He had left her unhappy and uncertain about his intentions. 'I know you'll do everything that occurs to you. You have been a good chap about the whole business. I wish your own stuff would work out somehow.' A month on, and his doubts were as strong as ever. 'I love Celia as much as I can see myself loving anyone, which is not enough to marry her. I know now, even better than I knew in England, that this would not work.' The only thing was to make a clean break, perhaps never to see her again. But how was this to be done? 'The only thing is for you to send me as many bulletins about her as circumstances allow and developments dictate. I can only hope for a change in her heart or some other fluke.'[38]

Rupert wisely took no action on these letters and when Peter got back from his Brazilian adventure he quickly decided that he did, after all, love Celia enough to marry her. Now it was his odious mother, Eve, who sought Rupert's sympathy. Presumably unaware that Rupert himself had previously wooed her future daughter-in-law, she wrote to express her dismay that Peter should be marrying out of his class. 'It hardly ever is a success,' she observed. 'I only know Celia Johnson very slightly, and I have never seen her act, so I am really not able to judge, but she seemed a quite ordinary personality . . . She may be very intelligent but she has no looks.' As it became clear that her son was paying no attention to her abjurations, her rage mounted. 'I can hardly believe it is true that Peter has joined that dim, grim family, penniless and suburban.'[39] Rupert, who was genuinely fond of Eve Fleming in spite of her malice and snobbishness, does not seem to have responded. The marriage duly took place and proved, if not extravagantly romantic, both durable and affectionate. Peter's letter to Rupert from the honeymoon set the tone of the relationship: everything was lovely, he said, 'and being married to the Crackpot is the best joke yet'.[40] Many years later Deirdre found an old photograph of Peter and Celia taken beside a swimming pool shortly after their wedding; it was typical, she felt, 'Peter treating Celia rather like a friendly cat that comes to lie on you, and totally absorbed in his book'.[41]

Deirdre herself had by now got married, in great state in Westminster Cathedral to Ronald Balfour. Rupert was unenthusiastic but overtly approving, an attitude which he found harder to sustain when his father remarried, with a girl whom he had picked up, according to his son, in some nightclub or brothel. Rupert's new stepmother was said to be the child of an exiled Russian aristocrat and a charwoman; there may have been some truth in this, thought Rupert, 'for she had a distinguished kind of beauty and the manners of the gutter'. As it happened he did not have to put up with her for long; after a brief and tempestuous marriage she was caught in bed with the family doctor and was duly divorced. She then married an English peer whom she had somehow entrapped and seems to have ended up impoverished if not destitute.[42]

Sibbie had died intestate. She had very little money of her own but shortly before her death had inherited £11,000 from her mother – about £250,000 at current values. Rupert, almost certainly with good reason, assumed that his mother would have wished this money to go to her children. Richard, however, decided to hold on to it. He gave his son an allowance of £300 a year, which was not ungenerous, but Rupert, who badly needed the capital, felt that he had been treated harshly. As a result, he seems to have regarded his father as a legitimate target whenever he was short of money. 'Received a demand of £37 from the Garrick Club,' he noted in his diary. 'Pa must pay.' By now the Piccadilly flat had been abandoned and Rupert was installed on the first and second floors of a house in Lawrence Street, Chelsea. Life was proceeding smoothly and the emotional wounds left by his rupture with Peggy were slowly beginning to heal.

Even in the months when he was half distracted by Peggy's loss Rupert had the spirit to flirt with his 'Irish colleen'; by the summer of 1932 he was ready for something more enduring. He found her at a garden party given by Heinemann's, to which he only went at the last minute because Alan Bott was too busy and wanted someone to go as an escort for his wife. Under a tree, sitting by herself, he saw a small, trim girl, notably

self-possessed, with fair hair and an attractive if not strictly pretty face –
a *belle laide* rather than a *jolie laide*, with eyes which promised more
excitement than might have been expected from her otherwise demure
appearance. Rupert approached her with a vague idea that she was
Daphne du Maurier but stayed talking to her with pleasure when he
found that she was in fact Comfort Borden-Turner, a typist in
Heinemann's London office. Comfort was, in fact, rather grander than
this job description might imply. Her mother, Mary Borden, was a
successful novelist from a rich American family (Rupert had read a
collection of short stories by her in 1926 – 'Nothing like first-rate – one
or two rather cheap – but not too bad' he recorded dismissively); her
father, Douglas Turner – now divorced and remarried – was a Scottish
lay missionary and Inspector of Prisons, while her stepfather, Louis
Spears, was an ambitious Conservative Member of Parliament with
abundant talents marred by his gift for making enemies. Rupert asked
Duff Cooper what he thought of him. 'If he had the word SHIT written
on his forehead in letters of fire, it wouldn't be more apparent than it is
now,'[43] Cooper replied.

Comfort turned out to have been at school with Celia Johnson; added
to which she was well read and had literary ambitions. Rupert quickly
decided that she was exactly what he most wanted. She responded
enthusiastically. Whatever sexual uncertainties that lingered from the
Ashcroft era seem to have been speedily dispelled: before long, Rupert
wrote, 'we became joyful lovers'.[44] But the course of true love ran as
turbulently as tradition decreed. Comfort dithered in a way which even
Peter Fleming would have found unconscionable. First all was rosy:
'Darling, your lovely deep voice and your smooth gentle hands. I do
love you so much . . . Please, please, love me darling and be happy for
me.' She urged him to put all thought of Peggy out of his mind: 'It is
awful to cling to a dead thing, an evocation of memories, however much
one longs to have the power to recapture it.' Then a note of uncertainty
crept in: 'I think I do want to stay with you Rupert and marry you . . .
When I say I am not sure I do, it is because I can't quite visualise a life
married.'

Early in 1933 Comfort went to Majorca for a few months. She left
with the best intentions – 'If you find yourself afraid that I lose my heart
to anyone else – well, just think that I could not if I would, leaving it as
I do in your keeping.' But then a former lover, Mark, appeared on the
scene, pleading with Comfort to return to him. She convinced herself
that he could not survive without her, while Rupert was strong enough

to stand alone and would anyway soon find somebody else. It was nothing to do with her feelings for Rupert, she protested: 'I love you more and am filled with sorrow and regret.' But duty called: 'Mark's need for me allows me no other course. It is something stronger than myself.'[45]

Many people confronted by so infuriating a message would have put it in the waste-paper basket and done their best to forget its writer. Comfort's father and stepmother, who strongly favoured Rupert over his rival, took it for granted that this would be his reaction. 'You may well think of yourself as a man who has had a spear thrust into his heart – a wound all but mortal,' Comfort's stepmother, Margaret, wrote to him. Since Rupert would presumably not now be going to Majorca to join Comfort, would he not come to stay with them instead?[46] But Rupert did not give up so easily. He flew to Majorca – an uncomfortable and dangerous experience which left him with a lifelong loathing of aeroplanes – and bullied or cajoled the by-no-means-unwilling Comfort into accepting that the path of duty led to him, not to her needy former love. He returned triumphant. Hardly had he settled back before he received 'a tiny letter to tell you of my love again, which I need not,' and 'to promise not to get into mischief again, which I will not'.[47] But she did: Mark reappeared; the dithering recommenced; when Comfort finally got back to London she was still in doubt. Rupert took advice from the latest recruit to the panel of judges of the Book Society, Margaret Kennedy, who as the author of the immensely popular novel *The Constant Nymph* might reasonably be expected to be an authority on all matters romantic. Encouraged by her, he met Comfort at the station and told her, lovingly but firmly, that unless she promised never to see Mark again, their relationship must end. The treatment worked; a week later a tearful Comfort telephoned to say that she was Rupert's for ever. Rupert celebrated in characteristically literary style. 'On 23 March I wrote in my engagement-diary the words "A Singing Bird", referring to Christina Rossetti's poem which begins "My heart is like a singing bird" and ends "Because my love is come to me".'[48]

All was not yet plain sailing. The Borden family had lost a great deal of their money in the Wall Street crash of 1929. 'If all dividends from America are going to stop, I shall have to get a job,' wrote Comfort.[49] Probably she would go back to Heinemann's. Rupert had no intention of letting his wife work for long for the loathed Heinemann's but the young couple had anyway promised Comfort's father to wait at least six months before marriage and he was content to let her spend that period in this ignoble employment. But there was another reason for the delay. Rupert was still a married man and Peggy had showed no interest in procuring a divorce. Now he wrote to her, explained that he wanted to marry, and asked her to co-operate. Her reply must have been mildly disconcerting:

> It certainly was a shock, although it is not really such a surprising thing. It does seem incredible, doesn't it, that I should at first have felt, not exactly jealous, but a sense of irretrievable loss. A sort of feeling of suddenly being left out . . . I am glad, darling, it has happened to you because I know it will make you happy and engrossed, at any rate at present.
>   One of the feelings I have had since your letter is that, if your love for Joan [sic] doesn't become permanent in a material sense – I mean marriage – but you do have a temporary love affair which could make you very happy, sometime in the future we might begin again in quite a different way . . . I think the experience of physical love would make an enormous difference to you, so much so that it would change my feelings to you. All this sounds grossly horrible and selfish and I don't mean in the least that I want to use your love for someone else for my own interest.[50]

The suggestion that Comfort might serve as a warming-pan to prepare the nuptial bed for the eventual return of Peggy was not one Rupert felt inclined to follow up. As was the practice of the day, he volunteered to do the gentlemanly thing and provide the evidence that would enable Peggy to divorce him as innocent party. All was proceeding smoothly until Peggy announced that she was living with the Russian director Komisarjevsky, intended to marry him, and so could not possibly pass herself off as innocent. The roles were reversed, which meant that it was now Rupert who had to divorce Peggy and present himself as the injured party. The disagreeable aspect of this was that, particularly in the months between the decree nisi and the decree absolute, he and Comfort had to behave with extreme discretion; otherwise the King's Proctor might conclude that the two principals were in collusion, the divorce was a put-up job and the course of justice would be best served by forcing the luckless couple to continue married.

In May 1933 the decree nisi was duly granted. The judge sagely remarked that this seemed to be a case in which all the facts were well established. 'Ha ha, little does he know of one small scarlet woman grinning in the background,' wrote Comfort exultantly.[51] But others did know, and Rupert feared that his housekeeper might spill the beans to the King's Proctor about untoward goings-on in Lawrence Street. It was a risk they were not prepared to take. All ideas of Comfort resuming work at Heinemann's were abandoned; instead she took off again for Majorca. There Rupert was able briefly to join her. 'Oh darling,' Comfort wrote in ecstatic anticipation, 'in six weeks you'll be here and close in my arms and we can forget about all the scandal-mongering old hags, God rot their guts!'[52] Whether Rupert's house-keeper or any other scandal-mongering old hag was in reality a threat to the divorce will never be known. Anyway, their prudence was rewarded. On 20 November the decree was made absolute. They were free to marry and did so five days later in the Chelsea Register Office. Deirdre and Peter Fleming were their witnesses.

Chapter Seven

Jonathan Cape's

Jonathan Cape's, when Rupert joined it in 1933, was one of the most enterprising and successful of the new imprints which had sprung up since the First World War. Its eponymous chairman was a man of extraordinary flair and determination. He had come from nothing, the son of a builder's clerk whose first job was as an errand boy in Hatchard's bookshop in Piccadilly. He had little education and no literary bent – if he had happened to start his working life a few doors down the street at Fortnum & Mason's he would no doubt have ended up as a Napoleon of the grocery trade. But though he had no particular affection for books or authors, he showed himself remarkably adept at picking winners in either category and then promoting them with skill and energy. He was 'a publisher of outstanding genius with the heart of a horse-coper,' wrote Eric Linklater.[1] His meanness was legendary; he felt it not merely his duty but his pleasure to restrict authors to the smallest possible royalty and to deal parsimoniously with his employees over salary and expenses. When he died Rupert gave him an unctuous obituary but commented to George Lyttelton that in fact Cape had been 'one of the tightest-fisted old bastards I've ever encountered'.[2]

In the tradition of Spenlow and Jorkins it might have been expected that Cape's partner, Wren Howard, would at least affect benevolence. He was, on the contrary, even more cheese-paring than his chairman. A trim, spruce figure of military appearance, his cautious precision complemented Cape's rather more swashbuckling approach while reinforcing his reluctance to part with more money than was absolutely necessary. He had a fine eye for design and it was largely due to him that Cape's books became highly esteemed for their good looks and high standards of production. Jonathan Cape may have felt little affection for authors, Howard actively disliked them; Rupert quickly learned that if any fraternisation was to take place beyond the normal demands of publishing, it would be up to him to provide it.

'He liked knowing the pecking order of authors,' wrote C. W. Wedgwood disparagingly of Cape, 'and had acquired a considerable surface knowledge of literature, knowing the titles of what sold.'[3] The slur was not wholly misdirected, yet did not do justice to Cape's feeling for quality or his readiness to venture where other publishers feared to tread. The firm's first publication was a reissue of C. M. Doughty's *Travels in Arabia Deserta*, an immense two-volume work which they had to sell at nine guineas to make even a modest profit. It seemed doomed to failure but proved a considerable success; still more important, it led to the establishment of a close relationship with T. E. Lawrence, which meant that in due course the firm published *Revolt in the Desert* and *Seven Pillars of Wisdom*. Cape too was one of the first British publishers to take American writers seriously and to pay regular visits to New York in search of new names to add to his list. Sinclair Lewis, Eugene O'Neill and Ernest Hemingway – all in due course won the Nobel Prize and added great réclame to the name of Jonathan Cape. Hemingway, in particular, also made the firm a great deal of money.

Cape was self-confident, even arrogant: William Plomer complained that he did not know how to listen but would invite people in 'for a talk' and then subject them to a relentless harangue on whatever subjects were in his mind.[4] Yet he had a shrewd awareness of his own limitations. He knew that he needed someone who would smell out latent talent as well as the ready-made best-seller and who could steer uncertain authors in the direction that would suit them best. To this end he employed Edward Garnett, son of the keeper of printed books at the British Museum, husband of Constance, the famed translator of Russian classics, and himself an editor of genius. Garnett, wrote H. E. Bates, was 'a semi-patriarchal, semi-diabolical figure in a floppy cloak-like overcoat, a grey scarf wound round his neck like a python, and preposterously small felt hat. He had grey hair, grey jowl-like cheeks that quivered ponderously like the gills of an ancient turkey.'[5] Whatever his appearance, nobody could have been less grey in character. A man of total integrity, he cared passionately about the quality of writing and the need for every author to realise his potential to the full. He was 'creative in a special sense', wrote his successor, William Plomer; 'far more creative, I consider, than most writers'.[6] Cape and Garnett disliked each other, in a sense despised each other, yet put a proper value on each other's strengths and made good use of them. Together, they were formidable.

Rupert had worked for a few weeks in Cape's office before beginning his year at the Book Society, so knew what to expect. 'JC likes everyone to be there by 9 am!!' he noted in his diary;[7] what's more, he was always there by 9 a.m. himself and usually stayed later than anybody else. In spite of his meanness, Cape in fact treated Rupert with reasonable generosity; he made him a director at a salary of £600 a year and agreed that, after the first year, he should participate in the regular profit-sharing agreement. But he expected great things in return. 'If you are to be a director, you must be able to direct,' he insisted. 'To do this you must know fairly intimately the processes of manufacturing and selling, although your principal work will be connected with the editorial side of the business.' Rupert could have asked for nothing more, and he must have responded too to the trumpet call with which Cape ended his letter of appointment: 'Jonathan Cape should become, in fact already is, an institution. It is greater and more important than any individual and is not run for my personal benefit or advertisement. I am its most faithful servant. It already has an unique status. We have to maintain this.'[8]

Every morning Cape, Howard, Rupert and sometimes Hamish Miles, fellow editor and translator, would meet in Cape's office to read the post and discuss the problems of the day. Rupert was relieved to find that his opinion was taken more seriously than it had been at Heinemann's. When he announced that his friend Peter Fleming was about to take off on a scatterbrained expedition up the Amazon and, if he returned at all, would undoubtedly do so with a highly entertaining book, Cape agreed to offer a contract and an advance of £300. His faith was justified: Fleming's *Brazilian Adventure*, one of the funniest and most high-spirited travel books in the English language, proved a great success and made the author's name. The Fleming connection endured and proved immensely valuable to Cape's; it was in the last analysis thanks to Rupert that Ian Fleming's preposterously profitable thrillers found their way on to the list. But his involvement with both camps sometimes caused him embarrassment. 'Don't you think Cape's are behaving rather mouldily to Peter?' asked Eve Fleming. 'Don't you think you ought to protect him a little more? I thought you might do something for him with Cape's, not because he needs the money but because I really don't think they behaved well.'[9]

Fleming's prowess must have boosted Rupert's reputation in the house. So too must the triumphant success of Duff Cooper's biography of Talleyrand, though the credit he earned from this must have diminished when for a later book Cooper took a literary agent and transferred to Faber & Faber's for a substantially increased advance. Nor were all his protégés successful. With some difficulty he persuaded Cape's to take on Alistair Cooke's first book, a collection of essays about the cinema. It flopped, and Cooke inscribed his editor's copy: 'To Rupert, patron, mentor and kindliest backer of the wrong horse.'[10] Nor did he always get his own way. Cape and Howard never hesitated to quash his more fanciful ideas. With some doubts but high hopes he introduced Nancy Cunard to his senior directors. She produced an enormously bulky dummy of her anthology *Negro*. Jonathan Cape pointed out that to print it in that format would mean that it was prohibitively expensive. Nancy insisted that there could be no question of any change. She was shown the door. She did not blame Rupert for her rebuff but Cape made it clear he thought his young editor had been guilty of introducing a dangerous lunatic into the premises. Nancy took her book to Gollancz's with equally little success; it was, she complained, like 'selling oriental rugs to manure merchants'. In the end *Negro* appeared under the imprint of a small, radical publishing house and at the author's own expense.[11]

As very much the junior member of the Cape triumvirate Rupert found that he was kept away from the more important authors and set menial tasks like the preparation of blurbs. This was not what he had envisaged when he became a publisher, but he found it an entertaining exercise. His reluctance to praise books beyond their proper merit meant that his superiors sometimes found it necessary to scatter superlatives over his copy, but he had a natural gift for producing concise and appealing summaries of books that meant little to him. On one occasion he was required to write selling copy for a novel by a successful lady author which was as yet unwritten and untitled but was going to be set in the same locality as seven of her previous best-sellers. To his gratification he accomplished the feat so successfully that the copy appeared unaltered on the dust-jacket of the novel.[12]

It is a fact of publishing life that the most junior editor tends to be made responsible for those authors who are notorious for their rudeness, inefficiency or uneasy temperament. Rupert had his fill of such cases. Robert Graves was notoriously tetchy. He took offence because his mistress, Laura Riding, had been invited to one of Cape's cocktail parties only as his partner and not as a poet in her own right: 'Her name on the Cape records is not a commercially brilliant one, she is aware,' he told Rupert sternly, 'but this seems to her all the more reason for an invitation in proper form.' In view of this discourtesy, he would boycott the party. Rupert contrived to appease the affronted Riding and both attended, but on another occasion he outraged Graves by shortening one of his poems in an anthology without prior permission. 'I am much displeased,' wrote Graves – presumably half in jest. 'An abject enough apology will be welcome; particularly one passing on the blame to someone else in a credible way.' The apology was forthcoming, though Rupert made no attempt to share the blame.[13] Wyndham Lewis, his mother's erstwhile love, proved still more troublesome. Rupert was in charge of one of his minor works, *The Roaring Queen*, which contained blatantly libellous passages about Victor Gollancz and the chief fiction reviewer on the *Observer*, Gerald Gould. Rupert pleaded for changes but could elicit none that would satisfy Cape's solicitor. In the end he referred the matter to Wren Howard who solved the problem by refusing to publish the book at all.[14] It was subsequently turned down by Chatto's and was finally published in 1973 after Gollancz's death.

One 'difficult' author whom Rupert inherited was in time to prove a benefactor on a grand scale. In fact Arthur Ransome, one of Cape's most important writers for children, was not himself difficult, but his wife, Genia – or, more correctly, Evgenia – more than made up for it. She had been Trotsky's private secretary, was still well disposed to Bolshevism and, if she lacked her former employer's Messianic vision, had inherited his distrustfulness, his venom and his guile. Rupert never wholly learnt how to handle her but he made a close friend of her husband. Ransome was a keen cricketer and Rupert persuaded him to raise a team to play an eleven representing Cape's. They also shared an enthusiasm for rugby football and Rupert took him regularly to matches at Twickenham. He drew the line only at adopting another of Ransome's passions, fishing. Ransome at one time convinced himself that he had made a convert and urged Rupert to take it up immediately: 'Start now and then, when next year's holiday comes, you will be fit to make proper use of it . . . Go to it. Every month you waste now will be heavy on your conscience later on!'[15] But Rupert had neither the time nor the temperament for such an occupation; he procrastinated, made excuses, in the end the matter dropped. Ransome forgave him: Rupert was to become his literary executor, editor of his posthumous autobiography and inheritor of a large part of his royalties.

Not all authors were difficult. Stephen Spender must have been the sort of writer junior editors dream of. Of course he would revise his book, he said, when Rupert pointed out its weaknesses; it needed revision and his only regret was that he had not seen the need for it himself. 'Moreover, if you are still not quite satisfied, I will go on rewriting it as many times as you like until I have got it right.'[16] Rupert was extraordinarily good at convincing his authors that he had the highest possible opinion of their talents. Edmund Blunden knew that Rupert believed him a great poet and so accepted from him criticism that he would have looked askance at from almost anyone else. He even asked Rupert to prepare a selection of his poems; a job which, Rupert replied, 'needless to say I should absolutely love to do, though I very much doubt my ability'. But not even an author as amenable as Blunden could be taken for granted. In October 1934 he protested when he heard that Cape's were printing 40,000 copies of a new book by that high priest of tabby cats and country gardens, Beverley Nichols. Rupert made the classic reply of the beleaguered publisher down the ages. It was all a question of demand, he explained. 'Certainly very few of the people you (or even I) see and admire read these books but the readers are there all right – tens of thousands of old women and goodness knows who. If they didn't read BN it would probably be something worse, or perhaps nothing . . . *Of course*, all this has nothing whatever to do with English literature . . . It is almost impossible, without some big seller or sellers on the list to take risks on good but uncommercial books.'[17]

As well as the 'difficult' he was often made responsible for the younger or less established authors. William Plomer was a contemporary of whom he grew very fond: 'He was such a darling, and so very funny,' he told Deirdre forty years later.[18] It was thanks to Rupert that Plomer brought his books to Cape's and in due course succeeded Garnett as principal reader. Only once did they come anywhere near to falling out; when Rupert insisted that Plomer was unnecessarily mealy-mouthed about the homosexual elements in his novel *The Invaders*. 'You don't say, and hardly even infer, whether they went to bed together or not.' Plomer refused to expand the passage, and for a time the relationship was frosty, but he bore Rupert no lasting grudge. A little later he was asking his editor to think of a subject for a non-fiction book. Rupert suggested a biography of the Albanian war-lord Ali Pasha, a somewhat recherché theme which Plomer nevertheless adopted and wrote on with great success.[19]

H. E. Bates was another writer who was pleased to have a younger editor with whom he could do business. 'We at once got on supremely well,' he remembered. 'Rupert was very much my sort of person and of my generation . . . [he] therefore became a liaison officer between the heads of the firm and myself, so that I found myself able to take to him problems, financial and otherwise, which I found it difficult to take to them.'[20] The problems were more often financial than otherwise. Bates was perpetually short of money. He was well into a new novel, he announced before visiting Cape's offices, 'But I can't go on as I would like unless I have not only your moral but also financial support. In short – it is the cash I shall come to talk about.'[21] On the whole Rupert thought that Cape's were being unnecessarily mean to an already well-known and potentially best-selling author; he fought to secure Bates better terms and was partly successful. But he could be harsh in his literary judgments. Bates recollected a luncheon at which Rupert and Edward Garnett's son, David, fiercely criticised his latest effort: 'I had spawned another monster; I was the begetter of a two-headed, crooked Mongolian monstrosity whose body would have to be put somewhere darkly away.'[22] Even Rupert on reflection thought he might have gone a little too far. He wrote to Bates (his tone as a correspondent was markedly less formal than Cape's or Howard's; he used Christian names habitually, which was unusual for the period, and ended his letter to Bates with 'Much love') to say that he feared he had made his author angry. 'It's not easy to write critically to someone one is very fond of and whose work one admires very much. As you say, I may be entirely wrong, but all I'm trying to do is to give you an honest opinion, and not to be an all-weather comforter.'[23] The solace was no doubt needed, but Bates was sensible enough to know that Rupert was a true friend and that his hostile criticism should be taken all the more seriously on that account.

Rupert's instinct was always to be generous and to pay an author as much as could be afforded. Under Jonathan Cape's tuition, however, he learnt how to drive a hard bargain if he had to. Denis Johnston, the Irish playwright, had elected to rewrite his latest book in proof. The extra cost would be £20, Rupert wrote sternly. Was Johnston prepared to pay? But even then, Rupert partially relented. After a heated wrangle with Wren Howard he was able to say that 'as a small gesture of confidence', Johnston's share of the bill was being reduced to a mere £5.[24] He had to learn to harden his heart, too, when friends wrote in asking if a job could be found for them at Cape's. Malcolm Muggeridge proposed himself but then professed to be relieved when he was turned down. As soon as he had posted the letter, he said, he had thought better of it: 'I always do this when I apply for a job, because I don't really want one.'[25] John Betjeman *did* really want one, but was disarmingly frank about his limitations. 'I know nothing about contracts for authors and very little about distribution to book-sellers,' he wrote: concluding more hopefully, 'I think I am pretty shrewd about what is likely to sell and what has no earthly chance.'[26]

Rupert made little effort to promote the causes of these marginal candidates, but he did better when Guy Chapman, whose book on William Beckford Cape's had already published, applied for a job in 1938. Rupert championed his cause with vigour and won the day. Chapman loved his new job. Much of his pleasure in it, he wrote, 'I owed to the third director at Cape's, Rupert Hart-Davis. I had known him well enough to respect his experience, self-possession and impeccable taste and I came quickly to feel a cheerful affection for him. He provided warmth and gaiety in the firm's somewhat arid atmosphere.'[27] It was Chapman who, when Arthur Koestler submitted *Darkness at Noon* and William Plomer 'disliked and despised it', took it home to read, was vastly impressed and passed it on to Rupert with a strong endorsement. Rupert shared Chapman's view, persuaded his fellow directors to accept it and thus ensured that one of the most influential novels of the 1930s and 1940s, a terrifying indictment of Stalin's rule, first saw the light of day under the imprint of Jonathan Cape.[28]

Though he could see the importance of such a book, Rupert took little interest in politics, national or international. When Douglas Reed's polemic *Insanity Fair* was published, H. E. Bates urged that a copy should be sent to every Member of Parliament. 'My dear boy, what's the use?' Rupert wearily enquired. 'They can't read anyway.'[29] He would far rather have seen Cape's list contain more poetry but here he had to combat the indifference if not hostility of Cape and Howard. Apart from Blunden, he notched up a few victories. Stevie Smith came to Cape's as a novelist but Rupert, who had edited her first book *Novel on Yellow Paper*, took advantage of its success to sneak in a volume of poetry and encouraged Smith to illustrate it herself with quirky Edward Lear-type illustrations. He became very fond of her, as well as an ardent admirer of her work, but was not able to protect her when Cape's tried to charge her £2 14s. 1d. for legal advice. Undiscomfited, she fought her own battle and won the day: 'You write like an angel, but you argue like a fiend,' Rupert observed respectfully.[30] He also succeeded in insinuating the American poet Robert Frost into Cape's list. Rupert admired

Frost greatly and felt that he had been far too long unrecognised in Britain. He suggested that the poet should prepare a selection of his poems for Cape's to publish. 'I can confess to you privately I shouldn't mind having a British public for my works,' Frost replied wistfully. 'Are you going to be able to get it for me? Don't feel too badly if you aren't. We'll stay friends just the same.'[31] Rupert rose to the challenge. The poems were published with introductory essays by, among others, Auden and Cecil Day-Lewis, and though neither Frost nor Cape's grew rich as a result, Frost found and never lost his British public.

Cecil Day-Lewis was one poet whom Rupert failed to acquire for the Cape's list. Day-Lewis, however, wrote successful detective stories under a pseudonym and Rupert, who loved the genre, was convinced that he could become a serious novelist. 'Actually, my seriousness at present runs into verse,' Day-Lewis told him. 'Also, for this type of book I am rather tied up with the Hogarth Press.'[32] Undeterred, Rupert kept up the pressure and offered an income of £300 a year for the next three years if Day-Lewis would give up his work as a teacher and embark on serious fiction. This was, Day-Lewis remarked in his autobiography, 'one of the few grave errors he [Hart-Davis] made in his publishing career'.[33] Day-Lewis wrote two novels for Cape's, neither of which was a disaster, though the critical reception was at the best lukewarm and sales were poor. In publishing terms, therefore, it must be counted an error if not a particularly grave one. But Rupert had made a friend. While he was trying to persuade Day-Lewis to write a novel, he visited the family in the country and was an instant success: 'Somewhat military in appearance and bearing,' Day-Lewis's son remembered him, 'yet funny and generously appreciative and compassionate'.[34] Day-Lewis was a committed Communist at the time; Rupert must have been aware of the fact, but it made not the slightest difference to their relationship. Friendship, for Rupert, was always far more important than ideology and, anyway, there were many much more interesting things to discuss than politics.

Rupert's capacity to make and retain friends from among his authors and colleagues was indeed one of his most notable accomplishments. Day-Lewis, Blunden, Plomer, Arthur Ransome, were all friends from the Cape's era who remained close to him all their lives. Another was Eric Linklater, now married to Rupert's one-time girlfriend Marjorie MacIntyre. Shortly before he joined Cape's Rupert had read Linklater's novel *Juan in America* and wrote in his diary that he had not been more amused by a new book for years. He was delighted to find that he would be responsible for Linklater's future works. But though he did not know it, he was dealing with what, in Jonathan Cape's eyes, constituted a 'difficult' author. Linklater thought that he had been meanly treated over *Juan* and, still worse, had been tied down to an unfairly restrictive contract for the next three years. His intention had been to leave Cape's as soon as he legally could. According to his biographer, when Rupert took over 'some of the resentment failed. A great friendship grew up between him and Hart-Davis.'[35] He quickly learned to trust Rupert's judgment; when he received handsome praise for the first few chapters of *Ripeness is All* he replied with relief that he had been fearing the book was not ripe but rotten: 'from these ugsome musings you have timely rescued me'. More politically conscious than Rupert, he made his opinions very clear when his German publisher wanted to change his translator. Rupert passed on the request. 'I don't know whether Goldschmidt is any good,' Linklater replied, 'but if Goverts Verlag refuse to employ him simply because he is a Jew, you can tell them to stuff a large bag of tin swastikas up their fundamental orifices and ride a tandem bicycle to hell.'[36]

Geoffrey Keynes, surgeon, literary scholar and brother of the economist, was another author who became a friend and played an important part in Rupert's life for many years. David Garnett greatly admired the catalogue of Gibbon's library on which Keynes had been working for many years and enlisted Rupert as an ally. Together they persuaded a dubious Jonathan Cape that this was a suitable book for his house to publish. The doubts were more than justified; as Rupert recollected with a hint of pride, the book 'achieved the splendid record of selling fewer copies than any other book published by Cape'.[37] But Keynes was unperturbed. 'Your collaboration has made a very big difference,' he told Rupert. 'Besides which, I have made a very nice friend, which is worth more than all. I really am grateful.'[38]

The charm did not always work. Rupert tried to lure Vita Sackville-West away from the Hogarth Press with talk of generous advances. She refused politely enough but told Virginia Woolf about the *démarche*; Rupert, she said, was 'too amiable by half'.[39] Osbert Sitwell was another failure though he took a more generous view of Rupert's efforts. 'I do want to let you know how *much* I appreciated all your kindness, and the energy you put into the attempt to secure me for Cape,' Sitwell wrote. 'If it had been a purely personal thing, you would have won, always.'[40] It was evidently not personal enough; Sitwell stayed with Macmillan's. But such setbacks were rare: by the outbreak of the Second World War

Rupert had established a reputation for being an excellent editor, a good judge of books and a man of generosity and integrity. Jonathan Cape had no reason to regret the decision to employ him.

Rupert had learnt a great deal during these years. He said in his memoirs that everything he knew about publishing had come from Jonathan Cape; so far as the tricks of running a successful business were concerned this was true. From Edward Garnett, however, he had learnt lessons which were to guide his conduct for the rest of his publishing life. 'Always remember, my young friend,' Garnett had replied when Rupert suggested that some otherwise worthy book might be unsaleable, 'that there is still in this country a residuum of educated folk.'[41] Rupert never forgot these words and it was for this residuum that he resolved to publish. The possibility that it might not be large or rich enough to sustain his efforts was regrettable but not a reason for changing his policy. Equally, he took to heart another of Garnett's aphorisms: 'The Scholar who does not correct his Proofs will soon have no Proofs to correct.'[42] Sloppiness was unforgivable, to hell with the publisher's schedule or the cost of rewriting books in proof, let the salesmen wail and the printers tear out their hair, what mattered was that the final product should be right.

Commercial considerations were always secondary. A typical exchange with Garnett occurred when Rupert proposed calling a volume of John Galsworthy's letters to Edward Garnett *The Making of the Forsytes*. This was a catchpenny title, Garnett retorted, and anyway not what the letters were about:

> We shall have to stick to my title, even though you lose shekels and your money bags get depleted by my obstinate adherence to Honour and Gentlemanly Feeling! Oh, my dear young friend, do you realise the truth of that old Scottish saying:
>
> > I'll take the High Line
> > While *you* take the Low.
>
> Seriously, this old scoundrel will always present to you the path of Spiritual Rectitude, while your associates are pushing you along the path of criminal commercialism.[43]

Rupert's reply is lost but it was presumably contrite enough to satisfy his mentor. Significantly, in Garnett's next letter 'Dear Rupert' replaced the more formal 'Dear Hart-Davis' of the earlier correspond-

ence. 'I am much pleased', he wrote, 'by your manly confession of your
error and by your resolve in future to endeavour to approach the High
Line. I trust, but I scarcely expect, that your example will lead your
associates into paths less profitable and more honourable.'[44]
    Resolutely and gallantly, Rupert stuck to the High Line throughout
his publishing career. The results were not invariably to the satisfaction
of his partners and his shareholders but he never saw reason to doubt
that he was right.

One of the more agreeable features of publishing as a career is that it
overlaps a range of enjoyable pursuits not directly connected with it but
still relevant enough to be defended as worth doing in the interests of
the job. Rupert had, if anything, grown more keen on cricket since he
had played it enthusiastically but ineptly at Eton. What more natural
then that he should organise a cricket team of Cape's staff and authors
to play sides from other publishing houses or from villages within easy
distance of London? Edmund Blunden was another fanatic who
regularly opened the batting with Rupert for the Cape's eleven. Peter
Fleming and H. E. Bates turned out for many matches. Cecil Day-
Lewis never played for Cape's but deposited his children with Rupert
and Comfort for ten days so that he could tour with another team.
Standards of batting and bowling were usually low and of umpiring
even lower. Playing against Bates's village eleven Rupert was top scorer
with twenty, only to be given out caught at the wicket off a ball which
he missed by several inches. Even the opposing captain felt bound to
remonstrate, whereupon the umpire said: 'Well, maybe he didn't hit
that one, but he hit the one before.'[45]
    But when Rupert was not publishing he was most often to be found
in second-hand bookshops or haunting the book-barrows in the
Farringdon Road. His enjoyment of book collecting had now become a
passion. In old age he chanced upon a list of purchases made between
1937 and 1939. He bought a total of 1,217 books at a cost of £74 8s. 4d.
– about 1/3d. a copy or £1.50 or so at current prices. Most of these
were first editions, some were bargains even at the time, others were
individually of little value but worth far more in the sets which he
lovingly and laboriously accumulated. It was the collection of a man
who was shrewd, patient and knowledgeable; he had not necessarily
read every book that he possessed but he was well acquainted with all of
them and he loved them with the fervour that the term 'bibliophile'
implies.

He reviewed books as well as bought, published and read them. At first he worked mainly for the *Spectator*, reviewing crime books from early 1935. It was in that paper that, in March 1936, he proclaimed his friend Cecil Day-Lewis had stepped into the front rank of crime novelists. Day-Lewis wrote under the name of Nicholas Blake – 'who derives in equal part from his great progenitors, William and Sexton,' Rupert observed. Then, during the war, he was invited to write a regular monthly round-up of crime books for Lady Rhondda's *Time and Tide*. He accepted with pleasure and for fifteen years carried out the task under the pseudonym of Norman Blood – 'Kind hearts are more than coronets, and simple faith than . . . ' He liked thrillers to be literate and logical, preferably with an element of quirkiness: as well as Nicholas Blake, Ngaio Marsh, Michael Innes and Edmund Crispin were among his favourite authors. He thought Dorothy Sayers readable but too snobbish, both socially and intellectually; Agatha Christie was workmanlike but uninspiring. His outspokenness sometimes got him into trouble. He gave Margery Allingham's new detective story, *Coroner's Pidgin* – admittedly one of her weaker efforts – so ferocious a notice that the editor wrote to protest. Miss Allingham was herself a long-standing reviewer for *Time and Tide*. There was no need to call her book a masterpiece, suggested the editor, but it did deserve 'a certain respectful attention . . . I wouldn't, of course, ask you to revise your estimate, but could you possibly send the book back for someone who really admires Mr Campion to tackle?'[46] If he *had* been asked to revise his estimate, Rupert's outrage would have known no bounds; as it was he returned the book with good grace while no doubt reflecting on the feebleness and fatuity of literary editors. His diatribe came as a surprise because Rupert was on the whole an admirer both of Allingham and her detective, Mr Campion, describing *The Tiger in the Smoke* as 'the best thriller I've read in years'. Even when he was at his most censorious he was never even slightly supercilious or dismissive of the genre; on the contrary, he much admired the leading practitioners and enjoyed their work. 'To me they are a great solace,' he told George Lyttelton, 'a sort of mental knitting where it doesn't matter if you drop a stitch.'

In 1933 he also began to review the occasional play for the *Spectator*, taking over for a few weeks when the regular critic was away. After 1935 this work dropped away, but for the first six months of 1938 he was employed as one of their two main theatre reviewers. Among other plays, he reviewed the celebrated production of *Othello* in which Ralph Richardson played the title role to Laurence Olivier's Iago. He compared Richardson's performance with that of Paul Robeson eight years before: Richardson, he judged, spoke the poetry much better, but where Robeson inspired 'pity and terror', Richardson inspired only pity. He avoided drawing any comparisons between the Desdemonas of Curigwen Lewis and Peggy Ashcroft, remarking only that Richardson was not well served by his heroine. In this he seems to have been charitable: the reviewer for *The Times* dismissed Miss Lewis as 'arch in manner and lifeless in intonation'. Doing a full-time job in publishing as well as spending evenings at the theatre and reporting on what he saw must have been a heavy load. Rupert had prodigious energy for doing what he wanted to do but he knew when the quantity of his work was militating against the quality. He reviewed his last play, Jean Giraudoux's *Amphitryon 38*, in May 1938.

Another curious by-product of his career was the preparation of Christmas quizzes for *Time and Tide* and, at least once, for *The Times*. Friends and acquaintances were enlisted in the search for suitable questions. Maurice Baring was particularly fecund as a source. The origin of clichés was one of his specialities. Few except he would have known that 'The long arm of coincidence' first appeared in a play of the 1880s called *Captain Swift*. Another of Baring's suggestions, which Rupert used, required the solver to state the time dinner was served at Patterne Hall, Mansfield Park, Courcy Castle and Todger's Boarding House.* Rupert kept the practice going when he joined the Army and enlisted his fellow recruits as a source of subjects. The literary level of the competition must have dropped; the themes on which the greatest expertise was exhibited were horse-racing, county cricket, the Duchess of Windsor and the novels of James Hadley Chase.

The Lawrence Street flat served Rupert and Comfort well for the first year or so of marriage but once Comfort was pregnant they concluded that something rather more spacious and sedate was called for. They moved to Lloyd Square in Islington and it was there that their first child, Bridget, was born on 13 January 1935. 'She looked perfectly hideous,' Rupert wrote in his diary, 'with a huge mouth, black and swollen head, a lot of fluffy hair and heavy red eyelids.' Eighteen months later on 3 June 1936, their son Duff followed; he was not quite as hideous as his sister had been but since by then Bridget had lost her swollen head and red eyelids and had become a particularly attractive

---

* Could this have been a malign hoax? Accurate times seem impossible to establish.

child, no invidious comparisons needed to be made. Another move was
deemed necessary, both to gain more space and to be near a park. They
found a house for sale in Stormont Road, off Hampstead Lane. Rupert
persuaded his father to put up £2,000; Jonathan Cape lent a further
£2,000; with characteristic generosity Peter Fleming offered to
contribute too. 'The new house sounds very exciting,' he wrote. 'Look
here, if you want a loan I will readily come across with a cool thou, or
any other sort of thou for that matter . . . No interest charged, but pay it
back when you conveniently can.'[47]

The offer was gratefully refused but a few months later Fleming was
able to be still more benevolent. He had recently been given a large
estate in the Chilterns near Nettlebed in Oxfordshire and offered
Rupert, for a far from economic rent of £90 a year, the lease of
Bromsden Farm, a partly Victorian partly eighteenth-century farm-
house about a mile from the new house that Fleming was building for
himself. It was not ideal – cheek by jowl with an extremely active
farmyard, with a petrol engine providing the electricity and only open
fires for heating – but it was wonderfully remote and yet within easy
range of London. 'It's not an elegant or a beautiful house, but it suits us
in many ways,' Rupert told Duff Cooper.[48] It took some time to put it
into order and they did not actually move in until 1939 but meanwhile
they often stayed with the Flemings at their bland neo-Georgian
creation, Merrimoles. In view of their past history, some men might
have found it a little awkward to have Celia Johnson so close a
neighbour, let alone as lady of the manor, but the idea never occurred to
Rupert. He had always been very fond of Celia and took it for granted
that she felt the same; besides, she was an old friend of Comfort. '*This* is
home now, and I grow fonder of it every day,' Rupert wrote in
satisfaction.[49]

Joyce Grenfell, whose father, Paul Phipps, had designed Merrimoles,
stayed there in January 1938. Rupert was also in the house. It was so
nice to see him again, Joyce Grenfell told her mother. 'He is so happy
nowadays. Two lovely, fit blonde babies, a house at Highgate and a fine
job in a successful publishers. He is so gay and amusing and makes one
feel warm when one sees him. You can't imagine how *fat* he's got!
Long, thin Rupert . . . ' A few months later he and Comfort were
staying with the Grenfells at their cottage on the Cliveden estate. Again
it was his fatness which surprised his hostess. He 'looks very well and is
so happy,' she wrote. 'She is very intelligent, quiet, cosy and the perfect
wife for Rupert.'[50]

The picture is of a happy man. As such it was true to life. Rupert rarely missed an opportunity to grumble but it did not often signify anything of importance. Other things being equal, or even close to equality, then it was his disposition to be contented. At the beginning of 1939 there was little to ruffle his satisfaction. He was more than delighted by his family. He complained to Eric Linklater that his son, Duff, seemed to spend most of his time crying but Linklater retorted that *he* was sharing his house with an Indian child 'with the appearance of an infant Bill Sikes, a perpetual voice like an angry guinea-hen and a nursemaid with a cart horse tread'.[51] Rupert had to agree that his troubles were trifling compared to this. He was a devoted if somewhat distant father who was apt to be immersed in books when he might have been romping with the children but was genuinely gratified by the fact that they existed. He had an interesting job in which he was appreciated if not lavishly rewarded. He was satisfied with his house in Highgate and delighted by his new-found country retreat. Life was good and there seemed every chance that it would go on getting better. The war put a stop to that.

Chapter Eight

Soldier of the King

'Chamberlain's a great gentleman. I'd always vote for him,' Rupert declared stoutly at the time of the Munich Crisis.[1] It seems unlikely that he gave much thought to the issues involved; certainly there is no indication that he ever discussed them with his uncle, Duff Cooper, who would have disagreed vehemently with his views on the Prime Minister and the policy of appeasement. By September 1939 Rupert had reluctantly concluded that war was inevitable and that it was essential that Hitler's Germany should be stopped before it committed yet more enormities. But he did not feel he was taking part in a crusade. Comfort wrote to tell him that she could not pretend to any passionate involvement in Britain's cause: 'I know that you feel just the same – you don't *believe* in the war any more than I do, though you have to do your part like everyone else.'[2] It was 1941 when she wrote this letter, by which time Rupert was, both emotionally and practically, rather more involved in winning, or at least not losing, the war than his wife suggested. It is true, however, that though he preferred the English way of life to any other, he was one of the least chauvinistic of men. He would, if necessary, have died for his country but he considered it quite as likely to be wrong as right and had no intention of ranting pugnaciously on its behalf. Rupert's war was to be conducted with quiet dignity and a touch of humour rather than histrionic heroism.

At the declaration of war Britain braced itself for devastating bombardment from the air and mammoth battles on the land. Nothing happened. Rupert was as taken aback as anyone: Comfort and the children had at once been packed off to Bromsden while he carried on with his publishing in London and awaited obliteration. His name was on the list of the Army Officers' Emergency Reserve but he was thirty-two and knew that many younger men would need to be called up before his turn came round, and he had no urge to thrust himself forward. His sense of priorities was unaffected by the coming of war. He had persuaded Winston Churchill to contribute a preface to the latest book by his stepfather-in-law, Louis Spears; on 4 September, the day after war was declared, he wrote to ask that Churchill's corrected proofs should be returned as soon as possible. The secretary to the newly appointed First Lord of the Admiralty politely replied that Mr Churchill was rather busy at the moment and hoped that somebody else could undertake the task.[3]

Rupert for his part was not busy enough. 'Publishing is semi-stagnant,' he told Edmund Blunden. It seemed reasonable to hope that the public would turn to books when the blackout began to curtail other pastimes, but at the moment few new titles were appearing and fewer being bought.[4] He went to the office every day, because there was nothing else to do and he needed the salary, but the work seemed pointless, made more so by the probability that in due course he would be called up, or at least found a job in some sort of national service. The war seemed as stagnant as the book trade; as the first eventless months slipped by Rupert was more preoccupied by the health of his son. In January 1940 Duff was diagnosed as having abnormal hip bones; a fortnight later the specialist's verdict was that the hip was tubercular. Expensive treatment and a long stay in hospital would be necessary. 'Darling, we have had such a good time so far,' wrote Comfort. 'I suppose it is our turn now to have a bit of bad – well, never mind – we got spliced for better or worse and we'll stick it out, eh?'[5] Friends rallied round: Peter Fleming offered to forgo a year's rent for Bromsden, Spears sent £25. Wren Howard belied his reputation for parsimony by making an indefinite loan of £50. As with so many other financial crises that he would have to face over the next forty years, Rupert remained unperturbed and in the end scraped through. There was more than a touch of the Micawber about him, and nearly always something *did* turn up. Comfort was far more concerned. 'Darling, I can't help feeling rather worried about our finances,' she wrote, a fortnight or so before Duff's illness added a fresh burden to the family exchequer. 'You never seem to have enough dibs and I don't know whether we are spending just a little too much or much too much . . . I don't see how we shall ever save up enough unless we do something drastic.'[6] Her first proposal was to close up the house in Highgate, a move which, since it would have left Rupert homeless, would have created more problems than it solved. Her only other suggestion was to reduce her smoking from twenty-five to twenty cigarettes a day.

Then the real war began. France was overrun, invasion seemed imminent, and Rupert joined the Local Defence Volunteers, first manifestation of what was rather more pithily rechristened the Home Guard. He drilled busily, erected pointless roadblocks and spent nights on watch in case German parachutists selected a cornfield in Oxfordshire as the site of their first drop. It was rather fun; it did not give him a taste for soldiering but suggested that the real thing might not be too intolerable. It was as well that he had something to occupy his spare time, for in July 1940 Comfort and the children departed for America to escape the threatened invasion, leaving him bereft. 'Don't be afraid, my love,' Comfort urged him. 'Nothing is certain as you say, and nothing much matters. We must live in the hope of seeing one another again, and if you are killed I will live for our children.'[7] This cheering message arrived just before Rupert was required to register for the Army. He could expect to be called up in another eight weeks or so. 'I'm not worrying about it at all – what's the use?' he asked Edmund Blunden, 'but am just waiting for whatever turns up.'[8]

In fact he was rather less fatalistic than these words suggest. He was by now thoroughly fed up with his daily work – or lack of work. 'At the moment I feel utterly sick of publishing,' he told Comfort. 'I feel v restless these days, can't settle much to anything and just marking time.'[9] He sounded out Duff Cooper, now Minister of Information, about the chances of a job of some kind under his auspices: many literary figures spent an unexceptionable and sometimes even modestly useful war doing propaganda work of one kind or another and such duties would have suited him well. Perhaps Cooper thought that to employ him would be too obviously nepotic, anyway the approach came to nothing. If he was going to join the Army, Rupert reflected, he might as well do it in the best possible way, which to his mind must mean that he joined the Brigade of Guards. The colonel who interviewed him when he went for his medical advised him to volunteer at once rather than wait to be called up. Strings were pulled, the old-boy net worked smoothly, he was told that if he did the statutory eight weeks in the ranks and four or five months in an officers' training unit there was every likelihood that he would get a commission in the Coldstream Guards. A scare followed when a disobliging doctor ruled that his eyesight was not good enough for the Guards. As soon as it was realised that he was going to be commissioned, however, the objection was dropped – short-sightedness, though an impediment in the ranks, presented no problems for an officer. He was told that he had a fortnight more of civilian life. 'I feel curiously and almost blissfully serene,' he told Comfort. 'I think it's the result of uncertainty being removed and the prospect of all immediate responsibilities being lifted from one's shoulders.'[10]

Rupert reported at Caterham on 20 September 1940, by which time the immediate threat of invasion had receded and London was the principal target for German bombers. Caterham, in fact, promised to be in some ways more peaceful than life in the capital. It was going to be strenuous, Rupert realised; he would be considerably older than most of the other recruits and would find it hard to keep up. But he was reasonably fit and felt sure he would survive; 'on the whole I am looking forward to it,' he told Blunden.[11] His friends were not all so optimistic: 'You will be every inch a Guardsman, but you won't much like being a cadet,' prophesied Geoffrey Keynes, while Charles Morgan commiserated gloomily: 'I hate to think of you in your present job. At the front, in France, it mightn't have been so bad [a curious observation at a time when there was no front in France], but here it must be bloody.'[12] Bloody it was in some ways but Rupert was unbowed. Jonathan Cape told David Garnett with obvious surprise that after ten days of Army life his reactions were 'wholly favourable. He appeared to be enjoying it.'[13] Jamie Hamilton, already an officer, sought Rupert out at Caterham, prepared to play a consolatory role. He found his friend 'in high spirits and looking very well. The life seems to suit him . . . And he doesn't in the least pine for *les neiges d'antan*, in the shape of Jonathan's frosty maw. In fact he says that publishing can look after itself for a bit.'[14] Rupert was scornful of his friend for having contrived to secure a commission without the gruelling preliminaries that he himself was enduring. 'I wouldn't really like to become an officer,' he told Comfort, 'without doing a day's drill or knowing anything about the men or their training.'[15]

His own knowledge of 'the men' was not particularly extensive. The twenty-two recruits with whom he shared a hut were all from public schools, the majority Etonians, and destined to be officers. 'We don't see much of the other squads (the rank and vile as you might say) except at grub,' Rupert told Comfort, 'but they're mostly v friendly.'[16] He did not get to know any of them at all well until he spent several weeks cooped up in a military hospital, but he would have managed perfectly well if his fellow recruits had come from the slums of Glasgow or the mountains of Wales. As his close and enduring friendship with Charlie Marford illustrated, he took people as he found them, with a freedom from social prejudice that was truly exceptional in the 1930s and 1940s. He could never be described as tolerant – he loathed pomposity and pretension and despised vulgarity of any kind – but if people amused or interested him he accepted them unquestioningly, without stopping to consider their accent or their antecedents. By the young Etonians with whom he shared a barrack room he was treated with an affectionate if slightly mocking deference; he was to their minds ancient, he was slightly odd, but they liked him and he fitted in.

They were anyway far too tired to spare much energy analysing their fellow victims. From reveille at 5.45 a.m. till an exhausted collapse into bed at 10 p.m., life was a treadmill of drills, marches, lectures, weapon-training and the endless cleaning and polishing of barrack rooms and equipment. Rupert found the routine demanding but acceptable: 'I'm by no means good at drill,' he told Comfort, 'but I'm better than some of the lads, and squads are passed collectively – which is just as well.'[17] He was rather more put out by the menial tasks to which he was assigned. Most mornings he was part of a fatigue party responsible for cleaning the latrines. But even this chore was made less onerous for the future officers: it's 'more directing than shit-shovelling', he told Comfort. And the more rigorous the demands made upon him, the greater the pleasure he found in surviving: 'There's a certain satisfaction in knowing that this is the toughest place in the whole Army – and if one can take it one can take anything.'[18]

What he did find jarring was the noise and the lack of privacy. At first he claimed that the latter caused him no distress; he was never alone for a moment but at least 'the others are all young and gently bred' (a phrase which he omitted from the version of the letter that appeared in his memoirs, presumably to avoid accusations of snobbery).[19] But in time he found that he craved a measure of seclusion, while the incessant battering of loud voices and louder music began to prey upon him. 'I can't say I'm looking forward to Caterham tomorrow,' he confessed to Comfort when spending a day or two at Bromsden towards the end of November. 'It's mostly the incessant noise that I dread, which dulls the brain.'[20] The food, on the other hand, caused him no distress. Throughout his life he enjoyed good cooking but preferred plain food to the more recherché confections he associated with abroad: his favourite dish was minced chicken with a poached egg – 'I'm crazy about rhubarb too, and rice pudding' – which he ate in great quantities and at still greater speed. At Caterham he found that the food was 'rough and starchy, but one's always ravenous and it seems delicious'.[21]

If he still felt hungry he could always eke out the fare with bangers and mash and beer in the canteen.

In some ways, indeed, life in the Army was actually to be relished. Rupert was one of the most sentimental of men; tears always sprang to his eyes, he said, 'at the first strains of a drum-and-fife band as at a glimpse of the King and Queen'.[22] The demands of war had attenuated some of the pomp and circumstance of regimental soldiering and a trumpet call is anyway less romantic if it summons one from bed at a quarter to six on a raw November morning, but there was still quite enough left to gratify Rupert's sense of tradition and to touch his sensibilities. He was particularly pleased by the sergeants who were charged with imparting the regimental history to new recruits. It was taken for granted that the country's story began with the formation of the Coldstream Guards in 1650; after that the history of Britain consisted of a series of isolated events in which the regiment played a part, with nothing very much happening in between. Rupert found this exposition a little unsophisticated but he was genuinely stirred by the battle honours and rejoiced in sharing in so noble a tradition.

The energetic but intellectually undemanding life, the freedom from responsibility, the feeling that he was fitter than he had ever been before, for a time at least appealed strongly to Rupert. 'There's obviously much to be said for an open-air life of semi-manual work,' he told Comfort. 'I wonder whether we could make a living out of any sort of farming?' 'I expect not,' he added gloomily, but Comfort, who had studied agriculture at Oxford, was by no means so sure. 'I don't see why you shouldn't learn to farm successfully,' she replied. 'It would take a bit of capital but would be the kind of life that would suit us both.'[23] If she really believed that it would suit Rupert to settle into an agricultural backwater and make his living as a farmer, she gravely misunderstood her husband. Rupert loved the country, but as a background to literary activity: to have to spend his days ploughing fields or tending cattle would have appalled him. Any such dreams were anyway quickly banished when, towards the end of 1940, his thirty-three-year-old body showed that it was not up to the strains of Army life.

First, in mid-October, he fell into a trench five feet deep and badly damaged his knee. He was in hospital for nearly a month, something which at first was a blessed relief from the relentless parades and fatigues but soon became a penance. He suffered from 'a complete mental and intellectual fatigue', a condition which he ascribed to the bromide with which the authorities were supposed to dose the Army tea

so as to quell any sexual urges that might survive the exertions of the
day. The worst part of it was that, once he had been out of action for a
couple of weeks, it became inevitable that he would be put back to begin
all over again with the next squad of recruits to arrive at Caterham. All
the travail of his first few weeks had thus been wasted. He had at least
the consolation of a fortnight's unexpected leave when he left hospital
and was excused physical training and some of the other more strenuous
pursuits when he returned to service. Even so, he was by no means sure
that his knee would stand up to the strain. 'If it goes again,' he wrote
resignedly, 'then I think the only thing to do is to get invalided out of
the Army, or at any rate the ranks, and try something else.'[24]

It was not his knee that let him down. On Christmas Day he was
afflicted by some mysterious bug, thought it was merely influenza,
reported sick and within a few hours was back in hospital with
pneumonia. This time he remained there for five weeks. 'Thank
goodness you are alive,' David Garnett told him. 'You have tried to do
what TE [Lawrence] did without his toughness. You remember
Uxbridge nearly killed him. It's all very well laying down your life for
your country – but to lay it down for a drill instructor is not sweet,
however decorous, and decorum is not enough as Nurse Cavell ought to
have said.'[25] The Army evidently agreed and took a commendably
pragmatic approach to Rupert's problem. Clearly he was unlikely to
survive a full course at Caterham, on the other hand there were a
number of useful jobs he could do as an officer in which his physical
stamina would be a secondary issue – solution: skip the last few weeks of
primary training and send him straight to Sandhurst.

After Caterham Sandhurst seemed almost absurdly luxurious. Rupert
shared a bedroom with one other man, hot baths were available, civilian
suits were worn at dinner. The NCOs treated the trainee officers with a
nice mixture of deference and contempt: 'Mr Fife, you look like a
bloody stuffed fish, Sir!' There was plenty of drilling and marching but
the merciless rat race of Caterham was a thing of the past. He fired a
machine-gun for the first time – 'and I did very well,' he told Comfort
proudly. He did less well on a motorcycle since he never really
mastered the principle of the kick-start. On their first outing the rest of
the squad roared away, leaving Rupert and one other cadet disconsolate.
Eventually even this last recalcitrant deserted him: Rupert flung in his
wake Meg Merrilies' gypsy curse from *Guy Mannering*, 'Ride your
ways, Laird of Ellangowan, ride your ways . . .'[26]

He spent one night in hospital during his time at Sandhurst, fearing at first that pneumonia had struck again but miraculously recovering within twenty-four hours. He found himself responsible for producing most of the material used at the concert which the cadets put on the night before passing-out. The previous entry had had William Douglas-Home to act as author and the evening had been a memorable success; Rupert provided a medley of 'topical skits, dirty jokes, jolly tunes and imitations of officers' and got quite as enthusiastic a reception as his predecessor. And so on 16 May a triumphant telegram was despatched to America: 'OLD BOY NOW AN OFFICER VERY SMART AND WELL BLESSINGS HART–DAVIS.'[27]

'Very smart' were important words for Rupert. He revelled in dressing up as an officer and did so with consummate self-conviction; no one seeing him in well-cut riding breeches, highly polished leather boots and swagger stick would have suspected that he viewed horses with mingled fear and loathing. He had a set back when the shop responsible for producing his boots and shoes was burnt down in an air raid a few days before the passing-out parade, but this problem was overcome, and he emerged refulgent in his new-found glory to dazzle Comfort's parents with his appearance (and delight them with his gifts of butter and sugar). He 'looked every inch a soldier', Douglas Turner told his daughter. 'You would have gone quite crackers over him. The only incongruous thing is the ridiculous one pip on his shoulder – at the very least there should be three and really he carried the appearance of a Major.'[28] In all the many photographs taken of him at the time he wears an air of fixed resolve: I am a stern disciplinarian, the image proclaims; I do my duty and expect others to do the same, I am fair but firm. Appearances did not altogether lie – Rupert really did possess these attributes – but they were nevertheless conscious and cultivated. He could be unsparing but not, as the pictures suggested, dour and grim. 'I find it almost impossible to manufacture a smile when I'm being photographed,' he explained many years later, 'so grumpy I'm likely to remain.'[29]

His first posting as an officer was to the camp at Pirbright, nicknamed Colony Bog after the adjoining tract of land and as ignoble an assembly of mean wooden huts as could well be contrived. In Rupert's eyes it was redeemed from squalor by the presence of the Coldstream Guards. On the notice board in the officers' mess only one piece of information was purveyed: 'In future on receiving the order Remove Head-dress all

ranks will cry Hip Hip Hurrah and not, repeat *not* Hip Hip Hurray.' On
the first day, the new arrivals were given a briefing on the behaviour
appropriate to their new position: the Commanding Officer must never
be referred to as the Colonel; when wearing a Brigade tie the dark blue
stripe should be at the top of the knot; pink should never be worn out
hunting when the Court was in mourning. The splendid irrelevance of
such information at a time when Britain was close to losing its battle for
survival seemed to Rupert comical yet curiously reassuring; a regiment,
indeed a nation that held firm even to its most trivial standards at such a
moment must surely in the end emerge victorious.

To the surprise of some of his friends, though not to himself, Rupert
proved to be a good officer. He was invariably well turned out,
punctual, efficient, hard-working and calm in crisis. Whether his body
would have stood up to the rigours of active warfare must be unlikely
but there is no reason to doubt that under fire he would have been
courageous and resourceful. In the non-combatant roles to which he was
assigned he quickly proved himself of value. After only seven months he
was promoted to full lieutenant and by the end of 1941 he had become a
captain: 'After promotion which is apparently something of a record in
the Brigade of Guards,' he boasted to Edmund Blunden, 'I am now
Adjutant of a new Battalion – and enjoying it.'[30] Unlike some others of
his former publishing colleagues, Daniel George – one of Jonathan
Cape's authors who played an increasingly important part on the
editorial side of the firm as the regular staff went to the war – was
unsurprised by his prowess. Rupert would be a great success in his new
job, George predicted; 'that it will, at the beginning, leave you little
leisure, I am equally sure. Application to business however, when the
occasion really requires it, is one of your many virtues.'[31]

Application was certainly called for: with no experience of administration on such a scale he found himself required to organise the
movement of eight hundred men with their equipment from a variety of
stations around Britain to form the new Sixth Battalion at Harrow.
Many of the school buildings were taken over; as an Etonian Rupert
must have derived some pleasure from the fact that he was occupying
enemy territory but since his Commanding Officer was himself a
Harrovian a degree of fraternisation with the indigenous inhabitants was
encouraged. Once the complications of the move were over Rupert
found the work well within his capabilities; he performed his duties with
admirable conscientiousness but without great pleasure. 'I am not much
in love with *la vie militaire*,' he told Blunden gloomily.[32] The battalion

was treated as a quarry, from which companies would every so often be extracted for posting to other units; the process was no doubt beneficial to the Coldstream Guards as a whole but dispiriting for the adjutant of the Sixth Battalion, who never felt that he was welding together a coherent unit that, when the time came, would acquit itself well in battle.

After nine months, for reasons which were no doubt apparent to the War Office but were never explained to the officers and men, the battalion was moved across London to a huge and grim former orphanage in Wanstead. 'My heart goes out to you,' commiserated Jonathan Cape. 'When I think of you quartered on Wanstead Flats I could burst into tears. Yet I can think of one place in London which is even more forbidding in its name and locality, Wormwood Scrubs!'[33] Certainly Rupert found Wanstead less congenial than Harrow and much more remote from Bromsden Farm, where he tried to spend the occasional weekend. The work was very much the same. 'How do you like being an adjutant?' Julian Maclaren-Ross asked him. 'Do you make your Orderly Room staff work all night? Ours does.'[34] Rupert's answers would have been 'Not much' and 'No'. Maclaren-Ross was a talented young writer whose short stories Rupert had admired and whom he had encouraged; he was also an extreme example of that too common species – the author who thinks the world owes him a living and is convinced that he is enmeshed in a giant conspiracy to do him down. The next thing Rupert heard of him was when he was under arrest and facing a court martial for desertion. What infuriated him, Maclaren-Ross told Rupert, was 'that I honestly did it because I hoped to be more use to the war effort in one of the ministries . . . It makes you feel that is the way writers are treated in this country, and to want to become a permanent deserter.'[35] Rupert gallantly trailed across London to visit the prisoner, lent him money and offered to defend him if it came to a court martial. He had some doubt whether Maclaren-Ross would be of much use to the war effort in any capacity but was quite certain that he was useless in the Army and would only involve endless trouble and expense if he were not allowed to go. He managed to persuade the major in the Medical Corps who was responsible for the case that the accused was unfit to serve and should be discharged. The Army insisted on its pound of flesh and first made Maclaren-Ross serve twenty-eight days' detention at the military prison in Colchester, then, to the relief of all concerned, sent him on his way.

Early in 1943 the Sixth Battalion was disbanded. Rupert was out of a

job: none of the other battalions was in need of an adjutant and none of
the combatant units was anxious to employ a thirty-four-year-old
lieutenant or captain whose health was suspect. He was assigned to the
Headquarters of London District, based in Mayfair, and moved back
into the house in Stormont Road, leading a life which, except for the
nature of the work, was close to what he had known before the war. The
office was conveniently close to Heywood Hill, the Curzon Street
booksellers, where Nancy Mitford was then working; Rupert looked in
there most days to pick up the latest literary gossip and see what new
books were on offer. 'Book-selling gets more gruesome every day,'
Nancy wrote to him. 'One now has to order 500 to get 3, but if the book
is going to be a flop one gets 500. So you see . . .'[36] The bookseller's
nightmare was the publisher's fondest dream. It was a period at which
almost any new book could be sold twice over. Like all its rivals, Cape's
was flourishing, and though Rupert felt no particular urge to rejoin it he
was beginning to hanker for civilian life. 'Dullish but not over-exacting,'
he found his work, while his daily routine constituted 'a reasonable
existence'. It could have been much worse, he reflected. Perhaps it
would have been if, as at one time seemed possible, he had gone to Staff
College. This would have involved a great deal of stressful work in
order to qualify as a major – a promotion which, anyway, he was by no
means sure he aspired to.[37] He was on the whole relieved when the
threat of Staff College was lifted, but he must have been regretful too,
for it would have been a remarkable tribute to his achievements if he
had been selected. Any disappointment there might have been vanished,
however, in October 1943, when he was told that he was going back to
Pirbright as Adjutant of the Training Battalion. 'I'm delighted,' he told
Deirdre, 'since I much prefer regimental soldiering with one's own
friends and troops to this dreary, impersonal staff work.'[38]

It was at Pirbright that he saw out the rest of his military service.
'Here there is discipline and drill and leaning towers of paper,' he told
Blunden.[39] For the first eighteen months or so it was exhaustingly hard
work; his Commanding Officer took a relaxed attitude to the problems
of administration and left it to Rupert to run the show more or less
single-handed. His companions were congenial, conditions were comfortable, food was good, he could get home to Bromsden almost every
weekend. If he had to be in the Army, this was as good a spot as any.
But increasingly he did not want to be at war. Daniel George struck a
sensitive spot when in July 1944 he wrote to say: 'God, you must be fed
up with soldiering, I hope the experience will not permanently warp –

or should it be "woof" – your spiritual outlook. Still, I have no doubt you will manage to save your darling soul from the power of the dog, and when peace comes, with your commercial instincts unimpaired, bring renewed force to selective publishing.'[40]

So long as the war was still raging and there was a constant need for fresh trained recruits, Rupert at least had a job that was active and obviously useful. By the spring of 1945, however, there was a sense that everything was running down. There was still enough to do but the pressure had slackened, he knew the job so well that he could do it with a minimum of effort and his staff were so well trained that they could largely carry the burden by themselves. He found time to read enormously; often he would shun the mess and take his dinner in bed. At one point he was reading eight books at once. His fellow officers must have thought him decidedly odd, but eccentricity has always been tolerated in the Guards and if he did his job well it was up to him how he chose to spend his spare time. 'Hitler is dead, the Germans say, and they ought to know,' was his diary entry for 2 May 1945. Now the countdown to peace began.

Even before the surrender of Japan Rupert's duties were concerned principally with repatriation and demobilisation. For a man longing to escape the Army and return to civilian life it must have been particularly galling to spend his working day arranging for other people to get ahead and do what he would so much have liked to be doing himself. As a veteran of thirty-eight, however, he was well up the list for demobilisation and did not have too long to wait. His diary recorded every step on the road to liberation. In June he delivered his standard lecture to the newly arrived officers – 'pray God for the last time'. On 26 September he went to London to try on his new civilian suits and buy some underwear. Two days later he spent his last full day in the Orderly Room. Finally on 29 October he was formally released and drove away from Pirbright to rebuild his life. He had lost five of what might well have been his most productive and fulfilling years, but so had almost all his generation and at least he had survived more or less unimpaired. He knew he had been lucky and did not feel that his time had been ill spent.

'It is difficult to thank you enough for all you have done, both personally and as Adjutant of the Training Battalion,' wrote a grateful Commanding Officer. 'No one could have coped with such a monumental job more efficiently than you have done, or more agreeably . . . I think your name will go down in the annals of the Regiment as an

Adjutant of quite unique ability.'[41] Rupert had every right to feel proud at receiving such praise, but probably he took still greater pleasure from a letter that he received nearly a quarter of a century later from a former clerk in his Orderly Room. 'We all liked you immensely for your wit and humour,' wrote his correspondent, 'and only in your presence did the gulf between officer and soldier seem unimportant.'[42]

Rupert's legal father, Richard Hart-Davis, playing the piano while cruising up the Nile.

Rupert's mother, Sibbie, with Gervase Beckett, the man Rupert believed was his real father.

Rupert and Comfort, photographed in Paris on their honeymoon in 1934.

Chapter Nine

Part-time Publisher

Most people who went to war between 1939 and 1945 served far from home, usually abroad, cut off from their families and peacetime pursuits. Rupert was never stationed more than twenty-five miles from Central London. For long periods of the war he was able to spend at least part of each weekend at home. He was in regular contact with the people with whom he had worked before he joined the Army. Far more than most people he was able to keep his personal and professional activities alive and ticking over. This did not prove to be an unmixed blessing.

Over his last year or two as a publisher Rupert had been becoming more and more dissatisfied with the way Cape's were run, particularly with what he felt to be the increasing incompetence and obstinacy of the Chairman himself. 'Jonathan is getting old, muddled and ever more repetitive,' he wrote in his diary in February 1940; by July he seemed 'slightly more ga-ga every day'; in October, when Cape announced that he thought he would be ready to retire in four years – by which time he would have been sixty-six – Rupert commented angrily: 'This will be at least four years too late! Who cares, anyhow?'[1] *He* cared for one; the success of Cape's and his relationship with the firm were always at the back of his mind, even when the demands of military life were overwhelming. It was no doubt in part at least the fear that he could never settle back satisfactorily into publishing so long as Jonathan Cape and Wren Howard were on the scene that caused him to dream of establishing himself with Comfort on a farm and seeking a living from the soil rather than other people's pens.

Even if he had not continued to take a close personal interest in his authors and their books he would have felt bound to help out whenever he could. Cape's were paying him a by-no-means ungenerous £450 a year – half his salary – as a retainer and when prosperity returned to

publishing in 1942 and 1943 he received occasional bonuses of £50 or
so. His seat was being kept warm by the historian Veronica Wedgwood
(who as literary editor of *Time and Tide* was responsible for employing
him as a reviewer of crime fiction). The future Dame Veronica had a
high opinion of Rupert's acumen and understanding of his authors and
was determined both to keep him fully briefed about what was going on
and to consult him whenever circumstances allowed. Stevie Smith, for
instance, put in a novel which Veronica Wedgwood thought repetitive
and diffuse. The author admitted that much of the offending material
had been in an earlier draft which Rupert had said should be heavily
cut. 'Is this the moment to say "Goodbye, sweet lady" to Stevie?'
Wedgwood asked anxiously. 'We get on so well, so far too well, that it
can probably be done without bitterness or tears.' Please telephone me
on Monday, the letter concluded.[2]

Her letters encouraged Rupert's suspicions that the firm was going to
rack and ruin in his absence. In a report on a typescript to Jonathan
Cape, she said, she had described an author's taste in literature as being
'somewhat undiscriminating'. Cape evidently considered that this was
high praise and used the phrase in his letter to the author – thus causing
some offence. In future reports, she concluded, she would have to stick
to 'words of one syllable and no cleverness'.[3] She was convinced that
Rupert was the only person who could keep Cape and Howard on the
paths of rectitude: 'The boys need the hell of a lot of controlling and I
wish you were back,' she wrote feelingly, after a particularly inept first
novel by a young woman had been accepted in spite of strong protests
from Daniel George and herself. 'And it isn't even by a blonde. It's just
Jonathan proving he has flair!'[4] The affairs of Arthur Koestler, whose
Darkness at Noon had caused a sensation in 1940, caused Wedgwood
particular concern. She had reported on his new book in terms which
she hoped would guide the way that Cape spoke to him, but she had her
doubts. 'I feel that if you could descend on Jonathan and be forceful . . .
it would have some effect . . . If you could come in and say something
emphatic about policy and the "long view" on the lines of what you said
to me, it would probably have a very good effect. Jonathan has very
definite views of what people do and don't know about, and he's never
going to listen to me on publishing policy.'[5] That crisis was
surmounted, but Koestler was a querulous author, quick to complain
about royalties, print quantities and advertising, while his written
English was not so polished as he imagined it to be. Wedgwood
reckoned that she could tidy it up without the author noticing, but then

Cape laid his hand on a typescript, 'scrawled totally inept alterations all over [it] and gave me a nasty secret morning's work with an india-rubber removing the traces'.[6]

Maclaren-Ross, whom Rupert had rescued from military prison two years before, was another author who caused Veronica Wedgwood to appeal to Rupert. She had talked Cape and Howard into accepting a synopsis of a new novel, only to find that a week later the author came in with an entirely different idea; conceived yet another one in the course of their conversation and skipped blithely down the office steps, twirling his silver-headed cane and announcing that he would have a first draft within six weeks. 'You know him better than I do,' Wedgwood told Rupert, 'and will know whether to interject some advice of your own or just to let him simmer. I gather you killed a book of his about vacuum cleaners, and it's clear you *can* kill his ideas if you want to. So, over to you, partner.'[7] For Maclaren-Ross Cape's now replaced the Army as arch-persecutor. They had procrastinated, refused him an advance, rejected his synopsis of a novel: 'I know that had you not been away from the firm on Army duty, these things would never have happened,' he told Rupert. 'Now I feel it is time to take some action to better my position. I'm terribly sorry, but you can't blame me.'[8] Rupert could and did blame him; the thought that he was spared the attentions of authors like Maclaren-Ross must have made the Orderly Room at Pirbright seem something of a sanctuary.

Usually Rupert's dealings with the firm were through Daniel George or Veronica Wedgwood but from time to time he found himself in direct contact with Cape himself. On H. E. Bates they thought as one. Bates had a high opinion of his own merits and made extravagant demands when he submitted his new novel at the end of 1942. Cape sent Rupert a copy of his letter and asked his opinion. 'The conceit of his letter, open and implied, is as colossal as it is nauseating,' stormed Rupert – '"what is now a considerable reputation", "hostile elements against me" (how can one be "hostile" to an insect?) God, if I had him in the Battalion!! . . . If you think I could help matters, by writing to him in moderate strain, which I think I could just bring myself to do – well then of course I will.'[9] If he did so it availed nothing. Bates moved elsewhere and proceeded to make a great deal of money for himself and other publishers. As with Maclaren-Ross, however, Rupert escaped the reproaches of the injured author. What prize idiots Cape and Howard had been, Bates told Rupert, for not making the minor concessions that would have retained his loyalty. 'However, I'm glad to think you had no part in it.'[10]

More often Rupert's relations with his Chairman verged on the acrimonious. Duff Cooper caused a minor spat. In 1942 he completed a biography of King David, a work based almost entirely on the Old Testament but lively and easy to read. Rupert liked the first part and encouraged Cooper to push on to the end. 'I hope your colleagues will share your view and come down handsome,' Cooper told his nephew.[11] They did not. Jonathan Cape told Rupert he thought the book 'pretty boring and conventional in presentation'. Biblical figures 'were not as a rule attractive to modern readers'. There was no comparison with Duff Cooper's *Talleyrand*. 'Let us not be bemused by the public figures who turn to authorship in their spare time and have £1,000 as a minimum advance.'[12] Somewhat unwisely, Rupert seems to have suppressed this letter and told his uncle that Cape's were enthusiastic about the book. He was glad to hear it, Cooper replied. His last book had been merely a rehash of already published articles, for *David* he would expect 'very much more favourable treatment'. £3,000 as an advance would seem appropriate.[13] Caught between a Chairman who was reluctant to pay £1,000 and an author/uncle who wanted three times as much, Rupert found himself in a delicate position. He told Cape that he thought he was quite wrong in his opinion of Cooper's new book and that a comparison with *Talleyrand* was not merely reasonable but must inevitably be made, while to his uncle he pleaded the paper shortage as a reason why printings must be kept small and a larger advance could not be justified. In the end both men grumblingly settled for £1,000 but Rupert was left with the feeling that he had used up valuable goodwill with Cape and would have greater problems in the future.

Another 'public figure who turned to authorship in his spare time' led to the relationship being still further strained. Field-Marshal Lord Wavell had compiled an anthology of his favourite poems which he called *Other Men's Flowers*. Peter Fleming, who was on his staff in India, persuaded him to submit it to Cape's and enlisted Rupert to plead the cause in London. It seemed that little pleading would be called for; Veronica Wedgwood was at once enthused and Wren Howard equally so. Then the typescript came to Jonathan Cape and he elected to write a letter to Wavell calculated to cause offence to any author, not least one who could reasonably feel that his position entitled him to a certain amount of respect. Peter Fleming sent a copy of the letter to Rupert with some blistering comments on its writer and Rupert telephoned

Wedgwood for an explanation. She was horrified, she replied; she had thought Wren Howard would nurse the typescript through, the problem was that since Jonathan Cape's regular secretary had left 'there isn't anyone who can keep an eye on what he writes. She used to seek advice if she was in doubt as to the wisdom of anything, but now, short of deliberate spying, I don't quite know what one is to do.'[14]

The damage was done, but it might not be beyond repair. Rupert wrote to Jonathan Cape a letter which he himself described as 'frank and brutal'. The Field-Marshal was considerably piqued, he said:

Wavell, like so many men of action, is extremely diffident about his literary leanings, and clearly needs even more 'jollying along' than most authors. He was dying to be told that his book was excellent and that his publishers thought so. Now the only place where you express any such sentiment is in para 3 of your letter, which is very cold and distant, and probably made Wavell think that you hadn't looked at the stuff at all. Further, to a man who is probably a bit shy about knowing and liking poetry at all, to describe his poetic treasures as 'familiar school recitations advancing in close formation' is tantamount to a sock on the jaw. Frankly, I'm quite surprised he didn't try to cancel the engagement straightaway. You see, he looks on the book as a life-long treasure which doesn't require much work on it. We know there's a lot to be done, but really that's quite a minor point. The important thing, surely, is that we have the complete bones of a tremendously saleable book. Your letter and memorandum rather give the impression that, if the book is any good at all, it will be the work of Daniel George (you mention him seven times). This of course is balls . . .

Lastly, since this letter is already thoroughly beastly, I must admit that I feel that I myself have been a bit carted. Your memorandum mentions me twice and suggests that I was associated with it and had seen the material – neither of which was the case. I wouldn't even have agreed to the former going as it stood, and though I did ask you to let me see the stuff, you didn't, and I wouldn't have seen it to this day if I hadn't by chance managed to get a glimpse of a second copy in the War Office Cabinet Office . . .

I'm afraid this letter is bound to annoy you. Don't think I'm trying to teach my grandmother how to suck eggs. I'm just trying to explain that Wavell and Peter are annoyed and why I think it is.[15]

Next day he followed up this letter by telephoning Cape and telling him that, as an Army officer who was still a director of the firm, he felt that he should now take charge of this project. Wavell was about to come to London: Rupert called on him several times at the War Office or his club. On one occasion, according to Chips Channon, he lunched with Wavell at the Senior – the pre-eminent club for military grandees – and Montgomery, from an adjoining table, joined them briefly.[16] It was unusual company for a mere captain and must have caused quite a stir at Pirbright if the news got back there. Rupert, however, had no recollection of such a meeting.[17] He got on very well with Wavell anyway, and the Field-Marshal's resentment was soon appeased.

The trouble was that, although he might deny it, Rupert *was* telling his grandmother how to suck eggs. Worse still, he was proved right when *Other Men's Flowers* got ecstatic reviews, became a Book Society Choice, and sold more than 60,000 copies over the next decades. Rupert's rebukes, Veronica Wedgwood told him, certainly shook Cape 'with whatever bluster of injured innocence he may have met them'.[18] But they rankled. Cape respected Rupert but already felt that he was too big for his boots, insufficiently deferential to a man who had been in publishing when Rupert was still only a boy and had, from nothing, carved out an empire for himself. He said little, even conceded that in the Wavell affair Rupert had played a valuable part, but he was left with a sense of irritated humiliation that was not going to make their relationship any easier in the future.

It was not only his publishing life that Rupert managed to keep alive during his Army years; more than the majority of his fellow soldiers he was able to maintain close links with his family and sustain the paraphernalia of a personal existence. Since July 1940 Comfort and the children had been in the United States, living with her Aunt Joyce, who had a house near the coast of Maine. Rupert and Comfort took pleasure in their correspondence. An impressive number of their letters to each other survives. They are not always easy reading. Most married couples evolve some sort of private language: expressions which are shorthand for an often-repeated sentiment, catchwords which evoke a common memory, affectionate diminutives the origin of which has often been forgotten. Rupert and Comfort carried the practice to extremes. When the 'tinkler' wakes him, Rupert tells Comfort, he will imagine her 'still deep down with your dwarf mug pressed sideways into the poo-o'. 'I am so glad we have got our tow language,' Comfort responded. 'It makes everything seem less dreadful to be able to write "my peepers were so pint clying" and so on. Our own private way of cheering oursowts up.' Since the letters were written peculiarly for themselves it is hardly proper for the prying biographer to complain, but there are still moments when one wishes that it had not been swote of the literary editor of the Spectagger to send Rupert a dwarf novel of Simenon's for Mit to review, rather than sweet of him to send Rupert a short novel of Simenon's for the same purpose.

But the letters convey deep affection. 'I have been so happy with you and fundamentally happy with our life,' Comfort wrote from the boat carrying her across the Atlantic. 'We do seem to be so *comfortable* together . . . I think the best proof of how happy I've been is how young I feel as long as I'm with you – although sometimes you arouse all my *old* maternal instinct.' She was constantly fretting about the possibility that Rupert would perish in battle. 'Don't feel any desperation, beloved,' Rupert replied. 'It's true I may be killed any day [hardly an imminent possibility since he was at the time in the middle of his training at Sandhurst] but somehow I don't think my number's up just yet . . . And if you do get the worst news don't let it get you down too much. It's bound to be a terrific shock at first . . . Later it'll all get easier. Don't worry when you begin to forget about me. It's bound to happen . . . You have made me happier than I ever dreamed of being. There is not one single thing that you could have done that you did not do, and oh, so much more besides. Whatever happens, you have made one person utterly and unbelievably happy for more than seven years. So don't forget it.'[19]

Comfort had barely arrived in America before she was making plans to come back after six months; otherwise, she said, she might begin to resent the children for keeping them apart. Rupert at first urged her to stay where she was. Bridget, perhaps, could manage by herself but 'what of our Haddock [Duff]? You can't leave him if he's going to have that ghastly, abandoned, desolate feeling, which is the worst thing in the world, especially for dwarvers . . . I can't believe the war will last into 1942, but I expect there'll be a bloody mess before it's over. Invasion and all. Oh, darling, it's so much safer and more sensible for you to stay in US with our dwarvers.'[20] Then Rupert began to think that after all the children could manage well enough with their aunt and it was Comfort who had second thoughts. Her decision not to come back caused Rupert bitter disappointment – 'I'm aching for, longing for, dreaming of our meeting' – but since he had argued that she should not return he could hardly protest when she took his advice. Then, in July 1942, she changed her mind again. The first that Rupert heard of it was when he got a message from the Orderly Room to say that his wife had landed near Bristol and would be arriving in Reading at noon.

One factor in her hurried decision may have been the news that a friend of Celia Johnson's, an attractive mother of a fourteen-month-old child with a husband who was a prisoner of war, had come to live at Bromsden and was entertaining Rupert at weekends. Rupert wrote enthusiastically to report that Mrs Gamble was now in full occupation 'and very well she's doing it. Nothing to touch my dwarver, of course, but pretty good considering. She looks after me marvellously at weekends – good grub, breakfast in bed, and goodness knows what.'[21] Comfort knew only too well that Rupert needed a woman in his life to cosset, admire and support him, to love and be loved by. The risk was obvious and unacceptable. Diana Gamble later said that Rupert never made any improper overtures but that she suspected that he might have done so if Comfort's return had been much longer delayed. She was sure that Comfort was equally alive to the danger and had no intention of leaving a potential rival in possession of the field. Diana returned to the house one day to find a small, determined woman furiously scrubbing a kitchen floor which, in her view, was quite sufficiently clean already. Comfort never said a word to suggest that she thought the house had been ill looked after during her absence and the two women in fact got on reasonably well, but it was never a totally comfortable arrangement. When Diana Gamble's husband returned from his prison camp and reclaimed his wife the ménage broke up to everybody's relief.[22] Comfort and Diana, however, remained close friends.

Comfort's last letter from America, which arrived at Bromsden several weeks after she did, had been written in a mood of foreboding. It seemed to her possible, almost likely that the Sunderland flying boat on which she had managed to insert herself would end up in the sea. 'If I don't get to you,' she told Rupert, 'you must know absolutely that I did not try to come just for your sake – it is for mine too. I can no longer abide with you so far away.' If she was killed then Rupert would have to look after the children – 'unless you are killed too,' she added as an afterthought. 'I particularly enjoyed "unless you are killed too",' Rupert commented wryly. The reunion was as rapturous as either could have hoped. 'After our year of enforced celibacy we made love passionately and often whenever I could get home,' Rupert remembered, and during the first month or two he managed to escape from Pirbright and make his way to the farm two or even three times a week.[23]

While still in America Comfort had told Rupert what pleasure she had got out of looking after a baby nephew. 'I dare say you wouldn't object to cherishing another dwarf babe of your own one day?' Rupert responded.[24] Comfort at first hesitated; in principle she loved the idea of another child, 'and yet when I think of the endless weariness and work and restlessness it seems not worth it'.[25] Keeping Bromsden going so as to have a base to which Rupert could retreat at weekends while at the same time helping out on the Flemings' farm was a gruelling routine which left her little energy for other pursuits. In October 1942 Rupert took her away for a week's holiday at a pub in Market Harborough. 'I'm urging it to have another dwarver,' he told Deirdre. 'It's longing for some more really.'[26] He must have done more than urge; within a few months it was clear that Comfort was pregnant. She insisted that it was going to be a girl, in which case it would have been called Kate. Rupert maintained they were about to have twin boys and was more nearly right than his wife: Adam, their second son and third child, was born on 4 July 1943.

By now all threat of invasion was past and air raids were relatively rare. Rupert and Comfort decided that it was safe to bring the elder children home. An unexpected problem now arose. Comfort's Aunt Joyce had grown attached to Bridget and Duff and convinced herself that it would be in their best interests to keep them in America until the war was over. She pleaded with her niece to let them stay, arguing that, even if Britain was now safe for children to live in, the Atlantic crossing would be desperately dangerous. The Hart-Davises stuck to their guns, whereupon Aunt Joyce suborned her local doctor into producing a medical certificate saying that the children were unfit to travel. Rupert decided that the only course was for him to go to the United States on a rescue mission. The War Office received his request with commendable calm; an indication, perhaps, of the triviality of the work he was doing at the Headquarters of London District. A few months later, when he was back at Pirbright, he might have found leave harder to obtain. As it was, a little vigorous lobbying was enough to secure him a berth on a ship carrying German prisoners of war to internment in Canada. He spent the journey reading *Lorna Doone* and *The Cloister and the Hearth*, on the grounds that these were among the most popular of British novels and that it was his duty to study the public taste. It cannot be said that his subsequent career as a publisher suggests he took whatever lessons he learnt seriously to heart.

Resistance crumbled as soon as he arrived in America. Aunt Joyce resigned herself to the inevitable and welcomed Rupert, if not effusively, then at least with good grace. He took a quick look at his sleeping children – 'blond, fat and lovely' he found them – then collapsed into bed after what had been an exhausting thirteen-hour journey in a crowded train from New York. Next morning Bridget and Duff were released into his room with the promise that they would find something nice inside. 'A magical day,' Rupert wrote in his diary. 'The children are *enchanting* and I have been bewilderingly happy. They came into my bedroom, expecting a "surprise", didn't know me for a minute, then leaped all over me. I realised in a wave how deeply I've missed and longed for them these three years. Bridget scarcely left me all day. They are very American, but so civilised, considerate and grown up. How Comfy will love them.'

Veronica Wedgwood wrote to congratulate him on his successfully accomplished mission: '"*Lieber Kamerad, quelle affaire*", as Blucher said to Wellington. Anyhow, I do hope it was the wicked Aunt's Waterloo and that the children are safe.'[27] In fact the children were still in Portugal at the time, with the last and potentially most dangerous leg of their journey before them. Rupert, who travelled back with fifteen thousand American troops on the *Queen Elizabeth*, was home in time to welcome them when they finally arrived in London. He took them at once to Bromsden, where they met their new brother and the family was at last reunited.

Deirdre with her children, Susie and Annabel, also back from America, joined them there a few months later. It was in the middle of a cold spell and Deirdre, who found the house almost unbearably damp and chilly, was dismayed to find Comfort nevertheless flinging open windows so as to air the rooms. The fire's were never lit except when Rupert was coming back for a weekend and even then did little to raise the temperature of the rest of the house. Comfort was a loving and conscientious mother and though the children can hardly have found life luxurious they had no cause to complain of being neglected. But most visitors found that there was a cheerless atmosphere about the house. In some way, the sense of fun had gone out of Comfort's life. She seemed indifferent to her looks and had no topics of conversation beyond the children and the rigours of wartime housekeeping. But she was devoted to Rupert's well-being and would happily sacrifice herself – or indeed anyone else who happened to be in the house – so as to ensure his comfort. Early in 1942 he had been laid low by a vicious bout of influenza. Comfort telephoned the Medical Officer and instructed him to keep a careful eye – or 'a v wow peeled peeper' as she retailed it to

Rupert – on her husband's health. She told the doctor that Rupert had only two winters before been dangerously ill with pneumonia, 'which, he said, you'd omitted to mention'.[28]

While she was in the United States with the children, Deirdre's husband, Ronnie Balfour, had been killed in a car crash. It had not been a particularly happy marriage and Rupert felt that in the long run his brother-in-law's death might even prove to be a blessing for his sister, but he realised that for this very reason she was bound to feel 'full of grief and remorse and regrets'.[29] He wrote to Deirdre with the best consolation he could muster: 'As you know, I don't believe in God or the life everlasting, but I do believe in eternal sleep, which doesn't seem so unwelcome to people who have been in London since the blitz began.'[30] It seems unlikely that his sister was conspicuously cheered by this message, but it was well meant.

The death of Hugh Walpole in June 1941 affected him more immediately. In literary reputation at least Walpole seemed to have outlived his time. Rose Macaulay commented on the grudging condescension of those appointed to pass judgment on his work. 'What extraordinary obits poor Hugh got!' she wrote. 'A new terror is added to death.'[31] She would have been still more astonished if she had known that Walpole's royalties would remain substantial until the late 1980s and that the conviction of various producers that a successful film or television series could be made out of the *Herries Chronicles* would ensure a substantial if erratic income for his heirs for even longer. When Rupert was told that he, together with his old colleague from Book Society days, Alan Bott, had been appointed Walpole's literary executor and trustee, he foresaw no such reward – merely a great deal of hard work at a time when he was already fully occupied (though he had been left a very useful £100 and a small portrait of a girl by Marie Laurencin which he sold for nearly £3,000 in 1968). Rupert was given leave to attend the funeral at Keswick and thereafter had to spend most of his spare time disposing of Walpole's twenty thousand books and eight hundred pictures and negotiating with the publishers over reprints of existing titles and the two unpublished novels that had been left behind. Most of the sales were deferred until the end of the war in the hope that the market would by then have recovered: no doubt to some extent it had, but Rupert was still able to buy at the auction five Hardy first editions at a pound apiece. The proceeds went to Walpole's brother and sister; Rupert's recompense was not to come for some time yet.

Rupert continued to meet his father for lunch or dinner once every two or three months though he rarely derived any pleasure from the encounter. 'He was more distrait than ever and listened to nothing,' Rupert told Deirdre after one such occasion. 'Next day he wrote and said what tremendous fun it had been.'[32] In the spring of 1943, when his business affairs had become more than usually embroiled, Richard suggested that he should move into the house in Stormont Road and take over its running costs while his son was away. Rupert hurriedly replied that the house was already fully occupied by people whom he could not possibly evict. The threat of a paternal incursion may have been one of the factors that induced Rupert to put the house on the market towards the end of the war. At one moment it seemed likely that Arthur Ransome would buy it but his wife took exception to the size of the garden and Ransome retreated hurriedly: 'If I again had landed my Missis into a house she did not like, the manufacturing of books for Cape's would have come to a sad end.'[33] He feared that his change of heart might cause ill feeling but Rupert took the news with equanimity; anyway, within a few weeks the house had been sold to a doctor from Wimpole Street for a respectable if unsensational £6,250.

It was time to prepare for civilian life. Rupert had no doubt that he would return to publishing: he enjoyed the work, believed he was good at it and, anyway, could think of no obvious alternative. His first loyalties had to be to Cape's, who had been paying him throughout his time in the Army and of which he was still a director. At the back of his mind, however, there did exist another possibility. Early in 1941 he had received a letter from David Garnett, known to his friends as 'Bunny' and son of the great Edward. David Garnett had written a first, extraordinarily successful novel, *Lady Into Fox*, in 1922 and had subsequently become literary editor of the *New Statesman*, continuing to write its lead book review until the outbreak of war. Rupert had got to know him when he was editing the *Letters* of T. E. Lawrence for Cape's, and though the two had not become close friends they liked and respected each other. Rupert was somebody with whom Garnett felt he could work, and enjoy working.

> I suppose if they don't kill you, or cripple you [he wrote in February 1941], you will remain in the Army till after the war. Have you thought of what you will do then? [It had occurred to him that Rupert might consider setting up as an independent publisher] and that I might conceivably join you if you have any capital at that time. I may have. After the war there will be a burst of intellectual curiosity of all kinds.

Thousands of soldiers will feel they missed a lot and will turn eagerly to reading books and some to writing them. We shall want to know about Europe too and shall hear what the French want to say – and, dare I say it, the Dutch, Danes, Poles, Belgians and all the different brands of German. I am afraid such words sound almost too much as though E[dward] G[arnett] was speaking from the grave. But if my suggestion makes you smile, so much the better.

I realise that, though you can say NO in emphatic terms, you can't possibly say yes. So tuck the idea away. Of course I don't really know that I want to be a publisher. What I do know is that I don't want to be a journalist.[34]

Rupert did not in the least feel inclined to say no, in emphatic or any other terms. In a letter to Comfort he described Garnett's letter as 'v swote' (amended to 'delightful' for the purposes of his memoirs) and added the comment 'Who knows?'[35] He met Garnett and talked the matter over: both felt that the possibilities were enticing, both agreed that nothing could be done till the end of the war. Rupert suggested a variant; that Garnett might join him in Cape's and that they should together take the business over when Jonathan Cape and Howard retired. 'Your suggestion that we should become the two blimps of Bedford Square appeals to me so much that I can hardly bear to forgo it,' Garnett replied. 'One side of you is cut out for it and the moustache need only begin to droop and the figure fatten.'[36] Rupert said nothing to the current blimps about his plans for their replacement, probably he never took the possibility very seriously, but this idea too was tucked away at the back of his mind for resurrection when at last he resumed life as a civilian and a publisher.

Chapter Ten

A Firm is Born

On 21 October 1945 Rupert addressed a letter to Jonathan Cape and Wren Howard. The tone was friendly but peremptory. If he was to stay on, he said, he would expect his 1940 salary of £900 to be doubled, he should be allowed to buy further shares in the company if and when the capital was available, and the directors' annual bonus should be split on the basis of 40 per cent to each of the two senior directors and 20 per cent to Rupert. To his former colleague, Guy Chapman, these terms seemed 'very just'.[1] Rupert probably expected that, even if they were not adopted in their entirety, they would provide the basis on which an acceptable compromise could be reached. He did not allow for the rancour which Jonathan Cape harboured towards him, viewing him as a relative tyro, who had had the impertinence to rebuke him roundly over his handling of Wavell's anthology and now presumed to lay down the law about his future conditions of employment. The firm did not need Rupert, Cape told him with some brutality, and he had not made a major contribution to its success. He still had a lot to learn and he would not be 'in a position to *earn* a vastly increased income from this Company for quite a while'. His proposals were 'neither reasonable nor equitable' and offered no basis for discussion. 'The gap is too impossibly wide.'[2] The relationship was over.

Rupert was disconcerted and indignant. His pride was hurt by the contention that he had made no important contribution to Cape's publishing: 'I could give you a list of books and authors that I brought you, but there seems little point.'[3] If that was what Cape thought of him, then the sooner they parted company the better. 'You must have something very promising in view,' Cape countered, taking it for granted that Rupert was being head-hunted by a rival publisher. Rupert replied, with something less than total frankness, that he had no other job in prospect. He was amazed, wrote Cape: 'It is a good maxim, I think, not to throw away dirty water before you have clean.' Michael Howard, Wren Howard's son and historian of the company, thinks that Cape was genuinely taken aback to hear that Rupert's future was not settled and that he intended this last letter as an olive branch opening the way to a resumption of negotiations.[4] If so, it came too late. Rupert had begun with doubts about the wisdom of renewing life where he had left it five years before, and Cape's rebuff convinced him that he must now strike out on his own. 'My chief feeling since has been an immense relief,' he told Duff Cooper. 'I have nothing whatever in common with those two chaps, and find them v tiresome withal. I think perhaps I've reached the stage (actually I'm 38) where one realises that one's only got one life, and that it's worth a lot to spend the working hours of it in congenial company! Also perhaps $5\frac{1}{2}$ years in the Brigade of Guards, while teaching one to bear fools gladly, rather puts one out of practice for tolerating business bores and shits.'[5] The bitterness was deep-felt, though in time it faded. When in 1959 the arch 'business bore and shit' celebrated his eightieth birthday, Rupert was among those who spoke at the dinner. 'There was, I felt, very genuine affection in what you said,' Cape told him. 'It was by far the best speech at the dinner.'[6] He deluded himself if he thought the affection was as genuine as all that, but Rupert never denied that he had learnt a great deal with Cape and felt some gratitude towards him for giving him so good a grounding in the world of publishing.

Duff Cooper had told Rupert that autumn was his favourite season; his nephew did not agree: 'Give me the cuckoo and the bursting buds of promise.'[7] Now it seemed that the buds were bursting and that spring with all its excitements and possibilities lay ahead of him. There was no shortage of kind friends to remind him that spring could also be a season of frosts and rain. There was something 'very restrictive about small publishing houses', J. B. Priestley told him. He would do far better to return to a powerful publisher like Heinemann and take over the editorial side.[8] Charles Morgan took it for granted that the difficulties of starting a new firm at the end of 1945 would be insuperable. He offered to put in a word with Harold Macmillan when next they met in the hope that there might be an opening there.[9] Rupert himself had no illusions about the difficulties that lay ahead. He had no earnings, no income except that derived from the fast dwindling capital obtained by the sale of the house in Stormont Road, no clear ideas for the future except for the cursorily discussed partnership with David

Garnett – he remained radiantly optimistic. 'My own firm may have to
wait a year or two until paper and other things are easier,' he told
Edmund Blunden; but that such a moment was fast approaching
seemed to him certain. If necessary, he would seek a temporary job to
tide himself over.[10] In the past Jamie Hamilton had often insisted how
eager he was that Rupert should join him in publishing. Now Rupert
amused himself by saying that he was ready to do so. Hamilton became
almost frantic in his protestations that there was nothing he would have
liked better if *only* he had not just taken on Roger Machell in the slot
that would otherwise so well have suited Rupert. 'It's no bad thing to
call his humbugging bluff occasionally,' Rupert commented dryly.[11] But
he had never expected his offer to be accepted and would not have been
best pleased if it had been. He had had enough of working for other
people; he might endure a short delay but, for better for worse, he was
resolved to go it alone.

David Garnett, he knew, was still ready to join in any such enterprise,
but, equally, Garnett had no wish to undertake the day-to-day running
of a London business. His idea was to remain in his country fastness in
Huntingdonshire, come up perhaps once a week, read and comment on
manuscripts and help form editorial policy, but eschew administration
and, so far as was possible, finance. He rightly felt that his temperament
was not suited to the grind of office work. Rupert once tried to persuade
him to give a lecture, saying how easily it would come to him. 'Nothing
comes easily to me,' Garnett replied. 'Not enough horse power. Not
even donkey power. I am really one of the original Galapagos tortoises
at heart.'[12] He belittled himself; he had formidable powers of
concentration and hard work when the subject appealed to him, but
nine-to-five in an office did not come into that category. Rupert would
have to look elsewhere if he wanted somebody to help him run a
publishing house.

He found him in Teddy Young, a dashing submariner who had won
a DSO as well as a DSC and bar and whose charm and glamour ensured
that all the girls in the office were half in love with him. Young had
worked with World Books before the war but his chief claim to
publishing fame was that he had drawn the original penguin which
became the trademark of Penguin Books. His naval colleagues delighted
in getting him drunk and persuading him to produce variants on this
theme; his masterpiece was said to be a pair of lesbian penguins.[13] He
was no more of a businessman than Rupert – his original, wildly

optimistic suggestion was that £10,000 would be more than enough capital on which to launch the firm and that £5,000 might be nearer the mark[14] – but he was a book designer of outstanding merit, could turn his hand to any facet of publishing other than finance, and was well equipped to keep the office running while Rupert found and worked on the books. The trouble was that he could contribute no more than a few hundred pounds to setting up the business. Rupert chipped in £3,000, raised from the shares he had been allotted in Cape's; David Garnett and his family put up £10,000; the rest came from friends and friendly authors. Eric Linklater was one of these; he denounced Jonathan Cape's 'dogged greed', contributed £1,000 to the kitty and promised that he would let the new firm have a collection of short stories which was now nearing completion.[15] Arthur Ransome put in £500, H. E. Bates £500, Geoffrey Keynes £2,000, Peter and Celia Fleming £2,000: by March 1946 the total was nearing £30,000. 'We've really got as much capital as we need – or at any rate can use in present circumstances,' Rupert told Duff Cooper. He would be delighted if Cooper felt like putting in a little but was not touting for investments: 'I've been besieged by rich men offering unsolicited assistance, but have kept clear of them, wishing to keep control in my own hands.'[16]

He was deluding himself. From the very beginning Rupert Hart-Davis Ltd was seriously underfunded: he never had the resources that would have allowed him to pay the sort of advances demanded by most established authors, to risk printing large quantities and holding substantial stocks, to spend freely on advertising and promotion. Authors and shareholders were extraordinarily generous: Peter Fleming recorded in his diary a dinner at Bromsden spent trying to persuade Rupert not to pay a dividend;[17] Arthur Ransome devoted many hours of work to the development of the Mariners Library and refused to accept any payment, a piece of benevolence which Rupert cancelled out by presenting him with a set of the complete *Oxford English Dictionary*. 'What chance has the firm got of ultimate success,' asked Ransome, 'if it begins by hurling the Great OED quite unnecessarily at people who never expected anything of the kind?'[18] Every little helped, but no amount of casual benevolence could substitute for a solid base of capital.

If the company was not to miss out on a critically important quota of the paper allotted quarterly to each publisher, it was essential that it should be registered within the next two months. This meant that quick decisions had to be made about a name and premises. The first was easy, in Rupert's eyes at least. 'Do you object to the firm being called by my

name?' he asked Young. 'I always prefer one-name firms, ie Jonathan
Cape is a much better name than George Allen and Unwin – don't you
agree?'[19] Teddy Young might have retorted that, if one-name firms were
so desirable, Young might be better than Hart-Davis, but neither he nor
Garnett was particularly concerned about prestige and both recognised
that Rupert was the driving force who would shape the firm's list and its
image.

Premises were more of a problem. John Carter, of the New York firm
of Scribner's, offered to lend a room or two in their London office for
the first few months, but though Rupert was amused at the idea of
setting up shop only twenty-five yards from Cape's, he did not wish to
be associated with a firm which, though once noble, he felt now to be
'no great shakes'.[20] By March 1946 the situation was becoming
desperate. 'If you hear of a cellar we could use as an office, grab it and
let me know,' Rupert urged William Plomer.[21] It might have come to
that, but a friend of Rupert's bought a house in Connaught Street, near
Marble Arch, found it too large for her needs, and let the firm use the
ground floor and basement for a tiny rent. David Garnett shopped
busily for furniture at country auctions; his proudest acquisition was a
vast partners' desk which he claimed to be: 'Suitable for the Chairman
of the Great Western Railway – or rather two.'[22] His wife, Angelica,
painted a signboard of a fox to hang over the office window; the fox was
chosen as a tribute to David Garnett's best-known novel but also,
Rupert said, because this was how both bookseller and author
considered the publisher.[23]

For the first couple of years or so Rupert and Teddy Young, with
some secretarial help, ran the business almost by themselves. June
Clifford was called in one Saturday to help out in an emergency and
found the two men performing almost every function known to
publishing; their approach was perhaps a shade amateurish but she
loved the atmosphere of casual enthusiasm. Sales were at first handled
by another small publisher, the Falcon Press; their London traveller,
Guy Fisher, soon jumped ship, however, and joined Hart-Davis's. At
first Rupert tried to pack the books himself but he made such a hash of
it (deliberately, Teddy Young suspected) that a young man, Deirdre's
brother-in-law, was hired to help with the work. Once parcelled up, the
books were thrown up the stairs and fielded by Young – in his day a
more than competent goalkeeper – before being loaded into the ancient
van which was the firm's only means of transport.

The shortage of paper threatened to be a crippling handicap. Every firm was allowed a percentage of what they had used in 1938; if they had not existed before the war they got no paper. An exception was made for ex-servicemen, who were allotted six tonnes each, but though all three of the new partners had been in the services only one ration was granted them. Rupert lobbied for an increase through the Publishers' Association, to such good effect that the allocation for ex-servicemen was doubled by the Board of Trade and Rupert was elected to represent small publishers on the Association's Council. He could never refuse an invitation; it was the first of many such appointments in which he served to the benefit of the literary world if not necessarily of Hart-Davis Ltd. Twelve tonnes were still only enough to produce smallish runs of nine or ten titles a year, but it was a start, and when a former publisher let Rupert have his unwanted paper quota at cost price the firm could really be said to be in business.

But what sort of business was it going to be? Rupert was a man of strong likes and dislikes and the dislikes were more easily defined than the likes. It is relatively easy to compile a list of the sorts of book Rupert was unlikely to publish. For financial reasons if for no other he would have to eschew the expensive, ready-made best-seller; some at least of his books would, he hoped, sell well, but he would have to find them for himself and make them work. He recoiled from anything that seemed to him vulgar or obscene. He felt, for instance, that *Lolita*'s 'literary value was negligible and its pornographic level high . . . I think it should not appear.'[24] But where the literary value seemed to him considerable he was prepared to swallow some decidedly ungentlemanly terminology. Norman Mailer's *The Naked and the Dead* he described as 'a 721-page American best-seller almost entirely composed of words not usually found in print', but his conclusion was that it was 'excellent, I thought'.[25] It was not the sort of book that any American publisher or agent would have been likely to offer him, but if they had he would have accepted it. He distrusted innovation. As a young man he had admired *Ulysses*, but it seems unlikely that in middle age he would have wished to publish it, while *Finnegans Wake* was far beyond the pale. He abhorred Beckett. 'Why do you bother with this nonsense?' he asked a niece. 'I turned down *Molloy* as unreadable rubbish.'[*26] He stormed out of *Waiting for Godot* at the interval: 'The ugliest, dullest, most meaningless twaddle I've ever had to endure.'[27] He had certain wholly

---

[*] This is probably vainglory. There is no reason to believe that anybody was ever silly enough to offer him *Molloy*, but he would certainly have turned it down if they had.

irrational prejudices. 'I have always been allergic to Indians, wherever they were born,' he told a friend, 'and have got along happily without reading one word of Naipaul's.'[28] Most comprehensively of all, he shunned the great ruck of cheap romances, badly written thrillers, tie-in books, celebrity biographies, tracts on self-improvement or do-it-yourself, which then as now provide the ballast in the list of most commercial publishers.

À part de ça, madame la Marquise, Rupert was prepared to take on anything which seemed to him to be well written and of some significance. His interests were wide and his tastes eclectic. He enjoyed re-publishing the lesser-known works of classic writers in scholarly and well-produced editions but was as ready to contemplate monographs on subjects of relative obscurity or adventurous attempts to challenge accepted dogmas. He admired quality, in almost any guise. Cautious, traditional, conservative: all these epithets can fairly be applied to Rupert as a publisher, but it is his total integrity that is his most striking feature. He was anxious to make a financial success of publishing; he rejoiced if one of his books became a best-seller; but he would never take on a book just because it was likely to sell well unless he also thought that it was good. A friend, knowing that he saw quite a lot of Daphne du Maurier, asked him why he had never published any of her work. 'Darling girl,' Rupert replied, 'but can't stand her books.'[29] It is only fair to say that du Maurier would never have entrusted one of her enormously successful romances to a publisher so little qualified to sell it; it is also possible to disagree with his opinion of *Rebecca* or *Frenchman's Creek*; but his sincerity and his readiness to pass up riches on grounds of literary judgment are impressive and, in their way, wholly admirable. His caution, too, did not preclude his taking risks with young authors who were unlikely to be financially rewarding. He criticised Macmillan's for notoriously fighting shy of unproven talent. 'Personally,' he told Arthur Ransome, 'I'd rather back my fancy with some young writers occasionally than build up an institution to which successful authors in middle age are bribed away from their original backers by big advances and red carpets. So there!'[30] When John Bayley won the Newdigate Prize Rupert wrote to ask him whether he was planning a literary career. Bayley replied that he would very much like to offer Rupert anything he might write but that he had no idea what that might be and, anyway, 'the Newdigate tends to be the climax rather than the prelude to most careers'.[31] That overture led to nothing, but Rupert would have been delighted if six years later Bayley's *The*

Romantic Survival had come his way and would have been wholly unconcerned by doubts about the commercial prospects for such a title. The writers from the past whom he particularly cherished were neither among the more fashionable nor necessarily the more celebrated. Kipling he believed to be 'one of the great literary geniuses of the Anglo-Saxon race', though he deplored the 'vulgarity, lack of taste, jingoism and cocksure brassiness'.[32] Yeats and Hardy were 'the greatest poets of the twentieth century'. Henry James, Peacock, Landor, were prominent in his pantheon. He re-read *The Egoist* with great pleasure: 'I much prefer Meredith to Miss Murdoch, Sir C Snow and the other misty highlights of the day.'[33] He urged William Plomer, whose writing he admired, to assemble his literary introductions and similar pieces into a volume: 'I know that *Belles Lettres* are now dirty words, but I much prefer them to many of those now universally printed.'[34] If challenged to choose the living authors whom he was proudest to have published, he would probably have included Edmund Blunden, Ray Bradbury, Charles Causley, Leon Edel, the Shakespearian scholar Leslie Hotson, R. S. Thomas, Andrew Young. He knew that none of these was likely to make him rich, other books from the Hart-Davis catalogues sold far better, but all of them measured up to certain literary and intellectual standards that to him were sacred.

Standards were the lode-star of Rupert's publishing. Michael Sadleir, bibliographer, novelist and director of Constable's, wrote to wish the new firm well. 'This is really rather noble and quixotic of me,' he added, 'as I fear you will be in direct competition for exactly the sort of book we like to publish. But at least the standards of the trade will be admirably maintained.'[35] David Garnett struck the same note: 'I could not agree more about keeping up a high standard. It is the only possible policy for us – because it is the only thing we can be sure of and can do better than other people.'[36] It can be argued that, by proclaiming and adhering to such standards, Rupert dug his own grave. He was well aware of the need to publish books which, if not runaway best-sellers, at least would make a respectable profit. He tried hard to find them. But the agents who controlled most of the more successful writers were deterred by his reputation as well as by his lack of selling power. Hart-Davis's from the start were identified as a last resort for the sort of highbrow literary product that more commercial publishers would baulk at. Rupert's Guards' officer manner and inability to conceal his disdain for what he felt to be trash, increased the agents' reluctance to deal with him. He was alive to the damage this did him, but unrepentant. If he were still a publisher, he told the youthful Scottish poet and novelist Robert Nye in 1973, he would immediately commission a volume of poems from him. He would not expect much financial success, however: 'I usually found that the sales of the books I published were in inverse ratio to my opinion of them. That's why I established some sort of reputation without making any money.'[37]

The exiguous paper supplies meant that Rupert was initially nervous about taking on the work of living authors, who would be indignant if their book sold out successfully but could not then be reprinted. By 1946 many classics had been out of print for several years. 'I'm expecting to cash in on this situation,' he told Duff Cooper.[38] He did indeed make a start with dead authors, though hardly with established classics. His first two titles, published in January 1947, were a collection of short stories by Henry James and an unpublished essay by Rupert Brooke on the arts under socialism, which it was vaguely felt would be relevant in the brave new world of Attlee's Britain.* Cooper thought that Rupert Brooke's thoughts would have better been left in deserved obscurity: 'I feel sure that had he lived, he would not have cared to see it in print.' He nevertheless hoped that it would prove profitable.[39] His hope proved groundless: the print run was optimistically large and the critics, though properly appreciative of the quality of the production, a hallmark of all Rupert's publications, were insufficiently enthusiastic about the content to kindle much excitement in the book-buying public.
     Later that year came the first book from a living author. Eric Linklater kept his promise to give Rupert any work which was not contractually committed to Cape's. In May 1946 he sent him the first of what he planned to be a volume of short stories. Rupert was enthusiastic. 'Am I wrong in spotting a new EL?' he wrote. 'An even surer touch, a different, simpler prose style?' If the other stories were anything like as good, 'the book will be colossal and the firm's fortune made'.[40] The book was illustrated by Joan Hassall – the fee for which Linklater sportingly insisted should be deducted from his advance – 'Give it me back some time if circumstances warrant it and you can afford it'[41] – but was not the runaway triumph the publishers had expected. 'We printed 25,000 copies and sold them all. The first big success in our first year,' Rupert wrote in his memoirs.[42] In fact they had

* For every aspect of the affairs of Rupert Hart-Davis Ltd I have found invaluable Richard Garnett's three articles in the *Book Collector*, Vol. 50, No 3, pp329–45; Vol. 50, No 4, pp493–506 and Vol. 51, No 1, pp34–7.

sold 16,000 after four years; respectable enough but not quite the 'big success' Rupert proclaimed it. It also contained one of the few production blunders of Rupert's time as an independent publisher. Linklater's dedication to the writer John Moore was somehow omitted. Rupert apologised in dismay. 'Say no more,' Linklater replied forgivingly. 'I have written to John Moore. I told him you were only a young publisher. That harsh reproof would bruise your tender spirit. I have promised to write another book and dedicate it to him. It will be a nuisance to write another book. But it is my trade. Oh dear!'[43]

Jonathan Cape's not-so-tender spirits were bruised by the threatened defection of this cherished author. Rupert's first few years as an independent publisher were marked by ill-tempered jousting with his former employer. 'What I *don't* want to do is to appear to be making a dead set at Jonathan and asking his authors to do this or that,' Rupert protested to William Plomer after urging him to undertake a selection from Augustus Hare's volumes of autobiography. 'The last thing I want to do is to cause trouble.'[44] His behaviour fell something short of the self-abnegation these words suggest. His stepfather-in-law, Louis Spears, was writing a book about the Second World War which Rupert coveted. It was pledged to Cape's. Rupert advised Spears to stand out for an advance of £2,000, 'which I think it very unlikely they would pay'. Spears protested that he was not concerned about the size of his advance. 'I don't see any point in raising this matter with Cape,' Rupert replied unblushingly. 'Once they're disposed of we'll discuss ways and means.'[45]

To the indignation of Cape's, Rupert published Duff Cooper's *Sergeant Shakespeare*, an ingenious attempt to prove Shakespeare had once been a serving soldier, in spite of the fact that Cape's had an option on Cooper's next book. They insisted that the option be transferred to the novel *Operation Heartbreak*, which Cooper was just completing. As in the case of Spears, Rupert suggested that his uncle should hold out for an advance higher than Cape's were likely to pay. Sure enough, Jonathan Cape turned down the book and compounded the affront by telling Cooper that he did not think he was cut out to be a novelist. Gleefully, Rupert took over. *Operation Heartbreak*, a splendidly romantic story based on a real-life wartime episode of which Duff Cooper had become aware while serving as Minister of Information, sold nearly 50,000 copies.

Rupert also made a bold attempt to prise Eric Linklater loose from his remaining ties with Cape's. He wrote of the great pleasure he had

had in reading *A Spell for Old Bones*. 'I realise that Cape's, though
clearly they neither appreciate nor like the book, have got to publish it.
But what it needs is some sort of special treatment. All they will do is
put it through the factory . . . But it's useless my creating mischief.'[46]
On this occasion it was Cape's who held on to their rights, as they did in
other cases where they felt Rupert was trespassing on their territory.
They offered Peter Fleming a contract to work with them in some sort
of loosely defined editorial function; at least in part so as to discourage
him from moving all his future books to Rupert.[47] When Francis
Meynell told Jonathan Cape that, as the idea for his new book had come
initially from Rupert it might make sense to transfer it to the Hart-
Davis list, Cape responded with a list of editorial proposals but ignored
the suggestion that the author might switch his loyalties.

Another refugee from Cape's who ended up with Rupert was
Stephen Potter, who presented *The Theory and Practice of Gamesmanship or The Art of Winning Games Without Actually Cheating* to the
assembled partners in March 1947. 'A real good honest laughing book is
what you really want,' Arthur Ransome had told Rupert,[48] and here one
was. They gambled their remaining stocks of paper on printing 25,000
copies. First reactions from the press were disappointing. 'Who is this
Potter?' Ian Fleming asked the literary editor of the *Sunday Times*. 'He's
just a jumped-up journalist.'[49] But then things improved dramatically,
the book became a cult, the word 'gamesmanship' was added to the
English language, a series of highly successful sequels appeared over the
following years. It was Rupert's first unequivocal best-seller.

It also marked the first overt sign of discord on editorial matters
between Rupert and David Garnett. Garnett had originally been as
enthusiastic about Potter's book as Rupert and Teddy Young but on
reflection he began to doubt whether it was really one for the Hart-
Davis list. The moral to be drawn, he concluded, was that they should
never 'let an author sell his own book to all of us together. Let us always
sniff around the MSS first.'[50]

The somewhat ambiguous division of responsibilities between the
usually-absentee Garnett and the omnipresent Rupert was always a
potential cause of friction. Once Garnett told a lady novelist that Hart-
Davis's would be delighted to publish her book. 'He'd got no business
to say that without consulting me,'[51] Rupert protested, yet he himself
often took on a book and only subsequently told his partner. An acerbic
note began to creep into Garnett's reports. On a collection of Gavin
Ewart's poems Garnett commented: 'Rupert (who may not have read

them) says these are good. I, who have, don't like them at all.' Even though his reading may not have been over-conscientious, Rupert can hardly have relished the suggestion that he praised work he had not looked at. Nor can he have been entirely pleased by Garnett's dismissal of Duff Cooper's translation of Louise de Vilmorin's *Madame de . . .* It was a slight novel, badly translated, concluded Garnett: 'We should tactfully reject it. If we can keep Sir Duff off translations in the future it will be no loss.'[52] On this occasion Garnett's view prevailed; the book ended up with Collins where it reprinted five times in the first two years. There was nothing approaching a rift in these early years but Garnett sometimes felt that he was being pushed into the sidelines and a latent irritation threatened one day to become more serious.

Though far from showing a profit in its first year – a contingency hardly anyone had envisaged – the firm had made a modestly successful start. Nineteen forty-eight was for consolidation. What every publisher badly needs is a backlist, a core of solid sellers which will go on from year to year providing the steady income that will finance new ventures and everyday expenses. A new firm by definition enjoys no such comfortable cushion. Those with ample funds may take a short cut by purchasing another publisher; the less fortunate have to manufacture their own. Hart-Davis's in part solved the problem by creating the Mariners Library. It began when Rupert and David Garnett had decided that Teddy Young deserved to work on some book which would engage his nautical interests. Garnett suggested Joshua Slocum's *Sailing Alone Around the World*, the journal of an intrepid American sailor, published in 1900 and long out of print. Arthur Ransome announced that it was one of his favourite books and volunteered to write an introduction free of charge. It was not a literary masterpiece, Rupert told Eric Linklater, 'but excellent reading for boys and sailors'. It would, he hoped, 'prove readily saleable, and should also broaden the basis of the list, which I am anxious should not appear too highbrow in the narrow sense'.[53] It proved an instant and, more important, an enduring success; Ransome chose a range of titles to follow it and contributed introductions to several of them; a book club and a paperback publisher took up the series; eventually the Mariners Library ran to forty-eight volumes and provided endless delectation for the armchair sea-goer unable to take to the water himself.

A further crop of Henry James reprints introduced a brilliant young American scholar to the list. Leon Edel, Lieutenant J. L. Edel of the Information Control Division, US Army, as he then was, had written a

thesis in French on Henry James's 'dramatic years'. He was persuaded
to prepare an edition of James's plays and then, with a punctiliousness
unusual at the time even among the most Jamesian of Americans, edged
his way cautiously through friendship to intimacy. 'Dear Hart-Davis,'
he began a letter in December 1946. 'By all means let us drop the
formality of "Mr".' It took another two and a half years before he
ventured: 'Dear Rupert – forgive the familiarity but I think we do know
each other well enough to drop formalities.' By then he had agreed to
write what was to be his classic biography of Henry James. 'I expect to
write from 150,000 to 200,000 words,' he announced. 'I will try to stay
in 150,000.'[54] The final biography ran to five volumes and must have
contained well over a million words. (This was by no means the most
inflation-afflicted of Rupert's enterprises. Early in 1949 he suggested to
Humphry House that he should edit a complete edition of Dickens's
letters. 'I can imagine you quailing at the thought, but truly I don't
think it need be unduly arduous. Very roughly, I visualise the book as
being in four volumes, price at something like six guineas.'[55] The series
is only just completed, it runs to twelve volumes, the total cost if bought
today would be over £1,000.)

The firm published sixteen books in 1948, most of them reprints or
new editions of existing books. They included a one-volume edition of
Peacock's novels, edited by David Garnett, though containing many
footnotes gleaned by Rupert in the Reading Room of the British
Museum. They were 'all credited to David', Rupert remarked in his
memoirs, an observation that seems to betray some pique. The year had
not been entirely unsatisfactory but the firm's basic weakness was
painfully evident. 'It's clear from the auditor's figures,' Rupert told his
sister in August 1948, 'that the business is unlikely ever to make a profit
until the capital is substantially increased. We also, of course, need a lot
more books to publish, but that part of it doesn't worry me so much.'
To add to his woes, the house in Connaught Street had been sold and
the new owner was demanding an increased rent and a £500 premium
for a five-year lease. 'I don't know how the hell we're going to raise the
money . . . If I was the worrying type I'd be like a stewed prune by
now.'[56] David Garnett remained optimistic. 'Don't be depressed,' he
urged Rupert. 'If we can survive we shall do brilliantly well and I am
personally convinced that we shall survive.'[57] Rupert was not depressed,
a state of mind which even in the unhappiest circumstances he rarely
indulged in for more than a few minutes at a time, but he was seriously
disturbed. The firm needed more books, it needed more staff, it needed

larger and more permanent premises, above all it needed money. Nineteen forty-nine must either see expansion or a slow and depressing death from inanition.

Chapter Eleven

Ruth

The staff was the least of the problems – though paying them promised to be difficult. The most important recruit was Harry Townshend, who had learnt his trade with his family business, the book distributor Simpkin Marshall. Townshend was a calm and capable manager, well qualified to take charge of sales and the business side of the firm. Someone once said of him that he was worried only if he had nothing to worry about; if that was true he must have spent peaceful years at Hart-Davis's, for his Chairman's extravagance and reluctance to accept that anything was impossible gave him endless grounds for anxiety. Rupert was a conscientious and exacting editor who believed that almost every sentence could be improved; the problem for Townshend was that Rupert found it almost impossible to work on a typescript and reserved his efforts for the printed proof. The resultant expense was horrendous; book after book that might have made a modest profit was tipped into deficit by the bill for corrections. When eventually a finished book emerged, Rupert was inordinately generous in presenting copies to all and sundry, not only costing the firm much money but often checking the instincts of readers who might otherwise have bought them. And production standards were never allowed to slip; even if it entailed buying small quantities of material at high prices, Rupert insisted that each title should be treated individually and given the paper and binding he felt it needed. Townshend was perhaps too amiable a man effectively to curb Rupert's lavishness; equally it is certain that without his steadying hand the firm would quickly have run on to the rocks.

Rupert's efforts to maintain the good appearance of his books – 'Neat but not gaudy,' wrote Arthur Ransome approvingly: 'Good for town or country and holding their own in any bookshop parade'[1] – were ably seconded by another new recruit, David Garnett's son, Richard. Richard Garnett, though a tyro when he joined the firm, learned quickly and was soon able to turn his hand to anything: a good eye for design, able to undertake major editorial repairs on the most faltering manuscript, adept at blurb and advertising copy, blessed with an excellent memory and much common sense, he played an important part in the firm through almost all its existence. But managers required supporting staff, the numbers crept up, by the end of 1949 there were thirteen people at work in Connaught Street. Since the office would have accommodated five or six in comfort, nine or ten at a pinch, the need for new premises became more pressing.

More people meant the capacity for more books. 'We simply *must* get out more books,' Rupert told Arthur Ransome in April 1949. 'You were wrong to tell me to keep The Mariners Library small.'[2] And they were not publishing the right sort of books, they needed 'a higher proportion of quicker-selling books and less that sold slowly and steadily over the years'.[3] Yet somehow this was to be done without any sacrifice in quality or change in the fundamental balance of the list. It would have been a tall order, even if Rupert had been prepared to set about it in the most efficacious way; as it was he was prone to immerse himself in the minutiae of daily publishing and hope that the books would come to him. His disdain for agents largely cut him off from the source of the quicker-selling titles which he professed to covet. 'I had never before heard of Ed Victor,' he announced loftily some years later of one of the most energetic and resourceful of the new breed of agents who successfully straddled the Atlantic. 'Is he a real person or a fiction of some computer? Eng Lit managed to give a pretty good account of itself for 350 years before any such parasites appeared.'[4] There is a Tennysonian grandeur about such scorn for lice in the locks of literature, but the literary agents were increasingly a fact of life and pretending that they were not there was hardly a helpful contribution to the building of a profitable list.

Quick-selling books, moreover, were likely to command large advances. Money was the most urgent of Rupert's preoccupations. Early in 1950 Harry Townshend invested £4,000 and joined the board. Geoffrey Keynes also joined the board as a non-executive director and contributed £2,000; he brought several scholarly additions to the list, but of the 'slow but steady' rather than the quick-selling variety. Rupert asked Arthur Ransome if he too would like to put in some more capital. 'I feel we are old enough friends for you not to mind my asking,' he wrote. 'Nor would I ask at all if my confidence in the firm's success in the long term was not great.' They needed another £10,000 on top of what they already had if they were to be able to publish enough books to ensure a profit. They lacked the security to persuade a bank to lend them the money, but if Ransome would invest £5,000 Rupert thought he could persuade his bankers to put up the rest.[5] Ransome could only run to £500 but a rich Swiss bibliophile called Dr Henry Goverts now appeared on the scene. Rupert quickly persuaded him that the firm would be both profitable and meritorious as an investment. All seemed set fair until the Bank of England suddenly vetoed the transaction. 'It really does seem insane,' wrote David Garnett. 'I will talk to friends of mine in the Treasury about it.'[6] He talked to good effect, the ruling was reversed and Dr Goverts put in £8,000. 'It will carry us on nicely for the present,' Rupert told his sister, Deirdre, 'but if later Tony [her third and penultimate husband, Tony Bland] is able to invest some more, that will be perfect.'[7]

The financial prospects seemed even more secure when they were approached by Book Tokens Ltd to produce a children's version of the token, to be known as Book Tallies. Rupert asked Arthur Ransome to commend the scheme publicly: not only would it bring in a steady income to the firm but 'if they are the success we all think they will be, they are sure to produce a lot more sales for the Ransome books'.[8] Sadly, they did not produce a lot more sales for anybody; the scheme limped on for a few years but was abandoned in 1952.

In 1949 and 1950, however, it really did seem as if Hart-Davis's were going to establish themselves as a profitable publisher. Their success was epitomised by *Elephant Bill*, the saga of Lt Col. J. H. Williams and his exploits with elephants during the war in Burma. Some member of the staff read an article on Williams in the *New Yorker*, on the basis of this he was approached and duly produced a turgid and ill-written typescript, David Garnett worked heavily on it and ended up with a colourful and compellingly exciting story. Rupert printed 9,000 copies and had sold three more impressions by Christmas. Personally, he took greater pride in the Reynard Library, a series of volumes collecting the key texts of great English writers, beginning with Dr Johnson and Goldsmith, but *Elephant Bill* came well within the criteria he set for his publications, being by the time it was published, literate, individual and of genuine interest.

Not all authors were so amenable as Williams to having their offerings reshaped or rewritten. 'During all those publishing years,' wrote Rupert as he looked back on his career, 'I came to realise that when authors ask for criticism all they really want is praise and encouragement.'⁹ Gavin Maxwell was a prime illustration of this truism. As a young and unpublished writer he was advised by the writer and critic Janet Adam Smith to take Rupert his first book, *Harpoon at a Venture*. 'It was all very like a dream,' he recollected, 'and everything exactly the opposite of how I would imagine publishers behave. They have, to cut a long story short, accepted the book without demur, and are sending me tomorrow a contract – and an advance of £100. Cor – the fools!' They were anything but fools: the book got excellent reviews, was a Book Society Choice and a *Daily Mail* Book of the Month and rapidly sold out its first printing of 25,000. But in time the publishers began to wonder whether the price was not too high. Maxwell would ring Rupert up every day, ask how many copies had been sold, work out what this represented in royalties and insist on coming round to collect the money on the spot. He would take his editor, Richard Garnett, to lunch at expensive restaurants and then find that he had forgotten his wallet. He ignored advice, resented criticism, and finally moved elsewhere in dudgeon when Rupert refused to pay a large advance to finance an expedition to Sicily in pursuit of a possibly mythical great-great-great aunt. He 'was one of the most tiresome authors I had to deal with,' Rupert concluded; the firm could ill afford to lose so profitable a writer but they saw him go with relief.¹⁰

It was the quest for more quick-selling titles which took Rupert to New York. He still professed to disdain the United States: 'They are a childish people,' he told Siegfried Sassoon in 1946, 'with, in places, a veneer of super-slick sophistication masking the emptiness.'¹¹ Such objurgations were not to be taken too seriously: he had a host of American friends, admired many American writers, and found his visits to New York exhilarating and challenging if also ultimately too exhausting to be endurable for long. 'Every time I come to this city,' he wrote in 1950, 'I go through a sequence of excitement, stimulus, heavy cold, wretchedness, longing for home.'¹² On this occasion, in his seventeen days in New York, his sensations were very similar. He visited 'twenty-four publishers, ten literary agents, perhaps six authors. I was entertained to the point of exhaustion, never paid for a meal, was seldom sober after 5 pm, never in bed till 1 or 2, up again by 8.30 . . . The first week was exciting in a savage sort of way, but thereafter I began to long for home.'¹³

'Bring back a new Huck Finn or some sentimental rubbish that will flood the female reading public with tears,' was Arthur Ransome's advice.¹⁴ Rupert, who was an ardent admirer of Mark Twain, would

happily have followed the first of these suggestions. Nothing of the sort
was offered, however. Instead he met an old acquaintance, Alistair
Cooke, and took on his study of the Alger Hiss case, *A Generation on
Trial*. He followed this up with a collection of Cooke's *Letters from
America*. Like most authors, Cooke thought that the publisher had
printed too few copies (15,000 against Cooke's anticipated 50,000) and
was not doing enough to sell those which he had printed. 'Can't you
bribe Harold Nicolson to proclaim in a double-column *Observer* piece
the deceptive importance of our book?' And wouldn't Rupert adopt the
slogan used by the *New Yorker* for its album of cartoons: '"Everybody's
first choice of Christmas present"? Or does this make you groan?'
Evidently it did; the people's choice did not receive the advertisements
its author felt it merited.[15] The other important acquisition from this
trip for the Hart-Davis's list was Ray Bradbury, one of America's
leading science-fiction writers who, unusually among practitioners of
this genre, contrived to be literate, intelligent and a writer of poetry as
well. This was not the sort of established writer Rupert often managed
to recruit; he won him by promising to publish him in hardback and
promote him as the serious novelist he was. The gamble worked; the
firm published ten of Bradbury's books and he stuck with them even
though tempted by offers of generous advances from richer and more
powerful publishers.

'The business is progressing as well as I expected – in fact rather better,'
Rupert told Duff Cooper exultantly early in 1949. They were likely to
break even that financial year 'and I'm confident that next year we shall
show a profit'.[16] By March 1950 he was telling Arthur Ransome that a
profit, though a small one, now seemed certain. But there was still a
need for more capital; the letter to Ransome was also an invitation to
increase his investment. 'I can't even dream of buying any more shares
at present,' Ransome replied. 'Sir Stafford Cripps's bony fingers grip
my throat.'[17]

In 1950 the firm published twenty-five books, in 1951 forty. Rupert
sometimes gave the impression that he had coped with the majority of
these single-handed, almost rewriting some, reading all of them with
critical attention. 'You say I have been working hard since first we met,'
Rupert wrote to Edmund Blunden, 'but in retrospect the years at Cape's
seem those of an idle apprentice in comparison with the hurly-burly of
today.'[18] He certainly did work long hours: in the first few years the
great majority of the books on the list were his personal selection, he

spent many hours on those which particularly appealed to him, most weekends were largely devoted to some sort of editorial work, he was closely involved in matters of design, sales, advertising. Yet when he told Blunden 'I have time for *none* of those things I truly want to do,'[19] he both exaggerated his commitment and belittled his capacity to keep a great many balls more or less successfully in the air at the same time.

He was not exactly a busybody, and yet he could rarely resist an opportunity to put his finger into a new pie or to occupy himself with matters that did not need to be his business. In May 1949, for instance, he heard that the Poet Laureate, John Masefield, was near to death. At once he began to scheme for the appointment of his successor. 'If the dear old thing should peg out, every string must be pulled in favour of Edmund Blunden [to replace him]. I plan somehow to enfilade Downing Street.' He sought to recruit Duff Cooper for the cause, though regretting the fact that 'he has little influence with these Labour boys'.[20] Cooper promised to join the campaign; he was all for Blunden 'and very much against that American Anglo-Catholic who thinks *Coriolanus* a better play than *Hamlet* and despises Jane Austen'.[21] Rupert, who liked T. S. Eliot, admired his poetry and also had little use for Jane Austen, wisely did not respond to this provocation but urged his uncle into battle. His efforts were both premature and unavailing: Masefield lasted for another eighteen years and was eventually replaced by Cecil Day-Lewis. Rupert was more successful in his efforts to ensure that his friend Janet Adam Smith became literary editor – or at first deputy literary editor – of the *New Statesman*, though ill-advised in one of his choices as an ally. 'My own intervention in that quarter would be likely to do more harm than good,' wrote T. S. Eliot. 'I fear that they would suspect that any recommendation by myself was part of a Tory plot of infiltration.'[22]

Individually such activities took little time and effort; collectively they represented a formidable drain on his energies. One of Rupert's problems was that he was *par excellence* the sort of man whom people wanted to invoke as an advocate for their cause; another was that he found it almost impossible to resist such appeals. Just occasionally he drew the line. Rosamond Lehmann urged him to remonstrate with her long-time lover Cecil Day-Lewis when the poet decided to stick with his wife rather than transfer his loyalties to his mistress. 'Rupert, tell him that there is not one of us, *not one* of his true friends, who thinks this decision is the right one. Tell him . . . that I'm worth staying with and worth something better than being thrown on the dust heap.'[23]

Even Rupert could see that this was one imbroglio in which he should not become involved. The anguished appeal was resisted. He continued to read enormously and held to his view that every author liked to receive a fan letter. His praise inclined towards the effusive: *The Echoing Grove*, he told Rosamond Lehmann, was 'a great book . . . written with the utmost intelligence, heart and guts'. Its story was 'almost unbearable in its hopeless, doom-laden inevitability and yet true and beautiful as well'.[24] The recipients of such accolades rarely seem to have felt them inappropriate; Rebecca West inscribed a copy of *The Return of the Soldier*: 'To good, kind, clever Rupert Hart-Davis who makes me feel as if I were all these things by praising me.' When writing to Nancy Mitford, he was particularly enthusiastic about the childhood passages in *The Pursuit of Love*. 'Uncle Matthew is my father and all the early part is absolutely autobiographical which is why it rings more true,' she replied. As a bookseller she had formed the conclusion that ordinary readers loathed their own childhoods and didn't want to read about other people's, so she had hesitated to go on about hers. 'Now I wish I had, as everybody seemed to like that part.'[25]

His social life was relentless: dining out three or four times a week, frequently visiting the theatre, lunching most days at the Garrick. When the Garrick closed for August and its members were forced into temporary exile he grumbled petulantly: 'I hate the Savile, where one is more than usually the prey of squalid bores.'[26] The houses he frequented unsurprisingly inclined towards the literary: at dinner with Rosamond Lehmann was Cecil Day-Lewis and 'another poet (epileptic they say but certainly charming) called Laurie Lee'. After dinner Day-Lewis sang Irish ballads accompanied by Rosamond Lehmann on the piano and Laurie Lee on the recorder: 'Altogether an enchanting evening.'[27] He enjoyed organising dinners to celebrate the publication of a book or some other momentous event: his dinner at the Garrick for Edmund Blunden featured poems written for the occasion by Cecil Day-Lewis and William Plomer, T. S. Eliot and Walter de la Mare attended, Siegfried Sassoon contributed the Burgundy, Rupert toasted Blunden's 'modest shining genius'. Blunden's wife Claire was not invited since there was no room and, less convincingly, 'the presence of ladies would probably over-excite the diners'. Evidently no umbrage was taken; Blunden thanked Rupert for 'a golden evening. I shall be talking of it even more than of the Battle of the Somme, the innings of 224 by R. H. Spooner, the pike I hooked on a sullen winter afternoon at Cheverny.'[28]

*

But the enterprise which was to prove the gravest distraction from his work as a publisher was writing the biography of Hugh Walpole. Ever since Walpole's death in 1941 Rupert, as literary executor, had been trying to think of somebody suitable to write the author's life. The more he thought about it, the more it seemed to him that he was the only person who could be trusted to handle the issue of Walpole's homosexuality without either being blatantly dishonest by ignoring it altogether or causing offence to surviving friends and relations by describing it in detail. He put the idea to Walpole's publisher, Harold Macmillan, who at once offered him a contract. The Walpole family said that they would advance him £700, a proposal particularly acceptable at a time when his publishing house was still to get off the ground. 'There's no particular hurry, but I shall get on with it as fast as I can,' he told Duff Cooper.[29] He began the task of working through Walpole's voluminous correspondence, including a host of letters from Henry James, Virginia Woolf, Arnold Bennett, Conrad, Galsworthy and other literary worthies; analysing and annotating the diary which Walpole had kept throughout his life; tracking down Walpole's letters; reading and re-reading the fifty or so books that the author had produced; and inviting from the public any recollections they might have of the writer and his surroundings. This last produced 'sheaves of stuff from lunatics, hideously repressed spinsters, disappointed novelists and Mr Michael Ayrton', whom Walpole had helped and who, unlike so many others, felt 'grateful and affectionate towards his benefactor'.[30]

In 1931, while staying with the Nicholsons in Ireland, Rupert had had his horoscope drawn and had been told that the conjunction of the sun with Venus and Mercury gave him 'a very strong literary and poetic mentality . . . it is likely that you will take to writing at some time or another'. He relished the prospect but, when it came to putting pen to paper on so substantial a project, felt curiously inhibited. He might have spun out the agreeable process of accumulating and collating information almost indefinitely if Walpole's family, 'most justifiably and in the nicest possible way', had not asked him to get a move on. In May 1948 he retreated for three weeks to North Yorkshire and began to write. Sometimes he found himself at a loss for words. 'Never mind,' a friend advised him. 'Just put something down. You can always alter it later.' He did as he was told, 'and funnily enough' he later told his sister, 'those passages hardly ever needed any attention'.[31]

There were certain problems that called for early solutions. He decided to make no overt mention of Walpole's homosexuality, but

instead to include coded references which made the situation abun-
dantly clear to the better informed: 'Hugh was always to some extent
afraid of women, certainly he never made love to any, he was always
easier in the company of his own sex'; 'Often . . . he would frighten off
new acquaintances, who he thought might be ideal friends, by the
extravagant vehemence of his immediate insistence on their friendship';
Turkish baths, he somewhat coyly commented, provided 'informal
opportunities for meeting interesting strangers'. Today such reticence
seems quaintly prudish, in 1948 it was almost obligatory – 'my story
was plain enough for many homosexuals to write and congratulate me',
he wrote much later.[32] He decided, too, to keep himself out of the story:
when he appeared he was disguised as 'a friend', for example as 'the
friend' who was present at Walpole's last meeting with Virginia Woolf.
His private passions were indulged, however: only a bibliographer at
heart would have told his readers that the 112 copies of *The Dark Forest*
which survived a fire at the bindery were 'bound in black cloth and bear
at the end the imprint of the Ballantyne Press. All copies of the
published edition, whether bound in black or red, carry the imprint of
Spottiswoode & Co.'[33]

He had hoped to have a first draft ready by the end of 1949: the book
was in fact not published until 1952. For more than four years it took
up any spare time he had in the evenings and most of his weekends as
well. 'I dare say that later in the year I shall be compelled to take some
time off from publishing,' he told Blunden in 1948, 'but am loth to
burden my already sweating colleagues with my share of labour.'[34] He
managed to confine his absences from the office to his annual holidays
but in the eyes of one at least of his sweating colleagues he devoted a
disproportionately large part of his time and energy to his work on
Walpole. In those years it mattered less because of the restrictions the
paper shortage put on the number of books any publisher could initiate,
but it gave him a taste for extra-curricular activity which was in the
long run to prove damaging to his firm. When several years later he
took on the task of editing the letters of Oscar Wilde he not merely gave
up much of his own time to the work but recruited junior members of
the staff to help in the search for references and thus kept them from
more pressing duties. Rupert's activities as author and independent
editor did not make the difference between success or failure as a
publisher, but they imposed a handicap which made success more
difficult.

Meanwhile, his marriage was falling to pieces. His own picture of what happened is clear, coherent and not entirely convincing. After Adam's birth in 1943, he wrote, Comfort had gone off sex; worse still, she seemed to withdraw more and more from any human relationship. She remained an excellent housekeeper and a conscientious mother but: 'The laughing, loving girl I had married ten years before was turning into a benevolent automaton.'[35] For some reason he later ascribed this transformation to Buerger's disease (he usually referred to it as 'Huerger's'), a circulatory disorder provoked by heavy smoking which was mainly confined to men, prevalent particularly among Jews and had no known psychological by-products. The element of heavy smoking was certainly present: since her time in America Comfort had become hopelessly addicted to the habit. She would start the day with a cigarette and keep one going until she went to sleep, irrespective of what she was doing – she even smoked in the bath. But though this was in the long run disastrous to her health, in the wartime and immediately post-war years the damage was still slight. A more likely explanation of her condition is that after the birth of Adam she suffered from acute post-natal depression. Rupert at the time was fully occupied as a soldier. If he had had more time, more patience and more understanding it is at least possible that Comfort would have come through her crisis and the relationship have been renewed. It would not have been easy, though. Physically, she let herself go. A friend who visited her towards the end of the war was dismayed to find her podgy and afflicted by acne, her faced covered with yellow blotches. Rupert, to whom a woman's looks were of great importance, could not help being repelled; and some of his revulsion showed. Instead of emerging from her depression, Comfort grew more morose and withdrawn. She made little effort to respond to such overtures as Rupert brought himself to make; when he triumphantly appeared with a primitive form of washing machine she was brusquely tactless in her rejection of so newfangled a device. She took no interest in Rupert's publishing or his other London activities. Her letters to Deirdre, who was one of her few confidantes, suggest that she had become obsessively tidy-minded and frugal; Deirdre felt sorry for her but refused to take sides and would do no more than lend a sympathetic ear.

During the week Rupert was alone in London, at first in a bedroom in the same building as the office in Connaught Street, then in the basement of Deirdre's house in Wellington Square. Even if he had been welcomed rapturously by his wife at weekends he would have found such an existence difficult; as it was it became intolerable. It was inevitable that he should look elsewhere for company and consolation. In August 1946, on a family holiday in Tenby, he met an attractive and intelligent woman called Ruth Simon. She had been born Ware and her father had captained Herefordshire at cricket, which meant that she was predisposed to share one of Rupert's ruling passions. Her husband, Oliver Simon, was a distinguished printer and designer, Chairman of the Curwen Press: 'She was never in the least in love with him,' Rupert told George Lyttelton; 'he had a fearful inferiority complex and a nervous grin.'[36] He was nevertheless a force to be reckoned with in the world of publishing. 'Yesterday I met Mrs Oliver Simon in the street,' Rupert wrote to Teddy Young. 'She and Oliver are staying around the corner, so I shall get to work on him on the beach.'[37] Presumably he had some question of design in mind; in fact it was Mrs Simon on whom he got to work.

'Charm' is the word which occurs most often in the description of Ruth; she was small – after Celia Johnson all Rupert's favoured women were below average height – not particularly striking in appearance, but a neat, attractive and vivid personality with a capacity for making whoever she talked to feel uniquely interesting and exciting. 'She glowed,' said one admirer. Joyce Grenfell praised her 'exquisite nose with a tiny tilt at the top',[38] but it was Ruth's congeniality as a companion which most impressed her. Men nearly always liked her enormously: George Lyttelton, who was usually censorious of extra-marital relationships, viewed her with almost idolatrous enthusiasm. Women were more cautious; the warmth and affectionate interest which men inspired in Ruth was not so easily evoked by somebody of her own sex, the shyness which men admired could seem like stand-offishness or a cool reserve when another woman encountered it. Rupert enjoyed her outspokenness. At one of their first meetings she told him that, in her experience, almost all publishers were frightful bores; on reflection, he told the historian G. M. Young, 'I realised that her observation was profoundly true. I have called my partners' attention to this and . . . we are hoping to make our name by being the only non-boring publishing house in London.'[39]

To Rupert the most important thing was that she obviously loved and admired him. This was what he needed. 'We fell in love like steel-filings rushing to a magnet,' he told George Lyttelton.[40] Soon after they returned to London they began to meet. The entry in Rupert's diary for 22 October 1946, 'Lunch Ruth 12.30', is marked with a red X.

Thereafter red Xs proliferate. Their exact significance will never be known though, unlike the Xs which marked the record of his relationship with Celia Johnson, it can safely be assumed that a little more than a sisterly kiss was in question. In March 1947 they escaped together for a few days to Wales; then four months later they went to David Garnett's cottage in Swaledale in North Yorkshire. Their stay there, Rupert told Deirdre, was 'lovely beyond dreams – lovelier than anything I've known. We both wanted, still want, to stay there for ever. We did nothing – everything, you know . . . we were simply so happy to be together without *anyone* else that the four short days seemed as long and bounteous as they do to children.' Deirdre felt sympathy for Comfort but she rejoiced in her brother's happiness. 'I feel your relationship has brought to life a whole new side of you,' she wrote, 'the most important side too, which up till now has been quite dormant. In spite of all the difficulties therefore and the complications, I can't feel anything but immensely glad that this has happened to you.'[41]

Though to Rupert's mind they behaved with exemplary discretion, their relationship soon became widely known in London. By 1949, when they ran into friends while staying at a hotel in Falmouth, Rupert was not in the least embarrassed and suggested that they all four met for a drink after dinner.[42] Anthony Powell used to lunch at an inconspicuous pub called the Chester Arms. It was something of a rendezvous for illicit couples who slipped in and out in a suitably clandestine manner; Rupert boldly advertised his presence by 'parking outside the entrance a publisher's van on the side of which was inscribed in large letters the words: "RUPERT HART-DAVIS".'[43] It would anyway have been hard to keep the affair secret when, towards the end of 1948, Rupert offered Ruth a job. Nobody could question her qualifications for playing a useful part in the office. Not only did she have considerable experience in book design and sound editorial skills; she had also for some years done an important job as secretary and book-keeper for the *Fleuron*, a journal of typography.[44] What she could have done is easily established; it is harder to decide what she actually did do or was supposed to do.

In the eyes of her critics, usually but not exclusively female, she contributed very little. Any usefulness she might have had as an editor and designer was more than outweighed by the time Rupert devoted to looking after her and the encouragement she gave him to pursue his private interests. In so far as she had influence over the company's activities, it was frequently ill-directed: 'The trouble with this firm is that it's run from the bedroom,' an employee once indignantly remarked. Her champions held that, on the contrary, she played an important role. She did excellent work on the design side, was responsible for most of the jackets, looked after the publicity for certain important titles and acted as editor for selected authors. Rupert did not necessarily agree with her judgment in every case – when she persuaded Verily Anderson to cut large parts out of her book of wartime reminiscences, *Spam Tomorrow*, he told the relieved author to put them all back again – but he had taken the book unread on Ruth's recommendation and generally left her a free hand in her editorial work. She continued to edit Verily Anderson's books, though the author found her patronising and decidedly off-hand; on the one occasion that an invitation was given to lunch at Ruth's house in Hampstead Verily was fobbed off with food left over from a dinner party the night before. '*Somebody* had to eat it,' Ruth explained.[45]

That Rupert found her of use is incontestable. She could turn her hand to most things and was always happy to take on the odd jobs that did not seem obviously to fall to the lot of anyone else. In so far as anyone in the firm tried to sell film rights it was likely to be Ruth and she would type certain letters and minutes which Rupert was reluctant to entrust to the *mêlée* of the secretaries' room downstairs. She was an invaluable intermediary between Rupert and junior members of staff who hesitated to beard the Chairman; if he was proving difficult a quiet word with Ruth would often lead to the problem being solved without any overt confrontation. The truth seems to have been that she did help a lot but that she was inhibited by the ambiguity of her position from making her presence felt or doing as much as she was equipped to do.

Their relationship in the office was conducted with extreme decorum: too much so indeed; the fact that Rupert referred to everyone else by Christian names but to her as Mrs Simon was calculated to arouse rather than allay suspicion. She was possessive of Rupert yet curbed any undue display of proprietorship; the only time that June, at that time his secretary, detected any sign of jealousy was when Ruth came into the room just as she was taking a bite out of a chocolate Swiss roll which Rupert, while still dictating, was holding out to her from across the desk. June's predecessor, who was more conspicuously alluring, several times felt that Ruth was viewing her with some disapproval; but there was never any direct rebuke. This did not stop the girls in the office resenting Ruth's presence; when she and Rupert took a day off to go to Brighton to do their Christmas shopping, the other secretaries urged June to suggest that everybody else should be allowed some time off as well.

Rupert wrote to Ruth every weekend and the letter would arrive on Monday morning; when they sorted the post the girls would giggle and hide it under other papers. In 1947 alone he wrote her ninety-two letters: 'They are beautiful love-letters meant only for each other, and I shall burn them when I've extracted useful factual data,' he told his young friend Paul Chipchase years later.[46] He did so too; in his attitude to his own archival sources he showed a ruthlessness which he would have deplored in other people. Of Ruth's letters to him it seems that only one survives. It was written some time in 1950, to await Rupert on his return to London. Alistair Cooke had been in touch trying to arrange dinner and she had been busy with Bill Williams working on the publicity for *Elephant Bill*: 'I have been feeling immensely important all day, so there! But all the same, darling, I'd rather feel like a small child with you lovingly around. So don't make a habit of leaving me for the day.' She urged Rupert to telephone her as soon as he got back. 'Goodnight, angel, for the moment. It's not very loving to type letters, is it? But this is half "Business".'[47]

Fairly early on in the relationship both Ruth and Rupert told their respective spouses what was going on. Oliver Simon was distressed but took the line that it was only a passing affair and would soon blow over. Comfort, by Rupert's account at least, was positively relieved. She had felt some guilt at rejecting his sexual advances and was glad to know he was now satisfied elsewhere. This could be wishful thinking on Rupert's part but Diana Gamble confirmed that this was her impression,[48] and Joyce Grenfell, who knew the couple well, felt Comfort was glad to be spared an unwanted burden: 'She is *so* buttoned up and simply cannot and apparently doesn't *want* to communicate. Absolutely no warmth. Frigid too, I suppose . . . He speaks with much affection of her in a compassionate, almost fatherly way, and said, if *only* she could talk to someone.'[49] The only person to whom Comfort did in fact talk with any freedom was Celia Johnson. It is perhaps significant that Celia was one of the few people who found it difficult to accept Rupert's new attachment, retiring to her bedroom with a rapidly contracted migraine when Rupert brought Ruth unexpectedly to Merrimoles.

Comfort's only condition was that, for the sake of the children, there should be no question of a divorce or formal separation. Rupert was happy to agree: Ruth also had children and was hesitant about breaking up her family. A situation in which Rupert and Ruth spent the week largely together in London and he returned to his wife at weekends seemed a compromise acceptable to everyone concerned. With the certainty that he would find Ruth waiting for him in London Rupert enjoyed his time at Bromsden. Most of it was spent reading or writing; he mowed the lawn and occasionally cut wood but Comfort took charge of any serious gardening. Though he loved the country, he was no countryman; he found little to interest him in either flora or fauna, and resisted all Peter Fleming's blandishments to take out a rod or gun. One Christmas, when rationing was at its worst, a cock pheasant perched temptingly on a fence outside the house. Egged on by his children Rupert got out an ancient .22 rifle and fired at the bird from an upstairs window. The only result was that a second pheasant appeared and stood beside the first one, crowing loudly. Since Rupert only had one cartridge, the family rations went unaugmented. He quite enjoyed walking, though. He apologised to Edmund Blunden for failing to write to him. 'When I reach home on Friday evenings I am usually exhausted,' he explained. 'A couple of long nights of sleep and some walks in the countryside set me up again. I walked a good 10 miles yesterday, in the Brigade of Guards fashion, and enjoyed every moment.'[50]

As a father he was kindly but remote. His son Duff can only remember Rupert once losing his temper. After a heated argument Duff had rushed from the room, slamming the door behind him. With a shout of 'Horrible boy' Rupert pursued him and whacked him on the behind. This served admirably to clear the air and peace then reigned. He would occasionally coach the boys at cricket. 'Our season has begun on the home meadow,' he told Blunden, 'but I fear Duffy is rapidly becoming too good for me.'[51] That concluded his parental efforts, however. He took pride in Adam's striking academic prowess but was baffled by his scientific bent. It might have been expected that he would try to broaden his son's cultural horizons but in fact he showed little wish to do so. When Adam remarked that he wanted something to read his father replied unhelpfully: 'Well, there are plenty of things in the house.' He only once offered advice of a literary nature. Adam said that he wanted to be able to write good English: 'Keep your sentences short and don't start them with the word "it",' were Rupert's words of wisdom. It was not a bad piece of advice, as pieces of advice go, but more could have been hoped for.

The children were remarkably unscathed by their parents' marital arrangements. There were no overt rows or obvious tension and they assumed that it was normal for a father to be absent throughout the week and then spend most of the weekend secluded in his study. It was not until well into the 1950s that Bridget, the eldest child, became aware of Ruth's existence as more than a figure occasionally encountered in London. She was disgusted when she realised what had been going on but felt no inclination to blame anyone: Bridget was never fond of Ruth, who made little effort to establish a relationship with her, but she accepted the situation as inevitable in the circumstances. Duff and Adam liked Ruth rather more but neither of them had much chance to get close to her.

Linklater was one of the few people to whom Rupert spoke about his situation, and he advised Rupert to soldier on at least until the children were grown up. Rupert later said that he regretted accepting the advice.

Chapter Twelve

Shipwreck

By the spring of 1950 congestion in Connaught Street had become so impossible that Richard Garnett was forced to work in the basement of a nearby house. The need for larger premises became urgent, especially since Rupert had had more than enough of living in the spare room of his sister's house and was longing for a flat where he could entertain Ruth in decent privacy. In July 1950 he took the plunge and leased 36 Soho Square, a ramshackle eighteenth-century house with a large basement suitable for invoicing and packaging, a big ground floor for the receptionist and secretaries, four or five other rooms which could be used as offices and a large room at the back of the first floor where Rupert reigned and board meetings were held. A cubby hole gave off Rupert's room, which his secretary felt was hers by right but where, in the event, Ruth was installed. On the top floor Rupert had a comfortable flat, separated from the office by a floor on which lived the actress Pamela Brown. Her presence added a pleasantly louche atmosphere to the premises; she entertained generously and was always ready to offer the use of her sofa to a friend. Drinking would go on deep into the night and the following morning the fascinated staff of Hart-Davis's would watch as the likes of Kenneth Tynan, Robert Helpmann or Peter Shaffer would totter tentatively into the light of day.[1]

Living above the office had the additional advantage for Rupert that he was almost always first to arrive in the morning and thus could open the post himself and find out what all his colleagues were engaged in. He also possessed a further bedroom, which rapidly became a repository for other people's books. Soon after he moved in he offered to accommodate nearly 7,500 volumes from Edmund Blunden's library and in 1955 Alan Wade's Yeats collection was added to the pile. 'What used to be my spare bedroom is now breast-high in Eng Lit,' he told George Lyttelton,[2] but this did not deter him from crowding in his friends as well if need arose. Rupert and Ruth frequently disappeared together into his upstairs fastness; the staff tactfully pretended not to notice what was going on though on one occasion, when Duff Cooper arrived unexpectedly on urgent business, June had to beat on the door until she could gain her Chairman's attention.

The atmosphere in the office was as carefree as in the flat above. 'It was great fun to work there,' Teddy Young remembered, and the word 'fun' is one which recurs repeatedly in descriptions of the daily routine. A lot of work in fact got done, but there was always time to joke or gossip. The directors took long and usually bibulous lunches and nobody complained if the junior staff from time to time indulged themselves as well. Rupert himself rarely appeared on the ground floor but when he did he was invariably affable and encouraging; he liked people to pursue their own ideas, was not in the least disconcerted by originality or even eccentricity and, on the relatively rare occasions that he noticed, was quick to give credit when it was due. When Francis Steegmuller translated Lear's poem 'The Owl and Pussycat' into French as '*Le Hibou et la Poussiquette*', Rupert greeted the absurd project with delight, encouraged Richard Garnett to commission illustrations and was only slightly surprised when the book sold 12,000 copies at Christmas. He had a proper sense of priorities and would often disappear with Teddy Young to Lord's if there happened to be a good match in progress. When test matches were being played he would give Rover tickets to any enthusiasts on the staff. June, applying for the job of secretary, was asked only whether she expected soon to have a baby and whether she liked cricket. She said that the first was most unlikely but admitted to watching cricket from time to time. 'The first Test starts on Thursday, you know,' said Rupert. 'Oh, will you be going?' 'The first Test is *always* at Trent Bridge,' said Rupert, amazed that anyone should be so ignorant. She still got the job, though.

June Clifford, as she had been when she first helped out in the early days at Connaught Street, had now married an optician and become Mrs Williams. She proved to be outstandingly efficient as a secretary; she attacked the typewriter with such fury, Richard Garnett noticed, that he thought she must be working off repressed emotions. Perhaps she was, but concealed passion for Rupert was not among them; she was happily married and, anyway, thought Teddy Young much the most glamorous of the directors. Sadly for Rupert, her husband was moved to Cheltenham and she had to give up the job; Rupert wrote to her regularly and never ceased to hope that she might one day be lured back.

Louis Spears disapproved of Rupert's treatment of his stepdaughter, Comfort, but he did not allow such considerations to interfere with his literary projects. In 1951 he sent Rupert the first draft of his book on the fall of France. 'It's going to be a smashing book,' Rupert replied. 'I don't think that the business of cutting and tightening it up a little is going to prove very difficult.'[3] He must have suspected that serious problems lay ahead. To Spears's indignation, when the time came Rupert demanded cuts of 75,000 words. Spears rejected this out of hand. 'I have spent more than twenty years advising other people about their books,' wrote Rupert, 'and, while I am naturally not always right, I have no doubt whatever about what ought to be done to this book, and I only pray you to look at it again with a cold and objective eye.'[4] When Cape's and Collins' followed Rupert's lead, Spears moved a step towards objectivity by proposing a small two-volume edition and a much larger printing of the truncated version. Rupert pointed out that this was economically inconceivable and Spears once more withdrew his book. He had the last laugh when Heinemann's eventually published the uncut book in two volumes to great acclaim and considerable financial profit.

Spears was not, therefore, particularly well disposed towards Rupert when, at the end of 1953, Duff Cooper's autobiography, *Old Men Forget*, neared completion. Cooper loathed Spears and the sections in which he dealt with Spears's role in the Middle East during the Second World War made it painfully clear that he considered him an irresponsible mischief-maker. Spears was furious and threatened legal action and an acrimonious squabble followed, which carried on after Duff Cooper's sudden death in 1954. Rupert was thus exposed to the full blast of Spears's indignation.[5] 'The greatest living shit,' Rupert described him. 'He let me down with a bang and I have never seen or spoken to him since.'[6] Duff Cooper's death left Rupert 'more stricken and cast down than I would have thought likely'.[7] Apart from Deirdre Duff was the last link with Rupert's mother and to lose him seemed almost like losing the father whom Rupert felt he had never had. His funeral at Belvoir Castle was splendidly spectacular. The mausoleum was lit only by a few guttering candles while the handsome young Duke of Rutland, 'all in black, looked like Mr Rochester in *Jane Eyre*'. On the way back to the castle one of the cars stuck in the snow. In his best adjutant's voice Rupert decreed: 'I'm very sorry but someone will have to get out and push.' Meekly the French Ambassador obeyed.[8]

Old Men Forget, which had sold 25,000 copies by Christmas 1953, was only part of what proved a sensationally successful season for Hart-Davis's. The place of honour was taken by *Seven Years in Tibet*, Heinrich Harrer's account of his escape from internment in India to Tibet, where he became tutor to the young Dalai Lama. It was by far the most successful book the firm published, and with 200,000 copies sold and Teddy Young's account of his wartime experiences, *One of Our Submarines*, also selling strongly, it seemed as if commercial success was at last about to be achieved. The year had been 'extremely lucky and prosperous', Rupert told George Lyttelton in one of the occasional letters that preceded their published exchanges. Not only had they made their first profit, but they had been able to write off the accumulated losses of the six previous years. 'I say luck,' Rupert went on, 'because one book such as *Seven Years in Tibet* can, in only a few months, alter one's whole financial position almost incredibly.'[9] Gratifying as this was, however, he personally took more satisfaction from the first volume of Edel's majestic biography of Henry James. Best-sellers like the Harrer were a legitimate reason for pleasure but the point of such success was that it made possible the publication of less profitable but more meritorious work. 'A few more like this, and I'll be able to lose on a few young poets!' Rupert told Edmund Blunden triumphantly.[10]

It proved a false dawn. In its obituary of Rupert *The Times* suggested that the firm's failure arose because this rush of best-sellers caused an expansion which could not be sustained over the following years. Certainly the unexpected best-seller has proved disastrous for many small, fledgling publishers. In the case of Hart-Davis's, however, the flurry of success disguised an endemic weakness. Shortage of capital and an inadequate flow of profitable books was the natural condition of the firm: the successes of 1953 and 1954 distracted attention from its failings but did not cure them. A number of books did well enough to make a modest financial contribution but inadequate marketing or profligate self-indulgence in the editorial process ate away the potential profit.

A case in point was G. M. Young's biography of Baldwin. The author had wanted to abandon work on the project when less than halfway through and had then caused despair at his publishers by proposing that all illustrations should be removed and the book subtitled 'A Political Portrait'. These difficulties were overcome and various objections by Walter Monckton on behalf of the Duke of Windsor were taken into account. Only when the book was in galley proof, however, did Rupert realise that the text of debates in the House of Commons quoted by Young often differed from the official version in *Hansard*. Changes had to be made at considerable cost. But this was only the beginning. When the book was already printed and bound and serialisation in the *Sunday Times* was about to begin, Churchill and Beaverbrook took violent exception to certain passages. Rupert thought their objections frivolous but had no intention of going to court to confront a man with Beaverbrook's litigious nature and limitless money. The offending paragraphs were rewritten and the pages tipped into the finished books. 'God knows what it is going to cost, but I fear that it will be quite a lot,' wrote Rupert gloomily. It was, and the lawyers' bills added to the damage. The author bore the bulk of the expense but the publisher's loss was also substantial. 'Don't take these things too much to heart,' Young told Rupert philosophically. 'We are the victims of fate. I always said that Baldwin would kill me, and it looks as if he has done it.'[11] Rupert would have endured Young's extinction with regret but resignation. The fact that his firm might well be included in the holocaust was less acceptable, especially since he knew that if he had been rather more alert to the risks, much of the expense could have been avoided.

It seemed always to be a case of jam tomorrow. Economies were introduced, Rupert's cherished production standards were in some respects lowered, Teddy Young went on to half time and young Richard Garnett took over most of his work: it was still not enough. In the summer of 1952 an accountant assured the directors that the difficulties could be overcome without the introduction of new capital if further savings were made. An office on the first floor was to be let; the Swiss investor, Dr Goverts, was asked to waive his yearly payment of £100; most significantly, Harry Townshend, David Garnett and Ruth Simon agreed to work without salaries for a year, 'on the understanding that these would be made up when the Company had made some profit'. No one suggested that Rupert should also waive his salary since it was obvious that he could not survive financially without it. David Garnett reluctantly accepted that this was reasonable, but the fact that he was being asked to make a sacrifice from which Rupert was exempt must have increased the brooding resentment which threatened to mar their relationship. Rupert also put forward, with some initial enthusiasm, a proposal from Robert Maxwell, Chairman of Simpkin Marshall, that he should put some capital into the firm and take over the sales, accountancy and distribution. Henry Townshend, who had already suffered at the hands of Maxwell, vigorously opposed the proposal, and it was quickly dropped.[12]

Within a few months it was clear that such cheese-paring would not be enough. A putative saviour now appeared in the form of Herbert Agar, a wealthy Anglophile American of patrician stock, distinguished appearance and literary tastes. Agar volunteered to put in a substantial amount of capital on the understanding that Rupert be joined as joint managing director by another American, Milton Waldman, who had been chief editorial adviser in the British firm of William Collins and had written readable books about Queen Elizabeth and Walter Raleigh. Waldman, it was assumed, would bring in a flood of new and profitable titles which would transform the turnover of the ailing firm. This Rupert and the other directors accepted, though Rupert at least must have found it unpalatable. David Garnett, however, took violent exception to a second condition; that the existing ordinary shares should be written down to half their original value. He argued that this was monstrously unfair: the reconstruction of the firm would be at the expense of the original shareholders who had backed the enterprise when prospects seemed far worse than they did now in 1953. Garnett and his family would be severely penalised, Rupert – with a far smaller shareholding – would emerge substantially unscathed. He urged Rupert to defer discussion of the proposals at the forthcoming board meeting since he would feel bound to oppose them as they stood at present.

Rupert refused, and a monumental row ensued. At the meeting on 6 June Garnett accused Rupert of exploiting the firm for his own purposes and of riding roughshod over the wishes of the other shareholders. The proposal that Rupert's salary should be increased, he argued, must be rejected, 'every economy must continue to be made so as to make the loss of the shareholders' money as little as possible'. When Rupert protested that he was having to borrow money and was unable to pay his children's school fees, Garnett retorted: '*I* had to borrow money last autumn and winter. *My* children go to the Council school because I cannot afford to send them elsewhere. If I brought up these facts you would rightly intimate that they were irrelevant. You must apply the same argument to yourself.' He claimed that with judicious economies and the aid of a few more dedicated investors the firm could survive without such drastic restructuring: 'It is not the profit and loss account that matters but the prospects in the future and the reputation of the firm.'[13]

The other directors either lay low or took Rupert's side. Geoffrey Keynes said that he was horrified by Garnett's outburst: 'He must have been brooding about it in his fastness at Hilton and has developed a complex in which he is persuaded that he is the victim of a plot.'[14] Certainly Garnett had been intemperate. He had the reputation of being short-tempered; once, when over eighty, he was bowled over by a car entirely through his own carelessness, and was so incensed that when the driver came over to see if he was all right he knocked him down. On that occasion he was appropriately contrite, in this case there was no contrition. He had some reason to feel misused. Rupert had failed to consult him properly and had presented the proposed reorganisation almost at the last minute and as a *fait accompli.* As a co-founder and far larger shareholder, Garnett felt that he had been shabbily treated. With proper handling, he could probably have been brought to accept the scheme, but he was ready to take offence and would have been suspicious of any radical proposal which Rupert had put forward.

Rupert subsequently told Frances Partridge that the real reason for the falling-out had not been financial but the unreliability of Garnett's literary judgment.[15] His doubts were not apparent at the time. Rupert had certainly on occasion ignored Garnett's advice and both men had been guilty of expressing their opinions with some brusqueness. But disagreements about books – relatively rare – were only symptoms of a deeper malaise. Garnett felt himself neglected and unappreciated, entitled to an equal voice in major decisions about the firm's future yet rarely granted it. Rupert must bear at least part of the blame for this disaffection. The result was that a deal was acrimoniously thrashed out, by which Garnett got three-quarters of the value of his shares instead of the half originally proposed. He withdrew in dudgeon from any association with the firm. His son, Richard, was away at the time and saw no reason to take sides in the dispute. He remained at Hart-Davis's; his father made no attempt to persuade him to do otherwise and was delighted when in due course he was made a director.

There was never a reconciliation. More than twenty years later Rupert asked Richard Garnett whether he thought the relationship with David could be renewed. 'I doubt if he still bears any active hard feeling,' wrote Richard, 'but . . . I don't see much prospect of your being *friends* . . . I would say the dog is sleeping – not snarling – now, and I don't see any useful way of doing anything but let it lie.'[16]

One unhappy result of the contretemps was that the Garnetts' cottage in Swaledale was no longer available for blissful weekends when Rupert and Ruth could be alone together and he could work contentedly on whatever literary project was involving him at the time. For two years they rented a small house at Thwaite, then they bought a derelict cottage at the top of the hill above the village of Keld. It was damp, it was dilapidated, its floors were encrusted with many years' accumulation of straw and sheep-droppings, it could only be reached by a gruelling scramble on foot up the steep hill, it pleased them in every way. They did not actually move in until 1956, but for the next two years much of their time while in the north was spent on supervising work on the cottage or picking up pieces of furniture and kitchen equipment at country sales. 'Reading by lamplight,' read Rupert's diary entry on their first evening in the new home. 'The downstairs fire has behaved perfectly and we are enchanted by our domain and the simple happiness of being alone.' The work of making a home brought them still closer together. Their marital status while in Yorkshire was deliberately left obscure; a letter from the farmer who looked after the property when they were away was addressed to 'Mr and Mrs Davis'.

Each year the pain of breaking off their idyll and returning to London became more intolerable. On 25 May 1955, the first day after coming south, Rupert had a series of meetings, a working lunch, drinks with the accountant in the evening, dinner at the Garrick for discussions on the Walpole estate and then to Rosamond Lehmann's, where he sat gossiping till half past twelve. 'Feel exhausted and longing for Swaledale, love and peace,' he wrote.[17] As with the Countess of Winchilsea when she prayed an indulgent fate to give her:

> A sweet yet absolute retreat,
> 'Mongst paths so lost and trees so high
> That the world may ne'er invade.
> Through such Windings and such Shade
> My unshaken Liberty

one suspects an element of self-deception. Rupert was not ready for an absolute retreat, however sweet it might be. But he had tested the illicit delights of a partnership which physically, emotionally and intellectually was totally harmonious, and he longed more and more to make it permanent. Early in 1955 Ruth's husband, Oliver, became seriously ill. He was 'most unfortunately recovering,' wrote Rupert uncharitably, 'as far anyhow as being a house-bound semi-invalid, which has been his goal for years.'[18] In March the following year he died. Ruth was now free to remarry. Rupert was not. Adam had only just gone to Eton, and by law Comfort was still his wife, but all the matrimonial delights that came his way were found with Ruth in London or in Swaledale. When William Plomer had given a dinner at the Café Royal to celebrate the publication of *Hugh Walpole* Comfort remained at Bromsden but Ruth attended as Rupert's proclaimed companion. 'Ruth has never enjoyed a party so much in her life,' Rupert told his host, 'and neither have I.'[19]

It soon became apparent that the infusion of new blood and new money – which was anyway much diminished by the need to buy out David Garnett – was not having the desired effect. Milton Waldman was a talented and constructive editor but he never achieved any sort of rapport with Rupert, so much so that he was not even mentioned in the account Rupert gave of the firm in his third volume of memoirs, *Halfway to Heaven*. Waldman seems almost to have been marking time before he was lured back to Collins'; he added a few German authors to the list but none of great significance. His relationship with Rupert was remote but reasonably amicable; the same cannot be said of Herbert Agar, with whom Rupert soon became seriously disaffected. Agar's role was never more than semi-detached but Rupert was quick to resent any suggestion of interference. Once he took on a book at Agar's strong recommendation, read it, disliked it, and with some relish withdrew his approval and struck it off the list. By the end of the first year of the new regime the two men were scarcely on speaking terms. 'He drinks heavily at lunch,' Rupert complained, 'and then comes back to the office and abuses Harry [Townshend] and me interminably.' Eventually Rupert lost his temper. 'After I'd let fly at him and left the room, he told Harry he wasn't coming back until he was sent for. I only hope he sticks to it.'[20]

One important author with whose acquisition Waldman was involved was Gerald Durrell. Durrell had written his first book for Faber's, but when they refused to offer a larger advance for the second book his agent, Spencer Curtis Brown, moved him to what he told Durrell was the 'up-and-coming' house of Hart-Davis. Durrell himself upped and came with a vengeance when as his fifth book for Rupert he submitted *My Family and Other Animals*. They said it was 'brilliant, the best he'd ever done,' Curtis Brown reported to the gratified author. 'They were sorry to hear the book had half-killed him, but the good news was that it was perfect as it stood and would require absolutely no editorial changes.' Durrell had been pleased by Hart-Davis's performance with his earlier books but had lost some of his enthusiasm when Rupert encouraged him to try his hand at a volume of short stories for children and then turned it down on the ground that it was 'too precious'. All was forgiven when *My Family and Other Animals* was hailed as a masterpiece and sold out its first printing of 30,000 within a few days. Rupert then excelled himself by persuading friends in the City to put up £10,000 towards the cost of the zoo that Durrell was starting in Jersey.[21]

Durrell was not a writer of great literary pretensions and he always remained mildly incredulous about his success. His affection for Rupert, however, might have been diminished if he had known how little the publisher esteemed his works. Richard Garnett dismissed *My Family and Other Animals* as 'unreadably facetious', and Rupert would not have put it very differently. He did no more than glance at Durrell's books himself, left the editing to others and felt mixed shame and gratification at their immoderate success. He approved the efforts made by Durrell's young editor, James Chesterman, to improve the syntax and remove some of the facetiousness but had no intention of intervening himself. When Chesterman argued that the latest book was unpardonably offensive about Durrell's relations and that the title, *My Family and Other Animals*, compounded the insults, Rupert privately agreed but offered his editor no support. Durrell's relationship with his family, Rupert felt, was his own affair. Personally, he liked the author, enjoyed his enthusiasm and ebullience and appreciated his extraordinary flair for getting on with and depicting animals. They were never close friends and their relationship was to end in tears, but whilst it lasted it gave satisfaction to both parties.

Durrell could be difficult as an author; Julian Maclaren-Ross was impossible. Rupert's intervention on his behalf during the war had convinced Maclaren-Ross that Hart-Davis's were his destined publishers. The trouble was that he assumed his publishers should also be his financial and legal advisers, available for confused consultations at any hour of the day and night and applying the full energies of the firm exclusively to his productions. Towards the end of 1952 he produced a volume of memoirs, *The Weeping and the Laughter*, for which he demanded a large advance and a contract within a week. Rupert refused to negotiate with a pistol at his head and returned the manuscript unread. Maclaren-Ross at once climbed down: 'There is no pistol, I am quite unarmed . . . I've always felt you were the best publisher to do it: so you in reality hold the pistol.' Rupert could spend as long as he felt necessary reading the book before making up his mind.[22] This sweet reasonableness lasted for several months, but soon Rupert was again being bombarded with demands for money. 'I am very fond of you,' he wrote, 'and I admire your books and like to publish them but I simply cannot act also as your banker and advancer of money which other people are going to pay you later. I do sympathise with your permanent financial worries, and I will do my damndest to earn you as much as possible in royalties. More than that I simply cannot do.'[23]

This dulcet response curbed but did not stop the flow of complaints and extortionate demands. The flow became a torrent when *The Weeping and the Laughter* was finally published. Rupert had failed to secure reviews and had been dilatory in forwarding letters; advertising had been pitifully inadequate; there were no copies in the Kensington branch of W. H. Smith's and they had not even heard of it at Whiteley's. Eventually Rupert had had enough. 'I didn't answer your last two letters,' he told the fulminating author, 'because they seemed to me petty and antagonistic, and I have no wish to quarrel with you. You always think you know best about everything and I can see it is no use trying to convince you to the contrary.' Several booksellers had refused to stock Maclaren-Ross's books because he had made himself such a nuisance in their shops. 'If you go on in this way, you will soon have every publisher and bookseller against you, which won't really be any help.'[24] Maclaren-Ross for his part was always glad of an excuse to quarrel with anyone. Rupert, he now claimed, had been arrogant, presumptuous and impudent; 'there are limits to my patience, and I have submitted to your uncalled for outbursts of asperity long enough'.[25] It was the end of the relationship. Rupert regretted it, for he genuinely admired Maclaren-Ross's writing and liked him when he was not at his most outrageous. He could never have met all Maclaren-Ross's demands but, if his firm had been richer, would happily have paid above the odds to keep him moderately happy.

If his firm had been richer he would also have spent much more money on publishing poetry. His taste in modern poetry was unadventurous; he was cautious about experiment and rejected anything which he felt to be exhibitionistic or wilfully obscure; yet he had a fine ear for rhythm, a deep appreciation of the beauty of words and subtle imagery; and a readiness to back whatever he felt to be sincere and heartfelt with a fine indifference to the vagaries of fashion. Among twentieth-century poets he had admired Hardy to distraction, and his eagerness to publish the collected poems of Andrew Young was justified by him on the grounds that he felt Young to be in that great tradition. Altogether he published thirty-two books of new poetry by seventeen living authors. Charles Causley was one who first figured on his list. 'I'd *very* much like to appear under your imprint,' wrote Causley, '(who wouldn't?); if I happened to be an actor, for instance, it would be a dash of the Old Vic *and* Stratford *and* of the nicer part of Hollywood.'[26] Causley became a friend and frequent visitor to the office. Once Rupert asked him whether he had passed anyone on the stairs. 'No,' said Causley. 'That was R. S. Thomas,' replied Rupert, oblivious to Causley's response. 'I'm still trying to work that out,' Causley wrote later.[27] It was a pity the two poets did not meet. They were both stars on Rupert's list, and though they differed widely in style and subject they shared an unflinching dedication to the truth and a clear-sighted but idealistic love of nature.

'It is lovely to be with someone who is enjoying their job as much as you and really doing what they want to,' his sister had written to him in the autumn of 1946.[28] Eight or nine years on and he was still enjoying his job, but the nature of that job had changed. He would still have described himself as a full-time publisher but an increasing amount of his pleasure was derived from enterprises which might have been related to his publishing but did not necessarily form part of it. His work on Hugh Walpole, both as biographer and literary executor, was particularly time-consuming as well as rewarding. Though Walpole as a novelist was generally scorned by the critics, the public refused to abandon his books. Rupert, who insisted that the executors should retain all the subsidiary rights, was constantly badgered about permissions for films, translations, plays and quotations. He even found himself responsible for a volume of short stories, called *Mr Huffam*, which was not published till well after Walpole's death. Walpole's editor at Macmillan's, Thomas Mark, was renowned for his skill at putting the most shambolic typescript into order; with some satisfaction Rupert wrote: 'I was particularly pleased with myself for spotting two howlers which seem to have escaped your masterly eye.'[29] Such labours kept him inordinately busy and brought no financial reward, since the royalties went to Walpole's brother. Rupert did not begrudge the time;

particularly since the brother was elderly and had no children and Rupert was next in line to inherit.

He found that he relished being the published rather than the publisher. 'Today was the first time I've ever been taken out to lunch as an *author*,' he told his editor at Macmillan's, Rache Lovat Dickson.[30] Some editors find it almost impossible to accept advice themselves, Rupert proved strikingly amenable. He asked both Richard Garnett and Daniel George to read his typescript and, in particular, eliminate all clichés. George was particularly keen on striking out the formula 'found him', as in 'April found him in Rome'. 'Got him again!' he would cry gleefully whenever an example caught his eye.

Hugh Walpole was published to considerable acclaim on 4 March 1952. Anthony Powell gave it a full page in the *Times Literary Supplement*; it was a warmly appreciative review and in his autobiography he paid a perceptive tribute to Rupert's 'no-nonsense style – a style apparently simple to the point of heartiness, while concealing a good deal of undercover subtlety'.[31] The comment, as he well knew, was as pertinent to Rupert's manner as to his writing, the affectation of bluff good-fellowness became so perfected as to become almost a reality but it cloaked a shrewd and nuanced judgment and an acerbic wit. Harold Nicolson, Cyril Connolly, Peter Quennell, Rose Macaulay: all the literary panjandrums of the day wrote glowingly of his achievement. It was the establishment saluting one of their own and as such to be viewed with mild suspicion; yet Anthony Burgess would not have been pleased to be included in any such *galère* and he told Rupert he had read the book twenty times: 'I found a copy in Borneo in 1958 and have always had the book with me ever since. It remains my touchstone for literary biography.'[32] Nor would Philip Larkin have wished to be lumped with the likes of Nicolson and Quennell, yet he told Barbara Pym that he was re-reading the biography and still found it fascinating.[33]

It was a balanced, thoughtful and well-written book. It deserved its success. Whether it is really a 'touchstone for literary biography' is another matter. Daphne du Maurier certainly had a point when she complained that Rupert was too preoccupied with the details of Hugh Walpole's diary and speculated too little about his thoughts and motives: 'I became almost dizzy with the ordinary social events of day-to-day throughout the years – where he lunched, dined, went to the dentist, even wearing waterproofs if it was cold etc etc – and could have done with so much more of inner life.'[34] Nancy Mitford asked Evelyn

Waugh if he had read *Hugh Walpole*. 'I'd looked forward to it as a terrific treat,' she wrote, '– can't get on with it. Tried skipping, tried the index, tried everything, no good, I can't. I believe the English buy books entirely on dullness, but perhaps I'm in a bad mood.'[35] Perhaps she was; nobody else found the book dull; but it is at times humdrum and Rupert's resolve not to refer to his subject's homosexuality meant that the picture of his subject was opaque and sometimes curiously out of focus. If he had written the biography twenty years later, when he could have treated Walpole with the honesty he showed towards his mother in *The Arms of Time*, it would have been a better book.

It was more than well enough received, however, to make Rupert think that he might do something else along the same lines. William Plomer suggested a biography of Aubrey Beardsley, but the idea was turned down. 'For all his reading and writing, he wasn't quite *literary* enough for my taste,' Rupert told Plomer. He didn't feel 'the remotest flash of that kinship without which no good biography can, I think be written'. But he urged Plomer to come up with more possible subjects, 'for I ache to sweeten these endless publishing chores with something I truly care for'.[36] In fact he was already engaged in the sort of project which he found that he cared for even more truly than the writing of biography: the editing of the letters of George Moore, the Irish novelist and autobiographer, to Lady Cunard. Rupert's delight in crossword and jigsaw puzzles, his insatiable literary curiosity, his determination to impose order on the world around him, united to make the editing of a collection of letters of this kind a uniquely satisfying experience. His patience and determination were limitless: he would happily spend hours in the London Library or the Reading Room of the British Museum so as to tease out the significance of a fleeting remark about a play seen, a book read, a dinner party attended. Some might have argued that nobody except Rupert *cared* what the remark signified and that he was wasting his time; this contention, in his eyes, missed the point. The information might be of importance to somebody else and, even if it was not, if the point was left obscure the editing would be less than perfect. Perfection, he accepted, was unattainable, but only if the editor had got as close to it as was humanly possible could it be said that the work had been properly done. Rupert's edition of Moore's letters to Lady Cunard was at least published by his own house, so that he could claim that he was, literally, minding his own business when he devoted his energies to this arcane pursuit. It is unlikely, however, that any accountant pursuing cost-effectiveness would have accepted that his time was well spent. This, no doubt, is part of the explanation for Rupert's abhorrence of accountants and his determination that they should play as small a part as possible in the running of the company.[37]

His work on the Moore letters also demonstrated Rupert's ability to persuade people to work for him devotedly for little recompense except gifts of books and much gratitude. Ernest Mehew was a civil servant by profession, who was to become the world's greatest authority on Robert Louis Stevenson. He seemed to ask nothing better than, on Rupert's behalf, to chase up obscure references or identify the fleeting apparitions who shimmer through the pages of any correspondence. In time Mehew was joined by Owen Dudley Edwards, Paul Chipchase and Nicolas Barker from within Rupert's own publishing house: scholarly figures whose patience, resourcefulness and above all generosity can only arouse astonishment and admiration. Rupert was a great editor, but he could never have achieved what he did without the dedication of this band of brothers.

Their help was going to be more than ever necessary when he took on his next, gargantuan enterprise. Ever since 1926, when he had first read Frank Harris's *Oscar Wilde* and Wilde's own 'De Profundis', he had been fascinated by Wilde's writings and personality and by his relationship with Lord Alfred Douglas. At first he viewed the playwright with some distaste: 'There seems little to choose between Wilde and Douglas,' he wrote in his book-list. 'A horrible blackguard.'[38] With time his view softened; he grew to believe that Wilde was both a greater writer and a better man than he was generally considered. In November 1950 he suggested to Wilde's son, Vyvyan Holland, that he should publish a volume – perhaps even two volumes – of the letters of his father. He got no answer but, undaunted, renewed the attack the following year.[39] This time Holland responded with some enthusiasm and the project was soon under way. Rupert's old friend Allan Wade was enlisted to collect and edit the letters. By mid-1955 the work was reasonably far advanced, though with a long way still to go. Then Allan Wade died suddenly. In his memoirs Rupert wrote: 'With the approval of Vyvyan Holland I recklessly said that I would finish the job.'[40] Vyvyan Holland's son, Merlin, believes that Rupert at first suggested that Vyvyan should do the work himself. Holland, however, who had just been bankrupted, was thoroughly preoccupied by his own misfortunes and was anyway shrewd enough to recognise that he was ill-equipped to undertake a job so meticulous and time-consuming. He said that he would prefer to play only a peripheral role. Rupert quickly accepted that the burden must be his. 'I hope and believe that he is prepared to leave most of the editing to me,' Rupert told Edmund Blunden towards the end of 1956.[41] Most of the time Holland was, though he took an active interest and was responsible for unearthing several useful caches of letters. Occasionally preoccupations about his father's reputation led to his becoming rather more involved than Rupert felt desirable. Once he questioned the need to include certain particularly intimate letters. Rupert brushed his doubts aside. 'I'm all for your criticising everything that catches your eye,' he replied, 'but I don't want it to worry you, and you must trust my editorial judgment. I am quite certain that this book will be a major contribution to literature.'[42] In spite of the insights into the homosexual world which he had acquired when working on Hugh Walpole, he still felt himself at something of a loss when detecting the covert significance of some of Wilde's comments. 'We need a bugger on board,' he told his most assiduous though heterosexual collaborator, Owen Dudley Edwards; but to have served the purpose it would have had to be a late-nineteenth-century bugger and no such paragon appeared to join the editorial team.

Rupert's first guess was that there would be eighteen months' work required for the completion of the collection. In fact it took seven years. Throughout this period his work on Wilde took first place in the competition for whatever time he had which might be considered 'spare'. The five days of the Christmas holiday, he told Blunden at the end of 1956, had 'enabled me to become so engrossed in the dating, arrangement and annotation of the Wilde letters that I now regard all else, particularly publishing, as an intolerable intrusion'.[43] Dedicated publishers do not have spare time and would never consider the intrusion of their work into their private life as intolerable, or indeed as an intrusion. Rupert was not a dedicated publisher. In 1957 he wrote fifty-six letters to American provincial newspapers, ranging from the *Great Falls Tribune* to the *Fargo Forum*, seeking to track down possible deposits of Wilde letters. He was at least as preoccupied by the replies as he was by the sales figures for Hart-Davis books or the acquisition of some promising young writer.

His inability to refuse invitations or to turn down requests for help meant that there were many other distractions in his life. The Literary Society was a dining club where a disparate group of people who had written books, or at least enjoyed reading them, met once a month at the Garrick Club to eat, gossip and usually drink too much. At the end of

1955 Alan Lascelles, just retired as the Queen's Private Secretary, became President and prevailed on Rupert to take over from John Sparrow as Secretary. The task was not extravagantly arduous but organising the menus, establishing who was going to be there, sorting out the finances and coping with the idiosyncrasies of the members, took up more time than Rupert could afford. A fortnight or so before each dinner a card was sent out to all members which they were supposed to return if they intended to be present. The formula read: 'I propose to attend . . . ' 'Surely not the right word?' T. S. Eliot scrawled on his card. '"Propose" to whom?'[44] He said that he would come but failed to turn up; so did Harold Nicolson; the Duke of Wellington, on the other hand, did not return his card but arrived all the same. A secretary's lot was not a happy one.

Arthur Ransome too took up a lot of time. In 1952, when he was about to have a major operation, he told Rupert that he wanted him to act as his literary executor and make a publishable book out of the autobiographical fragments which he had accumulated.[45] After the death of his wife Genia, a large part of his royalties would go to Rupert. The prospect was enticing, since Ransome's children's books still sold enormously well, but it was long delayed; Ransome did not die until 1967 and his wife survived another eight years. In the meantime, however, Rupert found himself acting as unpaid literary and financial adviser. It was sometimes a wearing duty, not least since the Ransomes lived in Putney and Rupert was required to find his way out there every two or three weeks and eat the enormous dinners cooked by Genia: 'That's salmon in the Polish style,' she would say, covering everything with a thick yellow sauce and then standing over him to make sure he ate it all. Rupert, who was trying hard to lose weight – 'I couldn't bear any longer being so Falstaffianly fat,' he told Blunden[46] – could have done without both the time-consuming journey to Putney and the extra calories.

Another burden was still more gratuitously self-inflicted. Many years before, while still at Eton, Rupert had written in his diary that he was doing Literature Extra Studies with George Lyttelton, 'who is *most* amusing'.[47] Since then Lyttelton had enthused many generations of Eton schoolboys with a love of reading: Aldous Huxley, J. B. S. Haldane, John Lehmann, George Orwell, Cyril Connolly, Peter Fleming, John Bayley all experienced his inspiring, exuberant and vastly enjoyable teaching. In October 1955 Rupert met Lyttelton at a London dinner party. Lyttelton had long retired and now lived quietly at

Grundisburgh in Suffolk, occasionally doing some work as an external examiner but more often feeling under-employed and rather out of things. He complained that no one ever wrote to him. It was a gambit he had tried with several others in the past, including Neville Cardus and his former colleague at Eton, C. R. N. Routh; each time a correspondence had begun but had soon petered out because of a lack of staying power on the part of his interlocutor. This time he had chosen better: Rupert promised to write a weekly letter, did so for the first time on 23 October 1955 and kept it going unflaggingly until Lyttelton's death some seven years later. Rupert's side of the correspondence was inevitably the more eventful, with literary parties, theatres, publishing scandals to describe; Lyttelton's was more quietly ruminative; but they had a large field of interests in common – books first, and as runners-up, Eton and cricket – and were never at a loss for a subject. They showed off to each other, rejoicing in their displays of arcane references and obscure minor poets, but they were genuinely interested in what the other had to say and eager to try out new pleasures at the other's instigation. Rupert always maintained that the idea of publishing the letters never entered his head until long after Lyttelton's death. It seems in fact unlikely that the possibility of making an entertaining and even modestly profitable book out of the correspondence *never* occurred to him, but what is certain is that he was not writing for that purpose. He would have kept it going even if Lyttelton had destroyed his letters as soon as they had been answered; because he liked his old English teacher and wanted to give him pleasure, but still more because he got great fun out of it himself.

He wrote the letters on a Sunday in his study at Bromsden. Every Sunday he also wrote a letter of at least four sides to his sister Deirdre. For almost all the time he was writing to Lyttelton he was also sending a weekly letter to Edmund Blunden in Hong Kong or Tokyo. The material covered by the letters sometimes overlapped but on the whole they were strikingly individual in approach and content. They took much time and thought. Most Sundays he wrote to Ruth as well. His partners may sometimes have thought that it would have been better if the same effort had been devoted to finding new books for the firm to publish; his children may have wished that he would emerge from his study and spend more time with them. Such reflections, though natural, would have been based on a misconception. If Rupert had had the extra time at his disposal he would have devoted it to Oscar Wilde. That was the sort of man he was.

*

His publishing business had always had crises, Rupert told George Lyttelton in October 1955, but 'this year has been causing me even more grievous worry. How long can it survive independently? Should I not amalgamate with X, Y or Z? Could I then preserve my independence?'[48] By the time he wrote this letter, the Agar/Waldman solution had clearly failed and Waldman was on his way back to Collins'. Losses for the previous year had been unacceptably high, yet it seemed likely if not inevitable that in the next financial year they would be higher still. Peter Fleming, with typical generosity, offered to waive the rent for Bromsden, but this was not something Rupert felt he could accept and even if he had it would barely have affected the situation. A more drastic solution was essential.

The most promising prospect seemed to be a merger with Eyre & Spottiswoode's, whose managing director, Douglas Jerrold, was said to be about to retire. It was suggested that Rupert might replace him and, while keeping his own firm's identity, 'integrate the whole caboodle and run it as one unit with several imprints'. With the promise of a salary of £5,000 a year it seemed too good to be true. It was: 'It became apparent that Jerrold (a loathsome fellow) had no intention of going for several years, and that therefore I should not in fact have a free hand.'[49] The possibility of some sort of deal with Eyre & Spottiswoode's was not abandoned but it receded temporarily into the background.

Now Rupert's first employers, Heinemann's, loomed on the scene. There was no question of a merger here, only of outright purchase, but Lionel Fraser, a successful businessman who ran Thomas Tilling, a vast conglomerate which owned a controlling interest in Heinemann's, thought highly of Rupert and offered him editorial independence and the possibility of promotion within the group. Rupert was flattered but suspicious: 'I'd do almost anything rather than accept what would in fact be perpetual serfdom, with an outside chance of one day running the whole caboodle – which I don't in the least wish to do.'[50] The offer was rejected. Now he tried not just 'almost anything' but almost everything. A plan for a merger with Penguin Books was considered but abandoned, since it would take too long to implement and the need was urgent. Max Reinhardt of Bodley Head entered into negotiations, but he had no money and alliance with him 'would simply prolong the agony very uncomfortably'.[51] Rupert dined at the Garrick with Michael Sadleir of Constable's to discuss a merger 'but could see little benefit to be derived therefrom'.[52] The Eyre & Spottiswoode's option was revived and re-examined but they offered Rupert only a seven-year contract and a directorship. He might have swallowed this but the negotiations dragged on and he lost patience: 'Their whole behaviour has been so tricky and stalling that they're beginning to sicken me.'[53] One by one the options closed; 'we can't go on more than a month or two alone,' Rupert told Deirdre despairingly.[54]

Rupert always claimed that he could put any problem out of his mind and sleep contentedly. His ability was now being tested to the full. 'The reserves of energy, optimism and stamina are getting a bit low,' Ruth told Deirdre. Chatto & Windus's, Gollancz's, Hamish Hamilton's had all expressed a wish to help but could do nothing useful. 'Everyone is devoted to Rupert and cannot bear to think that the firm should lose its identity. I get seriously worried about him one moment and then the next he is up at the top again, gay as a lark, but it cannot go on much longer without his having some sort of collapse. I am amazed at his resilience and unfailing (or almost!) cheerfulness.'[55] The cheerfulness was wearing thin though: he told his sister that he was suffering from headaches, deafness and insomnia, even at Bromsden he was finding it hard to sleep. To his doctor he said that he feared he must be suffering from a brain tumour; to his mingled relief and irritation he was told that it was no more than nerves.[56]

Then Heinemann's renewed their offer. What had seemed so inconceivable a few months before suddenly became acceptable, even desirable. 'I'm now beginning to see the advantages,' wrote Rupert. 'No more shareholders or financial worry of that kind; a larger income (I am to start at £2,500); more time for actual publishing, which lately I've been compelled to neglect. I shall have complete freedom in the choice and production of books and shall stay in Soho Square with most of the existing staff.'[57] Soon he found it hard to remember why he had ever opposed the deal. Heinemann's reputation as a literary publisher stood low at the moment but there was no reason why the name of Hart-Davis should be publicly associated with it; if the directors of Heinemann's did try to drag him down to their level he had 'an all-powerful friend at court' in the shape of Lionel Fraser. Given half a chance Rupert was always ready to manifest a Panglossian ability to believe that all was for the best in the best of possible worlds. Such a chance was provided now. 'I am much relieved,' he told Edmund Blunden, 'and begin to feel the clouds rolling away from my tormented head.'[58]

Chapter Thirteen

Back to Heinemann's

Not everyone was as euphoric as Rupert about the new arrangement. Eric Linklater urged him to preserve his independence whatever the cost. 'I know as much about publishing and book-selling as anyone not in the trade,' he boasted, 'and there's no doubt you are still the best animal over the literary jumps since 1945 . . . Go *on* – take in new stable boys, new jockeys, new corn-merchants, but run under the same colours, and to hell with the notion of "pulling" at this stage.'[1] Rupert might have replied that the going was too heavy, the handicap too great, the jumps too high. It was all very well for Linklater to trumpet defiance; Rupert had not merely his own future to consider but the continued existence of his firm with all the jobs dependent on it. The tone of most of his correspondents was regretful resignation. Arthur Ransome was one of the original shareholders who now received a cheque from Tilling's for the – marked down – value of his holding. It was a venture, he wrote, 'that I have thoroughly enjoyed and not regretted for a moment'.[2]

Tilling's policy, according to the official historian of Heinemann's, was 'to buy companies with good management and not to interfere apart from asking for annual budgets and agreeing targets'. The plan was to build up a stable of 'good family firms that needed very little interference'.[3] Hart-Davis's, under the Tilling strategy, would continue to publish its own books but for administrative and financial direction would fit snugly under the umbrella of Heinemann's. It seems unlikely that Hart-Davis's could ever have produced what an accountant would have considered a reasonable return on capital, but if things had run smoothly the loss might have been small enough and the gain in literary prestige sufficiently significant to make the investment defensible, if not obviously worthwhile. Unfortunately things did not run smoothly, partly because Rupert felt no particular wish to make them do so, still more because Heinemann's itself was a mess. Financial control was weak, leadership inadequate, its leading authors were elderly and falling out of fashion, good young writers were not being attracted to the list. Worst of all, from Rupert's point of view, the board room was a welter of venomous feuds and, try though he might to stand aloof, he found himself drawn into the in-fighting.

The most immediate result was that Harry Townshend was removed to Heinemann's and in future paid only occasional visits to Soho Square. He continued to be on the Hart-Davis board but was joined by two directors of Heinemann's, whose presence, it was made clear by Rupert, was to be endured only if they maintained a decent silence on most occasions. Herbert Agar remained on the board but contributed very little to the proceedings. Geoffrey Keynes soldiered on for another year or so but then retired on grounds of old age and absence from London. In his place, Rupert told Edmund Blunden, 'we have instated Richard Garnett, who has designed all the firm's books so well for many years'.[4] Apart from the fact that Garnett was involved with every aspect of the firm's activities except sales and had proved himself an indispensable support, his appointment was, for Rupert, a comforting link with the past, reassurance that the hopes and ideals which had been cherished when the firm was founded still lived on a decade later. The other most visible sign of the takeover was that the trade counter for the whole Heinemann Group tried to crowd into the basement of Soho Square. 'Goodness knows how they will fit in,' Rupert observed.[5] They did not, or did so only with grave loss in efficiency.

The quest for efficiency was one of the main reasons that had impelled Rupert to throw in his lot with Heinemann's. It proved illusory. He had been promised a reduction in overheads. The opposite happened: the two dedicated part-time packers who had worked for a pittance in Soho Square were replaced by a far greater number of union members, working to strict rules and demanding higher pay. He had been promised an improvement in deliveries. The opposite happened: the two days which Hart-Davis's had usually taken to process an order became three weeks and then four weeks, by which time Heinemann's were listed as worst in a table of forty-two publishers. Most vexatious of all were the interminable meetings in which he became involved. A. S. Frere, who was in charge of Heinemann's, was a man whom Rupert despised and disliked. He was constantly calling meetings at Heine-mann's Mayfair base to discuss means by which the various operations of the group could be streamlined or centralised. This was bad enough, but once a week Rupert was required to trail down to Heinemann's headquarters at Kingswood, where he had begun his publishing career a quarter of a century before. The Kingswood directors thought the Mayfair directors were gilded wastrels, the Mayfair directors thought the Kingswood directors were coarse bumpkins, Rupert loathed them all. He was convinced – probably with some reason – that they were jealous of his greater renown in the publishing world: when *The Times* commissioned him to write an article on the problems of contemporary publishing they felt that it was they who should have been approached. They were unable to comprehend why someone of apparent ability, who had been so long in the business, should insist on publishing so many books that were doomed from the start; he was baffled by their readiness to churn out the sort of mediocre pap which at that time was a staple of Heinemann's list. At meetings he spoke rarely and then usually in terms which conveyed a sense of their inferiority. The relationship was not a happy one and it seemed unlikely to grow happier.

'I don't in the least care whether Heinemann's lose their money or not,' Rupert told George Lyttelton in 1958.[6] It was not a hopeful basis on which to construct a working partnership. The takeover meant that Rupert was now spared the more urgent business worries which had plagued him over the previous years but this did not mean that he applied himself with greater assiduity to activities that his colleagues at Heinemann's would have thought desirable. 'Do you, as I do,' he asked Blunden, 'generally experience an inclination, not exactly towards idleness, but towards some work or study other than that which must be done at once? All my inclinations are literary, but they hate being dragooned.'[7] It would be more accurate to say that they – and he – did not mind being dragooned provided it was in a direction that he had chosen for himself; once he had picked his path and embarked on it then he would pursue it with formidable energy and single-mindedness.

A case in point was the London Library, that admirable institution founded in 1840 by Thomas Carlyle, largest private lending library in the world and haunt ever since its inception of a multitude of scholars and dedicated readers. Rupert was already a member of its Management Committee when, in 1956, the Library was suddenly deprived of its charitable status and told that in future it would have to pay substantial rates. The decision was appealed against and further appeals made at a higher level to the Lands Tribunal and finally to the Court of Appeal itself. By this time the Chairman of the Library Committee, Harold

Nicolson, who was more than seventy years old, very deaf, and hopelessly out of his depth when problems of rates and taxes were involved, had asked Rupert to take his place. Rupert accepted 'with a mixture of pride and trepidation', the trepidation relating to the amount of time the job would take rather than his own ability to manage it. 'Thank God we've got a chairman at last,' a member said to him after his first meeting in the chair; Rupert passed on the comment to George Lyttelton, adding uncharitably, 'truly I hadn't much to surpass'.[8] He stayed in the post for twelve years. He was, in fact, an excellent chairman: constructive, firm without being too authoritative, inspiring in his defence of the Library and its standards. He encouraged members to express their views and make their presence felt but was quick to curb anything that he felt to be extravagant or inappropriate. A lady member wrote to say sadly that in her many years at the Library she had never exchanged more than an occasional 'excuse me' with another member. Could not occasional opportunities be made for friendly gatherings in the Reading Room? He sympathised, Rupert replied, but 'I'm afraid that the majority of the members would consider a social "get-together" such as you suggest an intrusion on their privacy rather than an innovation to be welcomed. The Library was never intended to be a social gathering place and I think it would be difficult to arrange anything of the sort.'[9]

But Rupert's main responsibility was to rescue the anyway precarious finances of the Library from disaster after all appeals had been rejected and the burden of rates imposed. His first device was to persuade his fellow publishers to donate to the Library the books which otherwise it would have been forced to buy. Nearly all of them agreed. One exception was the redoubtable Sir Stanley Unwin, who insisted that the Library should take pride in supporting scholarly authors. 'For such an institution to "cadge" new publications by living authors sickens me. So strongly do I feel about it that I will make a personal contribution to the Library of £500 if they will desist from such an unworthy practice.' Rupert in his reply said that he felt so strongly about the role of the London Library in the literary life of the nation that 'I am willing to endure even your obloquy on its behalf.'[10] In his memoirs Rupert claims that he urged Unwin to let his good nature override his principles: 'And by heaven it did!'[11] If this was so the effect was not long-lasting; in future years Allen and Unwin's gave the Library a discount on its purchases but offered nothing free of charge.

Rupert disliked fund-raising but could be persistent and persuasive if he felt the cause was good enough. The Library was such a cause and he proved adept at wheedling money out of institutions and rich acquaintances: 'There's a certain irony,' he remarked to George Lyttelton, 'in trying to collect all this money when I'm at my wit's ends to pay my sons' fees at Eton and Oxford.'[12] After the last appeal on the rating issue had been turned down he and T. S. Eliot, the President of the London Library, wrote to *The Times* to appeal for help. Winston Churchill was prevailed on to write a supporting letter to *The Times*; the BBC contributed £1,000; £17,000 was quickly raised. It was enough to tide the Library over its immediate crisis but provided no cushion for the future.

Christie's now offered to hold a sale of books, manuscripts and pictures on behalf of the Library. For the next five months Rupert devoted getting on for half his working time to soliciting contributions for the sale. The star item was the manuscript of E. M. Forster's *A Passage to India*. Forster apologised that the text was messy and incomplete but it still fetched £6,500 – at that time the highest price ever paid for a modern English manuscript. 'It would be gentlemanly,' wrote Forster, 'to add that I wish to remain anonymous, but that is not what I wish. I am proud to show where my heart is.'[13] To collect the manuscript Rupert paid a special visit to Cambridge; he did so again when G. M. Trevelyan produced drawings by Domenichino, Romney and Edward Lear. T. S. Eliot had been asked to write out a copy of a poem to put into a similar sale in aid of the National Libraries. He told Rupert he felt more inclined to make the effort on behalf of the London Library and offered to write out the whole of *The Waste Land*. It would be wonderful, replied Rupert, 'I think it might fetch £1,000 – just think of that.'[14] Eliot then took off for a holiday in North Africa, whence Rupert soon received a triumphant postcard: 'Oh Chairman, my Chairman, the fearful task is done.' (In fact he originally wrote 'the long day's task' but presumably checked his Whitman and amended the paraphrase accordingly.) Rupert's prediction of the price proved modest: the University of Texas paid £2,800 for the manuscript and felt that they had got a bargain when they found that Eliot had included a line left out of the published version.

The same university bought the E. M. Forster manuscript. 'These inflated prices seem rather ridiculous,' Siegfried Sassoon commented. 'The world has gone crazy on paying huge sums for everything. I suppose Tom Eliot's umbrella will ultimately be bought by Minneapolis for £999.'[15] His irritation may have been exacerbated by feelings of guilt; when Rupert asked him for a contribution he refused: 'The fact is that I am so attached to my manuscripts that I can't bear to give them away.'[16] Rupert had been an admirer of Sassoon's ever since the 1920s – *Counter Attack* was 'white-hot poetry'; 'Everyone suddenly burst out singing' was 'a poem in a thousand' – but the two men had never met until Rupert boldly invited himself to lunch at Heytesbury in the autumn of 1958. The occasion proved a great success: 'I truly believe Siegfried Sassoon enjoyed the visit as much as I did,' Rupert told Lyttelton. 'He confessed to being terribly lonely.'[17] The visit was repeated again and again: Sassoon carefully reporting to Blunden on the quality of the duck and the quantity of the claret which Rupert consumed each time – 'good friend that he is'.[18] Predictably Sassoon asked Rupert to become his literary executor: Geoffrey Keynes and Edmund Blunden had already been recruited but there was no doubt who would have to do the lion's share of the work. No less predictably, Rupert accepted the task. Sassoon had kept diaries for most of his life and would tantalise Rupert by showing him the volumes and occasionally reading out a brief extract. Eventually, at a Literary Society dinner, Rupert asked him what he wanted done with the diaries after his death. 'They'll need some editing,' Sassoon replied quizzically. Rupert had little doubt who would be undertaking that task as well.

'In answer to your question, "Does Rupert ever refuse to do something he is asked to do?" the answer is, alas, NEVER,' Ruth told George Lyttelton.[19] He was asked to join the General Advisory Council of the BBC. It was 'a body I had never heard of and I'm sure it's quite useless', but he accepted just the same. He gave as his reason for doing so that another member was G. O. Allen, a cricketing hero whom he much admired, but he would have found some other excuse if it had been necessary. He auditioned hopefully for the BBC's *Round Britain Quiz*; he thought he had done all right but the project came to nothing. He sat on the Council of the Royal Literary Fund, a charity set up to relieve the wants of indigent authors. One day 'a young, sturdy, healthy man' wrote to ask for financial aid on the grounds that if he was required to do any other work it would disturb the flow of his poetry. Rupert indignantly protested that the fund was not there to help would-be poets but the old, poor and decrepit. This wastrel should be told to sweep streets for a living and write his poetry in his spare time. Many years later he reconsidered his position but saw no cause to change it. 'Now that the young man, Ted Hughes, has been made Poet Laureate I can feel sure that my harsh words were right.'[20] He spent several days in court ready to give evidence for the defence in the *Lady Chatterley* obscenity trial. When he had first read the book in 1928 he noted: 'Far the best novel of Lawrence's I have read but some things can well be left imagined.' By 1961 his views had grown more severe, he thought it 'sentimental, contrived and occasionally ridiculous'. Almost certainly he would not have published it himself but if Penguin chose to do so he thought it at the best absurd, at the worst outrageous to try to stop them.

He claimed not to enjoy speaking in public but rarely missed an opportunity to do so. He was a natural choice to propose the toast at dinners in honour of literary figures, high on the list of favoured speakers at memorial services, asked to open a Beerbohm exhibition, to address the annual dinner of the Booksellers' Association, the Hove Quill Club, International PEN. He trailed off to Preston to talk to an audience of two hundred on Francis Thompson, but since they were 'largely illiterate (in our sense) I doubt whether anyone enjoyed it much ... Poets should take care to be born in more civilised places, like the Tottenham Court Road.'[21] The Beerbohm exhibition was related to one of his more absorbing interests. When Beerbohm died Rupert at once volunteered to be of any help he could in connection with either the writings or the drawings. 'You mustn't hesitate to call on me to do things for you, in London or elsewhere, when it is possible,' he told Beerbohm's widow. 'It's true that I'm always busy, but I have a small army of willing helpers, and between us we can surely be of some help.'[22] At least in this case he could claim that there was some relevance to the Hart-Davis list; Rupert published a collection of Beerbohm's theatrical writings, a selection of his essays and an edition of his letters to Reggie Turner.

At least while his editorial work on Oscar Wilde continued he hesitated to embark on any new literary adventure of his own. In 1958 he was asked by Macmillan's to write a biography of the novelist Charles Morgan. 'It would surely be very thin stuff after Hugh,' he considered, 'particularly with a widow and two children to be considered.' He did not turn the idea down out of hand, however, but hesitated and imposed difficult conditions. Morgan's widow then changed her mind and decided that she did not want a biography to be written for twenty years. 'This seems rather hard on Charles,' Rupert observed; so far as he personally was concerned his main feeling was relief.[23]

He gave more thought to the suggestion a few years later that he should write the biography of Augustus John. John had been a close friend of his mother and had drawn Rupert as a child. It was a flattering and in many ways tempting proposition. 'A fine, flamboyant figure, unquestionably a genius, knew everybody for 60 years . . . BUT . . . Do I know enough about painting? Has he kept any letters? Would the family give me a free hand? How long would it take? . . . If I were not committed to publishing for at least another 5 years I dare say I should jump at it. As it is I waver and wobble. Hadn't I better stick to writers, and avoid a painter with a widow, seven children and goodness knows how many mistresses and by-blows? . . . I expect I shall say no.'[24] He did say no. John's admirers were going to have to wait well over a decade for Michael Holroyd's biography of the painter. A biography of Oscar Wilde seemed an obvious possibility but when Owen Dudley Edwards mentioned it Rupert replied that there were already too many such books in existence. Possibly he did not wish to gain the reputation of a biographer who specialised in homosexuals; when Richard Ellman came forward he eventually agreed that there was room for another study after all. But though he avoided engaging in any major project he still indulged in the occasional newspaper article or review. Until the paper ceased to appear in 1960 he continued to review three or four thrillers a month for *Time and Tide*. He sometimes wondered whether he could justify the time this took but comforted himself with the thought that he was a quick reader and that the actual work of preparing the article took only two or three hours. Besides, the pay was useful.

His letters of the time abound in phrases deploring the tempo of his social life: 'I *used* to enjoy it immensely, but now do so less and less. It's such an expense of spirit and waste of gin-and-prattle.'[25] He claimed that he was getting better at refusing invitations but his engagement diary suggests that his success was limited. As for everybody else aged in the early forties or above, prices seemed unreasonably high. His best-selling American author, Ray Bradbury, took him to dinner at the Mirabelle. 'Probably the most expensive in London,' Rupert protested. 'Admittedly we had a very good dinner, with two bottles of reasonable wine, but the bill for the four of us came to £16!! Even our American hosts were a little shaken.'[26] He could never decide whether the business of entertainment was more damaging to his purse or his figure. He strove from time to time to combat the effects of too much rich eating, but to little effect. In 1958 he appeared in a *Brains Trust* programme on television. 'The cameras seem to have had a benevolently thinning effect, so that instead of Holbein's Henry VIII I looked more like an old

Cavalry Colonel painted by El Greco. Thank heaven the cameras can still lie!'[27]

One field in which he wasted little energy, either as a publisher or a citizen, was politics. He told George Lyttelton that he had lost what interest he ever had, 'particularly since the disappearance of Winston, the last of the giants'. When he went to the *Daily Telegraph* election night party in 1955, 'reluctantly' as he insisted in his diary, he recorded the food, the drink and to whom he talked but never mentioned the results. The victor, Eden, he considered a nonentity, deploring his 'toothy complacency, total lack of oratory, and record of indecision'.[28] He met the Labour leader, Gaitskell, at a dinner party and was disconcerted to find him 'very likeable, intelligent, amusing and easy to talk to'. He could not understand what such a man was doing in politics and assured Blunden that the experience would leave his 'diehard Toryism' unaffected.[29]

His prejudices had been confirmed by the Suez Crisis. Temporarily he revised his opinion of Eden. 'I have thought Eden right from the beginning of this crisis,' he wrote, ten days after Anglo-French forces attacked Egypt. 'It looks more and more as though in the nick of time we may have prevented a general war in those parts, backed by Russian arms and armour. I fancy that what was basely thought collusion between Israel and us was simply the fact that the Israeli intelligence was as good as ours, and they too realised that it was now or never.'[30] He went on believing that the Anglo-French intervention was justified, but soon reverted to his earlier views of Eden. When the former Prime Minister's memoirs appeared, Rupert reported that 'they struck a new low in tedious clichés. He deserves to have them read back to him at dictation speed by a "Foreign Office Spokesman". I always thought him a weak, dull mediocrity and here is proof positive.'[31] At least his replacement revived Rupert's faith in the future of the nation. 'I hail Harold Macmillan,' he told Blunden. 'Eton, Balliol, the Brigade of Guards *and* a publisher – what more could one ask for?'[32]

Into the interstices of this crowded life had to be fitted his family. By now Bridget and Duff were grown up. In June 1956 Duff's twentieth birthday was celebrated. The three children gathered at Bromsden for the occasion. 'They were all very young and gay and handsome and happy,' Rupert told Lyttelton, 'and they unknowingly provided one of those rare occasions when one can see in one glance that all the hideous sacrifices entailed in their education have not so far been wasted.'[33]

Bridget, who as a girl was considered by Rupert to require less education, involved fewer sacrifices. She went to agricultural college, achieved considerable distinction there, and displayed a passion for horses which her father found endearing but distinctly odd. Duff was less wedded to horses but deeply committed to country pursuits, rivalling his godfather Peter Fleming in his enthusiasm for the destruction of furred or feathered creatures. 'Duffy and some farmer friends today shot 106 hares,' Rupert recorded with mild dismay. 'The older I get, the less do I sympathise with the slaughter of animals.'[34] Duff was 'an excellent boy, and clever,' his father judged; 'but without any literary bent' – a curious misconception of one who was to earn his living almost entirely by the pen.[35] He won a bursary to Oxford but after only a few months threatened to leave. 'Since I voluntarily left Oxford myself after two years, and have never for a moment regretted that action, I don't feel justified in trying much persuasion,' Rupert explained to Blunden.[36] His reticence did no harm. Duff changed his mind and stayed on.

Rupert took the same relaxed view of his parental role a few years later when Duff, shortly after starting his first job at the *Sunday Telegraph*, became engaged to Phyllida Barstow. George Lyttelton hoped that Duff would not make the mistake of marrying too young. 'Since I was first married at twenty-two, and again at twenty-six, I am not in a strong position to tell him that he is too young at twenty-four and a half,' Rupert retorted.[37] Given the disaster Rupert's first marriage had proved, it might have been thought that he was well placed to issue a warning, but he restrained any such inclination and Duff duly entered into a marriage that was a source of unbroken gratification to his father. Two years or so later Bridget followed her brother's example, marrying a successful lawyer, David Trustram-Eve, whose father, another lawyer, was shortly to become Lord Silsoe. Rupert found the experience daunting. 'I feel it's lucky that I have only one darling daughter,' he told Blunden, 'for the business of the wedding is occupying the greater part of my life. There look like being 250 at the wedding reception, and I am wondering whether 144 bottles of champagne will do. There must be *some* teetotallers about.'[38] Evidently there were; in the event only 120 bottles were drunk.

Financially Bridget and Duff could now look after themselves. Adam, however, was still at Eton and in 1956 the situation seemed bleak. 'How long can dwindling income and non-existent capital continue to meet missing fees?' Rupert demanded rhetorically. 'Never mind, it's so long since I was able to see more than a month or two ahead (if that) that I've given up that sort of worry altogether.'[39] As usual his insouciance was justified. Hugh Walpole's sister died and left him £1,000; it was not a fortune but in those days it was enough to see Adam through the last years of his schooling. He emerged festooned with honours – 'he remains withal his old self, very affectionate and simple and undemanding'[40] – and his Open Scholarship to Merton College, Oxford, ensured that the rest of his education would not put an intolerable burden on his father's scanty funds.

The time had almost come when Rupert's marital impasse was to be resolved. For the moment his double life continued. Comfort, though she continued to make a secure home for her children, was in a sad way. She suffered from anxiety and depression and was fed a battery of drugs to make her existence possible; her heavy smoking was beginning to do serious harm – she was 'coughing continuously like a sea-lion,' Rupert wrote unsympathetically.[41] She still from time to time appeared in public as Rupert's titular wife: when Rupert lectured at Oxford on Oscar Wilde she came to the dinner party that David Cecil gave afterwards – 'All very agreeable and I *think* Comfort enjoyed herself,' Rupert reported.[42] A less happy occasion must have been the silver wedding party that he gave at the Garrick Club. He looked forward to this occasion with deep foreboding. 'My old father is equal to at least four wet blankets, and now Comfort has invited her mother, with whom I am barely on speaking terms, to come for a preliminary drink,' he told Lyttelton. 'Why did I suggest it? Why was I ever married at all?' To make things even more unfortunate, the fact that he was having the party made Ruth unhappy: 'I think she's all right now, but her misery made me feel miserable too.'[43]

They were not entirely happy years, made less so by his health. Though outwardly robust, Rupert was both something of a hypochondriac and unusually vulnerable to bad colds and influenza. He made things worse by occasional bouts of fasting; whenever he was following a regime he felt alternately ravenous and bloated, 'also rather frail, light-headed and irritable'.[44] Some of his afflictions were probably psychosomatic, but there was nothing imaginary about the jaundice which he contracted in May 1959. He was in bed at Bromsden for several weeks. Comfort, who was working as a teacher and enjoying her job, felt disinclined to stay at home to nurse her husband. Instead she sent for Ruth. 'Ruth was knocked sideways by this astonishing invitation,' wrote Joyce Grenfell, 'but came not knowing how it would be, simply because there was real need.' The two women quickly established a relationship which, if not affectionate, at least was based on mutual tolerance. 'Comfort was quite easy in a shy way,' Grenfell went on, 'and as Ruth is very shy too I imagine they hopped round each other like birds. But it worked and they got on quite well together for *three weeks!*'[45] Rupert was probably equally surprised but accepted the situation gratefully: 'The two of them get on well,' he told Lyttelton, 'so I am wonderfully looked after and not separated from Ruth.'[46] The disease was less pleasant than the treatment. 'Sorry young Hart-Davis has the jaundice,' Evelyn Waugh wrote breezily to Rupert's aunt, Diana Cooper; 'may be cancer of the liver.'[47] It wasn't, but it felt as bad. Diana herself was more sympathetic but her consolation was not calculated to make Rupert notably more cheerful. She was so sad, she wrote, to hear of Rupert's 'yellow predicament'. She had had it twice herself and knew 'that melancholy and suicide are rampant supporters'.[48] T. S. Eliot was more obscure but almost equally unhelpful. His comfort was 'one which I have given myself when lowered by some ailment – to reflect that my inclination to murder, mayhem or suicide is due to physical causes. Let me hope you can apply the same poor salve to your affliction.'[49] The affliction lingered on for several months; it was July before he was able to venture back to the office.

Through 1960 he was physically more or less unscathed, then in 1961 he began to feel listless and ill. At first it was thought to be a recurrence of the jaundice; then a diverticulum in the duodenum was diagnosed; then he was said to have lumbago; then an osteopath discovered a displaced vertebra. He was 'under observation' he told Arthur Ransome. Ransome was perturbed: 'Doctors and surgeons are so damned inquisitive. They always want to look round the corner and hate letting their patients get out of reach.'[50] After a few days at the Middlesex Hospital he was released and in the end his affliction disappeared. Nobody seemed to have any very clear idea as to what had been the matter, nor was he given any good reason to believe that his troubles would not recur. It was not a comforting background to the turbulent publishing scene that awaited him in the office.

Somehow the books continued to appear – though not enough of them and far too few that yielded even a modest profit. In the six years in which the firm was owned by Heinemann's 286 books were published – all of which, Rupert was accustomed to boast, 'I had to read, and often edit, punctuate and even rewrite'.[51] His contribution was, indeed, substantial but he overstated it. Some of the books he not merely left unread but preferred to pretend were not on the list at all. With reluctance he admitted the existence of 'a frightful book by Stanley Cullis about the Wolverhampton Wanderers Football Club'.[52] His firm had been saddled with this because Heinemann's were the official publishers for the Football Association and, though they were committed to this title, it did not bear the Association's imprimatur. A book that even Heinemann's would not publish – earth had not anything to show less fair. The final insult was that it sold out its first printing of 5,000 copies before publication, 'which is more than can be said of most of my precious literary books. It only goes to show!' But though he deemed it 'frightful' it is highly unlikely that Rupert even glanced at it. Nor can one imagine that he devoted much attention to Erma Harvey James's *Unusual Vegetables* or Kenyon Goode's *I Couldn't Cook Either*.

Whatever he might say, editorially Hart-Davis's was by no means a one-man band. Richard Garnett was by the mid-1950s taking on an increasing number of the books, while James Chesterman was responsible for one or two of the most important authors. Chesterman, after barely a fortnight with the firm, had found the typescript of Harrer's *Seven Years in Tibet* thrust into his hands. The translation from the German was appalling, he had been told, and needed complete rewriting; it was far too long and should be cut by almost a half – a substantial book club order hung on the result and, to meet it, a revised text was necessary within two weeks. Ruth was temporarily evicted from her office and Chesterman left to get on with it. It was a remarkable act of faith on Rupert's part, seeing how little he knew about his new recruit, but his confidence was rewarded. He did not habitually get round to praising anyone in the office but on this occasion Chesterman earned a gruff 'Well done!'

When Chesterman moved across to Heinemann's – a change of allegiance which Rupert was initially inclined to view as treachery but which later he forgave – the young novelist and translator David Hughes took his place. Hughes had been styled 'Literary Adviser' when working for his previous publisher and one day asked Rupert whether he could use a similar title in his new office. 'I don't need advice, literary or otherwise,' came the stern reply. Hughes had been taken on specifically to bring in new and younger authors. He did not find the task an easy one. When he proudly produced the typescript of David Storey's *This Sporting Life*, insisting that it was a work of striking merit,

Rupert took it, read it – or at least looked at it – overnight and returned it next morning with a scornful 'inexorably third rate'.

John Gross, future editor of the *Times Literary Supplement* and a man of letters up to even Rupert's exacting standards, was also brought in as reader and part-time editor. He had in the past been a junior editor with Victor Gollancz and found his new employer far more stylish and enjoyable to work with, if not necessarily more likely to make both ends meet in commercial terms. In 1959 Nicolas Barker, scholar and bibliophile who was one day to occupy Rupert's position in the chair at the London Library, arrived to take over the production work, thus freeing Garnett to spend more time with authors. It was an energetic and talented team: the pity was that Rupert did not make full use of its members, but kept the business of commissioning new books almost entirely in his own – horribly over-committed – hands.

John Gross, who had considerable knowledge of New York publishing, had hoped that he would be called on to suggest new American writers and put his contacts to good use. He was disappointed. Rupert kept all dealings with American publishers to himself. In 1961 he took Ruth with him on a visit to New York. 'I happen to have been in that violent city when both King George V and King George VI died,' he had told G. M. Young some years before. 'I wonder what the Royal Family would pay to stop me going there again!'[53] No offer was made so off they went, travelling by sea since Rupert's morbid fear of flying was unabated – the airport bore the same relation to the aeroplane, he once remarked, as the tumbril to the guillotine.[54] For three weeks he followed the same hectic schedule, six or more business appointments a day and an avalanche of theatres, dinners, cocktail parties. With Ruth there to help read the typescripts and bear the brunt of the entertaining it was the most enjoyable of his publishing visits to the United States. It was not notably successful, however. 'I didn't get any exciting books to publish, but I'm sure we gained a lot of good will instead,' he wrote in his memoirs.[55] Goodwill was a commodity of which Rupert was never short; his colleagues would willingly have traded some of it for a few exciting books.

For himself, he remained dedicated to his 'precious literary books' which had been so badly outsold by Cullis on Wolverhampton Wanderers. George Lyttelton told Rupert of a conversation he had overheard in which somebody had referred to a huge and scholarly critical study of the fifteenth-century Lancastrian poet Sir Richard Roos, which had been written by an Oxford don and was shortly to appear on the Hart-Davis list. There wouldn't be much money in that, some cynic had remarked, whereupon someone else observed that 'Rupert Hart-Davis didn't worry very much about that side of publishing.'[56] As it happened, in this case the book was handsomely subsidised so the accusation – if that was how it was intended – was beside the mark. Even though it was not actually going to lose money, however, it was certainly not going to make much; and Rupert, indeed, did not worry very much about that.

Nor was the firm likely to make much profit out of a collection of sonnets by Charles Tennyson Turner, younger brother of the Poet Laureate. These were taken on at the urging of John Betjeman, who agreed to select the poems and write a preface. He was paid £25 for his work. 'I am afraid this seems a very small reward for all your trouble,' Rupert wrote apologetically, 'but the book will be hard enough to sell at fifteen shillings.'[57] Rupert already knew and admired Turner's work and little urging was needed to persuade him to take it on. Sometimes he proved less receptive, even to the most literary of proposals. In 1962 Frances Partridge tried to persuade him that a collection of the letters from the critic and conversationalist Desmond MacCarthy would be a publishable proposition. 'I greatly respect Hart-Davis's scholarship,' Partridge wrote in her diary after an initial discussion. 'He's also a natural all-rounder, a Bonham-Carter almost, but does he deliberately set out to charm?' If he did, there were limits to the efforts he was prepared to make. He returned MacCarthy's letters with a brisk dismissal: 'He's a charming person with very little to say and no great gift for letter writing.'[58] His verdict would have been just the same, the dismissal indeed would have been still brisker, if the letters had been crammed with salacious and commercially exploitable scandal. The question of their saleability was a secondary consideration in Rupert's mind.

Fortunately, not all scholarly books or books of literary quality were for that reason unprofitable. Michael Howard's brilliant study of the Franco-Prussian War made nobody rich but brought the firm cash as well as credit. Patrick O'Brian's *The Unknown Shore*, the last of his naval books before he began on the great Aubrey/Maturin series, was also comfortably in the black; he was one of the staff's favourite authors – 'punctual, courteous, deferential and realistic in his expectations.'[59] But a disquietingly large proportion of Rupert's books were caviare to the general: eminently worth publishing, impeccably produced, but not calculated to stir much enthusiasm among the directors of Heinemann's or run-of-the-mill booksellers. It was always with great reluctance, too, that he refused a friend or dropped an established author. The third volume of L. E. Jones's delightful memoirs, *Georgian Afternoon*, sold over 6,000 copies but it was clear that with it Jones had shot his bolt. Nevertheless Rupert stuck with him and published a fourth volume of autobiography, a collection of poems and two volumes of short stories. The sales crept ever downwards, from the derisory to the disastrous.

There were a handful of profit-makers among his close friends and relations. Duff Cooper had already done Rupert well, now the memoirs of Duff's wife, Lady Diana, became a striking success. These had been undertaken at Rupert's urging; Diana, from the start, had doubts about the enterprise. She wrote ten thousand words of colourful, haphazard and gloriously uninhibited prose, was dismayed on reading them and sent them for rewriting to a journalist friend. The result was tidier, grammatically correct and pallid in comparison with the original. Diana sent both versions to Rupert, who was delighted by the first and dismayed by the second. The revise was abandoned: 'My editor insists on making a proper monkey out of me,' Diana explained to her rejected friend.[60] Rupert also did a lot to the text but contrived to keep the vitality and high spirits of the original, and both sales and critical acclaim were enough to convince Diana that she must engage in a second volume. This too sold well. She had a triumphant signing session in Hatchard's. Evelyn Waugh maintained that 80 per cent of the 500 copies sold were to members of the bookshop staff queuing up in different guises; Rupert's story was that Waugh appeared 'extremely tipsy and bullied everyone who came into the shop to buy a copy'.[61]

By the time Diana got to the third and saddest volume, leading up to Duff's death, inspiration and energy were running out. Rupert had cut out all her favourite bits, she complained to Waugh, who was quick to make mischief. 'I'm sorry you let Hart-Davis over-rule you into curtailing it,' he told her. 'The artist is the sole judge of his own scope.' There was trouble too about the title. Diana wanted to call it *Noisy Years*; Rupert argued that the first two books had taken their titles from Wordsworth's 'Intimations of Immortality' and the third should follow suit. He suggested *Trumpets from the Steep* and had his way – 'the silliest possible title,' Diana wrote crossly, 'most unsuited to the cover picture'.[62] At one time there was talk of a fourth volume to cover her widowhood. Rupert glanced through Wordworth's poem to find a possible title and emerged triumphantly with: 'The Pansy at my feet'. Sadly the book was never written and the title remained unused.[63*]

Peter Fleming was an old friend who continued to support the Hart-Davis list. In all Rupert published ten of his books. The seven from the Heinemann years included some of his best-sellers, among them *Invasion 1940* which involved much tedious and expensive rewriting to suit the whims of the Cabinet Office. Fleming knew that many other publishers would be delighted to take him over and would probably sell considerably more copies of his books, but it never occurred to him to abandon ship. His loyalty and generosity were unwavering. Only with extreme reluctance and under pressure from his agent did he ask Rupert to do like every other tenant on the estate and take on a repairing lease for Bromsden. 'Sorry to be so mercenary,' he apologised; though since the house had just been refurbished at the cost of the estate it was unlikely that any expense would be involved for the next few years.[64]

Not all Rupert's old friends were so undemanding or so profitably productive. The case of Nancy Cunard shows well the enormous pains to which he was prepared to go on a project to which he felt personally committed. In November 1955 she sent in an impressionistic biography of the man whom she believed to be her father, the novelist George Moore. Rupert welcomed it enthusiastically and then subjected it to harsh criticism. The proposed title was meaningless: 'I don't go quite so far as Samuel Butler, who said that a good title was one which told anyone who knew anything about the subject that they didn't need to read the book, but I am tremendously in favour of titles being as informative as possible.' Her style, he went on, was in many respects deplorable, the balance of the book was wrong, the epilogue was unnecessary: 'it seems to me to lie like a dead weight, far too heavily flavoured with religion'. 'Don't let all these minor criticisms dismay you, darling Nancy,' he concluded disarmingly. 'This is, after all, my job, at which I have spent 25 years, and I shouldn't feel I was being the least use to you if I didn't tell you exactly what I thought.'[65]

Over the next few months he took endless pains to check up on dates and references, to track down obscure illustrations, to identify unknown names. He wrote her thirty-two letters between 1 November 1955 and 1 June 1966. She was duly grateful and on the whole took his strictures meekly. Her only insistence was that the epilogue should remain,

---

* 'The Pansy at my feet/Doth the same tale repeat.' The earlier titles had been *The Rainbow Comes and Goes* and *The Light of Common Day*.

though in a truncated form; when two of the reviewers singled it out for special praise, Rupert handsomely admitted 'how right you were'.[66] But now the trouble started. Nancy suggested she should come to work in Soho Square. Appalled at the prospect of this supremely disruptive egoist on the loose in his office, Rupert explained that, much though he regretted it, there was no vestige of a vacancy. He urged her to go on writing.[67] She suggested a travel book on Africa. There were too many already, Rupert replied: 'The book for you to write is the story of your own life – the one book that *only you* can possibly write.'[68] It could indeed have been an enthralling and enticingly scandalous story, but when she finally put in a first draft Rupert found to his dismay that it was beyond redemption. He told her that 'it was fragmented, lacked direction and was not sufficiently personal and lively'.[69] If she had seen the force of his criticism and had appealed to him for help then, in spite of misgivings, he would undoubtedly have sunk himself in the task of trying to salvage something from the wreck. It was too much to expect, however; depressed and angry she withdrew her manuscript. Rupert was genuinely saddened, for he was fond of Nancy and respected her talents, but he also felt some relief. He had been saved a great deal of hard work on an enterprise which could never have been entirely satisfactory, either in literary or financial terms. The directors of Heinemann's would have applauded his conduct but were more alive to the fact that he had devoted hundreds of working hours to Nancy Cunard's published book, *GM: Memories of George Moore*, even though only 3,000 copies had been printed and many of those remained unsold.

By the end of 1960 Rupert was telling George Lyttelton of a two-hour meeting, 'outspoken and acrimonious', at which the future of the group had been discussed without any very constructive ideas being put forward.[70] Hart-Davis's continued to record mounting losses: about £15,000 in 1961, nearly £22,000 the following year. Rupert would have said that this was because of the size of Heinemann's overheads and the incompetence of the services they provided; Heinemann's blamed Rupert's insistence on publishing unsaleable books and his indifference to commercial success. Both parties had a point. Worse still, the board of Thomas Tilling was becoming restive. As Lionel Fraser's co-director, Sir George Briggs, kept demanding: 'How much longer, Mr Chairman, are we to go on throwing money out of the window just to satisfy the whim of being civilised – which we are not?'[71] The answer, though nobody suspected it at the time, was 'not that long'.

In 1960 the problem had almost been resolved, at least as far as Tilling's were concerned. Rupert told George Lyttelton that his spies reported a plot was afoot to sell Heinemann's to 'an American tycoon . . . I don't much like the sound of it.'[72] The spy was Harry Townshend, who had come across a copy of a memorandum which showed that the whole concern was on the point of being sold to the American publishing giant McGraw Hill. He at once alerted Rupert, who found an ally in Fred Warburg, head of Secker & Warburg's, which had also been sucked into the maw of Heinemann's. Warburg, and Heinemann's export manager, Alewyn Birch, liked the sound of it even less than Rupert. Together they set out to block the sale. 'The three of us were constantly in touch during that hectic period,' recalled Birch. 'None of us was in any sense anti-McGraw Hill . . . But we believed very passionately that a country's culture cannot be represented by a publisher from another country.'[73] They appealed to Lionel Fraser, who had been led to believe that everyone was in favour of the sale, and at once broke off negotiations. Alan Hill, another director of Heinemann's, had regretfully come to believe that the sale was desirable. Hill considered Rupert to be 'professionally the archetypal, almost Edwardian man-of-letters rather than a down-to-earth publisher' and deplored the fact that a sensible solution had been thwarted by 'a fringe group, drawn from two small, recently acquired, loss-making companies, together with Alewyn Birch'.[74] Like it or not, however, the deal was dead.

The problem still had to be resolved. Heinemann's by now were in a desperate plight. In April 1961 a merger with Bodley Head was mooted; once again Rupert opposed it; once again the idea was dropped. It would anyway not have served its purposes. The relationship with Heinemann's became every day more strained and Rupert felt himself as much under pressure and as physically debilitated as he had done during the original takeover six years before. Then suddenly a white knight emerged, eager to rescue Hart-Davis's from the dragon's cave in which it was immured. Rupert's objections to McGraw Hill had always been based more on the fact that the house was heavily biased towards scientific and technical publishing than that it was American; he agreed with Birch that in an ideal world British publishing should remain in British hands, but the world seemed ever less ideal and this beggar at least recognised that he could not be a chooser. It was with the ardent support of Rupert that Bill Jovanovich, President of the American firm of Harcourt Brace, opened negotiations with Heinemann's for the purchase of Hart-Davis's.

Chapter Fourteen

False Dawn

Bill Jovanovich was the son of a Yugoslav peasant who had found his way to the United States and made a decent living in a Pittsburgh steelworks. From this modest and far from cultured background Jovanovich rose with startling speed, achieved every sort of academic honour and by the age of thirty-four had become President of one of America's mightiest publishing houses. Rupert had met him several times in London and New York and had been impressed by his energy, authority and respect for literature and learning. Jovanovich for his part found that Rupert personified the Old World dignity and integrity which he most admired. The two men were quick to identify each other's qualities; it took longer for them to discover that these were not the whole story and that what seemed so admirable on first acquaintance might begin to appear less so when subjected to the wear and tear of a publishing business.

Harcourt Brace – or at any rate Jovanovich – were looking for a London presence; a firm of solidly established reputation whose productions would bring credit to their name. The plan was that whatever British subsidiary they selected would gradually be enlarged to accommodate the sort of book they had to sell, including their large and important academic list. It is today difficult to conceive what led them to imagine that Hart-Davis's would prove a suitable instrument for marketing their wares in Britain. For Rupert, the main attraction of Harcourt Brace was that they were not Heinemann's. In principle he was quite prepared to expand on the lines Jovanovich anticipated; though he did not imagine that this would amount to much. What mattered most was that his new owner would be in New York rather than Mayfair, would pump in new funds, and would leave him in peace to carry on with what he was already doing though on a larger scale. The long-term aspirations of the two parties were in fact widely different, but the miasma of goodwill with which Rupert and Jovanovich enshrouded themselves ensured that both men were satisfied their minds had met in total harmony.

Heinemann's were at first curiously reluctant to sell their ailing protégé. 'They seemed to think that selling anything to America was in some way selling the pass,' observed Rupert censoriously;[1] a somewhat uncharitable comment given his own fierce opposition to the takeover by McGraw Hill less than a year before. After a few weeks, however, Heinemann's relented and let Hart-Davis's go at a price based on the value of the assets plus a more-or-less nominal £5,000 for goodwill.[2] Commercially they had done a very reasonable deal; their pride was damaged, though, by the overt determination of their most distinguished literary subsidiary to escape from their control in favour of a transatlantic raider. For Rupert the stakes were high. Heinemann's not only paid his salary but owned his office, his flat, his car. If negotiations broke down the atmosphere, already sour, would become intolerable and his future alarmingly uncertain. As it was, after what he described to Edmund Blunden as 'nerve-racking negotiations', a deal was done and his firm became the property of Harcourt Brace at the beginning of 1962. 'I'm sure this is the right answer,' he wrote, 'and for the first time in years I can feel hope and enthusiasm flowing back. Doubtless most of my illnesses have had their origin in the hopelessness of my business situation.'[3] He seems never to have wondered whether his firm was qualified to undertake the sale of substantial quantities of American text books. 'This seems to me to make admirable sense,' he told T. S. Eliot confidently. 'In these days I can see no other way of a business like mine surviving.'[4]

He himself benefited dramatically by the change. His flat and car were safe and his salary was raised to £4,000 a year, a considerable amount by publishing standards. Almost for the first time in his working life he had no overdraft. The office seethed with new energy and an ebullient sensation of going places; a representative of Harcourt Brace was sent over to help set up an education department, to be based in a separate office in nearby Dean Street. The list of directors swelled impressively; Margaret Lane commented that it was rather like the 'beginning of a symbolic novel, with Jahveh, Jehovah or God the Father taking a part'. She added a prescient word of warning: 'I hope it turns out like that, though the Jehovah of the Jews was never a character I felt I could put much trust in.'[5] Rupert seemed busier than ever but for the first time in years he felt that he was in control of and relishing his activities. 'The new publishing arrangement is so exciting and many-sided that my office time looks like being pretty full,' he told George Lyttelton. 'I already have more work than one secretary can cope with.'[6]

One of the best things from Rupert's point of view was that Harry Townshend was persuaded by Bill Jovanovich to return from Heinemann's to throw in his lot with his old firm. From the point of view of his own future it was a brave, even gallant decision, but Jovanovich assured him that, come what might, he would never let Hart-Davis's down, and Townshend quashed whatever doubts he might have had. Distribution was now once more handled from Soho Square and the calamitous inefficiency of the Heinemann regime was quickly forgotten. There was, indeed, only one galling feature about the new arrangements. Jovanovich insisted that Ruth must leave the firm, according to Rupert because 'she and I were living together'.[7] Another view is that Ruth did not fit into any accepted organisation pattern and that Jovanovich recoiled from what he felt to be the messiness and inefficiency involved. Rupert was distressed by the development but was in no position to make it a breaking point. In fact Ruth was not treated ungenerously; she was given a golden handshake of £500 and her departure was made into more of a phased retreat than an abrupt dismissal.

It was a stroke of good fortune that the launch of the new enterprise more or less coincided with the completion of Rupert's work on Oscar Wilde. This had absorbed a substantial part of his energies over the previous seven years: it was the sort of work he most enjoyed, he told his sister, 'making order out of chaos, turning a great many bits of paper into a readable book'.[8] There was an element of self-indulgence in his labours. If a reference amused or intrigued him he would pursue it relentlessly, even though its relevance to his central subject was at best tenuous; for instance, he told Edmund Blunden, he could not resist adding a footnote saying that the architect of St Aloysius in Oxford, a church frequented by Wilde as an undergraduate, was Joseph Aloysius Hansom, who also invented the Hansom cab.[9] But there was much of real importance among the trivia. There had been a prolonged debate about whether it was appropriate to include in the collected letters the text of Oscar Wilde's great apologia, 'De Profundis', the letter written in Reading gaol and, formally at least, addressed to Lord Alfred Douglas. The original editor, Allan Wade, thought that to include it would throw the book out of balance; Rupert at first agreed, then reconsidered. All doubts were dispelled when he and Ruth became the first people to see the original manuscript of the letter which had been deposited in the British Museum under a fifty-year embargo. He at once realised that this differed in many respects from the published version. Thus he achieved the considerable *coup* of including in his volume the first correct rendering of Wilde's most important letter.

Over the twelve months before the corrected, re-corrected and re-recorrected proofs were finally consigned to the presses, the luckless printer received a constant flow of last minute additions, emendations, afterthoughts. Those in charge of the accounts at Hart-Davis's were perhaps still more luckless; Richard Garnett estimates that 'the corrections bill must have been at least a fifth of the book's total production cost'.[10] The consequence was that the book made a much smaller profit than might have been expected from its sales. The results, however, were still satisfactory, particularly so far as the income from foreign rights was concerned. Half the royalties went to Vyvyan Holland; even so Rupert recorded with some satisfaction that his share would pay for the whole of Adam's Oxford career. Perhaps, he told George Lyttelton wryly, 'one day I'll produce a book whose royalties I can spend on myself.'[11]

The book's reception, however, meant far more to Rupert than the money he might earn by it. It could hardly have been more gratifying. The same assembly of critical big guns as had applauded his biography of Walpole – Harold Nicolson, Cyril Connolly, Raymond Mortimer, Anthony Powell, John Sparrow – now thundered respectfully. They were, except perhaps for Connolly, personal friends and thus disposed to be generous in public; but Nicolson's diary entry, not intended for the author's eyes, was approving: 'He really is a scholar, that man. He has taken immense trouble in his editing.'[12] Friends were still more effusive in their letters. 'You needn't bother to do anything else. This is your sufficient monument,' wrote Eric Linklater, while Peter Fleming was enchanted by the footnotes which, 'like Oriental servants anticipating one's need for a *chotah peg* are at hand before it has occurred to one to summon them; they succeed each other in the same sort of aura of omniscience, indefatigability, courtesy and resource that used to emanate from good Chinese servants.'[13] It was, indeed, a prodigious achievement, and one in which Rupert could take great pride.[14]*

---

* Fifteen years later he learnt that the British Museum copy of the *Letters* had been stolen. 'Some poor wretch must have been desperate,' he observed with satisfaction.

The completion of the *Letters* left him free to devote himself more wholeheartedly to his publishing. Anxious as he was to prove that Harcourt Brace had been right to put its faith in him, he rejoiced in his new-found liberty. And yet he found himself curiously deflated. 'I am so accustomed to having some editing or kindred work on hand that I feel rather empty without any,' he told Lyttelton.[15] For years he had been accumulating the published works of Edmund Blunden, in every form and edition. Now he began a long-meditated bibliography. The author himself was due back from the Far East for a few months. 'Bibliography would like to claim a good share of your time,' Rupert warned him. 'As well as EB I have started working, whenever MSS and proofs permit, on the letters from Max Beerbohm to Reggie Turner, which have been held up for years by my Oscar labours.'[16]

But such diversions, though time-consuming, did not make demands on Rupert's energies remotely comparable to his labours on the Wilde *Letters*. Other burdens also were removed; though Rupert would never have admitted that his correspondence with George Lyttelton was in any way burdensome. 'Oh, George, how many books there are to read and re-read and enjoy and talk about, and how little time I seem to have for this, my greatest pleasure,' Rupert had lamented when they first began to exchange letters.[17] 'Talking about books' was at the heart of their correspondence, and the writing of the weekly letter gave Rupert a pleasure almost as great as reading. He carried on until the week of Lyttelton's death from cancer; by this time he knew that his old friend was too ill to take in what was going on, but 'I clearly must go on writing, in case he improves and asks for my letter'.[18] Even before he died, Rupert was at work on Lyttelton's obituary. The problem was that very little had actually happened in Lyttelton's life to disturb the even tenor of his career as schoolmaster, 'and somehow one must avoid making him sound like Mr Chips, whom George abhorred'.[19] He died on 1 May 1962. 'I still can't quite accept his disappearance,' Rupert told Blunden, 'and find myself making notes in my mind of things that will amuse him.'[20]

The writing of the weekly letter – with all the surreptitious checking of references, and search for felicitous quotations – had taken at least an hour, sometimes two or three hours every Sunday. That time was now free. So was the time which he had used to devote to the monthly round-up of new crime novels for *Time and Tide*, since that long-faltering journal finally expired in 1960. Nobody who knew Rupert would have believed that he could totally free himself from the many preoccupations that beset his daily life, but the fact remains that, in January 1962, at the age of fifty-five, he addressed himself to publishing with an energy and wholeheartedness that he had not exhibited since those heady, early days when the firm was just beginning.

It was high time. Though never altogether in the doldrums, the pace of his publishing had grown sluggish over the final years with Heinemann's. Some of the old staples had ceased to figure in the lists. The Mariners Library was fast drying up and booksellers were increasingly unenthusiastic about additions to the existing corpus. The Countryman list – never close to Rupert's heart with its homespun manuals such as *Keeping Pigs* and *Wine Growing in England* – had almost run its course. The Soho Bibliographies, whose range extended from Lucretius to the Sitwells, was a distinguished collection of great use to scholars but unlikely to generate much in the way of cash flow. Important series, like the fifteen volumes of Ibsen translated by Michael Meyer, the seventeen volumes of Coleridge, and the monumental edition of Dickens's letters, redounded to the credit of the house and were kindly viewed by Harcourt Brace. To Rupert's critics, however, they seemed more appropriate to an academic press which could view its annual profit or loss with slightly greater detachment than an allegedly commercial publisher.

New turnover was urgently needed, and the quickest way to achieve it was by taking over another publisher with an existing list. One such was Adlard Coles, a small nautical publisher based in Southampton. Coles himself – 'rather a muddler but certainly honest and a most agreeable man', Rupert described him[21] – remained on the south coast and left the administration of his firm largely to Richard Garnett. The faintly patronising tone of Rupert's judgment sums up his attitude towards the undertaking: indifference tinged with kindly contempt. Nor was he more directly concerned with another new undertaking. 'People' – by whom he meant Harcourt Brace – 'tell me I should have a children's list,' he complained to Tom Wilson of the Harvard University Press. 'But I don't know what to do.' 'Hire my sister,' suggested Mrs Wilson. Her sister was Marni Hodgkin, an American editor married to an immensely distinguished Cambridge professor of biophysics and wanting a proper job in England. Rupert, the Wilsons told her, was 'a sweet old thing', looking like 'a very large white rabbit'. They liked and admired him, but considered Ruth was the more forceful of the two, both as a person and as a publisher. In this they were wrong, but their view is a useful corrective to the more usual judgment that Ruth was a doormat who asked for nothing better than to sustain Rupert in all his whims and wishes. Rupert met Marni Hodgkin, liked her, asked her how much she felt she ought to be paid and met her wishes, and installed her, first with the packers in the basement, then briefly in his spare bedroom, finally in a different building at the back. That more or less concluded his interest in the children's list.[22]

Knowing that new initiatives were called for, David Hughes contrived to infiltrate into the firm a young editor and would-be writer with a background in magazines – Brendan Lehane. Together Lehane and Hughes cooked up an idea for a series of quick books on current issues to rival the celebrated Penguin Specials. Lehane swiftly prepared a memorandum setting out his plan, presented it to Rupert and sat back to await a lengthy discussion and, with luck, action to follow. Instead he found himself fobbed off with odd jobs, checking stock for the catalogue or proof-reading some of the twelve volumes of Henry James's short stories which were being edited by Leon Edel. From time to time Rupert would mutter to Lehane that they really must fix a time for a proper discussion of his interesting ideas, but such a moment never seemed to come. In an effort to get things moving Lehane bearded John McCallum, a vice-president of Harcourt Brace who happened to be visiting London, and gave him a copy of his memorandum. McCallum was delighted; the project, he felt, was just what the firm ought to be undertaking. Within an hour Lehane was summoned to Rupert's office and was told that his ideas were most impressive, meetings would shortly be arranged, progress would be made. Then McCallum returned to the United States; with relief Rupert pushed to the back of his mind a proposition which he had always found unappealing and which was anyway inappropriate to his firm. Lehane found himself back with the catalogue and his proof-reading and after a few more weeks resigned and went elsewhere. Rupert was characteristically courteous, made a decent show of appearing regretful and was patently relieved at his departure.[23]

The truth was that, though Rupert was well disposed towards Harcourt Brace, was grateful for their investment and anxious to see the firm's publishing expand, he did not intend substantially to adapt its output to suit the new proprietor. If suitable best-sellers came along then well and good, but he did not mean to lower his standards so as to accommodate them. Unfortunately his 1962 list contained little in the way of best-sellers, suitable or otherwise. The nearest approach to a

sensation was Frances Donaldson's *The Marconi Scandal*. This landed
Rupert in an unpleasant contretemps, since Donaldson wished to
include Kipling's ferocious and decidedly distasteful poem 'Gehazi'
which denounced Rufus Isaacs, the Attorney-General at the time of the
scandal and possibly himself involved, as 'Judge in Israel, a leper white
as snow'. Stella, Marchioness of Reading, who as Gehazi's widow not
unnaturally took exception to the poem's inclusion, urged Rupert to
remove it. Rupert, however, felt that the poem was so well known that
to exclude it would attract more comment than to leave it in. Anyhow,
however nasty its tone, it was a fine piece of invective that deserved
another airing. He ruled that it must stay in. 'Poor Stella,' Joyce
Grenfell commented, but it was poor Rupert too. He had no wish to
offend a woman whom he respected, even if he did not particularly like
her, and the unpleasantness caused by the episode was one of the several
causes which contributed to his growing disenchantment with publishing as the year wore on.

Another was his limited enthusiasm for the titles that Harcourt Brace
added to Hart-Davis's list. One of these, *Conversations with Stalin* by
Milovan Djilas, the dissident Yugoslav politician, deservedly created
quite a stir and sold well, but the others were worthy, respectable but
neither significant in content nor distinguished in style. It was a very
different Harcourt Brace title, however, that provoked the first overt
breach between Rupert and Bill Jovanovich. Mary McCarthy's new
novel, *The Group*, had created a great stir in the United States and sold
extremely well. Re-read today it seems a brilliantly written if rather
unpleasant book; the author displays an icy dislike for her characters
and for contemporary society which is shocking in its intensity but not
in its sexual explicitness. In 1963 it was the sex that shocked. Rupert
was not necessarily averse to strong meat but he took against what he
felt to be the drab prurience of *The Group*. He tried it on two or three
members of his staff and was fortified in his dislike. Although the book
had already been advertised in the trade press he now told Jovanovich
that he would not continue with it, giving as his main reason a legal
opinion – of unspecified source – that it contained obscenities and that
its publisher would probably be prosecuted. In considerable irritation,
Harcourt Brace then sold the rights to Weidenfeld & Nicolson, who
took a less serious view of the legal dangers. In fairness to Rupert it
should be said that he was not alone in his assessment of the book.
Another leading British publisher, Dwye Evans, told George Weidenfeld that Mary McCarthy's novel was 'Too American, too dirty. It

won't sell more than two thousand copies.' Weidenfeld & Nicolson in fact sold 200,000.[24]

To Jovanovich, Rupert's behaviour seemed a betrayal. He had championed the cause of Hart-Davis's against the mounting complaints of his colleagues and yet now, when he offered Rupert a book in which he personally believed and which he felt would transform the finances of the British house, he found it scornfully rejected. To Rupert it was a question of literary taste and good judgment; to Jovanovich it was a matter of loyalty and of sound commercial principles. The two minds failed to meet, and the failure poisoned the future relationship. The disagreement over *The Group* did more than any other single factor to make Jovanovich feel that he had been wrong when he chose Rupert as his standard-bearer in the Old World.

But this was only a stage in a gradual erosion of confidence. Harcourt Brace was heavily dependent on its institutional investors, who poured money into scientific publishing and expected a respectable profit in return. At first these people had barely noticed the acquisition of Rupert's firm, or accepted Jovanovich's assurance that it would provide a satisfactory instrument for the sale of academic books in Britain. Gradually, however, a series of visitors to London came back with alarming reports of how Hart-Davis's was run: it was too gentlemanly, too slow, too lackadaisical, too preoccupied with the appearance and literary quality of its books, too slow to push them in the market place or pick material that would have a better chance of selling. Harcourt Brace's academic titles failed to make the impact that had been anticipated in New York: partly because they were unsuitable for the British consumer, partly because Rupert's sales force had no real idea how to reach the market. Gradually discontent grew in the Harcourt Brace boardroom and Jovanovich, whose position was strong but by no means impregnable, found himself more and more beleaguered. Rupert could legitimately complain that the investment had been made on the basis of a five-year plan and that his firm had in no significant way fallen behind its undertakings; to Jovanovich the long-term prospects seemed bleak and the costs involved in defending his irritating protégé against the assaults of his fellow directors grew increasingly unacceptable.

His decision to cut his losses and dispose of Hart-Davis's as rapidly as possible was unheroic but forgivable. What cannot be condoned was the way the execution was carried out. In spite of his personal assurances to Rupert and other members of the firm that he would support them through thick and thin, he made no attempt to explain his position or to explore ways by which the ill effects might be mitigated. He never even came to London but sent over a relatively junior employee, Ed Hodge, to do the dirty work. Hodge appeared, unexplained, in Soho Square early in August 1963. Rupert provided him with office space, wondered why he had come and asked him whether he would like to visit Bromsden at the weekend. 'I'd better not,' said Hodge apologetically. 'I'm here to close you down.'

It was, Rupert told Edmund Blunden, 'one of the basest and most ruthless betrayals I have ever heard of in the publishing trade'.[25] He felt that he had been let down as a friend and condemned as a publisher; his own future was relatively secure since he had a five-year contract with Harcourt Brace but his staff, for whom he felt responsibility, faced dismissal and, in one or two cases, virtual destitution. 'On one of my flights to New York at your behest,' he reminded Bill Jovanovich, 'I was shown into your office and you jumped to your feet, put your arms round me and embraced me. To your secretary, who looked somewhat startled, you said: "In Montenegro, where I come from, when a man greets another man like that it means that whatever happens he'll never let him down." Too bad we weren't in Montenegro at the time.'[26]

Hodge's instructions were that he should first give Rupert the choice of going it alone. The offer was not ungenerous. If Rupert and Harry Townshend would waive their contractual rights as directors, worth some £32,000 over the next three and a half years, then they could have the firm and all its assets for nothing. The trouble was that there was no reason to believe it would show a profit in the immediate – or, indeed, on past record, distant – future, and, as Rupert explained to Blunden, 'we couldn't carry on for more than a month without financial assistance'. He did not rule out the possibility of finding a millionaire to buy the firm but time was short and August was not the best time to track down a benevolent plutocrat. His heart, anyway, was not really in the chase. 'In fact I shouldn't at all mind saying goodbye to publishing, of which I have had quite enough – 34 years – but not in this way, with so many sufferers and loose ends.' Meanwhile he sought solace in his own way: 'On Thursday Ruth and I sneaked away from the turmoil and spent a happy afternoon at the Oval.'[27]

A few millionaires flickered briefly on the horizon, but their promise came to nothing. The *Daily Express* at one moment seemed to be in an acquisitive mood – 'That would surely be a fate worse than death,' Rupert noted grimly – but their interest too proved fleeting. At one point he hoped that Thomas Nelson and Sons would take over the business, 'pay everyone and let it slowly and decently expire. This would avoid the danger of a liquidation, and they are very decent people.'[28] Quite what would have been in it for Nelson's it is hard to see; a point that presumably occurred to its directors for the negotiations quickly petered out. By this time Rupert had invoked the help of Arnold Goodman: solicitor, future peer and Master of University College, friend of the mighty and most consummate of fixers. Goodman was confident that a satisfactory solution could be found, but the danger always existed that Harcourt Brace might grow impatient and simply close the business down. On Rupert's birthday, 28 August, he told Deirdre:

> The girls in the office combined to buy me a red carnation, which almost made me cry. We have now got an extension until next Tuesday, Sept 3, and indeed if this tension and suspense don't end by then, I shall be removed by men in white coats . . . My little friend is the utmost comfort and joy to me, and I don't know how I could cope without her . . . I'm sure you're right, and that this will all turn out to be for the best, but I am weighed down by responsibilities to the staff (29 of them) and to countless authors, printers and others, who may be heavy losers if things go wrong.

Then Arnold Goodman pulled out of his hat Sidney Bernstein, creator and Chairman of the conglomerate Granada, whose interests sprawled widely over the entertainment world, from motorway cafés to television. Bernstein admired Rupert and would probably have encouraged him to remain at the helm, but even if a firm offer had been made it would have been rejected. Rupert had had more than enough of publishing, and indeed of life in London. He was offered a deal which met his minimum requirements and jumped at it. Granada had recently taken over another small publishing house, MacGibbon and Kee. It would make much better sense, Rupert concluded, to let its managing director, Reginald Davis-Poynter, be responsible for the running of their new acquisition and for himself to retire gracefully into a distant though still watchful role.

> A number of my staff will stay, including Richard Garnett [he told Blunden], and I shall be 'consulting editor'. No books will be published over my imprint except those chosen and recommended by me. Since what they want is a 'prestige' publishing house, this will absolve me from doing anything I don't like. They believe that by absorbing all the

expenses in the other businesses, except my consultant's fee of £2,000 a year, they can make even my books pay – and they may even be right. I shall probably stay on full time for a month or two, perhaps even to the end of the year, and then switch to being an out-of-the-office editor. I hope to stay in the flat as long as I want to, but there are a thousand details still to be fixed. The great thing is that the imprint will go on, with only the right sort of books, including the Collected Coleridge, the bibliographies, Henry James and all. *Laus Deo!*[29]

It all sounded too good to be true. So, to some extent, it proved to be. Granada, even wearing the mask of Rupert Hart-Davis Ltd, was a hopelessly unsuitable house for massively expensive literary publications. Rupert's next few months were partly occupied with finding a new home for these ambitious enterprises. The Dickens *Letters* and the Soho Bibliographies ended up with the Oxford University Press; the *Collected Coleridge* stayed where it was so long as Richard Garnett remained at Granada but in the end found its way to Routledge's. Financially, Granada kept their word to Rupert but the flat in Soho Square was not available for as long as he had hoped. By the middle of 1964 his goods were being packed up. 'In a way I shall be sad to leave here,' he told Blunden, 'but it is so noisy now, and Mr Bernstein is longing to move the business into a few cells in some soulless modern building.'[30]

The news that Harcourt Brace were about to pull the plug on its British subsidiary spread quickly around publishing London. Gerald Durrell's agent, Spencer Curtis Brown, decided to remove his charge to safer pastures with William Collins'. Unlike Jovanovich he went round in person to break the unwelcome news to Rupert. His reward was a tirade of abuse; Rupert called him 'a bloody shit' and accused him of nameless malpractices.[31] The incident illustrates the strain under which Rupert was working: Curtis Brown was perhaps being somewhat too quick in his reactions but he was still right to protect his client's interests. From Rupert's point of view, however, it was a cruel betrayal; it came at a time when he was still hoping to find a sponsor who would sustain him as an independent publisher and the defection of so profitable an author greatly weakened his position. Within a few weeks he was resigned to the inevitable. When Verily Anderson broke it to him that she too was jumping ship and moving to Cape's, he received the news benignly. 'What a good idea,' he said. 'I was just going broke anyway.'[32]

His friends and fellow publishers were ardently sympathetic. 'You

have done so much for so many literary gents including yours truly,'
John Betjeman told him, 'have been such a wonderful publisher and
producer of good looking books, such a champion of causes, all on top
of being so excellent and scholarly and READABLE a biographer . . .
As you say, it's not the cash that matters, but the dependents – also, to
the English world of letters, the loss of a great publisher and
enthusiastic non-Leavis-Lewis-Wainite.'[33] To C. V. Wedgwood it was a
disaster for English publishing, 'and so *unfair*, so intolerably unjust after
all you have done and achieved. There has been no more enlivening and
distinguished imprint in the post-war years.'[34] Several London publishers swore that they would have no further dealings with Harcourt Brace;
an assurance which, as is usual in such cases, lasted until the next
tempting proposition.

Rupert appreciated the encomia and the support, but once the deal
had been done and the essential elements of his publishing house
preserved, his main feeling was one of relief, almost satisfaction. When
he told Blunden that he would not mind saying goodbye to publishing
he had been telling no more than the truth. Over the last ten years he
had been growing ever more certain that this world was not for him,
that his true happiness lay elsewhere. 'I'm not really *au fond* a publisher
at all, you know,' he had told Blunden some years before, 'though it
becomes increasingly difficult to make anyone believe it . . . I'm really
some sort of literary bloke, who likes reading, writing, ferreting,
compiling, classifying – all that, and the sausage machine of endless new
books can grow very tedious.'[35] Now, unexpectedly, a chance had arisen
to escape the sausage machine. The debacle of his breach with Harcourt
Brace left Rupert with the bitterness of the failed and the resentment of
the betrayed but it also offered the hope that, for the first time, he
would do what he wanted to do in the way that he wanted to do it. At
the end of 1963 Rupert began a new life.

Rupert with his son Duff in the summer of 1938.

Hugh Walpole, Comfort and Rupert,
outside the Hart-Davis' house in Stormont Road, Hampstead.

Rupert as a Guardsman Recruit in 1940 and resplendent as Captain and Adjutant some four years later.

he family reunited in the summer of 1944. Duff and Bridget flank the infant Adam; Rupert monstrates that even in the most relaxed circumstances he is incapable of smiling at the camera.

Rupert, Ruth Simon and the American writer, Leon Edel, outside the office of Rupert Hart-Davis Ltd at 36 Soho Square.

Osbert Lancaster's vision of authors flocking Soho Square.

Richard Garnett, who joined the firm in 1947, played an ever more important part and is now its historian.

Ruth Simon, drawn by Consuelo Haydon.

Rupert and June,
shortly after their
marriage in 1968.

June; Rupert's friend and invaluable factotum, Boyk Sekers; and Joyce Grenfell.

The cottage on top of the hill outside Keld. There was already a Kisdon Farm and a Kisdon Cottage, so they called it Kisdon Lodge.

The Old Rectory, Marske-in-Swaledale.

The seventieth birthday party. June and Duff are at the back on the left with Boyk's widow, Nellie, between them. Adam is at the back on the far right and his wife is on the extreme left. Bridget is seated behind Rupert, next to Duff, and her husband is in front of Adam. Deirdre is behind Rupert's left shoulder.

Rupert, aged about ninety, at work in study at Marske.

Chapter Fifteen

A New Life

'Next Christmas I hope to be in Yorkshire with my darling Ruth,' Rupert told Edmund Blunden at the very end of 1963. 'She has been wonderfully patient for $17\frac{1}{2}$ years but is naturally longing for a husband and her own home.'[1] Nineteen sixty-four was to be a year of uprooting and renewal.

For many years Bromsden had been a place where Rupert's children lived and where he would go at weekends to write letters, work on books and renew acquaintance with his wife and family. Because he had never owned it, he had always been reluctant to spend much money on improvements. In winter it was damp, dark and cold; when a friend of Adam's who had spent most of his life in India came to stay he was 'almost rigid with cold. We keep buying him bedroom slippers, thick jerseys and bottles of cayenne pepper, but they don't seem to help him much.'[2] Even at its best Bromsden fell short of Rupert's ideal. 'The weather is perfect,' he reported one June when he had just returned from a few days with Ruth in Yorkshire. 'The house is covered with huge red roses, and the laburnum blossom is drifting down on me as I write. A flycatcher has a nest outside the library window, a pied wagtail in the clematis over the porch, and countless house martins under the eaves. A lush pastoral scene, in fact; but my heart still yearns for the windy uplands, green valleys, and surrounding peaks.'[3]

He had only stayed on at Bromsden for the sake of Comfort and the children; now the children had left home and Comfort seemed to have accepted that there was no point in continuing their sterile relationship. In January he wrote gratefully to Peter Fleming to tell him that he had decided to move north. 'It is ludicrous to suggest that you owe me any gratitude,' Fleming replied; 'the boot, if I may coin a phrase, is on the other foot, since for 25 years I have had – built in, as it were – the best of friends, the wisest of counsellors and the most entertaining of *raconteurs* within a biscuit toss of my house.' There was no point in looking back regretfully, Fleming urged him, still less in self-reproach. 'Press on regardless with your Yorkshire plans, and you'll soon be engrossed in a new life – an unusual privilege for persons of our age, unless they get sent to prison.'[4] Fleming's sorrow at the loss of an old friend was mitigated by the fact that his godson and favoured companion, Rupert's son Duff, was eager to move into the house. It was a perfect solution: ensuring that Peter Fleming would still have somebody whom he liked and trusted at close quarters, providing Duff with a home, and giving Rupert the satisfaction of knowing that a house in which he had experienced much happiness would remain within the family.

The problem of where Comfort was to go was less easily solved. Their daughter, Bridget, provided the answer. All the Hart-Davis children, whatever their private views about the situation, had contrived to remain on excellent terms with both their parents and to avoid taking sides in a conflict which they regretted but understood. Now they rallied to their mother's aid. Bridget made available a cottage adjoining her new house, a mile or so from Bromsden Farm. Duff and Adam busied themselves in painting it and putting it in order. There were still difficulties to be overcome, not least financial, but the most immediate problem had been solved.

On Monday 27 January Rupert left Bromsden for the last time. 'I think my departure was a relief to most people,' he told Blunden, 'but sentimentally I couldn't help feeling a little sad.' It had been his home for so many years, so many happy memories were associated with it as well as frustrations and disappointments. There were serious inconveniences, too. There was not yet anywhere in Yorkshire which could accommodate his books. They were assembled into 197 tea chests and stored to await the provision of a suitable home. For Rupert to be cut off from his books was a deprivation second only in horror to being isolated from those he loved; some would have said, indeed, that for him to lose human companionship might have been the lesser sacrifice. Yet he did not seriously doubt that he was doing the right thing: 'It will be a wonderful relief to live only one life, and that with my darling Ruth.'[5]

Temporarily they would live in Kisdon Lodge, but though love in a cottage had given them enormous pleasure in the past, its inaccessibility and primitive facilities meant that it could not provide a final answer. For more than a year they had been looking around the neighbourhood in search of a more suitable home. In June 1962, they had visited the

Swaledale village of Marske, to inspect a house which they had been told was for sale. Next to the church they found what they thought must be it, a large, rambling eighteenth-century building with Victorian extensions, no architectural gem but solid and pleasant and standing splendidly with a view across the valley. They peered through the windows, tramped through the undergrowth, and then went to the Post Office to ask if it could be viewed. This was not the house they were looking for, they were told; it was the Rectory, which was not on the market. It had been standing empty for five years, however, and the word was that the Church Commissioners had almost made up their minds to sell. The postmistress obligingly gave Rupert and Ruth a key and they prowled around the interior. Much work was needed, but there were thirteen rooms, several of them quite large, two bathrooms and a plethora of outhouses. A few days later they went back for a second look and were confirmed in their good impressions. 'Much taken with the peaceful situation and possibilities of the house – all very exciting,' wrote Rupert in his diary.

Even if the house were for sale, the purchase price and the cost of putting it in order would need much more money than Rupert had available. The contretemps with Harcourt Brace could hardly have been better timed; the Americans bought him out of the rest of his contract for £12,000 and thus provided a larger capital sum than he had ever possessed before. Rupert had hoped to be able to buy the house direct from the Church Commissioners but too many other interests were involved and in the end it was decided that it must be put up for auction. The agent told Rupert he did not expect it to fetch much more than £1,000, a local builder assured him that it was structurally sound but that, in view of its condition, he would be ill-advised to spend more than £2,000; in the end the opposition of a speculative builder from Darlington forced the price up to £4,200 – but still Rupert felt that he had got a bargain. Repairs were at once put in hand and an army of carpenters, electricians, masons, plumbers and painters surged each day up the hill to the Rectory to renew the wiring, install central heating, put a new fireplace in what was to be the drawing-room and, above all, to construct hundreds of yards of shelving to house the books with which Rupert was longing to be reunited. By the end of October, though the work was far from complete, it was advanced enough to allow them to spend a first night in their new home.

In the village they were known as Mr and Mrs Hart-Davis; Rupert did not actively propagate the fiction but he saw no reason to correct an impression which he hoped would soon become reality. Comfort had become reconciled to the fact that divorce was inevitable if not desirable. Both Bridget and Duff had now got children of their own and Adam showed signs of himself being on the verge of matrimony. Financially, the situation was slightly eased by the death of Rupert's father. It was nearly twenty years since Duff Cooper recorded that Richard was complaining how ill he was, 'which he has said ever since I have known him, but he looks wonderful'.[6] Since then he had continued to grumble about his health and continued to look wonderful. In 1952 he had annoyed Rupert by asking him to surrender his interest in the trust fund which had been established after Sibbie's death. Rupert refused, pleading his obligations to his wife and children: 'I am, and have for years been, damned hard up,' he protested.[7] After that, the two men met rarely; usually for morose dinners at the St James's Club which gave neither of them much pleasure but instilled a sense of duty done. Gradually hypochondria gave way to genuine illness. 'My old father (85) seems near his end,' Rupert told Edmund Blunden in 1963. 'Last week his doctor telephoned to say he couldn't last many days.'[8] He lasted in fact 356 days, 'almost blind and utterly gloomy'. Rupert visited him once or twice but found the experience dispiriting and did not feel that his presence gave any pleasure to his father. 'It's rather like visiting a corpse,' he remarked, adding sadly, 'but I'm sure he'll outlive us all.'[9] No doubt he would have done so if he could, for he clung tenaciously to life. When finally he died Rupert could not bring himself even to pretend to grieve. 'It was a great relief to all,' he told Janet Adam Smith.[10] Rupert put on the appropriate dark suit and black tie and dutifully journeyed to London but his routine was otherwise unaffected: his diary for the day of the funeral records only the birthday dinner he had that night at the Epicure restaurant. They ate a whole roast grouse each; 'a very happy sunlit birthday'.

    Richard Hart-Davis died with substantial debts but there was still something like £14,000 left over. The lion's share of this went to Deirdre but Rupert got £500 and what was left of his mother's money. It was not a fortune, but it slightly eased what would otherwise have been an economically difficult year. It was not enough, however, to solve the problem of how Comfort was to survive alone. As so often when Rupert was confronted by apparently insuperable financial difficulties, a kindly providence intervened. Rupert was now sole owner of Hugh Walpole's archive – a rich treasure house of manuscripts, diaries and letters. The University of Texas, always voracious for British literary manuscripts, offered to buy it for $50,000. Rupert held out for $56,000 – about £20,000 at the then rate of exchange – and got it. 'It's the only money I've ever had,' Rupert told Genia Ransome, 'and I'm getting rid of it immediately by making it into a trust with a life interest for my wife.'[11] Comfort was therefore provided with a home close to her children and grandchildren and a modest income. For Rupert this removed a great weight from his conscience. A few weeks later he told Edmund Blunden that he had spoken to Comfort on the telephone: 'She sounds very happy, and much more cheerful than she has been for years – which is naturally a great relief for me.'[12] There may have been an element of self-deception about this – Rupert wanted to believe that Comfort was happy and therefore happy she had to be – but certainly things had worked out far better than he had thought was possible a year before.

By this time a start had been made on the dismal charade which the British divorce laws then still imposed on those resolved to end their marriage. 'Evidence' had to be provided that Rupert was guilty of adultery and to this end an enquiry agent, in the form of 'a buxom widow of sixty, very civilised and agreeable' arrived by appointment at Soho Square to take them by surprise. She refused anything alcoholic but accepted a cup of tea, they gossiped affably for a quarter of an hour or so and she then departed, armed with information that proved their guilt.[13] On the basis of this Comfort was granted a decree nisi divorce which became absolute on 14 October 1964. Ruth had let her flat in Hampstead on a three-year lease, Rupert was hanging on in Soho Square but with no expectation that he would be there for long, the last ties with London were wearing thin. Five days after the decree absolute Ruth and Rupert came up to London to be married at Caxton Hall. It was no more than the formal endorsement of a situation which in their own minds had been established for many years but for Rupert its significance was still immense. 'Very near to tears immediately afterwards,' he noted in his diary. He was easily moved to tears but these were tears of relief and happiness.

Their honeymoon was as reduced in scale as their wedding celebrations. They took a train to Darlington where they had left their car and drove to Edinburgh, to a country-house hotel whose windows looked out on to rose gardens, peacocks and a distant prospect of Arthur's Seat. They dined off 'delicious scallops from Oban, duckling with salad, white and red Burgundy and *marrons glacés*. A perfect end to a magical dream-like day.' They spent four nights there, breakfasting in bed and eating enormous meals. The final bill was £32 – a figure which seems strikingly modest even for 1964. By day they pottered around bookshops, admired the beauties of Edinburgh, saw one or two old friends, braced themselves for the battles with builders and decorators that lay ahead. And so it was back to Marske and a new life, or rather the old life under a new guise.

That Christmas they went to Holy Communion in the church beside their house: 'our first for perhaps forty years. Both enjoyed it all.' Probably what they most enjoyed was the beauty of the words and the surroundings and the sense of continuity with the past. Neither Ruth nor Rupert had any deep religious convictions, still less any respect for the established church except as part of a social order which they hoped would survive. They felt no regret that they had not been married in church, nor any wish to have their union blessed in some subsequent ceremony. 'I believe in none of it,' Rupert had told George Lyttelton, with more than a tinge of regret. 'Don't think that I wouldn't like to believe: of course I would, and of course I realise that the lack of belief is at the bottom of most of our troubles today – not an atheist, you know, but an old-fashioned agnostic.'[14] His agnosticism did not prevent him becoming a regular attender at the little thirteenth-century church which lay just outside the Rectory wall. From time to time he fell out with the vicar but otherwise got much pleasure out of reading the lesson to a congregation which usually consisted of a dozen or so elderly villagers. Not for nothing had he trained at the Old Vic. At the carol service he was always entrusted with that great and mysterious lesson from the first chapter of St John. 'I read very loud and very slowly,' he told Deirdre, 'which electrifies the villagers, who are used to the largely inaudible mumbles of the dear local clergy.'[15] He would have been affronted if anybody else had been asked to take on this starring role, and was delighted to have the vicar round for a glass of wine after the service. He liked to think that he was thus part of village life. But it was the community that he valued, not his immortal soul. God was rarely referred to during the many hours that he and Ruth talked together.

Books, on the other hand, were rarely for long out of their conversation. The unpacking, arrangement and rearrangement of his ten thousand or so books, with which Ruth's far smaller but still not inconsiderable library had to be integrated, provided one of Rupert's most engrossing occupations for the next six months, indeed until the carrying to and fro of books became physically beyond him. Hugh

Walpole, he had written in his biography, 'had all the true bookman's passion for arranging books'.[16] Rupert was happiest when arranging his own but took considerable pleasure from doing the same thing with other people's; in 1940 he told Comfort that he had just spent a happy afternoon trying to put some sort of order into Peter Fleming's library – one of his specialities, he admitted. A room without books was, for him, a room impoverished; the library was the heart of a house from which all life emanated. Lord Melbourne's ideal home, which consisted of a bedroom with libraries leading off it in every direction, would have appealed strongly to him. Anthony Powell dedicated to him his novel *Books Do Furnish a Room* – 'rather suitable, *n'est-ce pas?*' Rupert commented with some gratification.[17] At Marske, for the first time in his life, he was able to concentrate all his books under one roof, so ordered as to be instantly accessible. It was one of the many reasons why his new home was uniquely precious to him.

But there were plenty of others. It was spacious, dignified yet unpretentious; set in one of Yorkshire's loveliest valleys with the open dale stretching away only a few hundred yards beyond the house; in a village just large enough to provide a viable community yet small enough to be intimate and to give the inhabitants, once accepted, the feeling that they belonged. Rupert and Ruth *were* accepted; the Rectory had been empty for too long, the locals rejoiced to see life return to it, with all the social and economic advantages that a big house can bring to the village to which it belongs. The Hart-Davises were not entirely strangers to Marske; they had visited Swaledale often enough to be known, or known of, long before they had any idea of settling in the village. They were the sort of people calculated to be acceptable in that close-knit, intensely conservative society: gentry; well off by local standards without being affluent; unostentatious; friendly; with enough remote and mysterious connections with the great world outside to provide a touch of glamour, yet reassuringly homespun and down to earth.

The house and garden quickly took shape. Apart from the books it was Ruth who did most of the work. Her taste was individual and, within its own parameters, impeccable.

The place has a very happy feeling to it [wrote Joyce Grenfell, one of the earliest visitors]. She has a liking for colour . . . The dining room is red red. No pink, no touch of orange in it – absolutely red. Warm, but a bit strong, I think. White curtains etched in black horses. She has collected mugs for ages and has a pleasing collection and they sit on shelves and are used for flowers all about the house . . . The house is gay and light but Rupert's special joy, his library, is full of the glow of floor to ceiling books. There isn't one inch of wall space and the effect is wonderfully warm and attractive . . . Everything has interest and quality and it is a house of atmosphere and charm. They are mad about it and the garden.[18]

They were mad about each other too. Joyce Grenfell had hardly met Ruth before she visited Marske: she felt slightly possessive towards Rupert and was ready to resent this woman who had disrupted his marriage and had now removed him to this northern fastness. Within twenty hours she was writing with some relief: 'I like her very much. She is very shy, like a small bird. But when she begins to trust you she stays still and you see how steady her almond-shaped eyes are and how delicate her nose. She is quick, nervous in a way but not in the least neurotic. Rupert loves her deeply and the chords between them are deep and vibrate warmly and strongly. Such things are so good to behold.'[19]

Ruth had a great capacity to adapt to meet the needs of whoever it might be with whom she was associated. She would have made a good shot at being the wife of a dentist or a merchant banker and entering into their concerns with genuine interest. But with Rupert no redirection was called for. 'Ruth and I can't get over the unbelievable fact that we like doing *all* the same things and therefore do everything joyfully together,' Rupert told his sister. 'I'm afraid this doesn't happen to many people and we are indeed blessed.'[20] Rupert was apt to believe that people must enjoy what he enjoyed himself and that, if they failed to do so, it was only because of their obtuseness which could, and should, be corrected. Where Ruth was concerned, however, little correction was needed: books, the theatre, country walks, the crossword, cricket were all to the forefront of her delights, and those pleasures which Rupert did not naturally share – gardening in particular – were ones in which he could take an interest and play a part. Almost everything could be done in common. 'It was just so utterly good to see you both not just being happy together, which I've seen before, but living together in such happiness,' wrote Janet Adam Smith after a stay at Marske. 'Even the washing-up can be a pleasure when shared with one's dear one.'[21] Rupert would hardly have included washing-up among his favoured pastimes but he did share the delights and travails of everyday existence to an extent which he had never known before.

His friends rejoiced as reports filtered back of new-found happiness. Margaret Lane wrote to say how much she wished to come north to see 'the Old Rector pontificating in his study and designing the herbaceous border. I have evidence he doesn't do too much *digging*, but the Rector's wife, with basket and raffia hat, is sure to be good with the roses. It all sounds idyllic.'[22] It was idyllic, and an idyll which Rupert was increasingly reluctant to disturb. When in Marske it seemed to him inconceivable that he had ever wanted to live in London. He was apt to quote Andrew Lang's lines from the 'Ballade of True Wisdom':

> And I'll leave all the luxury, the noise and the fray
> For a house full of books, and a garden of flowers.

But though he had successfully left it, the noise and the fray from time to time reclaimed him. Rupert was still Chairman of the London Library; he was still Secretary of the Literary Society; less agreeably but more pressingly than either of these, he was still under contract to Granada with a residual but ill-defined responsibility for the publishing house that bore his name. It was a responsibility that was to cause him considerable chagrin over the next few years.

His duties were not particularly arduous. He was expected to go to London twice a month to attend board meetings – '2.45–4.30 incredibly hot, noisy, boring meeting,' he wrote crossly in his diary after one such occasion – and to advise anyone who wanted advice on literary matters – a contingency which rarely arose. He read and worked on typescripts which he had commissioned in the past. He kept up with his authors and recommended their new proposals to his employer. He suggested – or that was the theory anyway – new projects and writers. It could have taken up a lot of his time; in fact the lack of enthusiasm for the relationship on both sides ensured that not much was done. Rupert had a slightly grudging respect for Bernstein himself but little for his subordinates, and he made his attitude painfully clear. Shortly before the final takeover he was telephoned by the man who was to all intents and purposes Bernstein's second in command. With hardly a pretence at covering the mouthpiece he said loudly to the colleague who was with him: 'It's that yammering idiot again!'[23] No one likes being despised, particularly by somebody whom one feels to be in a position of inferiority. Rupert was resented by the employees of Granada who were responsible for the concern's publishing interests; they did nothing to encourage him to take a more active role and he did even less to make them wish to do so. They begrudged the £2,000 a year Bernstein was paying him; he felt no inclination to do more than the bare minimum to earn his money.

Harry Townshend had retired from publishing at the end of 1963. 'This would be most depressing,' Rupert told Edmund Blunden, 'if I wasn't able to look on his departure as some sort of prelude to my own liberation from office life.'[24] Richard Garnett lasted for another two years, but his departure ended Rupert's last real link with the firm. 'I am wondering what will be the fate of the Hart-Davis books in which I have an interest,' wrote Geoffrey Keynes early in 1966. 'Perhaps you don't know yet, but if you do I should be grateful for enlightenment.'[25] Rupert did not know, and if it had not been for the responsibility he felt towards his authors, he would not have cared. He was a director, but he directed nothing; he was merely a name at the top of a piece of writing paper. He was a consulting editor, but nobody consulted him and he had no wish to proffer unasked-for advice. Leon Edel was another author who was confused about Rupert's ambiguous position. 'How will things be worked?' he asked. 'I mean, will you want me to keep in touch about all working problems and ideas etc etc?' He had just revised and added several chapters to his book *The Psychological Novel* which Rupert had originally published in 1955. Would this be something Rupert would deal with, or should he approach Richard Garnett, or was there somebody else who would be responsible? 'In other words, to what extent will you be disengaging yourself by leaving London? I am all in the vague . . . '[26] Rupert was in the vague too, but every week that went by, every meeting in London he attended, he became more certain that total disengagement was the best, if not the only answer.

He was slightly disconcerted to find that Granada fully shared his views. One by one his authors had been jumping ship. Alistair Cooke protested that he felt undying loyalty to Rupert as an individual but had no wish to be published by Bernstein: 'I like Sidney very much as a person; I don't care for his network or his public performance.'[27] Charles Causley told Rupert that his next volume would be appearing under another imprint: 'I hope you will forgive me, and understand me when I say that I would wish it so only so long as my relations with the firm of Rupert Hart-Davis remain as they always have been: one of the happiest and best.'[28] The loss of Causley Granada could have endured with equanimity; Cooke was the sort of writer they valued and for whose sake Hart-Davis's had been acquired. If Rupert could not retain his services, indeed if he seemed ready actively to speed such writers on their way, what case could there be for preserving the association? When Rupert's contract ran out he was offered only £250 a year as recompense for his name continuing to appear as a director. 'This offer seemed to me insulting and derisory,' Rupert told Deirdre. 'No mention was made of my editing or doing anything. I never much liked being listed as a director when in fact I had no control over anything, but £2,000 a year was not to be sneezed at.'[29] He let a few days pass and then politely refused the offer.

His friends greeted this latest turn in his fortunes with predictable indignation. He was not surprised, wrote Leon Edel; he had always expected the association to end in tears. Why did Rupert not use his new-found freedom to undertake a lecture tour of the United States? 'I know you shrink from the thought. But it's a very genial, rapid and almost painless way of acquiring assets in a short period.'[30] Rupert did indeed shrink from any such undertaking: to address audiences across mid-America would have been an occupation second only in horror to permanent incarceration in a Granada boardroom. He accepted his exile from the latter with profound relief. But he would never be entirely free so long as there were authors whom he felt a duty to protect. Sometimes that protection was best given by a refusal to become involved. Shortly after Rupert's contract terminated Geoffrey Keynes wrote to ask whether he still had enough influence with Granada to extricate him from the obligation to offer them his new book.[31] Rupert could reasonably have replied that Granada were unlikely to be irresistibly attracted to a revised version of Keynes's 1948 *Blake Studies* and that the problem would have been to persuade them to take it on, not to relinquish it. He might have added that the only thing calculated to induce Granada to stick to their rights and insist on publishing Keynes's book would have been the thought that by doing so they might have been annoying Rupert. Possibly he did in fact privately tell Keynes something of the sort. Formally, he contented himself with a non-committal reply and seems to have said nothing on the matter to the directors of Granada.

Sometimes he still felt bound to intervene. In 1970 Janet Adam Smith at last produced the new edition of the *Collected Poems* of Robert Louis Stevenson, which had long been contracted for by Hart-Davis's. To her dismay she got a brusque reply to the effect that publication would depend on whether Granada could secure an order for unbound copies from an American publisher. She sent the correspondence to

Rupert with an indignant covering note: 'I really was madly angry.'[32] Rupert was even more so. He wrote furiously to the now ennobled Sidney Bernstein: 'I have long since given up worrying about idiocies apparently carried out in my name, but this off-hand betrayal of an old friend and distinguished scholar seems to me one over the odds. Such behaviour can only bring shame to the firm, and incidentally to you, since everyone knows that you own it.'[33] Rupert told Janet that he understood Bernstein was now 'so dotty as scarcely to make sense,' but the reply that he elicited was both generous and dignified. 'I haven't given up worrying about the idiocies carried out in my name,' Lord Bernstein wrote ' . . . and am deeply sorry that you and Janet Adam Smith have been worried, disturbed or misled.' To Adam Smith he explained that the cause of offence was the work of 'a young man (public school, Oxford) not only misunderstanding instructions but writing a misleading letter. Everybody at Hart-Davis Ltd is blushing and full of apologies – as I am.'[34] Publication of the *Collected Poems* proceeded without further mishap.

Two years later Rupert found himself still further removed from his original creation when he was told that Granada had decided to merge its publishing subsidiaries and that the firm would in future be known as Hart-Davis, MacGibbon. 'The amalgamated companies will retain their respective editors and editorial policies,' he was told, a reassurance which gave him little confidence.[35] Books published under the Hart-Davis imprint became progressively more rare, but so long as the possibility remained that something wholly unsuitable might appear to heap shame upon his name he continued to be vexed by it. As late as 1983, when the Granada publishing houses came under the control of Collins', Rupert had to be reassured that there was no possibility of his name being used in a way that might cause him any distress.[36] In fact it was not used at all. Effectively Rupert's publishing had ceased entirely within three years of his establishing himself at Marske. He was free at last to devote himself to the exacting but far more congenial task of being 'some sort of literary bloke'.

Chapter Sixteen

Triumph and Tragedy

Literary blokes may have a thoroughly agreeable existence but they do not usually earn much money. Rupert was still almost entirely devoid of capital. His £2,000 a year from Granada was useful but not enough to live on and anyway was not likely to continue beyond the expiry of his contract in 1968. The money from Harcourt Brace had largely gone into the purchase and refurbishment of the Old Rectory. Luckily Ruth had some money of her own, no great fortune but enough to tide things over until some fresh source of funds came to hand. Rupert felt sure it would. In the meantime he had as little compunction in using Ruth's money as he would have felt hesitation in lavishing all that he had on her. Money meant little to him: he liked the things it bought but would sacrifice them without much regret if the money were not there and certainly would never put himself very far out to acquire it. On one holiday in Italy Ruth happened to have more money immediately available and therefore met all the cost. Rupert told George Lyttelton about this, adding with some relish that he had always felt that to be a kept man was 'a consummation devoutly to be wished'. He was half joking, but where his money came from was genuinely a cause for little concern; it was enough that it was there and that he could do with it as seemed proper.

It was fortunate a little money was available, since he and Ruth had many friends who missed seeing them in London and would happily travel a long distance out of their way to visit them in Yorkshire. Marske could not really be said to be on the way to anywhere but it was not so far off the main routes from north to south as to make it impracticable as a stopping-off place. They opened their doors, effectively, towards the end of January 1965 and by the end of the year had given a bed to nearly sixty people, some of whom came several times. First to arrive was Janet Stone. Her husband, Reynolds, was a

distinguished engraver and painter who had been responsible for the
sitting fox that graced the firm's writing paper, not to mention the
running fox – more economical in the space it took up – which was used
for advertisements. Janet was herself a talented photographer. She spent
two nights at Marske. Rupert's diary entry after she left was typical of
many hundreds that were to follow: 'She was an ideal guest and yet
we're blissful to be alone again.'[1] Almost always Rupert viewed the
incipient arrival of guests with dismay, enjoyed their company greatly
while they were there, then rejoiced when they departed. To John Bell,
who shared with Rupert responsibility for managing the Ransome
estate, he admitted that as he stood on the steps of the Old Rectory to
wave visitors goodbye he was consumed by fear that their car might not
start and they would have to come back to the house. Once it happened
to Geoffrey Keynes and Rupert was upset for weeks thereafter. In these
early days at Marske his yearning for privacy was still well under
control; it was to swell alarmingly in future years.

   When his guests did arrive Rupert wished them to have decent food
and wine. The wine he could look after himself, the food he left entirely
to Ruth. He was a competent and reasonably willing washer-up and
layer of tables but cooking was beyond him. He liked to eat large
quantities and did so at a great rate. He was 'a man of incredibly speedy
eating,' Joyce Grenfell described him. 'What's more, he can't sit and
wait for the rest of us to finish but gets up at once, as he gobbles his last
mouthful, and starts to clear away . . . restless and, I think, rather
discourteous.'[2] He was markedly unfussy about what he ate. 'I'm very
lucky in that I like almost all food,' he boasted to his sister, after
remarking that he was as happy with fish fingers as smoked salmon.[3] He
made a few exceptions, though. Deirdre, in the bleak days of rationing,
once served him a horseflesh steak without any indication as to what it
was. Rupert ate it with relish, but when later told what it had been,
rushed to the lavatory and was violently sick. Almost anything else was
acceptable, but he did like his food to be well cooked and took a keen
interest in what he had been given. He regularly recorded in his diary
and letters the dishes that had been served to his guests and seemed
sometimes more preoccupied by the food than by the people concerned.
When Kathleen Raine came to lunch at Marske, Rupert made no
mention of the conversation nor referred to the fact that her *Collected
Poems* had recently appeared. Instead he told Deirdre that she had been
given 'melon, cold chicken with lemon sauce (delicious), that splendid
sweet of seedless grapes soaked in orange juice and Boursin cheese'.[4]

When she first stayed at Marske, Joyce Grenfell noted that the house was 'cosy and controllable' which, since they only had help in twice a week, was just as well.[5] The 'help' was provided by Boyk and Nell Severs. Boyk was a former farmhand whose job as warden of the Army range at the top of the hill above Marske left him plenty of time to garden and do odd jobs around the house; Nell for her part was always ready to clean and do what else was needed. They were 'two of the nicest people I've ever known,' wrote Rupert,[6] and they came to be among his closest friends. Rupert was fascinated by Boyk's wisdom, knowledge of the countryside and shrewd if detached appreciation of world affairs. There was nothing remotely patronising about the relationship: Rupert genuinely enjoyed Boyk and Nell's companionship, was interested in their views and basked in the affection that they showed towards him and his family. Within a few years it seemed to him that the pleasure he derived from his life at Marske depended largely on their presence.

Increasingly he resented the duties that regularly took him away from Yorkshire. Extra excursions were avoided whenever possible but sometimes became essential; one such which he could not have brought himself to miss was the award of an Hon. D.Litt. at the University of Reading. The other graduands, who included Geoffrey Keynes and Wystan Auden, were relatively old hands at such occasions, but for Rupert 'it was a first (and almost certainly last) appearance in such a role'.[7] It was all rather fun, he told William Plomer, 'except that my comic hat was hellish tight. Ruth enjoyed it greatly. Wystan's face is now furrowed like a close-up of the moon but he was very sweet and friendly.'[8] A few months later it was a sadder occasion which took him away. He had grown to know T. S. Eliot well and to value his friendship during the years he had spent as Chairman of the London Library and Eliot's death early in 1965 caused him real sorrow. He wrote an obituary for the *Sunday Telegraph* and dragged himself to London for the memorial service. 'Saw many friends in the distance,' he wrote in his diary, 'but afterwards ran for taxi, picked up luggage and drove to King's Cross. The bliss of being home again . . . '[9] He could not be quite so precipitate in his departure when in September 1965 he went to East Coker to unveil the tablet which recorded that Eliot's ashes had been deposited beside the church. He had never spoken from a pulpit before and relished the powerful position that it gave him, but his words were eloquently informal and patently from the heart.[10]

He was too good at doing this sort of thing for his own peace of mind. Whenever an address was needed at a memorial service, celebratory dinner or other occasion honouring a literary figure, Rupert's name was likely to be canvassed as a suitable contributor. In November 1966 he made a speech at Edmund Blunden's seventieth birthday party. 'I couldn't refuse for Edmund,' he explained to Deirdre, 'and feel I must say a word for R. C. Hutchinson next week, but otherwise NO!' It very rarely was 'NO!' when it came to the point, of course; X was such an old friend, Y's widow's feelings would be hurt. He relished the sound of his own voice and got satisfaction from the fact that he was doing a job well, but he still paid a high price. Such speeches were always agony, he told his sister: 'not so much the actual delivery, which if I've prepared it properly and the audience is friendly, is quite fun: but the days of dread beforehand, the putting-off and last minute rush . . . and the impossibility of uncoiling afterwards. I never sleep properly that night and the words go on and on in my head, sometimes with improvements added, and I feel pretty low next day.'[11]

Such distractions, however, only made his returns to Marske more pleasurable. In October 1965 he wrote in his diary that they had been in the Old Rectory exactly a year, 'the loveliest and most exciting year ever'. The excitement lay in the absence of excitement: at Marske and with Ruth Rupert had discovered that the greatest excitement was to be found in tranquillity. Almost the only new departure in their first year in the north was the introduction into their lives of the jigsaw puzzle. Rupert already wasted several hours a week on crossword puzzles, now jigsaw puzzles of extraordinary size and complexity were added to the entertainment. Often he would work on two at once, rented from a jigsaw club and set up on large baize tables in different rooms. Joyce Grenfell, who like so many comedians took both herself and life with marked seriousness, deplored this frivolous pastime. 'I find it psychologically interesting,' she wrote, 'that people of intelligence like Rupert set themselves terribly arduous tasks like these giant puzzles . . . rather than cope with life, or, in Rupert's case, writing, at which he is so gifted. It isn't idleness because they keep busy at their idiotic tasks. But it *is* laziness. In Rupert's situation it is escapism and self-indulgence.'[12] It *was* escapism, but it was justified. Rupert spent many hours working on editorial tasks which called for meticulous attention. A break was needed. Reading purely for pleasure was the obvious diversion, but even Rupert found that unbroken immersion in a book imposed a strain on the eyes and reduced the satisfaction. Another man might have taken out a gun or exercised the dog, but Rupert had neither gun nor dog and had no wish for them. Jigsaw puzzles required concentration but were neither physically nor intellectually demanding. They suited him, and if Joyce Grenfell or other visitors thought the pastime childish, then, he would have felt, so much the worse for them.

Some years before, George Lyttelton had told Rupert that he was bound one day to be knighted. Rupert dismissed the idea as a 'delightful fantasy'. If he were offered a knighthood, though, he admitted he would accept with pleasure. 'I have no worldly ambition . . . but while one is engaged in the merry-go-round, it seems churlish to refuse any rewards from the sideshows.'[13] Now he had stepped off the merry-go-round and he assumed that whatever chance he had once had was gone for ever. Then, one evening in the early autumn of 1965, when at the Garrick Club for a dinner of the Literary Society, his old friend Sir Alan 'Tommy' Lascelles, private secretary to the Queen, asked him whether he would like to become a knight. Rupert replied – untruthfully – that he had never considered the idea but – truthfully – that he would be delighted. 'Leave it to me,' said Lascelles. Siegfried Sassoon, who had discussed the matter with Lascelles, got it into his head that the New Year Honours' List of January 1966 would contain the news. 'He'll be Sir Rupert on Jan 1st,' he told Blunden, 'a very perfect gentil knight and Ruth a worthy ladyship.'[14] More embarrassingly, he wrote to tell Rupert how pleased he was, 'anticipating the spate of congratulations'.[15] Edmund Blunden did the same. Rupert read the letters, was surprised because he had received no notification of the honour, but looked at the List on 1 January 1966 with some expectation. It was disappointed. 'Your lovely congratulations are, alas, misplaced,' he told Blunden. 'The whole thing was a plot between Siegfried Sassoon and Tommy Lascelles which seems to have misfired – but I shall treasure your letter with its knightly address on the envelope.'[16] Sassoon was mortified by his blunder. 'I understood from Tommy that it was a dead snip for today. Never mind. You need no titular advancement.'[17]

The plot had not misfired but Sassoon had underrated the cumbersome nature of the honours system. Rupert had initially felt acute disappointment but he was soon cheered by the assurance that all was under control and the knighthood would be his in January 1967. He received the formal notification in November but told nobody except Ruth, Deirdre and Comfort. He made no pretence of greeting the news with indifference: the desk diary for 1967 which he began to fill up from the late autumn of the previous year was headed proudly 'THE

KNIGHTHOOD YEAR'. Victor Gollancz had told him that when he
had received his knighthood five hundred letters of congratulation had
flooded in. Rupert assumed that he would get at least as many: 'I'm
prepared for the worst,' he told Deirdre, 'and have ordered 500 extra
sheets of writing paper and envelopes. We're both very excited about
the whole thing.'[18] On the eve of the announcement they had a dinner
party for a few favoured neighbours and broke the news. 'They were all
delighted,' Rupert recorded in his diary. Then the congratulations
began to arrive. Peggy Ashcroft was the earliest to telephone; Rupert
had bet Ruth that Jamie Hamilton would be the first to call but he had
to be content with second place. Boyk and Nell were summoned for a
drink at 11 a.m. and shown the announcement in the *Sunday Times*.
They were suitably gratified and later that day left on the Old Rectory
doorstep a paper bag containing a few potatoes, onions and other
vegetables. 'Boyk and Nell felt that a present was in order and gave us
all they had. We were deeply touched.'[19] A neighbouring farmer
pronounced that the knighthood was an honour to the village and
brought his own tribute in the form of a load of manure. Rupert
anxiously counted the letters and telegrams that arrived each day,
professing to deplore the work that would be involved in answering
them but privately resolved to do better than Victor Gollancz. The final
tally was 454; annoyingly less than his rival's total. Rupert comforted
himself with the reflection that Gollancz was notorious for overstating
the sales of his books and was no doubt doing the same with his
congratulatory letters.

The investiture at Buckingham Palace was scheduled for 7 February.
A week before that they decided to go to Edinburgh to attend a friend's
wedding. The train was late on arrival so they walked briskly while
looking for a taxi, eventually hailed one, and then relaxed for the last lap
of the journey. 'Have you told him where to go?' asked Ruth. 'Yes,
darling.' She gave two choking sighs and collapsed into his arms. Long
before the taxi reached the hospital she was dead. She had had slight
trouble with her heart a few years before and from time to time since
then had visited a specialist. Always she had been reassured and told
that there had been no apparent deterioration. Her death was as abrupt
and unexpected as if she had been struck down in some tragic accident.

The next days passed for Rupert in a dazed dream. He went back
home, spent a few hours in drugged sleep, returned to Edinburgh to
make arrangements for the disposal of the body, planned the funeral,
drove to the station to meet his sister Deirdre who had at once come

north to look after him. He decided it would be best to go through with the investiture rather than postpone it to another date, and the number of arrangements that had to be made and people that had to be talked to carried him through the intervening week. The funeral was on 4 February, two days later he and Deirdre left for London. He stayed with Janet Adam Smith and her new husband, John Carleton, headmaster of Westminster School, at their house in Dean's Yard which was to be his London base on many occasions in the future. Rupert had taken a handful of tranquillisers before the ordeal but the effect was beginning to wear off by the time he had been waiting in a queue for an hour or more. Only the excessively dilapidated actress Margaret Rutherford was allowed a chair; everyone else had to stand. Fortunately for Rupert, the man immediately ahead of him in the queue was his old friend Neville Cardus, whose grumbling was so vociferous as to keep those around him entertained and occupied. 'I've been through all this before when I got my CBE,' Cardus complained. 'You can't sit down, you can't get a drink and you can't spend a penny. I can't go through it all again. If they offer me a life peerage I shall turn it down!'[20] Eventually the ceremony was over and Sir Rupert returned to Marske. For the first time he really took in that he was going to have to face life without Ruth.

For the last two years they had done everything together; for twenty years she had been the most important person in his life. For anybody the shock of the sudden loss would have been devastating; for Rupert, whose capacity to depend emotionally and physically on those he loved was alarming in its intensity, it seemed as if life had become impossible. The grief was agonising, sudden shafts of pain that seemed to rend body as well as mind; but worse than the grief was the despair. He told Joyce Grenfell that 'he'd like to be dead, now, this minute, but couldn't kill himself in case it separated him even further from Ruth'.[21] He had little belief in a Christian deity and anyway was not prepared to accept the existence of a God who would allow such casual cruelty, but he was convinced that in some way Ruth was still present in his life, watching his actions and applauding the way in which he managed to keep his home going, to preserve the structure of normal life. He did not have the consolation of believing in an after-life where he and Ruth would be reunited, yet equally he could not bring himself totally to dismiss the possibility. 'I can't say I *believe* in survival after death,' he told Deirdre many years later, 'but just *hope* there may be some, though if there is there'll be a huge scrum struggling for our attention.'[22] In 1967 he came very close to such belief; though he based his conviction not on any religious construct but in obstinate persuasion that no spirit as vital and resolute as Ruth's could be extinguished by a mere corporeal failure. Deirdre most definitely did believe in survival after death. She was a close friend of Rosamond Lehmann, who was a committed devotee of spiritualism and was convinced that through it she had established intimate contact with her dead daughter, Sally. Now Rosamond put Deirdre in touch with Ena Twigg, one of the most celebrated mediums of the age. Mrs Twigg was a woman of apparently striking normality and common sense, who lived with her husband, a retired engineer, in a semi-detached house in Acton. Mervyn Stockwood, a Church of England clergyman whose advanced views sometimes verged on the heretical but whom nobody could have accused of gullibility, described Mrs Twigg addressing a potentially hostile audience in the University Church at Cambridge: 'She came through with flying colours. What won the sympathy of her hearers, including the sceptical, was her sincerity.'[23] Believing that Rupert would be consoled by some communication with his wife, Deirdre visited Mrs Twigg a fortnight after Ruth's death. The result was much what could have been expected: totally convincing to those who wished to be convinced, unconvincing to the hardened sceptic.

Ruth was quickly persuaded to speak. 'I didn't suffer at all,' she – or Ena Twigg – told Deirdre, 'but my first thought was of my darling. Tell him that nothing is wasted, not to have any regrets. Every day of those two years was a blessing and she says they had more in that period in that house together than most people have in a life time. Tell him, I am far more alive than he is.' Ruth had met Victor Gollancz, who felt warmly towards Rupert, and was getting on very well with Rupert's mother. Sibbie sent her own message. 'Tell Rupert not to worry about Ruth,' she said. 'I will look after her.' A month later Deirdre went back again. 'Nothing has ended,' Ruth assured her. She urged Rupert to look forward: 'You are not to let go. You have a lot of writing to do.' He was given instructions about what to do with the garden and told not to move out of their bedroom. 'I so loved that place. It was so cold and draughty and shabby when we found it and we made it so lovely.' 'If this is being dead it is a wonderful experience,' she concluded.[24]

Rupert was more than ready to be convinced. None of the words attributed to Ruth seemed in any way discordant or out of place. 'If I had been there,' he told Deirdre, 'Mrs Twigg might have been able to read my mind, but I was 300 miles away up here.' Ruth had been quoted as saying: 'You weren't frightened of me when I was dead. You simply bent down and kissed me on the forehead and then went away.' That was exactly what happened, Rupert said; only he and a nurse who was present could have known it.[25] He decided that he must visit Mrs Twigg himself. She was heavily booked up but it so happened that Rosamond Lehmann had been offered a seance at a time when Rupert had to be in London. Unexpectedly, Rosamond found that she had to go away and suggested that Rupert took over her slot. 'This is the first time *ever* that she has offered me a sitting that I haven't been able to accept,' she told him. 'It flashed on me that this might be "meant" for you all along, with me as the link. Anyway, I do hope you will go and that you will feel a renewal of hope, strength and confidence afterwards. I believe you will.'[26]

The seance took place on 27 July. Deirdre was also there. Ruth was delighted by Rupert's progress. 'You are alone but not lonely,' she declared. 'You are looking so much better and now you are looking forwards instead of backwards all the time. Isn't it marvellous?' Turning to more practical matters, she urged Rupert to get the damp patch on the ceiling fixed as soon as possible, though on no account was he to try getting up on a ladder himself. Rupert protested that it was difficult to get a builder to do so small a job. 'I will have a look round,' promised Ruth, 'but they seem to be mostly over here.' She had been determined to get through to Rupert. 'You didn't ever think you would be able to come and talk to me like this, did you? Why doesn't everybody know about it?'[27] Rupert told Rosamond Lehmann that his visit to Mrs Twigg had changed everything, 'and provided a steadfast light at the end of the tunnel. I truly do believe it – it's impossible not to believe it – but I still find existing alone from day to day a terrible burden.'[28]

He never repeated the visit, although Rosamond urged him to do so. This does not seem to have been because he lost confidence in spiritualism. Early in 1968 he was urging Vyvyan Holland's widow, Thelma, to have recourse to Ena Twigg. One of the main drawbacks to spiritualism, he said, was 'that it is so open to fraud of various kinds, and we are lucky to have such a patently honest and immensely gifted person as Mrs Twigg. I particularly like the absence of mumbo-jumbo, don't you? I'm sure that if our beloved dead want us to get in touch with them, their greatest need of such communication must be immediately after death, when everything is strange and new.'[29] Possibly he felt that Ruth no longer needed to get through to him; more probably, as he made new commitments and took on new concerns, he felt less need to get through to her.

Three years later, when Deirdre and the Grenfells were staying at Marske, they discussed the letters which Rosamond claimed to be still receiving from her long-dead daughter. Deirdre was sure that they were genuine; Joyce Grenfell believed the contrary; 'Rupert stays silent on the subject,' she wrote. 'I think he tried to get in touch with Ruth once – to please Rosamond? – but he never did it again, and I think he is totally unconvinced.'[30] She deceived herself; Rupert was not unconvinced. On the contrary, he told Deirdre nearly twenty years later that he still believed 'there *is* some connection with people after they're dead, but only psychic go-betweens like Mrs Twigg can get in touch with them'.[31] But though the thought gave him some satisfaction, once the immediate horror of Ruth's death had faded he felt little inclination to renew communications. Rosamond Lehmann's consuming and all-absorbing grief for her daughter was alien to his nature. He never forgot Ruth, always missed her, but after this one adventure he felt no need to pursue her on the astral plane. It was enough to keep her memory alive by tending her garden and planting flowers around her grave. One afternoon a few weeks after her death he and Boyk spread earth around the grave and put into it clumps of snowdrops taken from the field behind the house: 'Boyk refused payment for his afternoon's work. Most touching. Felt a fraction happier.'[32]

Letters of condolence poured in; all of them welcome, though the thought of replying to them at times overwhelmed him. The letter which moved him most came from Siegfried Sassoon, whom he and Ruth had visited only a few weeks before. 'I don't know when a friend's bereavement has caused me such poignant and prolonged distress,' Sassoon told him. 'Dear Rupert, you have shared the bereavement of others in your noble heart, and you know that we just *have* to go on somehow. And Ruth would tell you that you *must*, though your ideal companionship has been so cruelly destroyed . . . One thing I *can* offer you – my deep and devoted friendship, for you have come to be . . . a source of strength and encouragement beyond anyone else . . .'[33] His 'poignant and prolonged distress' was not a mere figure of speech, as is shown by Sassoon's letter of a few days later to Geoffrey Keynes. He had been 'horribly upset about Rupert and Ruth,' he wrote, 'and have found it almost impossible to think of anything else. His life is broken in half. But he must go on somehow, making what he can of his mental resources when the desolation has abated. It is the worst shock I've had for years.'[34]

A string of devoted women travelled north to sustain Rupert, organising a sort of roster so as to ensure that he was never left alone. Deirdre, his daughter Bridget, Peggy Ashcroft, Janet Stone, Janet Adam Smith, Joyce Grenfell: each in turn was assured that they were uniquely precious and his most valuable source of consolation. Each time he meant it; Rupert loved each ministering angel in turn with a fervour that was without a trace of insincerity. Given the shipwreck of his brief, almost abortive marriage, his continuing devotion to Peggy Ashcroft was perhaps the most remarkable. They had never lost touch but had not really renewed their friendship until 1956. 'I can remember exactly what I used to feel about her, but I don't feel it any more,' Rupert had told George Lyttelton, 'just a deep and tender affection surrounded by memories. All rather moving and agreeable.'[35] The affection was reciprocated. Peggy Ashcroft put everything aside to be with him, stayed at Marske for more than a week until relieved by Bridget and devoted the best part of a day to cooking dishes that would see Rupert through in case the system temporarily failed. 'I feel still half in Marske with you,' she wrote the day after her departure, 'sharing your life and your grief, wanting to lighten it but knowing one is really powerless. But it was so sweet to be with you and you made me feel I was a little spar to cling to. And now I feel closer than ever to understanding what your agony is – only such a loving heart as yours can know that complete emptying, but because you *have* such a heart you must and *will* survive in spirit.'[36]

Janet Adam Smith had been 'the greatest sustaining force and joy in all these agonising weeks'; Janet Stone was 'a source of comfort such as I have never hoped to find'; but it was Deirdre who was above all precious to him in his travail. Rupert wrote to her the day she left, exactly four weeks after Ruth's death. 'All our lives you have been so dear and close, so tender, thoughtful and loving – but never so deeply as now. All these years you have been all I had left of Mummy and now you are so much of my darling Ruth, because you loved each other, and you know so instinctively and exactly what I feel. Like my darling, I am a very loving and giving person, and now you must expect a great part of the affection which I have to lavish.' The following day he wrote again: 'I am really better, and the fits of weeping and despair are fewer. Oh darling, the pity of it.'[37]

Deirdre loved her brother and would have done a great deal to spare

him pain, but this *cri de coeur* must have caused her some alarm. To be
the only remaining link between Rupert and his mother had sometimes
proved onerous; to have to take on the same role for Ruth as well might
be too much. She had a life, a family, responsibilities of her own; there
was a limit to the number of times she could rush north to succour the
emotionally demanding Rupert. Her recourse to Mrs Twigg may in part
have been inspired by her wish that some other power should be called
in to help her brother in his desolation. But though communication with
Ruth's spirit might have provided a temporary answer, she can hardly
have hoped that it would suffice to appease his agonising loneliness.
Some more overtly physical aid was needed. Quite where it would come
from Deirdre could not be sure, but she must have known Rupert well
enough to be hopeful that he would soon find for himself someone who
would – not replace Ruth, but fill the gap her death had left.

'I know most certainly that you must love someone enormously, for
that is your nature,' Peggy Ashcroft had told him many years before.[38] It
was inevitable that once the first shock was over, even while it endured,
he would look for somebody to love. The danger that occurred to his
friend Dickin Moore was that he would be too precipitate in his quest.
'The greatest mistake I ever made,' Moore wrote, 'was my attempt to
solve the problem of loneliness by getting married. I regretted it as soon
as the ceremony was over, when I realised I had married a *solution*.'[39]
This was not at all how Rupert saw it. It never occurred to him that the
problem might be soluble and he took it for granted that he was doomed
to a lifetime of loneliness. When what he felt to be the miracle happened
and a solution presented itself there was no question of it being *a*
solution, it was *the* solution, the only possible solution, the solution
which he believed Ruth would wholeheartedly have approved and
which he even convinced himself that she had brought about.

It was, indeed, Ruth's doing that June Williams came to Marske.
Though Ruth was a capable typist, ready to devote long hours to her
husband's service, the build-up of work, swelled as it undoubtedly
would be by a flood of correspondence about the knighthood, was
becoming too much for her. Ruth knew that June had been Rupert's
favourite secretary, that her husband was now dead and that the job she
was doing for the Warden of Radley College left her with long school
holidays which she might be pleased to fill by a visit to Marske.
Towards the end of 1966 Ruth suggested to June that a working holiday
in the north might suit everybody concerned. June accepted with

alacrity, and agreed to come to Yorkshire at Easter, in mid-April 1967. She was now in her early forties: small, even by the standards of Comfort and Ruth; trim; alert and decidedly attractive. She had liked and admired Rupert but viewed him with slight awe; Ruth had never particularly appealed to her but for Rupert's sake she was dismayed and shocked by her death. She wrote a letter of condolence, in which she implied, without actually stating it, that her visit to Marske would now be off. 'Had my darling Ruth arranged a time for you to visit us?' Rupert responded anxiously. 'Could you still come? Or would it be too improper for you to stay alone in a large house with a weeping widower? We could cook between us – say if it's possible.'[40] It was possible, but was it wise? June consulted an old friend, Joan Astley, who knew Rupert well. 'If you want Rupert to propose to you and intend to accept him, then go,' Mrs Astley advised. 'Otherwise don't.'[41] June had considered the possibility of embarrassment, of feeling that she was intruding where no visitor was welcome, but the contingency envisaged by Joan Astley seemed absurdly remote. She decided to go, but hedged her bets. If she found the atmosphere difficult or Rupert hostile she would send an SOS to a friend who would then telephone to say that her mother was ill and that she must come south at once. With her line of retreat thus secure, she set off for Marske.

She arrived in a considerable fluster. Normally the most efficient of people, she was in a sufficiently anxious state to confuse Doncaster with Darlington, try to change trains at Sheffield and end up having an argument with a ticket inspector. How could anyone in their senses confuse Doncaster and Darlington? demanded the inspector. 'They both begin with D and are in Yorkshire,' June suggested. 'Darlington isn't in Yorkshire,' retorted the inspector, kindly but crushingly. She took a taxi and eventually ended up at the Old Rectory. Mr Cave, the vicar, was there and seemed mildly surprised when Rupert greeted her with an enormous hug. Rupert, she felt, was in a highly emotional state; his manner in the past had often verged on the histrionic but now he seemed almost out of control. She happened to mention that her cat had died, whereupon he burst into tears. There was no real need for grief, she assured him; it had happened some years before and she had quite got over it. 'I don't even like cats,' said Rupert dolefully.

'In hindsight it seems as if the whole thing had been *meant*,' Rupert wrote in his memoirs.[42] Two nights after June's arrival, Rupert was playing her Tchaikovsky's *Symphonie Pathétique*, a composition which even at the best of times he found intensely moving. At the end of it, he

said abruptly: 'I'd like to go to bed with you.' 'I don't think that would
be at all a good idea,' said June, with an attempt at firmness. 'Why not?'
'Because you'll be sorry about it next day.' Rupert eventually prevailed
and *was* sorry the next day, not out of regret or shame but because the
experiment had been something of a disaster. This did not deter him
from trying again, however – this time with better results. By the time
June left, after five days, they were committedly in love.

Rupert had no glimmering of doubt that he was doing the right
thing. He wrote lovingly to June before she had even left the house:

> Darling, darling little June, my beloved midget. I have just crept out of
> your soft warm arms, and am scribbling this scrap so that you will get
> something on your first bleak morning back at Radley. I am half asleep,
> in no state to write sense, but full of love and gratitude to you. In these
> five extraordinary days you have brought me from death to life, from
> despair to hope, from desolation to renewal. You think I shall relapse
> when your gentle presence is removed, but I am determined not to let
> that happen . . . Oh darling, darling June, you are the most blessed and
> peace-bringing of girls, as well as being so terribly exciting. I love you, I
> rejoice in you, I thank you, I long for you.[43]

He realised that, to the outside world, he might seem to be finding
consolation with undue rapidity. It was, after all, less than three months
since Ruth's death. To all except his intimates he continued to protest
his grief; to present himself as still being trapped in that desolation from
which he told June that she had rescued him. He was not being
insincere – he did miss Ruth with passionate intensity – but in no way
did he feel that his love for June was incompatible with his duty to his
dead wife. On the contrary, the two were closely, inseparably linked.
'The whole of your coming seems to me to have been *meant*, and
planned by Ruth, as indeed it was,' he told June. 'I shall never stop
loving her or forget a moment of all those years – any more than you
will forget or stop loving David, but let us turn happiness [*sic*.:
'unhappiness'?] back into happiness.'[44] He bombarded her with letters;
each day reiterating his love for her and the continuity that existed
between her and Ruth. 'You have given me back a point and purpose in
my life,' he told her, 'to make you supremely happy, and at the same
time to do all the things that Ruth wants me to do. In all of them your
help and presence are essential. I simply couldn't begin without you –
and that was one of the deepest causes of my despair. Do you
understand? Of course you do. You are all perception and sensitive

sympathy. You were sent by God and by Ruth, and I am your servant and lover for ever.'[45]

Deirdre was one of the first people to whom he confessed his new attachment. He was afraid that she would disapprove and was delighted to find that her first reaction was relief that he was escaping from his obsessive grief. June was '100% non-irritating,' he told her, 'very neat and competent, and I find complete peace and content in her company.' Again and again he went over the arguments that had convinced him that he was not being disloyal to Ruth; he was, one feels, more intent on reassuring himself than convincing his sister but he knew that Deirdre had been fond of Ruth and felt that she was bound to question his decision. He had no real interest in himself, he told her, but for the first time in his life he had been forced into some sort of self-analysis.

Directly I realised that I should never see my beloved Ruth again in this life, I was forced to the conclusion that I should never be able to do all the things Ruth would like – in house, garden and books – without a loving companion. I am full of love and affection which must be lavished on someone if I am to keep sane and active. June knows that Ruth was the love of my life, of my maturity from 40 to 60, and that I shall love her always. But when she hesitantly says: 'How could I compete with Ruth?' I tell her there is no question of competition: they are totally different, and what she can do is to turn my agony back into the love and joy and peace that caused it. She would be perfectly happy to chuck her job and come here as my secretary-companion, but I tell her that is not realistic. We are in love with each other, and I need a lover as well as a companion and secretary. She would marry me tomorrow, but somehow I must first convince her that I am in my right mind. Perhaps a few months will do the trick . . . It's hard to disentangle selfish motives from unselfish ones – perhaps they are always confused. At first I felt disloyal and unfaithful to my darling Ruth, but now – it may be wishful thinking, though I fancy most good thought is in some way wishful – I have come to feel that Ruth couldn't wish me to spend the rest of my earthly life celibate and alone.[46]

Gradually, the news that he had found solace spread among his friends. One or two of them felt that, if only for reasons of decorum, he should have waited a little longer. Most of them rejoiced. Joyce Grenfell, who had grown to love Ruth, felt that she was in no way being supplanted; rather, it was 'an extension of something Ruth gave him that he needed'. She felt that in some ways it was a tribute to Ruth that

Rupert felt so desperate a need to marry again. She herself, she wrote, could never contemplate remarrying if her husband were to die, but she was different to Rupert and she could well understand how he felt. 'There's no doubt that Rupert is *no good* alone,' she concluded.[47]

Chapter Seventeen

Life Renewed

On 23 October 1967 Rupert wrote to congratulate his old friend Richard Church on his remarriage. 'I daresay I shall follow your example one day,' he said. 'Living alone is not for us. Nothing can be the same again, but we must salvage what fragments we can . . . I am just, after nine months, beginning to feel I may be able to work again.'[1]

The letter was disingenuous. By the time he wrote it June had given up her job at Radley and had for nearly a month been installed in Marske. She at first insisted that she could give Rupert both the secretarial assistance and the companionship he needed, she could even give him the love, without going through the formalities of a marriage. The thought of becoming Lady Hart-Davis strongly appealed to yet also appalled her. She genuinely doubted whether she could give him all he wanted and expected, or come to terms with his grand and intellectual friends. He had proposed to her, she believed, on impulse, while borne on a flood of desperation; he would repent at leisure and she could not endure the thought that he might come to regret or, even worse, resent her presence. Rupert would have none of it. Her fears were, to him, incomprehensible and the disadvantages of their living for long 'in sin' together were overwhelming. In a flat in the centre of London it might have been possible: 'But in a tiny village like this, the indefinite presence of a poppet alone in a house with a widower, however old and decrepit, would cause endless scandal. I don't in the least mind for myself, but refuse to let you in for that.'[2] At first he thought that they could not survive the censoriousness of the neighbours for more than a few weeks in August, then he decided that cohabitation for several months would be acceptable provided everyone who mattered knew that they planned to marry in due course.

The villagers of Marske seem to have accepted the situation with equanimity. June was, of all people, most likely to appease whatever disapproval they might have felt for so irregular an arrangement. She was friendly without being effusive, shy without being timid, attractive without being flamboyant or extravagant. Nobody could have been less like a scarlet woman. 'She is very pleasing to look upon,' wrote Joyce Grenfell, 'tiny: shoes size 3 and I suppose she wears dresses size 8 at most. With her grey hair and hazel eyes, straight nose under a high forehead, she has an eighteenth-century look even though her hair is cut in a modern way. She has a good little figure like a sixteen-year-old, and dresses very simply with definite style. Sweaters and skirt and little neat bright coloured shifts to change into. She . . . is orderly and calm.'³ She was eighteen years younger than Rupert but in some ways the more mature; he recognised and respected her quality. 'I am not a fickle or changeable sort of person,' he told her, 'and you are lodged in my heart for ever. It isn't just physical lust, I promise you – though there's plenty of that, too – but rather the joy and serenity of your presence, and the sweetness and utter goodness of your nature. I am in love with you in every way.'⁴

  While they were still debating the pros and cons of matrimony, June's mother – Mumsy – arrived to stay. If June was small, Mumsy was minuscule; a seventy-four-year-old bundle of energy whose idea of a relaxing morning was to clean the oven or wash the bedroom curtains. She tip-toed in and out of the library with exaggerated reverence, convinced that Rupert was engaged in some work of seminal importance even though he was patently doing a crossword puzzle or dozing placidly. Finally she plucked up her courage and asked directly whether Rupert planned to make an honest woman of her daughter. Rupert might have replied that it was June who should be asked that question but by good fortune the debate had been concluded only the night before. June, he was able to reply, had agreed to marry him – in June as it turned out.

  Before that, the anniversary of Ruth's death came and went. Rupert attached an extravagant importance to anniversaries. A letter to Deirdre dated 25 November 1967, for instance, was headed: '34th anniversary of my wedding to Comfort. Tomorrow Mummy will be 81.' He was particularly keen to share with his sister the memories kindled by his mother's birthday. On 26 November 1986 he noted in his diary: 'My darling mother's hundredth birthday. Rang D.' A similar entry announced the 101st and 102nd anniversary. Ruth's death added an item of unique importance to the list. 'I felt wretched and weepy all Wednesday,' he told Deirdre. 'but had a good cry at twelve o'clock, which cleared the air a little . . . June was unbelievably sweet and right and comforting all day – as indeed she is every day.'⁵ On this occasion he felt no compunction at involving June in his sorrow; in later years he was torn between a propensity to indulge his grief and a feeling that it was rather unfair to his present wife to mourn too ostentatiously for the old one. By the third anniversary he was more alive to June's feelings and began to make greater efforts to accommodate himself to them. 'Time does undoubtedly blunt and blur the edges of sorrow,' he admitted to Deirdre,' and those great waves of grief come seldom now, though that last terrible hour in Edinburgh returns to haunt me. Mostly I am able to concentrate on all the loveliness of those twenty years, with loving gratitude.' Then he was struck by an awareness of present loyalties. 'Don't mention any of this in your letter,' he enjoined his sister.⁶

Rupert and June got married on 13 June 1968 in the register office at Richmond. Boyk and Nell were the only witnesses. It was a brilliant day of blue skies and sun, and when Arthur Cave, their friend and rector, conducted a service in the little church beside the Old Rectory, Swaledale was at its most refulgent. As they came out, Boyk flung his arms round June, kissed her soundly and cried in triumph: 'Lady June!' Then they retired to the Old Rectory for a glass of champagne. 'An acquired taste,' commented Boyk cautiously, having not yet acquired it. Nell did not share his doubts, with the result that when they got home she could do nothing but collapse into a chair and laugh. Unused to such excesses, Boyk called in a friend from next door – a trained nurse – to diagnose her condition. A glance was enough. 'She's tight,' pronounced the neighbour.

For their honeymoon they drove north in leisurely style and took the ferry to Arran. There was a little desultory sightseeing, much bathing and lying about in the sun, undemanding walks: 'an enchanted week in this enchanting island,' Rupert wrote in his diary. They vowed to return and since, for Rupert, habits once formed were rarely shed and precedents were binding, they did so regularly over the next decades. 'Beautiful sunshine all the time and I'm unbelievably happy,' June rejoiced to Deirdre. 'I can hardly believe it's all true.'⁷

Rupert now began the business of breaking it to his friends how life had changed. He took it for granted that they would be as happy as he was. In London a few days before the wedding he had told a few people about his intentions. Duff, he recorded in his diary, 'seemed very pleased. Tea with Katy, who was also pleased. A drink with Adele, she too delighted. Told Danny news at breakfast. She *delighted*.' Rupert was apt to assume that his friends felt what he wanted or expected them to feel and any reservations on their part would probably have been overlooked. In fact, however, there seems to have been unequivocal approval from every side. Joyce Grenfell wrote exultantly to her friend, Virginia Graham: 'Isn't it GOOD. I am so pleased. And somehow I *know* Ruth would be too. The news has quite lit up the day for me.'[8] Peggy Ashcroft was equally enthusiastic. She claimed to have sensed that something like this was going to happen when Rupert had visited her in Stratford a year before. 'How strange intuitions are, but they are seldom wrong about people one loves . . . You have a wonderful gift, my darling, for knowing what you want, and not hesitating to reach it. Now I feel you will have won peace and serenity back with a dear companion.'[9]

The children were delighted by their new stepmother, though she was nearer Bridget in age than her husband. The thought of Rupert morose and lonely in the north would have been a constant worry to them and a burden on their consciences if they did not regularly visit him. They would have been disposed to welcome the advent of June whatever her nature. As it was they liked her greatly and appreciated that she was superbly qualified to keep their father happy and well cared for. Bridget remained totally loyal to her mother but she found June warm and more approachable than Ruth and got on very well with her.

Only Comfort looked on the new Lady Hart-Davis with some disapproval and thought her unworthy of so great a charge. June and Comfort met in July when Rupert took his new wife to meet Duff at Bromsden. The encounter gave little satisfaction to either party but left Rupert with the comforting illusion that all wounds had been healed and good order now prevailed within the family.

Comfort was in a sad state. It seemed that decades of heavy smoking had finally caught up with her: she had been afflicted by hardening of the arteries, gangrene set in, and she had a foot amputated in 1966. She struggled on, looked after by Bridget, until a stroke two years later and another in 1969 brought her to the brink of death. 'The children are being excellent,' Rupert told Deirdre, 'but I can't help feeling a certain distant responsibility for the poor little creature.' He went south to visit her in hospital – a pilgrimage which involved more of a sacrifice than might appear, given the extreme reluctance with which he now left Swaledale – and found her frail and despairing: 'Poor little thing, she looks like a ghost. I feel full of compassion for her, and yet I can see how easily and quickly I should be maddened again if I saw much of her.'[10] She held on for nearly eight more months until at last Duff telephoned to say that his mother was dead. 'It was a sad day,' Rupert told Tommy Lascelles. 'We were divorced nearly six years ago, but now of course my thoughts skip all the later unhappiness and concentrate on those golden days of youth. As Oscar so truly said:

> He who lives more lives than one
> More deaths than one must die.'[11]

Rupert was on his fourth wife, and so his fourth life at least; death was to obtrude upon him often in the next thirty years and each time he relived the happiness and regretted the sorrows of the past. But the actual disposal of the remains of the dead was of increasingly little concern to him. He dutifully went south for Comfort's funeral but slipped away at the end without even saying goodbye to Deirdre; his excuse being that he feared he might otherwise be trapped into conversation with Comfort's stepfather, the abominable Louis Spears. June, he told his sister, had been 'so sweet, sympathetic and understanding all this week. How very *very* lucky I am! Perhaps to be born lucky is the greatest gift the gods can bestow.'[12]

He stayed with Bridget the night before Comfort's funeral; she was somebody on whom he knew he could depend and whose company he enjoyed, yet he had singularly little in common with her. She read few books and was absorbed by her children, her horses, her country occupations. Adam's scientific interests were quite as mysterious to Rupert, but his intellectual curiosity and ebullient energy meant that the two men had more to talk about to each other. Adam had always enjoyed the privileges of a youngest child: while Bridget and Duff had regarded Rupert with slight awe, to Adam he was 'dear old dad'. In 1965 he had saddened his father by marrying a woman who did not fit in at Marske and, in Rupert's eyes at least, made no effort to do so.[13] The young couple had spent three years in Canada where Adam taught at the University of Edmonton – 'Adam to farewell lunch – chops and apple pie. Felt very weepy and low all day,' was Rupert's characteristic diary entry – but shortly after his mother's death he returned to England. He joined the Oxford University Press, where he was notably successful: his zest and enthusiasm were such that he won a round of applause from the hard-boiled travellers at the seasonal sales conference. Rupert was proud of his success, but horrified when Adam announced that he was thinking of investing some money which he had inherited on setting up his own publishing house. 'DON'T!' was his father's alarmed response; and Adam reluctantly accepted that this advice at least deserved attention as being based on a sound body of personal experience.

Duff had by now become a successful journalist and author. His godfather, Peter Fleming, died in August 1971 on a grouse moor having just brought off a successful left and right. Rupert was dismayed. 'He was my oldest friend,' he told Tommy Lascelles; 'never has he ever failed in generosity, loyalty and undemanding friendship.'[14] A few weeks later Duff was invited by Jonathan Cape's to write Fleming's biography. 'He asked whether *I* wouldn't do it,' Rupert told Deirdre, 'but I said I had enough on my plate, and I think it would be an excellent thing for him, putting him on the map as a serious writer.'[15] Celia Johnson was not entirely convinced, and pressed Rupert to take on the task. He was 'too old, lazy and busy with other things,' he told his sister. Duff would do an excellent job: 'With her [Celia] and me behind him he can't go wrong.'[16]

Deirdre, the recipient of so many of these confidences, was herself in trouble. Her third husband, Tony Bland, was a man of charm and talent but emotionally unstable and unable to resist embarking on affairs with women considerably his junior. Rupert was indignant on his sister's behalf. 'He is a monster of egotism and selfishness,' he declared. 'The only way to stop this ghastly sequence is for *you* to tell him that this is the end, and mean it and keep to it.'[17] Deirdre could see the wisdom of the advice but was not yet disposed to follow it; in the meantime she was miserably unhappy and Rupert in his turn felt distressed and impotent.

Apart from this, however, Rupert had fully regained his normal condition of cheerful contentment. Deirdre for some reason seems to have felt that it would do him no harm to be reminded of past sorrows. She once more got in touch with Ena Twigg and emerged with a fresh batch of messages from Ruth. Rupert received them appreciatively. 'I do indeed think of her a great deal with the tenderest feeling,' he assured his sister. 'Oh, how lucky I have been. I do thankfully appreciate it all, and my blissful life with June now. Sometimes she quite wrongly gets the idea that I'd like to see my friends, but the truth is that I'm completely content in our peaceful routine alone together . . . Calm of mind, all passion spent.'[18]

In the first years of their marriage June's doubts about her ability to cope with Rupert's friends caused her endless turmoil. Two 'charming people' came to stay, she told Deirdre. 'She was very sweet and helpful, and he was a dear, but I felt so *stupid*. She was extremely well read and kept asking me if I'd read Scott and Thackeray and all sorts of French literature (in the French of course). Finally she asked if I'd read Dickens. "Yes", I stumbled out, but could think of no more to say! I was *awful*! I could weep (I did in fact). I wonder if I could have a crash course on Coleridge for next w/e?' (when Kathleen Coburn, the Coleridge scholar, was coming to stay).[19] June was, in fact, more than intelligent enough to hold her own and Rupert, who had not married her for her knowledge of Thackeray or Coleridge, was proud to exhibit her to his friends. She was convinced, however, that she was letting him down and causing him embarrassment.

Guests were soon arriving. Rupert told Deirdre: 'I love them all, but wish they would keep away.'[20] His concern was mainly for his wife. Things got so bad that when Peggy Ashcroft invited herself to stay Rupert felt bound to put her off: 'It's rather touching that anyone should feel so possessive about a broken-down old wreck like me.'[21] June saw the envelope, guessed what it contained and was so upset that Rupert tore up the letter and asked Peggy to come as she had suggested. But June was still on edge and unhappy about the prospect. In the end Rupert asked Deirdre to telephone Peggy, explain the situation and ask her to write saying that she had changed her plans and would now not be able to come to Marske: 'She knows I am devoted to her, as she is to me, but we can get along very well without seeing each other just now.' Peggy Ashcroft at once did as she was asked, wrote a friendly letter of excuses and 'from the moment it arrived Junie has been her old self again – gay and happy'.[22]

'Burn this letter!' Rupert ended – an injunction which had its usual effect of ensuring the recipient kept it with special care. '*Please on no account refer to this, in letter or conversation*,' he asked in an earlier letter. When he had had his horoscope read in 1931 he had been told that the moon in Taurus showed 'that the woman you love will always call out all that is noblest and best in your nature'. Love had not lasted in the case of Comfort but neither Ruth nor June had cause to complain of his dedicated devotion. He felt intensely protective towards June and was prepared to make considerable sacrifices to spare her pain or anxiety. When she was ill he was delighted to have the opportunity to cosset her; he adopted elaborate subterfuges to keep her in the dark if anything threatened which he felt might disturb her equanimity. 'I simply adore my little June,' he told Deirdre. 'She grows sweeter and dearer every day, and we are blissfully and effortlessly as one. I try feebly to combat her immense unselfishness.'[23]

But though his devotion was real it came at a price. Their being 'effortlessly as one' nearly always seemed to mean that she was required to conform to him. He used her shamelessly as an excuse for not doing things he himself had no wish to do. June would have rather enjoyed going to a royal garden party or a reception at Windsor; Rupert ruled that it would make her anxious and the invitations were refused. When the Grenfells suggested taking them out to dinner at a nearby pub, June's eyes glinted. 'Oh, no!' said Rupert. 'June loves cooking.' Joyce Grenfell was horrified when she discovered that Rupert expected June to show him all the letters she received and even the letters she was sending. 'He likes to know what I write,' June explained; but as Joyce Grenfell added: 'He doesn't show her all of his!'[24] Everything in the Old Rectory had to be kept as it was; if curtains needed to be replaced or a room repainted the new look must approximate as closely as possible to the old. He begrudged her any kind of independence. She had got out of the habit of driving and longed to have some practice: 'Of course, darling, perhaps tomorrow,' he would say, but tomorrow never came. 'She is a willing slave,' said Joyce Grenfell, though she conceded that June was happy in her slavery. June told Deirdre that Rupert was at a meeting, 'so I've got what he calls "free time". He organises my every moment when he's here, which is practically always, and I love it.'[25] She did love it, but at times it grated. It was only tolerable because she knew it was the mark of Rupert's love for her and that her husband had no idea how heavily he imposed on her. 'I wish he were more imaginative and sensitive to her,' Joyce Grenfell complained. 'None so insensitive as the very sensitive.'[26]

Insensitivity could sometimes lead him to inflict the very pain which he was so anxious to spare her. June remembers one awful day when Edith Evans and an old friend of Comfort's were both staying the night. Edith Evans breakfasted in bed, so the first part of the morning was given up to a discussion of Comfort's transcendent qualities. Comfort's friend then left and Edith Evans descended; the conversation turned to Peggy Ashcroft who, for two hours, was praised to the skies. Edith Evans in her turn left and a relation of Ruth's came to tea. For another two hours they discussed Ruth's virtues. 'I found that very exhausting,' Rupert said, when they at last had the house to themselves. 'What about *me*?' June longed to retort, but of course she didn't. Rupert would have been surprised and hurt, and that was something she could not contemplate. He snored ferociously and sometimes in desperation she would tiptoe to another room to try to get some sleep. When he found out he was deeply offended. 'I don't do it on purpose,' he protested. 'He wants her in his bed and that is that,' wrote Joyce Grenfell. 'So she lies there raging and not sleeping – isn't it idiotic?'[27]

During their first years of marriage, money was a constant worry. Bridget and her husband were most supportive where Comfort's welfare was concerned, but Rupert was still committed to contributing £40 a month to her maintenance. The Granada income had stopped in November 1968 and Rupert's earnings were minimal. Under Ruth's will he was supposed to have inherited £200 a year but it was slow in arriving in his bank. When he reached the age of sixty-five he would be slightly better off since he would then receive an annuity of about £800 a year and get an Old Age Pension instead of paying out National Insurance, but that was still some years off and even then he would not have nearly enough to live on. 'I keep telling him not to worry about money,' June told Deirdre, 'but of course it doesn't help at all to be told not to worry. I'm quite sure there are lots of people who would pay handsomely for his advice and reputation. If only we knew them!'[28] Until such time as these unsuspecting benefactors turned up Rupert decided that he must raise some money by selling a few pictures and manuscripts. The Marie Laurencin portrait he had been left by Hugh Walpole was sent to Sotheby's; Rupert had hoped it might fetch £1,000, in fact it went for £2,800. The manuscript of *Stamboul Train* which Graham Greene had given him was sold, with Greene's blessing, for £500; a packet of Ruskin letters also brought in £500. 'Clearly *all* the books here are worth a small fortune, and there are plenty more I can sell without heartache,' he told Deirdre with satisfaction.[29] But though the wolf had been temporarily repelled from the door, Rupert could not live for ever on sales from his library. Some more permanent source of funds was badly needed.

Rescue duly arrived. Since 1963, when Hugh Walpole's surviving brother died, Rupert had been the sole beneficiary from the literary estate. The sale of Walpole's library had provided Comfort with her main source of income, the royalties continued to bring in a healthy £1,500 or so a year. 'One can't expect this to last much longer,' Rupert told Edmund Blunden.[30] The detection of best-sellers had never been his strong point as a publisher and he was no more correct in this case than any other. Royalties continued steady for a year or two, then came explosion. First in 1969 Pan bought the paperback rights in the *Herries Chronicles* for £6,500; the hardback publisher took 45 per cent but Rupert's share was still handsome: 'Isn't it astonishing!' he told Deirdre. 'How delighted dear old Hugh would be.'[31] The following year Scandinavian publishers made offers for translation rights, then came the Japanese. A Norwegian paper paid £900 to serialise the Herries books: 'Another splendid windfall. This will enable us to get a new car . . . The Walpole cruse seems inexhaustible.'[32] And another cruse was about to open. Arthur Ransome's widow, Genia, was in frail health and seemed unlikely to survive for long. When she died, a quarter of Ransome's still substantial royalties would accrue to Rupert. While they lived, and indeed after their deaths, Rupert had devoted many hundreds of hours to the affairs of Walpole and Ransome. In doing this he had never stopped to consider whether he would one day be rewarded for his work. Rarely can bread cast so generously upon the waters have earned so ample a recompense.

Though Rupert took little exercise he managed to keep himself in good trim: from time to time he panicked about his waistline but a bout of dieting always seemed to restore good order. In 1963 he ordered the first suit he had had made for him since 1945, and proudly told Edmund Blunden that his measurements were unchanged.[33] But in 1967, perhaps made more vulnerable by the strains following the death of Ruth, he contracted a particularly unpleasant skin disease called psoriasis which caused almost intolerable itching. By way of treatment he had to be smothered in yellow ointment, powdered and then swaddled 'in a complete suit of mutton-cloth – two legs, two arms and a vest, all tied together with fiddly little tapes'. After twenty-four hours this carapace was removed with the help of olive oil and the process was begun again. 'June has to do most of it,' Rupert told Deirdre. 'She is an angel from Heaven, who grows sweeter, kinder and dearer every day.'[34] The treatment worked but the doctor cheerfully told him that the relief would probably only be temporary, he must expect the condition to recur and recur again.

    Like most Londoners, Rupert had believed that services obtained in the country would inevitably be inferior to those offered in the metropolis. Quite soon after moving to Yorkshire he accepted that the Richmond barber might be a possible alternative to Trumper's, but lawyers, accountants, doctors, dentists were another matter. Gradually, his reluctance to travel south overcame his prejudices. Early in 1971 he tentatively essayed a local dentist. He had the rotting stumps of five teeth removed in Richmond. The results seemed satisfactory: 'I begin to wonder whether we shouldn't transfer altogether to this chap,' he speculated. 'It could save us a good deal of money and would prevent our ever having to visit London.'[35] In June he repeated the experiment. This time, however, things went wrong, the dentist seemed somehow to have punctured a vein and Rupert ended up in the Military Hospital in Catterick, where a team of four dentists and two doctors worked for several hours to put him to rights. This might have been expected to revive all his scepticism about the skills of Yorkshire dentists but he persevered: in February 1972 he had nine stoppings and later that year one tooth and two further stumps were removed. When an extremely painful abscess developed in one of his few remaining teeth he wrote disconsolately to Deirdre: 'I fear that may be the end of my own pegs . . . what a nuisance the bloody things are.'[36] For several years he struggled on, in occasional pain and almost invariable discomfort and with the doleful prospect of false teeth looming ever closer. Since he was also increasingly deaf and suffered from painful bouts of lumbago, he was beginning to feel rather sorry for himself as the 1970s wore on.

But though these afflictions were unpleasant they were not as alarming as the mysterious fits of giddiness and nausea which began increasingly to plague him towards the end of 1972. Eventually this was diagnosed as Menière's Disease, two of the symptoms of which were ringing in the ears and serious deafness. Earlier victims had included Julius Caesar, Martin Luther, Dean Swift: a fact which may have lent the disease some intellectual and social cachet but gave Rupert small comfort. For nearly six months he hardly dared leave the house and was nursed devotedly by June who had not merely to cater for him physically but also to provide some stimulation when he felt too ill to read or even to do jigsaw puzzles.

At least he had now shed the remaining duties which forced him to go to London. He gave up being Chairman of the London Library in October 1969. Kenneth Clark, T. S. Eliot's successor as President, praised him to the skies and June 'swelled with pride, but the assembled members, perhaps stunned by the unaccustomed financial surplus . . . uttered no word'.[37] A year or so before, he had handed on the Literary Society to Peter Fleming, who for the brief period left to him kept Rupert posted about new developments. 'Some oaf suggested women should be invited,' reported Fleming, 'just shows to what excesses the

demon alcohol can drive us.'[38] Rupert, who like most other men of the
period relished female company but nevertheless believed that they
were unfit to be admitted to male clubs, would have shared Fleming's
dismay at so outlandish a proposition. That the idea should even be
mooted must have seemed to him fresh evidence that London was no
longer a city fit for the civilised to frequent. On one of his increasingly
rare visits he met Jamie Hamilton, 'just the same and v friendly', he told
Deirdre, 'but I got an immense impression of falsity and boredom.
Altogether London was hateful and I never want to go there again.'[39]
When Hamilton pressed him to come to his seventieth birthday party
he refused in the most affectionate terms but enquired peevishly of his
sister: 'In more than six years he has never made the slightest attempt to
come here; why should he think I'm any keener to go to London to see
him?'[40] He was equally disobliging when the widow of the writer Sir
Laurence Jones tried to involve him in an evening of music and reading
in honour of her dead husband. 'I think it's a frightful idea but can't say
so,' he wrote. 'The imperiousness of the very old is hard to counter
without being unkind.'[41] He hardened his heart, risked the charge of
unkindness and refused the invitation.

His occupations in Swaledale expanded to fill the gaps. A few weeks
after Ruth's death, an apricot tree that she had ordered arrived and
needed planting. Rupert's first reaction was to break down in tears but
then, Deirdre told Janet Adam Smith, he pulled himself together and
thought: 'To hell with it! I shall learn about gardening, it will be
something for me to do, and something that Ruth loved.'[42] He recruited
Boyk to help him and together they settled down to learn about
gardening and develop what Ruth had begun. 'My greatest solace has
been in finishing and looking after the garden which [Ruth and I] had
planned together,' he told Richard Church.[43] When June, an accomplished gardener, came on the scene, his energy dwindled, but he still
did far more and took much greater interest in the garden at Marske
than he had ever done at Bromsden.

Though he had contrived to shuffle off his London commitments,
Rupert had still not wholly mastered the art of saying no. Inexorably, he
was drawn into local life. One involvement was with the Georgian
Theatre at Richmond, a charming eighteenth-century relic which Lady
Crathorne had rescued from ignominious employment as a storehouse
and restored to something near its former glory. It was grand yet
intimate; Hugh Brogan told Rupert that it had 'more real character than
any playhouse I've ever entered . . . What wonderful, electric, nuanced

acting it would make possible. The intimacy of television with the excitement of actuality.'[44] With his London links and his theatrical experience Rupert was an obvious person to recruit as a supporter. He took on the task with relish and persuaded a series of distinguished friends to travel north to give solo performances in the theatre: Joyce Grenfell, Edith Evans, Emlyn Williams, Micheál Mac Liammóir. Such stars had to be entertained; a task which June found stressful but less alarming than when literary luminaries were involved. While driving Edith Evans to lunch with the Crathornes, June confessed that she always felt nervous going to grand places and meeting new people. So had she once, said Dame Edith, but now 'I just tell myself I'm *adorable*'. June was working in the kitchen when Micheál Mac Liammóir entered behind her back and exclaimed: 'You beautiful creature, no wonder so many come to see you.' 'What rubbish you do talk,' said June. 'No, darling,' replied Mac Liammóir. 'I wasn't talking to you. I was talking to myself in the mirror.'[45]

Arranging the visits and looking after the visitors took much time but worse followed when Nancy Crathorne was diagnosed with cancer and in due course died. Inevitably Rupert was asked to take over as Chairman. 'I haven't the time, the money, the contacts or the inclination,' he moaned. 'On the other hand it would be a thousand pities to let it die.'[46] The other hand prevailed; Rupert took office just in time to welcome the Queen Mother on her visit to the theatre. He had to say a few words from the stage to welcome her and in tribute to Nancy Crathorne; he dried up in the middle and had to look at his notes but June claimed he seemed totally unflustered. Certainly the Queen Mother appeared not to notice: 'How blue and beautiful her eyes are! She seemed delighted with everything.'[47]

Soon his letters to Deirdre were peppered with allusions to 'a meeting that lasted a good three hours', 'yesterday I had a *four-hour* meeting of this infernal theatre committee', '*another* long meeting. It's a great nuisance and I shall be thankful to be quit of it.' Until John Eccles came to the area, however, and joined the Committee, there was nobody whom he felt could be trusted to carry on the work. With relief he handed over to Eccles early in 1975. Some chairmen like to linger on after their formal departure and plague their successors with suggestions and criticisms; Rupert continued to support the theatre and attend most of its productions but he never interfered. 'I have had enough committees to last for two life-times,' he told Deirdre.[48]

Another local enterprise with which he became heavily involved was

the conversion of Marrick Priory, a deserted Benedictine nunnery a few
miles from Marske, into an adventure centre for boys and girls from the
industrial towns in Yorkshire or elsewhere. Rupert became Treasurer
and took over an enterprise heavily in debt and floundering in a mesh of
clerical bureaucracy; he enlisted the local grandees to help with the
fund-raising, pushed through plans to build a house for the Warden,
and in due course persuaded the Lord Lieutenant to attend the opening
ceremony. By this time he had become Chairman. As such, he was
largely responsible for the appointment of Jonathan Bailey, later to
become Bishop of Derby, as the first Warden of the centre. It proved an
inspired choice: Bailey had energy, imagination and organising skills
and got the Priory off to a triumphant start. Rupert was inclined to
believe that most clergymen would be better employed doing something
useful rather than spouting platitudes but in Bailey he had found a
churchman entirely to his taste; the two men never discussed religion,
or for that matter literature, but they worked harmoniously and
constructively together. To Bailey Rupert seemed particularly remarkable in that his work for Marrick was entirely altruistic. He had no wish
to win public recognition or establish a claim to some higher office; still
less did he hope to use Marrick as a stepping stone into local society.
Rupert was not himself one for the active life of hiking, pot-holing or
climbing but he saw the value of such activities for under-privileged
children from the cities who had barely seen a tree, let alone a landscape
as grandiose yet as beautiful as that of Swaledale. He knew how much
Swaledale meant to him and believed that it could mean as much to
many others. He abhorred what seemed to him the desecration inflicted
on the countryside by mass tourism, but if young people could be
taught to appreciate natural beauty and become fully aware of their
surroundings while at the same time stretching themselves physically
and psychologically, he believed it would be well worth some sacrifice of
time and effort on his part.

'Altruistic' is not the first adjective that one would apply to Rupert.
He was, indeed, capable of the most flagrant selfishness. He was once
told that one of his secretaries had said of him: 'Mr Hart-Davis is very
nice as long as his own personal comfort isn't interfered with.' 'The
older I get the truer that home-truth becomes,' Rupert admitted
ruefully.[49] To 'personal comfort' add 'habits' and 'freedom to work as
and when he pleased' and a recognisable if one-sided picture of his
personality emerges. But he was also capable of remarkable and
spontaneous generosity. When Harold Atkinson, a neighbour in

Swaledale but not a particularly close friend, was in hospital in Newcastle after a major operation, Rupert drove several times to visit him – a journey of some sixty miles each way – and wrote a letter to him every day in an effort to cheer him up. His beloved Boyk dropped dead when chatting to a friend in a nearby field. 'Junie and I are heart-broken and hardly slept a wink last night,' he told Deirdre.[50] But he did not merely grieve, he devoted much time and effort to ensuring that Boyk's widow, Nell, was well looked after, spoke at his funeral, and gave whatever help was needed in sorting out his affairs.

Boyk's death was doubly painful because it gravely damaged the pattern of existence which Rupert had constructed to sustain his old age. Boyk, with his goodwill, his charm, his range of talents, had become part of Rupert's daily existence. He was essential to Rupert's habits and, to an almost grotesque degree, Rupert was a creature of habit. Each day, each week, unwound according to a rhythm of unvarying rituals. New departures were ventured on only with extreme reluctance; if they proved successful then they were at once absorbed into the seamless scheme of existence so that it felt as if they had always been part of normal life. He resisted the installation of television until 1970 but, once it had been installed, watched it with rapt attention. He never missed a day of a Test Match, happily oblivious to the fact that, as June told Deirdre, it was 'an appallingly bad picture, colour coming and going, picture coming and going, atmospherics and interference galore – it's hopeless'.[51] Certain programmes were not to be missed, regardless of the feelings of guests or the most pressing invitations: *Dad's Army*; *Softly Softly*; *Z Cars*. But the medium was not deemed suitable for the serious or the adventurous. David Storey's *Home*, with Gielgud and Richardson, was 'switched off in boredom', so was *Citizen Kane*; *Monty Python* he dismissed as 'silly and pointless'.

Holidays followed an equally inflexible routine. The honeymoon visit to Arran had proved a great success; it was repeated year after year, with stops on the way at the same hotels, if possible in the same rooms. In 1972, inexplicably, they ventured as far as Elba. Rather to Rupert's surprise he enjoyed the holiday; they made bookings for the following summer and took the same journey for the next seven years until other commitments made it impossible. In principle he was prepared to accept that other places might be as agreeable, possibly even more so; but he knew Elba, he was known in Elba, his life there could be conducted to a secure pattern: what sense could there be in looking elsewhere?

*

Rupert would have maintained that the main point of leading a structured life was not because it pleased him but because it made it easier for him to accommodate the various literary tasks that lay in front of him. At last he had escaped from the day-to-day demands of publishing and could lead the life of a man of letters to which he had for so long aspired. 'As for laziness, I have now happily surrendered to mine, and very enjoyable it is,' he told his sister in 1969. He took some pleasure in boasting about his idleness; when Deirdre's daughter was about to visit him he suggested that she should be told to expect 'a balding, grey-haired, paunchy old square, selfish, lazy and intolerant'.[52] If to watch undemanding television, re-read old novels, do jigsaw and crossword puzzles, is to be lazy, then Rupert did indeed indulge himself for more of the time than a stern ascetic might have thought proper. The fact remains that, in his own time and way, he applied himself for what most people would have considered more than a working day to a series of books to which he was committed.

There was some conflict between the books of his own which he wanted to write and those which he felt bound to work on for the sake of other people. His long-term objective was a memoir of his mother, possibly expanding into a full-scale autobiography. He was making preparations for this even before he married June: a room in the Old Rectory had been assigned for the collection of papers, Deirdre was being badgered for details about Sibbie's education and early life. 'Soon I shall read everything through, making notes of all that's useful and relevant,' he told his sister. 'Are you sure you haven't got any other scraps?'[53] But somehow or other, more pressing commitments always seemed to interfere; five years later he was still 'sweating away at other people's manuscripts, longing to get cracking on my own'. Deirdre suspected that he was recoiling before the prospect of something that might prove to be painful and embarrassing; Rupert crossly rejected the idea. 'You're quite wrong about my building up any sort of resistance to my book – you mustn't believe all the psycho-analysts tell you. In fact it's just the opposite, and I can't wait to begin it.'[54] No doubt he was convinced by what he said, but it still seems likely that Deirdre had a point; it was much easier to tidy up other people's work than to start with a blank page, and Rupert may well have had qualms about a project which would involve far more in the way of introspection and self-examination than he felt comfortable or proper.

He could, however, legitimately claim that he had many other pressing responsibilities. His first was to Max Beerbohm. He had revered Beerbohm, both as writer and as caricaturist. Beerbohm's widow and, after her death, his sister-in-law, Eva Reichmann, depended heavily on Rupert for advice on how to deal with the mountain of papers and drawings that Max had left behind him. Rupert had already edited and published Beerbohm's letters to Reggie Turner, now he began to compile a collection of those theatre reviews which had not already appeared in Beerbohm's own selection, *Around Theatres*. There was some good stuff that deserved a second lease of life, but the enterprise was of marginal importance and the two volumes which he published, *More Theatres* and *Last Theatres*, achieved little in the way of reviews or sales. The first was 'filthily produced and chock-full of misprints,' he complained to William Plomer – the offence being made more painful because it appeared under his own imprint.[55] It was a delight to have escaped from the treadmill of publishing, but he was now finding that liberation carried with it the disadvantage that he could no longer control the production of his own books. Instead he fumed impotently at what seemed to him the shoddy workmanship and limited understanding of those who were still active in the field. It was worthwhile, all the same. A third volume, a collection of Beerbohm's prose pieces accumulated from various journals and newspapers and called *A Peep into the Past*, gave him particular satisfaction because he chanced on an unsigned article about William Archer in an ancient copy of *The Times*, thought he recognised the style, established that it was indeed by Beerbohm and triumphantly resurrected it. The fact confirmed him in his belief that, for an editor, informed serendipity could be every bit as valuable as a capacity for conscientious hard work. Rupert had both.

His catalogue of Beerbohm's caricatures demanded such qualities in full. Rupert had conceived the idea for this in 1958. A *catalogue raisonnée* was badly needed, he told George Lyttelton, 'since there's no way of finding out how many there are, or were'. There would be no money to be made out of it, in fact 'the job would get pretty close to that "pure scholarship" which is its own reward'.[56] Eight years later he had got down to work, putting a notice in the papers appealing for information. The response had been uplifting or appalling, according to his mood – more than 150 letters in the first week. For the next ten years he worked on the project, sometimes desultorily, sometimes with passionate intensity. The accumulation and attribution of the drawings was the easy part; their dating and the explanation of their subjects required endless research and speculation. It might have been spun out for ever if the centenary of Beerbohm's birth had not provided a deadline which the publisher insisted must be observed. In the end he tracked down 2,093 caricatures, of which he was allowed to illustrate 200. The critical response, when the book at last appeared in August 1972, was all he could have hoped for. All the usual allies rallied to his support in the British press while in the *Washington Post* the American critic Richard Freedman – probably the leading authority on the subject – called it 'splendid' and 'the most scholarly job ever done on Max's graphic art'. Only Roy Strong in *The Times* offended Rupert. He did a double review of the caricatures and *A Peep into the Past*, and wrote that the latter was full of 'charming slight pieces' which were professional in a way to which the drawings did not aspire. As a draughtsman, he asserted, Beerbohm was 'feeble to a degree . . . rising little beyond what might be categorised as "board-room doodles"'. Rupert rarely took hostile criticism kindly; Roy Strong was deemed doubly guilty because he had originally welcomed the idea of a Beerbohm exhibition at the National Portrait Gallery. Ignorant abuse, Rupert considered the review – 'that silly show-off whiz-kid'.[57]

The completion of this gargantuan task should in theory have freed him for work on his memoirs but new responsibilities seemed to arise as soon as the old ones departed. Siegfried Sassoon died in 1967. In his last months he had been made unhappy by his failure to secure the Order of Merit. Rupert told him that he had best forget the possibility; Tommy Lascelles was now retired and the new regime did not seem particularly well disposed towards him. 'The value of my work does not depend on the patronage of Michael Adeane and the Palace,' replied Sassoon haughtily. 'It depends on the appeal of its *humanity*.'[58] Rupert visited him for what proved to be the last time a few weeks later and then hastened south again for his funeral. As he felt certain would happen, he found himself appointed literary executor. The status of Sassoon's diaries was obscure but Rupert, afraid that they might be destroyed or sold, succeeded in carrying them away with him. Soon he would start preparatory work on them, certain that one day they should be published.

The affairs of Arthur Ransome made more immediate demands on his time. Rupert had encouraged the idea of an autobiography and Ransome had made a start but soon became discouraged: 'The wretched Ransome sticks fast in the quagmire,' he told Rupert,[59] and when he died he left behind him a jumble of uncoordinated passages, repetitive, inaccurate and with only three or four pages to cover the thirty-five years since the publication of *Swallows and Amazons* had launched him on a new career.[60] Rupert had promised that he would finish the book after the author's death and see it through to publication, but Ransome's widow fought a delaying action for almost four years and then expected Rupert to produce a finished text within a few weeks. 'It shouldn't be a long job,' said Rupert hopefully,[61] but he had not allowed for the wretched Genia, who interfered endlessly with his work and allowed her ferociously anti-semitic views to poison her relationship with Ransome's publisher, Cape's. The editor was Tom Maschler, one of the most enterprising and creative of contemporary publishers. This cut no ice with Genia, however. 'I have met Jews I have greatly admired,' she wrote, without specifying who was included in this privileged minority, 'but there is a type I just can't stand at any price and TM unfortunately is it.'[62] She waited until the work was almost complete and then proposed postponing publication for thirteen years. Rupert paid no attention, whereupon she sent him a mass of additional material which had to be assimilated: 'I'm heartily sick of it, and grudge all the time it's keeping me from my own book,' he told Deirdre.[63] It was 1974 before he got it finally into shape. Genia died before it went to press. Rupert refused to make any reference to her in the prologue: 'Short of destroying the typescript, she did everything possible to prevent the book's completion and publication, and gave up her rearguard action only a few weeks before she died.'[64]

Arthur Ransome safely out of the way, Rupert was at once enmeshed in the affairs of William Plomer. Rupert had long admired Plomer's writing. 'When I consider how many of our contemporaries have faded poetically,' he told him in 1972; 'Auden declined upon clerihews, Spender showing no change or improvement, poor Cecil [Day-Lewis] almost dead – I rejoice in the strength and fertility of your muse.'[65] When Plomer died at the end of 1973 Rupert was in Elba, where he got a telegram asking him to get in touch with the author's lawyer. 'So I probably *am* his literary executor,' he told Deirdre.[66] He was: the books and papers he disposed of to Durham University but he still found himself having to conflate two volumes of autobiography into one and to cobble together a book out of the many miscellaneous pieces Plomer had left behind. Rupert had been very fond of Plomer as well as respecting his work – 'Most people I am delighted to be away from but *you*, dear William, I miss,' he had written some years before[67] – and he did not resent the extra work, but it was yet another hurdle to surmount before he could tackle the memoir of his mother.

By now he was literary executor to Hugh Walpole, Duff Cooper, Siegfried Sassoon, Max Beerbohm and William Plomer – all demanding thought and time. Then came news that Edmund Blunden was close to death. 'I have a nasty (but I hope unfounded) idea that I may be his literary executor,' Rupert told Deirdre.[68] The idea was not unfounded; indeed, Rupert would have been as much offended as relieved if he had been spared the duty. He duly gave the address at Blunden's memorial service and took on yet another load of responsibilities.

Even when he did not feel himself bound by any such obligation he could rarely resist an appeal for help when an old friend turned to him. James Lees-Milne was 'the dearest and kindest of men', so naturally Rupert felt bound to read the proofs of all his books.[69] 'I think he is a great man in his way, which is scholarly without being pedantic,' Lees-Milne wrote in his diary. 'What an honour to be asked to let him read my manuscript. He is the successor to Eddie Marsh as England's proof-reader-in-chief.'[70] Proof-reading did not mean merely the correction of misprints; Rupert improved grammar and cut out redundant words with a vigour which must have alarmed cost-cutting publishers who had assumed that they had been given something close to a finished article. 'I have adopted almost all your suggestions and excised "of course" and "overall",' another old friend, Anthony Powell, told him, 'taking your severe strictures to heart.' But he refused to substitute 'contrast to' for 'contrast with', recalcitrance which Rupert regretted but admitted might be pardonable.[71]

Any job that seemed likely to involve an expedition to London was generally rejected but he could not resist becoming a judge of that then most civilised award, the W. H. Smith Prize, for which no books were submitted by publishers. The winner was chosen by three literary figures united by nothing but their knowledge of and love for books. Rupert took Elizabeth Bowen's seat in 1965 and remained a judge for twenty years. After the first year or two he rarely attended meetings in London but conducted all negotiations by telephone. His sheer obstinacy usually won him the day, though sometimes he was overborne. In 1967 he wanted the prize to go to Rebecca West, but Raymond Mortimer, another judge, black-balled the selection and argued successfully for Jean Rhys's *The Wide Sargasso Sea*. Mortimer was most anxious that Rebecca West should not hear that his opposition had cost her the prize. Inevitably she did. 'If you should have the chance to talk to her about the affair, perhaps you could make me seem not too much of a brute,' pleaded Mortimer to Rupert. 'But she is violent in her emotions, and I don't expect to be forgiven. I hate being hated.'[72]

Joyce Grenfell wrote two volumes of autobiography and each time hastened north to seek Rupert's comments. On the first occasion, she was unlucky enough to coincide with a Test Match. Instead of settling down at once to read her typescript, Rupert retired to watch the shadowy figures flickering in a snowstorm which was still the best that Swaledale had to offer by way of television reception. 'I think it's a little unkind because he knows it means a lot to me,' Joyce Grenfell complained, 'but he has grown *very* indolent and really does nothing he doesn't want to do and is self-indulgent to the point of paralysis.'[73] Fortunately the cricket did not continue. Rupert devoted the following day to reading the typescript, praised it lavishly and was at once forgiven. By the time he had finished he had read the complete text through at least three times – 'a kindness and privilege of which I am fully aware,' Joyce Grenfell wrote gratefully.[74] Her only complaint was that he would not let her make any reference to her visits to Marske and the work he had done on her book: 'He says "But I've done it for dozens of people ... " Frustrating.'[75] The paperback edition of the second volume, *In Pleasant Places*, caused Rupert mild irritation when he found himself referred to in the index as 'Hart-Davis, old Rupert'. 'The adjective is accurate,' he admitted to the publisher, 'but it seems a little unkind to publicise one's misfortunes in this way ... If you reprint the book, the substitution of "Sir" for "old" will do the trick.'[76]

Towards the end of 1973 June wrote excitedly to Deirdre to report that: 'Believe it or not, Mit [a family nickname] has *turned down* helping an old friend with her book! Very reluctantly and regretfully, of course ... It's the life of the Duke of Windsor and not really his cup of tea anyway. Isn't it good?'[77] Frances Donaldson was not as old or as close a friend as Joyce Grenfell or Jim Lees-Milne but Rupert had published two of her books and admired her writing. To turn down her plea was, for him, a formidable departure from precedent. He was getting better, too, at rejecting propositions for which he thought he was ill-suited. An editor at Collins' telephoned to offer him a minimum of £20,000 if he would write the biography of Somerset Maugham. He had refused, he told Deirdre: 'he was such a horrid little man, and I have plenty to do already – but it was fun pretending for a moment that I was going to do it.'[78]

As important a factor in dissuading him as the horridness of Maugham must have been the fact that the work would take him for long periods away from Marske, a possibility which he was less and less ready to envisage. The same was not true of Mountbatten's proposal that Rupert should edit the correspondence between Queen Victoria and her granddaughter Princess Victoria; this he might have undertaken but 'so far as I've seen it, it doesn't seem to me to add up to a book'.[79] As for Jamie Hamilton's suggestion that he should write a study of the five authors for whom he acted as literary executor – he dismissed the idea with derision.[80] Increasingly he began to think of reasons why he could not deliver addresses at the memorial services of literary figures or lecture to miscellaneous bodies. In 1969 Leeds University invited him to join them as an honorary lecturer. 'I said I would think it over, but have no intention of accepting,' he told his sister. 'Why should I? Still, it is quite gratifying to be asked.'[81] Partly his rejection of such offers was due to the increasing indolence of which Joyce Grenfell had complained; much more it was because he realised that time was getting on and that if he was ever to write the memoir of his mother he must soon address himself to the task.

Most of all, he stayed at home and minded his own business because he was a contented man. He had created a pattern of existence which suited him admirably and he was reluctant to do anything which would put it even slightly at risk. Towards the end of 1968 Rupert told Deirdre that he and June had been listening to a broadcast of *Any Questions*. The discussion had turned to the best ways of avoiding the stresses and strains of modern life. 'We suddenly realised that we have *no* stress or strain; aren't we incredibly lucky?'[82] Two or three years later an old friend from Army days looked in on the way south. Rupert gave him a drink and settled him on the terrace to enjoy the sunshine and the view. The visitor looked around appreciatively and said: 'You know, if you're living in this beautiful place and doing the things you want to do, you're halfway to Heaven.'[83] Rupert took the phrase as the title of the final volume of his memoirs; he would have claimed that it was a fitting description of the last thirty years of his life.

Chapter Eighteen

Halfway to Heaven

Some time in the mid-1970s, Rupert decided that he was an old man. There was no particular reason for it. He drew his Old Age Pension from 1972 but though he showed the usual signs of wear and tear he was intellectually almost as alert and quick-thinking as ever. 'My mind moves very fast,' he had boasted to George Lyttelton some twenty years before,[1] and though the wheels perhaps now spun round a little less rapidly he could still more than hold his own in any sort of literary discussion. His memory was formidably good; his judgment as clear, firm and occasionally wrong-headed as ever. He did not think or look like an old man, he just came to the conclusion that he was one and that he should therefore behave appropriately. Most conspicuously, this showed itself in a determination not to put himself out or to deviate by an iota from the course of life which he had established. New departures were rarely if ever sanctioned; one by one even the time-hallowed rituals which involved social effort or journeys far from Marske, were dropped, first temporarily, then for ever.

The phrase 'decided not to' became a reiterated motif of his diary and his letters to Deirdre. First it was distant holidays: 'decided not to go to Arran', 'decided not to go to Elba'; then local outings were similarly curtailed – they decided not to go to York or Harrogate. Occasionally this reflected genuine anxieties on behalf of June. 'She dreads the journey to Elba and I can see why,' wrote Joyce Grenfell in 1978. 'They have to take all the MSS of the book about his Ma as well as his colossal shoes, at least 3 pairs without which he cannot do. And NO porters. And distances to be traversed in the stations from one train to the next.'[2] More often it was Rupert's judgment that the pains outweighed the pleasures and that he could not be bothered to make the necessary effort. It was not only holidays that were circumscribed. The year after she wrote the letter about the Elba visit, Joyce Grenfell died, leaving

Rupert and June £2,500 each. Rupert assured her husband, Reggie Grenfell, that nothing would keep him from the memorial service. A few weeks later, he was beginning to look for an excuse not to attend, a fortnight later again and he had persuaded himself that nobody could seriously expect him to make the journey. The roads were so bad, the trains so crowded and unpunctual, the occasion would be vast and impersonal: 'Just think of trying to get to King's Cross afterwards in the rush hour! I'll make some convincing excuse to Reggie when the time comes, and I'm sure he'll be too exhausted to mind.'³

When he actually got somewhere he was still capable of enjoying it. A few years earlier he had made the effort and gone south for the memorial service for Janet Adam Smith's husband, John Carleton. Even more remarkably, he had gone on to spend a night with Deirdre at her home in Lewes. 'Wasn't Mit in rattling good form?' wrote June afterwards. 'He always is once he's made the huge effort of stirring his stumps! An extraordinary mixture of vitality and laziness and having many friends whom he loves but doesn't want to see! It is very beautiful up here, but I do think people are more important than scenery.'⁴ Rupert would have made a few exceptions – June herself being the pre-eminent example – but he was by now convinced that scenery was more important than people and books than either. To make him stir his stumps became steadily more difficult, in the end almost impossible.

One of his favourite quotations came from Thomas Carlyle: 'Empty grinning apery of commonplace creatures and their loud inanities ought to be more and more shut out from us as the Eternities draw nigh.' Even when the eternities were still a considerable distance ahead Rupert used to maintain, somewhat unconvincingly, that he was not at heart gregarious, even sociable: 'The fact that I am tolerably good at dealing with people is misleading,' he told George Lyttelton. 'I much prefer near-solitude, at any rate for long periods.'⁵ What had been at the most half true in London had become reality in Swaledale. Social life became restricted to an ever-diminishing circle of close neighbours: when Lord and Lady Zetland asked them to dinner 'to meet a lot of peers', Rupert firmly refused. 'I really think we have now succeeded in getting all our neighbours at longish arms' length.'⁶ When kind friends tried to press on him new acquaintances whom they thought would prove kindred spirits to cheer him in his exile, he reacted with suspicion if not hostility. Norah Smallwood, an old ally from the world of publishing, was anxious for him to get to know a couple who had settled about ten miles away; one wrote on Byron, the other on Tolstoy. 'I said I'd rather die,' Rupert reported with relish, 'as this was just the sort of time-wasting nonsense I'd come all this way to avoid!'[7] Even old friends became progressively less acceptable. Jamie Hamilton and his wife invited themselves to stay. Rupert professed delight but became more and more panic-stricken as the day approached. 'What can we do with them all the time?' he asked Deirdre. 'We have, thank God, no distinguished neighbours to introduce them to.' A fortnight later, and he had almost screwed himself to the point of putting them off: 'The thought of more than a day of small-talk, and Yvonne's high-pitched laugh, and Jamie constantly looking at his watch, and all that cooking and washing-up is more than I can bear.' Eventually Deirdre happened to meet the Hamiltons at lunch and gave Jamie a hint as to Rupert's feelings. The next thing was a charming letter saying that the Hamiltons had unexpectedly been called to Paris and so must put off their visit. 'I'm sure this must be your doing and it's an immense relief to both of us,' Rupert told his sister gratefully.[8]

The numbers of people invited to stay dwindled dramatically in the 1970s and 1980s and soon consisted only of a handful of very old friends or people who needed to consult Rupert's personal knowledge or manuscripts in his possession. Such people were increasingly unwelcome, though they were usually unaware of the fact, for his courtesy almost always remained unwavering. One of the later guests, a few months before she died, was Joyce Grenfell. She became the subject of a peevish letter to Deirdre. Her bossiness had increased, Rupert reported, 'and she treats Reg like an under-privileged slave . . . She must always have the last word. Whenever I tell a funny story, she immediately caps it with an unfunny one. After I had read some good poems aloud, she insisted on reading some poor ones very badly.' But then he relented: she was after all, 'a good, generous, talented creature'.[9] Her letters recording the visit make it obvious that she had no suspicion her host was nurturing such disobliging thoughts.

Just occasionally, however, what an old friend described as his 'resonant cantankerousness' overcame his innate civility. Deirdre's daughter, Lucy, somewhat rashly brought to the house a boyfriend who was bearded, Marxist, and worst of all, did not even pretend to take any interest in Rupert's anecdotes. The visit was not a success and Rupert did not conceal that he longed for it to be over. He blamed the failure entirely on the young man's uncouthness: 'The older I get, the more important do manners seem to be. They are the oil that makes the machinery of life run smoothly.'[10] June, more charitably, saw it as 'a simple case of what they call the "generation gap"'. Also, she told Deirdre, Rupert's increasing deafness made it hard for him to follow a conversation, and this made him tired and irritated: 'So let's forgive the darling brute for his flamboyant opinions.'[11] His irritation led him from time to time to behave with uncharacteristic rudeness. Deirdre offered to send him a copy of Lucy's first book, on sexuality and feminism. 'Do *not* send me Lucy's book,' Rupert replied sternly. 'I could not possibly be interested.' Lucy, who genuinely admired her uncle, was mortified by the rebuff.

His contrariness led him to decry almost any project for a book that was put in front of him. He urged James Lees-Milne not to write about the 6th Duke of Devonshire; Hugh Brogan not to write about Arthur Ransome; at least three authors to put aside any idea of tackling Siegfried Sassoon. Leon Edel was told that it would be a great mistake to turn to Bloomsbury for a subject while Richard Ellman was urged to eschew Oscar Wilde. When Selina Hastings came to talk to him about Evelyn Waugh: 'I tried to dissuade her, since there have already been two lives, and though he was a good writer, he was a horrible man. Even the appalling anecdotes I told her failed to put her off,' he concluded; a curiously imperceptive comment, since the more appalling the anecdote the more likely it was that any putative biographer would be attracted.[12] His argument to deter Kate Grimond from writing about her mother, Celia Johnson, was somewhat more cogent though equally ineffective: 'Except for the theatre, Celia had no interesting life at all.'[13] His heaviest guns he reserved for Professor Peter Alexander, who proposed to write a book on Leonard and Virginia Woolf. This suggestion, said Rupert, was 'one of the worst I have heard in a long time . . . Readers are sick and tired of blather about Bloomsbury and you would be writing for a non-existent public.'[14] In almost every case his lugubrious prognostications were ignored; he bore no grudge and did what he could to help the authors when in due course they applied to him.

His natural conservatism became more marked as he severed his ties with contemporary society. Melford Stevenson, a notorious hanging judge of alarmingly reactionary opinions, was remembered with approval as 'one of the only judges who hands out punishments that might be a deterrent. I'm all for him.'[15] In theory he kept an open mind about contemporary developments. He told Robert Nye that he was aware of the generation gap and the difficulty he found in appreciating younger poets and writers. 'I try not to say "This is rubbish",' he concluded, 'but rather "It means nothing to me".'[16] He did not try very hard. When he finally retired as judge of the W. H. Smith Prize his one piece of advice to his successor was to resist any pressure to award the prize to the poet Geoffrey Hill, a favourite of one of the other judges, Christopher Ricks. Hill wrote gibberish, Rupert contended, and should not even be considered let alone chosen.

Politically, his conservatism was as deeply encrusted as ever. 'Harold Wilson has resigned – good riddance!' was followed closely by 'Callaghan elected Prime Minister – God help us!' In 1974, after much anxious cogitation, he voted Liberal, but this was an aberration that was not repeated. Once Mrs Thatcher took power his loyalties were secured. She seemed to him 'the *only* politician in our time who isn't in the least devious . . . I wouldn't trust any of the others an inch.'[17] When Mrs Thatcher fell he lost what little stomach he had ever had for the political fight. On 6 February 1992, shortly before the general election, a letter from him to the editor appeared in *The Times.* 'I cannot be the only one of your readers who is satiated by the ghastly faces and voices of politicians trying to sling mud at each other every day. I remember the good advice of W. B. Yeats:

> A statesman is an easy man,
> He tells his lies by rote;
> A journalist makes up his lies
> And takes you by the throat;
> So stay at home and drink your beer
> And let the neighbours vote.'

Reactionary, curmudgeonly, misogynistic: such adjectives are suggested by the preceding pages but bear no relationship to what people found in the Old Rectory when they penetrated its defences. Rupert was as he had always been: friendly, amusing, a generous host, endlessly helpful, as tolerant in the flesh as he could be acerbic and condemnatory on paper. He was a warm-hearted and lovable man and his grumpy carapace concealed the truth only from those who did not know him. In Marske, where they knew him well, he was viewed with affection and respect.

He was also still a vastly productive editor and author. In September 1974 he at last began writing the memoir of his mother. He found the work exhilarating and fulfilling. 'I do think I was meant to be a writer,' he told Deirdre. 'Once, when we were in a taxi driving down Berkeley Street, Mummy suddenly said: "I know, when you're grown up you'd better be a man of letters", and that in fact is what I've become. Having no creative gift – I could never write fiction or poetry – and being a late-developer, I needed a lot of practice in the choice and arrangement of words before I was ready to start. And funnily enough I got it from correcting and rewriting other people's books! I was 45 when *Hugh Walpole* appeared, and then I knew I could do it.'[18]

He was resolved that he was going to be completely honest about his mother, though he accepted that this would mean exposing her weaknesses as well as extolling what seemed to him her extraordinary qualities. Being honest with himself, however, did not preclude indignation if anybody else allowed themselves a similar liberty. In his biography of Augustus John, Michael Holroyd made a passing reference to Sibbie as being nice and apologetic and 'determined to give up the drink'.[19] Rupert took extreme offence, deeming it a gratuitous attack on his mother, introduced maliciously by the author so as to get his own back for Rupert's refusal to help him in his work. Since in due course Rupert was himself to make it clear that Sibbie consistently drank more than was good for her and at times teetered on the brink of alcoholism, it is hard to see that he had grounds for his indignation. On the subject of his mother, however, a balanced judgment could not be expected; he loved too passionately and cared too deeply for objectivity. He wrote Holroyd 'the most scarifying letter', then wisely decided to sleep on it before sending it, postponed sending it again until he had finished reading the book and finally suppressed it altogether.[20]

The Arms of Time, its title taken from a sonnet by Charles Tennyson Turner, was a book of only 150 pages, but it took Rupert nearly five years to write and publish. Partly this was because of the difficulty he experienced in describing some of the more painful episodes, subjects he tackled with such reluctance that he unconsciously sought out any other work that would distract him; partly because those other distractions were enjoyable and engrossing enough fully to engage his attention.

The most time-consuming was the preparation for publication of the letters he had exchanged over six years with his schoolmaster friend, George Lyttelton. The idea that these might make a book had been exercising him for several years and when Jock and Diana Murray came to lunch in October 1976 he told them of their existence and gave them a batch to examine. Diana Murray read them first, liked them and recommended them to her husband. Jock Murray agreed. 'He was an inspirational publisher, always prepared to take a chance,' wrote Rupert.[21]

Murray was in fact not quite so inspirational and rather more cautious than Rupert supposed. He was by no means convinced that a book of letters of this kind would work and passed them on to one of his editors, Roger Hudson, saying that he wanted the opinion of somebody who was younger and neither an Old Etonian nor a lover of cricket. In spite of suffering from these sad disabilities, Hudson was enthusiastic and urged publication. Nevertheless, it was February 1977 before Murray finally decided that he would like to do the book. 'Jock telephoned to say that he wanted to publish all the GWL–RH-D letters. Great excitement!' Rupert wrote in his diary. Again he was too ebullient; Murray was at this point only prepared to commit himself to one volume. The book therefore appeared as *The Lyttelton Hart-Davis Letters: 1955–56* with no volume number. 'If these letters find favour there are plenty more to come,' Rupert promised in his Introduction. But though Murray may slightly have hedged his bets, it was still a brave undertaking. 'Has anyone else ever edited their own letters for publication?' Rupert asked Janet Adam Smith.[*] 'And for them to appear in the same list as Byron's letters is surely the height of presumption!'[22]

'I am busily hacking the dull, unkind and libellous passages out of the letters,' Rupert told Deirdre.[23] How much was hacked will never be known, for to the considerable irritation of George Lyttelton's children, he destroyed the originals once the series had been completed. Eton and cricket, as Murray had suggested to Roger Hudson, were indeed two of the recurring topics; so was the Literary Society to which Rupert had secured Lyttelton's election. He was doubtful how far it was proper to publish references to the dinners of a group which, without being secretive, had never courted publicity. He consulted Tommy Lascelles. He had always been told that he should never repeat anything told him in confidence, Lascelles ruled, 'but it has never occurred to me that one mustn't talk, or write, about clubs as *institutions*, as if they were so many Medmenhams, the scenes of nameless revels.'[24] But more than anything else the letters were about literature; the conversation of two extremely well-read and civilised beings about the books they were reading, had read, were about to read, were resolved never to read; a conversation

---

[*] A curious question. To take only one example; Rupert himself had been responsible for Lady Emily Lutyens' girlhood correspondence with an elderly clergyman, edited by herself and called *A Blessed Girl*.

whose urbanity and lightness of touch never concealed the passionate enthusiasm that lay just below the surface. Jock Murray thought that the rather pedestrian title did not do justice to the contents and asked another stalwart of the Literary Society, Bernard Ballantrae, to propose a livelier alternative. Ballantrae's suggestion was 'I Say, Rupert,' a phrase often occurring in Lyttelton's letters.[25] Rupert would have none of it: a title should say what the book was about and *The Lyttelton Hart-Davis Letters* did exactly that.

Rupert suspected that Jamie Hamilton, who was scheduled to publish his long-promised memoirs, would take umbrage at the fact that he had not been asked to handle the letters as well. He was proved only too correct. It was not a question of profit, Hamilton protested, but of friendship; he resented the fact that he, who felt Rupert to be his oldest friend and who had originally introduced him to publishing, should be left so brutally to one side. Hamilton would never have taken on the letters, Rupert protested, 'so please forget and forgive. Let Jock lose his shirt on these interminable letters, and wait for my own book, which with any luck won't lose you more than your collar and tie. Come out from your umbrage. I love you.'[26] Hamilton was not so easily appeased and though Rupert would much rather not have upset him, he in fact felt little pity for the affronted publisher. To Deirdre he wrote crossly: 'He still behaves like an insecure little boy, which at 76 is hard to sympathise with.'[27] It was several years before Hamilton could bring himself to admit that it had perhaps been for the best, 'as I was bought up and Jock remained independent'.[28]

Ex-publishers do not normally make easy authors and Rupert was exigent beyond the norm. When Faber's published Siegfried Sassoon's letters to Max Beerbohm, he demanded galley proofs, once provided as a matter of course but by 1986 an unusual and expensive luxury. Instead they produced 'lousy page-proofs' and pleaded that the request for galleys had not 'filtered through' to the appropriate department. He had some reason to complain about the lousiness of the proofs. The indented passages were in the wrong typeface – an error which he insisted must be rectified – while the settings, he complained, appeared to be 'the work of a mutinous computer'. But what galled him as much as anything was that the covering letter was addressed to Mr Hart-Davis. 'I was knighted in 1967,' Rupert replied sourly, 'but clearly the news hasn't yet filtered through to you.'[29]

When it came to the *Letters*, Murray's perpetrated nothing as heinous as this but they refused to provide a revised specimen page. 'I suppose I shall have to lump it,' Rupert grumbled. 'Tetchy old pub,' Jock Murray scrawled in the margin of this letter. Unlike Cape's and the Oxford University Press, Rupert wrote in congratulation, Murray's seemed capable of predicting when proofs would be available. 'Ha! Ha!' was Murray's comment on this. 'I pray our unique knowledge turns out truth.'[30] He urged Rupert to come south for a party on publication and when Rupert explained that he would be in Elba on that date he made various other proposals for celebrating the event. 'You are very charming and very persuasive,' Rupert replied, 'but I am by now inoculated against charm and persuasion. So please forget all your delightful suggestions.'[31]

The *Letters* were published in June 1978. The reviews were for the most part friendly, even effusive. 'One of the most winning books I know,' Raymond Mortimer described it, while in the *Daily Telegraph* David Holloway called the letters 'splendidly and unrepentantly civilised'. The book provided, said the *Economist*, 'a singular insight into the opinions, quirks and prejudices of a certain literary, gentlemanly England'. The perception that it was a book written by insiders for other insiders was in general seen as a merit but irritated some readers. Helene Hanff, whose *84 Charing Cross Road* might have been thought to share some of the same characteristics, wrote to Roger Hudson to complain: 'Two men can't just decide to Have a Correspondence and expect anyone else to care. You don't write letters that way. And you don't sit and think up things to write in your letters and you don't write and lavishly praise your correspondent for *his* letters, as if an ordinary letter were something portentously earth-shaking for anybody to manage to write.'[32] She was right in pointing out the artificiality that pervades these letters but wrong in assuming that nobody would care. On the contrary, a surprising number of people felt that they were privileged to enter the world of these two cultivated and on the whole affable English gentlemen. The sales were not prodigious but as good as Jock Murray had hoped and a great deal better than he had feared. Rupert was content, though he found things to grumble about. Too few of the reviewers, he felt, had done justice to the jokes, 'but perhaps such things are out of fashion, along with elegance, wit, style etc'. Worse still, the *Guardian* had failed to mention the book at all. 'I fear they won't now. It nowadays seems interested only in books of poems by dissident Bulgarians and such riff-raff.'[33]

The question now was whether there should be further volumes. Rupert claimed that at a convivial dinner with Janet Adam Smith, on what must have been one of his increasingly rare visits to London, Murray had promised that there would be at least a second instalment. 'Was he or I in his or my cups?' Murray asked Roger Hudson. 'I do think worth continuing with our cautious front, even if we know we will weaken, because it may strengthen our hand when it comes to selecting a second vol. Suspect his ideas won't exactly correspond with ours.'[34] In fact, once the principle of publication had been conceded, there was not much room for manoeuvre over the selection of the material. The appeal of the correspondence depended on its leisurely pace and amiably discursive nature; to abridge it fiercely would have been to destroy its quirky individuality. Rupert paid enough attention to his critics to prune the passages on Eton and cricket and also to remove 'a good deal of the mutual admiration which some readers found cloying'[35] but there was no way by which the balance of the correspondence could be substantially changed. Still less was it possible to address the complaint which Virginia Graham made to Joyce Grenfell, that the letters dealt almost exclusively with a man's world: 'About once every three months a woman is mentioned . . . not a woman has a thought or opinion – a beautiful cerebral arrogance with females in their proper place, mutely serving in the background.'[36] Rupert might have accepted that the criticism, though exaggerated, had some truth in it, but would have pleaded that it was a fact of life. There were many women in his life and they in fact featured quite prominently in his letters, but most of the publishers and authors with whom he dealt, not to mention all the cricketers and members of the Literary Society, were male and it was they who commanded the lion's share of the space.

It turned out that the reading public did not want any changes. Except for a few veterans who had died in the intervening twelve months, it seemed that everyone who had bought the first collection acquired Volume Two as well, and a certain number of new devotees were added. Sales were slightly up; reviews were quite as friendly and rather more extensive. Rupert was surprised and slightly put out by Daphne du Maurier's piece in the *New York Times Review of Books*. George Lyttelton, she argued, now appeared the less conservative and hidebound of the two. 'A strange inversion is thus seen to have taken place by the end of this volume: the man of the world is revealed as a cautious *littérateur*, while the provincial *littérateur* is revealed as instinctively worldly, with a bold interest in all that's new.'[37] Rupert felt that his interest in all that was new, if hardly bold, was at least as strong as Lyttelton's; he knew that he was hidebound, even in some respects reactionary, but whenever he remembered to do so he did his best to keep an open mind. Though some new departure might mean little or nothing to him, he conscientiously reminded himself that it was not necessarily worthless or contemptible for that reason. Sometimes he even believed what he was saying.

There were to be six volumes in all. Each time Jock Murray professed uncertainty about the practicality of continuing the series, each time it became more obvious that it would be a mistake to cut it off. 'The same grapes are being pressed,' Roger Hudson reported on Volume Four, 'but the flow of juice is still brisk enough and the wine is still piquant, warming and nourishing. If we can do 3,000 at a bearable price and make our margin, why cannot we continue? There are few enough regular staples around to cast this one aside.'[38]

On the whole Rupert's relationship with his publishers remained friendly though there were occasional acrimonious spats, caused usually by what seemed to him unwarrantable delays. When the proofs of Volume Three had been unexpectedly held up, Jock Murray reported that at last there was light at the end of the tunnel. 'The light at the end of the tunnel may be an oncoming train,' suggested Rupert balefully. Things went even worse on Volume Four. On 14 April 1980 Murray told Rupert that he and Roger Hudson were fighting over who should be first to read the typescript. Two months later no comments were yet forthcoming. 'I begin to wonder whether the fight ended by your knocking each other out, like Tweedledum and Tweedledee,' wrote Rupert. 'Time, no doubt, will tell.'[39] Time did tell, and gave the right answer, but the problems between publisher and author did not end there. Hudson made a large number of editorial suggestions; he had accepted most of these, Rupert assured him, but rejected a handful 'for reasons too long and boring to bother you with'. In fact he had ignored almost all of them – 'which I feel is a pity,' Hudson noted sadly, 'but difficult to press the point.'[40]

By the time the final volume appeared, Rupert's irritated outbursts had become more frequent. 'In my long experience,' he told Hudson, 'these are the most incompetent printers I have ever come across.' 'Rubbish. Hyperbole!' Hudson scrawled across the letter, and passed it to Jock Murray who added: 'This is Rupert doing his Guards adjutant number!'[41] But though Rupert might from time to time rend his publishers, he accepted that they were in the last analysis allies in a common cause. The same was not true of hostile reviewers. He was less than ever ready to tolerate criticism which he felt to be unfair or misconceived and almost any hostile comments seemed to fall into these categories. Geoffrey Grigson he had long identified as the standard-bearer for the Leavisite school of literary criticism, a movement which he felt to be joyless and humourless, the exaltation of acerbic pedantry over everything that gave colour and life to the art of writing. When Grigson, in the *Guardian*, gave a harsh but by no means unreasonable review to Volume Three, Rupert was incensed, not just by the tone of the piece but by the fact that, given his known prejudices, Grigson had been asked and had agreed to review the book at all. 'Grigson is a louse and a failure,' he told Deirdre, 'with a grudge against anything which is generally praised. To read his review you'd think I had at some time done him an injury, but in fact I have never, happily, had the faintest contact with him.'[42]

The series gathered momentum with each volume and by the time all six had appeared reprints of the first two were already in train. They were not spectacular best-sellers nor even noticeably profitable for Rupert – the royalties were split 50–50 with George Lyttelton's son, the jazz trumpeter Humphrey, and Rupert reckoned that the greater part of his share was dissipated on sending free copies to his innumerable friends – but they were unequivocally a success and made a mark far greater than the sales figures might suggest. Rupert acquired a devoted fan club which looked forward eagerly to each volume: from Queen Elizabeth the Queen Mother to a retired schoolmistress in New Zealand, a pair of colonels in Virginia, an Italian publisher and an ex-Communist from Scandinavia who wanted to know how he could study the rules of cricket. Philip Larkin wrote that he had bought all six volumes: 'I find them enormously entertaining and with some excellent jokes.'[43] A Mr Beadle wrote to propose that he should don the mantle of George Lyttelton and engage Rupert in a new correspondence. Though not a cricketer, he confessed, he had for many years been secretary to the local ramblers' association and was a keen Rotarian. With such qualifications he felt sure that he could play his part in an exchange of 'anecdotes, jokes and comments on the passing scene'.[44] The offer was politely refused.

Penguin were eager to publish a one-volume selection of the *Letters* in paperback and Murray's strongly backed the idea, maintaining that it would not be intended as a substitute for the whole series but instead would lead readers on to tackle the longer work. Rupert would have none of it; once the ding-dong of the weekly exchange had been lost the whole point of the correspondence would have vanished. 'Obdurate fellow!' commented Roger Hudson. 'He is letting the best be enemy of the good.'⁴⁵ The fellow remained obdurate, abetted by Jamie Hamilton who mischievously reintroduced himself into the scene by offering to publish all six volumes in three substantial paperbacks. He had just been going to make a similar suggestion himself, Jock Murray protested. 'As you know, I still hanker for that really wide new audience that only a Penguin selection would reach, but now we have this new formula before us, I feel we could be just as effective as Hamish Hamilton with it.'⁴⁶ A selection from the *Lyttelton Hart-Davis Letters* was eventually published, but it had to wait till after Rupert's death.

The Arms of Time finally appeared in September 1979, at almost exactly the same moment as the second volume of the *Letters*. To those who were accustomed to consider Rupert as a correct and buttoned-up figure who had his emotions well under control and would hardly admit to having any dirty washing, let alone to launder it in public, the book was a startling revelation. One of Rupert's reasons for delaying the writing had been that he did not wish to publish while his father was alive: 'Not that he is my real father, I feel pretty sure, but he's the only one I've known, and tiresome as the poor fellow is, I don't want to hurt his feelings.'⁴⁷ Richard Hart-Davis would indeed have been hurt by a book which portrayed him as a snob and a bore, mean, self-pitying and with little interest in the finer things of life. His marriage was shown as at the best a sterile sham, more often hell for both parties. Sibbie, on the other hand, was extolled as a figure of radiant charm, beauty and high intelligence, though also self-indulgent, promiscuous and capable of a childishness which her admirers found charming but must have driven her husband to desperation. But the element in the book which to some seemed most shocking was the intensity which it revealed of the relationship between mother and son. Each was the most important figure in the other's life, and Sibbie's unbridled craving for Rupert's love and support seemed to many of those who read about it to be unusual certainly, unnatural perhaps, and probably unhealthy into the bargain. Rebecca West, whose tragically warped relationship with her own son had so marred her life, reviewed *The Arms of Time* in the *Sunday Telegraph*. She could not bear to admit that it was about the love of a mother and son, Rupert told the novelist, Jane Gardam; so she 'described it as the story of a failed marriage'.⁴⁸

Rupert himself had had some doubts about whether he was giving too much away. He sent a typescript to his favoured arbiter of matters of taste, Tommy Lascelles, and asked him whether he thought it was good and should be published. As a literary record, Lascelles concluded, it was above criticism, but if published it would encounter the same sort of hostility as Gosse had met with for his *Father and Son*. People would be bewildered by a 'son revealing in a book for sale . . . the intimate details of the emotional life of one or another of his parents'.* The book was sentimental, something which was to be condoned in many cases but not, in Lascelles's opinion, where this sort of relationship was in question. Rupert had been hoping for reassurance but it is unlikely that any strictures from Lascelles would have deterred him. Deirdre was all for publication, he told his friend, and he thought his mother would have felt the same. He realised that he would certainly be accused of bad taste but 'my withers are now too old and hardened to be wrung'. As to the charge of sentimentality, of course, it was justified, 'but this is a love story, and a love story without sentiment is like a meal without wine'.[49]

The Lyttelton Hart-Davis Letters had incensed a certain type of critic as being insufferably snobbish and complacent. *The Arms of Time* stirred up no such reactions. Rupert would probably have preferred it if it had; he enjoyed his outbursts of fury in which he excoriated the excesses of fashion-conscious modernists. But he was pleased by his reviews, in particular that of Anthony Powell in the *Daily Telegraph*, who praised the memoir as 'sad, funny, moving, intensely felt'. Only Rupert, he said, could have written it because of the delicacy and dexterity which had been so evident in his biography of Walpole and which here made totally acceptable a story that in other hands 'might have been too inward-looking, even embarrassing'. Rupert's only disappointment was that it was not more prominently reviewed and did not sell better; 1,700 copies had left the bookshops by Christmas – 'a pathetically small number', he considered.[50] In fact the figure was quite respectable and certainly compared favourably with many of the titles he himself had published. Rupert could never bring himself to be wholly realistic, however, when the sales of his own books were in question. He knew, in principle, that the childhood memories of a retired publisher living in seclusion in North Yorkshire were unlikely to stimulate great popular demand; he would not seek to create such a demand by adorning his

---

* Lascelles always felt that indiscretion was compounded if it appeared in a book for sale. He condemned the Duke of Windsor's memoirs, *inter alia*, on the grounds that it was 'obscene to write gainfully about one's own love affairs'; leaving open the question of whether it was any less obscene to write about somebody else's love affairs, or to describe one's own free of charge.

book with elements of the scandalous or sensational; he would do as little to help Hamish Hamilton's promote the book as he had done for Murray's with the *Lyttelton Letters*: but he was still disappointed when his work did not prove to be an acclaimed best-seller.

Apart from *The Arms of Time* and the second volume of the *Letters*, Rupert edited two other books in 1979, a fact which may go some way towards, explaining why each individual project took him longer than he had at first expected. *Two Men of Letters* comprised the correspondence between R. C. Hutchinson and Martyn Skinner. Hutchinson was a novelist who had teetered on the brink of greatness yet never quite achieved it. Rupert admired him extravagantly, ensured that he won the W. H. Smith Prize and, when he died in 1975, pronounced with confidence that posthumous glory awaited him. So far his day has not dawned and it now seems unlikely that it ever will. His friend Martyn Skinner was even less celebrated, though he could proudly claim to have been the only working farmer to have won the Hawthornden Prize and the only working poet to have won a prize for his malting barley. He specialised in interminable epic poems which seem even less likely to be revived than the novels of Hutchinson. Their correspondence was intelligent and interesting but the title, chosen by Rupert as a deliberate defiance of current fashion, was calculated to deter both the academic purist and the general reader. The book sold pitifully few copies and won only limited recognition from the handful of men of letters who still graced the literary pages of the day.

The second book, *The Selected Letters of Oscar Wilde*, was what it sounded, an attempt to reduce to a slightly more manageable size the collection which had been published seventeen years before. Since the first collection had come out, however, an alarmingly large number of unpublished letters had come to light. Rupert was by now convinced that what was needed was a second volume of Wilde letters or, best of all, a mammoth volume which would assimilate old and new in one truly comprehensive collection.

'This house is like a non-stop book-factory with no working to rule,' Rupert complained to Jane Gardam, whose novels he admired greatly and who was one of the very few new friends whom he allowed to penetrate his seclusion.[51] So crowded was the literary assembly line that it was clear any new Wilde collection would have to wait. The next candidate for editing was the diary of Siegfried Sassoon, which he had successfully rescued from Heytesbury before Sassoon's son, George, sold the remaining manuscripts at auction. The diary was 'a big problem', Rupert admitted to Deirdre. It was enormously long – over a million words for the period between 1921 and 1940 alone – and packed with important literary material as well as revelations about Sassoon's own life and personality and much scabrous gossip about his contemporaries: 'Cutting and selecting won't be easy.'[52] At least there was no problem about finding a publisher. Faber & Faber's, Sassoon's own publishers, were delighted to take on the diary and paid an advance of £5,000 for the first volume – to be split 50–50 between Rupert and George Sassoon.

The first volume in fact turned out to be the second; Rupert began with the diaries for 1920–1922, which were published in 1981, and then moved back to the diaries covering the First World War. The reason Rupert gave for this was that Sassoon's own autobiography, though presented in fictional guise, had carried him through as far as 1920 and had drawn so heavily on the diaries that there was no need to publish them. The argument never seemed particularly cogent – the three George Sherston books were not linked closely to the diaries – and Rupert presumably reconsidered his decision. It was fortunate that he did so, since the wartime diaries proved much the more profitable. Duff persuaded his employers on the *Sunday Telegraph* to pay £3,000 to serialise the more dramatic episodes. 'There's nothing like nepotism,' Rupert commented appreciatively.[53]

A third volume took the story up to 1925, but now the problems became intractable. The later diaries were largely dominated by Sassoon's relationship with Stephen Tennant, who was described with a ferocious loathing that made publication difficult if not impossible during Tennant's lifetime. Tennant finally died early in 1987 but now George Sassoon developed belated scruples about publishing material which dwelt too directly on his father's homosexuality. 'I have reminded him that Sassoon often told me he wanted his diaries to be published, and made me literary executor so as to bring this about,' Rupert told Ernest Mehew.[54] If Sassoon in fact did express his wishes so unambiguously, the occasions were not recorded by Rupert; references to their meetings on the contrary give the impression that the poet rather enjoyed leaving an element of uncertainty about the eventual fate of his diaries and made a point of not giving any precise instructions. It seems likely, however, that he knew what Rupert planned to do and neither sought to veto it when he was alive nor turned resentfully in his grave once he was dead. George Sassoon, anyway, soon recanted and agreed that later volumes of the diaries could be published. By the end of 1987 the way was clear, but now it was Rupert who dragged his feet. He wanted to get ahead with the second instalment of his own memoirs, he was engaged in editing Max Beerbohm's letters, everything seemed to take longer than it had used to – 'it'll be some time before I get back to Sassoon, if I ever do', he told Deirdre.[55] He never did.

By then he was almost eighty years old. The fire was still bright but it was beginning to burn low.

Chapter Nineteen

Dying Fall

All birthdays mattered to Rupert and in 1977 his seventieth had seemed to him particularly momentous. He was downcast at breakfast when nobody appeared to be paying great attention to the anniversary. He can hardly have supposed that June would let such an occasion pass unmarked. All three children, with wives and husbands and the six grandchildren, arrived in the morning, a day's celebration followed, Adam produced a pipe and seventy different types of tobacco, the family jointly presented him with a music centre. 'Who could have asked for a happier birthday?' he enquired.[1]

Part of his happiness was founded on the fact that his children were not merely loving and dutiful but had themselves made lives that were prosperous and contented. Adam was the only one who caused him concern. He was a model son and Rupert had every reason to be proud of his achievements but his marriage was not a happy one. It held together after a fashion for another fifteen years but Rupert barely concealed his hope that it would one day disintegrate. 'He should have done it years ago,' was his disobliging comment when told that his younger son had at last gone off with another woman.[2]

Duff and Phyllida, on the other hand, seemed admirably well suited to each other. In 1977 their fortunes took a dramatic turn, when Phyllida sold a novel about the Indian Mutiny to the American publisher Bantam Books for $200,000. The book had been tried on the telephone operator at her British publisher, Futura, who had approved it heartily on the grounds that she liked books to be 'sexy but not sordid'. 'Clearly she has a gift for writing this kind of rubbish,' Rupert told Deirdre. He admitted to having thoroughly enjoyed it himself.[3] His somewhat solipsistic view of life was shown when Duff and Phyllida decided to seek a temporary tax refuge in Ireland. 'And if I die, they won't even be able to come to my funeral,' Rupert complained indignantly. He rejoiced at their successes, though; as he did at the continued prosperity of Bridget. In 1976 her father-in-law had died and she became Lady Silsoe. 'Fancy one's daughter suddenly becoming a peeress!' was Rupert's gratified comment.[4]

He was as close to his sister, Deirdre, as ever and still wrote to her every Sunday. Usually he had her previous letter in front of him and his style grew disconcertingly staccato as he dealt with each succeeding point. One complete paragraph read: 'I always thought ouzo a horrible drink. Can't you have hand-rails fixed to the cellar steps?' In 1978 Deirdre remarried for the fourth and final time to William Inman. Rupert thought him a kindly bore and did his best to avoid having to talk to him. Deirdre knew her brother quite well enough to detect his feelings; she was hurt but unsurprised. Rupert, she knew, would put himself out for her sake to an extent which he would contemplate for few others, but there were limits to what could be expected of him. Her children discovered this when they made their plans to celebrate her seventieth birthday and hoped to include Rupert in the occasion. They were going to have a dance, they told him. 'This is grave news,' Rupert replied. 'For more than fifty years I have detested, and largely managed to avoid, dancing of any kind. Moreover, being stone deaf in one ear I can, in any big gathering, hear only a jumble of parrot noises.'[5] The festivities took place without him.

June was the still centre of his life. She organised his birthday parties with the unobtrusive efficiency and consideration for others that was the hallmark of her life. He policed her doings as systematically as ever but somehow she managed to get the arrangements made without him noticing. The effort must have been considerable. On one occasion Janet Adam Smith asked for a photograph of the Old Rectory so that she could have a special mug made and surprise Rupert with it. June obliged but only at the price of 'a very stealthy morning, tip-toeing around in soft shoes, starting with guilt every time he talks to me'. She urged Janet not to make the mistake of thanking her: 'He reads all my letters. If you need anything else, please write in code and send it by carrier pigeon.'[6] Deirdre was belatedly outraged when she discovered the regime to which her sister-in-law was subject. 'It shocks me that you open all her letters,' she wrote. 'It's no good telling me that she doesn't mind, it just seems to me insulting.'[7] Rupert did believe that June didn't mind, and up to a point was still correct. She knew that her husband's vigilance was based on love and not distrust. But she would have relished slightly greater freedom and appreciated the efforts of friends such as Deirdre or Joyce Grenfell to win it for her.

Even Rupert could not insist that June remain at home when, early in 1981, she was told that her mother was ill and on the point of death. She hurried south. It was the first time since their marriage that she had left him alone at Marske and almost the first time that they had spent a night apart. The separation lasted ten days. Rupert had no illusions about his self-sufficiency but he was still taken aback by the desperate loneliness which afflicted him. 'You are so much a part of me that I feel only half alive when you're not here, unconsciously waiting for your call or your footstep,' he told her. 'I love you more and more every day, and need you every moment. You are my light and life and joy, and you have made me the happiest and most spoiled old man in the world.'[8] Rupert claimed that his worries over how June would manage alone after his death were an important element in the misery caused him by their separation. No doubt such thoughts did preoccupy him from time to time, but during the ten days that June spent away from him he had little inclination to reflect on anything except his painful plight – 'Oh, I do miss you so!'

Mumsy's death saddened him, if only for the distress he knew that it would cause June, but it did not touch him deeply. If asked, he would probably have said that only if something disastrous had happened to June, Deirdre or one of the children would he have felt real pain. Almost without his noticing, however, a third member of their household had taken possession of his heart. In 1978 a stray kitten of indeterminate type had presented itself at their door and demanded attention. Rupert had always professed to dislike any sort of pet, but he preferred cats to dogs and rather grudgingly allowed this one to find a home with them. They called her Pesky, and within a few weeks she dominated their lives. Soon the need to look after her was being put forward as a reason for abandoning the annual trip to Elba. She had been with them for nearly two years, however, before Rupert took in how strong his affection for her had grown. Pesky disappeared. 'After Ruth died,' he told Deirdre, 'I thought I was anaesthetised against grief for good, but it isn't so.' In the awful weeks after Ruth's death he had repeatedly played Mahler's Third Symphony; now in the absence of Pesky, the custom was revived: 'We feel as though we have lost a child.'[9] On this occasion the child was back, safe and sound, by the end of the week, but ten years later old age and kidney failure forced them to put her down. Rupert's contemporaries by this time were dying thick and fast but none of them provoked grief a tithe as deeply felt as Pesky did. For days afterwards Rupert wept almost continuously; seven weeks later, he told Paul Chipchase, 'we still miss her every day and talk of her continually'.[10] Deirdre became concerned about his extravagant reaction and sought to administer some bracing comfort. 'You must call a halt to the grieving as you will make yourself ill and it is not fair to Junie,' she wrote severely. 'You said in your last letter that you had had no grief for 22 years, and I doubt if there are many people who could say the same. It is surely time now to turn all thoughts of mourning into those of thanksgiving for those happy years?'[11] It was easier said than done, but gradually Pesky slipped into the background of his mind.

At least he was soon to spare himself further worry about June's financial position as a widow. One by one, he began to turn into money the treasures which he had accumulated throughout his life. His remarkable collection of books and manuscripts relating to Edmund Blunden was sold to an American university for £50,000. The copy of Max Beerbohm's *Zuleika Dobson*, illustrated by the author and presented to Rupert by Beerbohm's widow, fetched £10,000 from an American university. Most notable of all, in 1983 the University of Oklahoma at Tulsa bought his entire library for £210,000. £25,000 was paid immediately, the rest in instalments, but the books were to remain in his possession until he died. The money, as it accrued, was invested in June's name, thus ensuring that she would be, if not a wealthy widow, at last one who could face the future with some security.

Quite apart from these windfalls, Rupert's income was more substantial than at any period of his life. The Walpole estate continued to bring in handsome returns and from 1976 he began to get a share of Arthur Ransome's royalties. Royalties from his own books and his fee for judging the W. H. Smith Prize were not as large as either of these but they were by no means negligible, averaging something under £3,000 over the last twenty or so years of his life. His total annual income varied wildly according to the whims of film producers and foreign publishers, but usually it was between £10,000 and £20,000 a year and on one occasion leapt to £45,000. He was never a rich man but he had quite enough on which to live out his life in comfortable seclusion.

He continued with his own work, though the rate of progress became more sluggish with every year. *A Beggar in Purple* – the title taken from a phrase of Kipling's: 'He wrapped himself in quotations as a beggar would adorn himself in the purple of Emperors' – was published by

Hamish Hamilton's in 1983. It comprised extracts from the common-place book which he had kept all his adult life and which was remarkable for the consistency of judgment which marked his selections. Most people look back with slightly abashed incomprehension at the writing which they considered of transcendent beauty when they were young. Rupert saw little or nothing to be ashamed of. Johnson, Carlyle, Tennyson, Emily Dickinson, Landor among the classics; Sassoon, Hardy, Henry James, Yeats for the twentieth century: they were not the most fashionable of names but all of them have withstood the test of time. Rupert's tastes had evolved with the years but he had always remained faithful to old favourites; the boy who had recited Macaulay to his uncle Duff could have done as much, with almost as great relish, seventy years later or more.

In 1985 came *More Letters of Oscar Wilde*. This produced some monumental rows with the publisher, John Murray. First Roger Hudson produced a drawing of Wilde and suggested it be used for the jacket. 'You, and the Wildenstein Gallery may say that this drawing is of Oscar Wilde,' retorted Rupert, 'but I say, categorically, that it is not. It is more like Billy Bunter, and bears no resemblance to all the portraits and photos of Wilde. If you printed it anywhere in my book you would hold yourself up to hatred, ridicule and contempt.' Hudson passed the letter to Jock Murray. 'Ha! Ha!' Hudson annotated it. 'He does enjoy slapping me down. Of course it is nonsense to say that the picture "bears no resemblance at all".' 'He loves being dogmatic,' Jock Murray added. The drawing was returned to the gallery.

Then Rupert mauled the first set of galley proofs so comprehensively that Jock Murray sent him corrected galleys rather than the more usual page proofs. 'You are honoured and privileged,' Murray told him. 'Only Paddy [Leigh-Fermor] equals your correction efforts and he only gets page-galleys at second go.' Finally, at the last minute, Rupert discovered a photograph of Oscar Wilde's hand, showing his lifelines, which he wanted inserted as a frontispiece. Murray replied that this would cause delay and much extra expense. Rupert was indignant, the expense could easily be absorbed, 'I beg you to trust my judgment on this matter'. He was becoming an old tyrant, Murray told Hudson; anyway, a picture of a podgy hand was too kinky to serve as a frontispiece. In the end Rupert grudgingly agreed that the hand might appear at the end of the book on text paper. He made it clear that he felt Murray's had fallen down badly on the job.[12] Jock Murray wrote privately to Merlin Holland, Oscar Wilde's grandson and assiduous guardian of the flame: 'Would it be indiscreet to comment that in the preparation of this book Rupert has combined the toughness of a publisher (which he was) with the eccentricity of an author (which he is)? I am his admirer.'[13]

It took Rupert another five years to complete his second volume of autobiography, *The Power of Chance*. He found the task uninspiring. *The Arms of Time*, he told Ernest Mehew, had had 'a subject (my mother's life), a shape (that of her life) and a theme (the love between mother and son)'. The only subject of this new book was himself, and this was not something in which, or so at least he said, he was particularly interested.[14] He told Deirdre that he was persevering only because he enjoyed the actual business of constructing phrases and shaping paragraphs and so as to get as many facts as possible on paper for the benefit of anyone who might one day want to write his biography.[15] If the latter was indeed a serious purpose he did not serve his putative biographer particularly well. Far more than had been the case with *The Arms of Time*, he took drastic liberties with his text, amalgamating letters or diary entries and changing words, dates or names for no apparent reason. Why, for instance, in the quotation of a diary entry describing dinner with Charlie Marford, should the date be changed from 3 March to 5 May and the phrase 'Charlie has neither money nor job, but he is cheerful and amusing' be amended to 'He without job or money but cheerful as ever'? Why should 'dinner' with Walter de la Mare be transmuted to 'lunch'? Such changes do not seem to have been calculated to deceive or to give a better impression of the author, but they indicate a casual indifference to the written word which he himself would have deplored a few years before.

The main defect of *The Power of Chance*, however, was that it was a drab catalogue of events with few reflective passages and little space devoted to the personalities of those he met. Deirdre was sent a typescript and urged him to enlarge more on people and episodes: 'Often it is not even like a diary but almost more merely an engagement book.'[16] Rupert could see that there might be some force in the charge but he was disinclined to do anything about it and felt that the reader was being told quite as much as he needed to know. He was put out when Anthony Thwaite in the *Sunday Telegraph* said that there was too much name-dropping, too few revealing anecdotes, too little real information about either him or the women he loved. The book was boring 'partly because Hart-Davis is obviously such a nice man: unselfish, affectionate, looking for the best in everyone, scrupulous in his dealings, decent in his manners'. Thwaite had been nice about him, Rupert admitted to Deirdre, 'but nasty about the book. You were right in not taking to him much.'[17]

Rupert had originally intended to polish off his life in a single volume. His decision to stop *The Power of Chance* in 1945 and follow it with a third volume was inspired by my own biography of King Edward VIII. He was reading this with interest, he told Deirdre, 'but with considerable physical discomfort. It has 600 large pages.'[18] He would inflict no such burden on *his* readers. If progress on the second volume had been slow, on the third it was snail-like. He had started his next volume, he told Paul Chipchase in May 1992, but was suffering from what he hoped was temporary writer's block: 'Senile inertia, and now the sunshine, keep me idle.'[19] His main problem was that, even more than with the previous book, work on *Halfway to Heaven* bored him. 'I've written another paragraph . . . I must try to make it less dull than it now seems to me,' he told Deirdre.[20] In 1991 he professed himself disappointed by Frances Partridge's *Hanging On* – 'one of the most depressing books I've read in years' – and Sybille Bedford's *As It Was* – 'a collection of newspaper articles, mostly about food in various part of Europe'. 'These two old ladies should be quietly stopped from publishing anything more,' he concluded.[21] It was advice he did not heed himself.

His family, who had seen enough of the work-in-progress to realise that the book was beyond redemption, urged him to give it up. He refused, out of an obstinate resolve to finish what he had begun. By the time he had done so he was almost ninety. What he would have recognised twenty years before as a series of jejune and spiritless jottings from an engagement diary now seemed to him to possess real merit; the tedium of writing was forgotten, the satisfaction at having put his life on record remained. He was surprised and hurt when Murray's, with all the barrage of apologetic explanations so familiar to the rejected author, refused to publish his book. A few weeks later Faber's gave the same reply. Duff suggested a third possibility but this too came to nothing. 'In my publishing days it would have been accepted immediately,' wrote Rupert indignantly, 'unless I had published it myself.'[22] In the end it was taken on by the Gloucestershire firm of Sutton Publishing as a pendant to the reprint they were doing of his Walpole biography. They paid what was, by that date, a more-or-less nominal advance of £1,200 but knew they had little chance of getting it back. The book got scant attention from the reviewers; Rupert still had many friends and admirers on the London literary scene but any even half-honest report on *Halfway to Heaven* could only have been offensive to the author and silence seemed the kinder policy.

By the time it appeared in 1997 he had more or less stopped working. His last serious piece of editorship, *Letters of Max Beerbohm*, had appeared in 1988. Murray's had once again been the victim of authorial tantrums that may have persuaded Jock Murray to harden his heart and refuse to publish *Halfway to Heaven*. Once again the page proofs were 'the worst I've ever had', unsightly running headlines had to be removed, the footnotes were too small, the lettering on the binding cramped and inelegant: the book was going to look like 'a cheap Routledge reprint of a century ago with everything crammed in as small as possible to save space and money'. The last straw for Rupert came when he found sales copy for the book relegated to page 21 of Murray's catalogue 'behind a lot of rubbish'. 'Most publishers would have put it a bit nearer the front,' he told a friend indignantly. 'Let us speak on Friday as to what to do with this cantankerous old man,' his editor, Roger Hudson, wrote wearily to Jock Murray.[23]

Even in the 1990s, as work on his memoirs ground painfully on, he still from time to time took on other jobs, but the demands made on him became ever more occasional. He wrote the odd piece for the *Dictionary of National Biography*, and an article about Maurice Baring for a special number of the *Chesterton Review*, but by the early 1990s even such trifling commissions were drying up. He was still called in as an ultimate authority on a variety of subjects – in 1987, for instance, he found himself mediating between Richard Ellman and Merlin Holland over the former's contention, on what seemed decidedly shaky evidence, that Oscar Wilde had contracted syphilis at the age of twenty – but he felt less and less disposed to undertake anything which called for serious research or concentration. 'I'm terribly sorry,' he told Ernest Mehew in 1994, 'but I fear you can't rely on me any more. Old age is making me struggle with the final volume of my life-story, since I can write for only half an hour before I'm tired out. Your huge pile of galleys has been on my conscience for weeks, but I can't promise any more corrections. Forgive me, please.'[24]

'Are you fit?' the village postmistress had enquired towards the end of 1981. 'Fit!' Rupert replied. 'I haven't been fit for twenty years!' But though he suffered from aches and pains and often, in the middle of the night, convinced himself that he was the victim of a probably fatal

heart attack, by the following morning he still felt tolerably hale. Within
a few years, however, he was undergoing irritating prostate problems.
He had the operation at the end of 1985 and told Deirdre that he
remembered being told that, if it was successful, it would add fifteen
years to his life: 'If true, that would take me to 93, an awesome prospect
for my precious Junie.'[25] The operation was a failure, or at least
improved things very little, but he still survived to ninety-two. He was
unsurprised by the fact that there had been no dramatic improvement in
his condition; he used to quote with approval the gloomy observation of
Ivan Illich: 'Most treatment of the old requiring professional intervention not only tends to heighten their pain but, if successful, protracts it.'
    Arthritis was so painful even without professional intervention that
any treatment was acceptable. In 1992 his right knee caused him such
trouble that he had a cortisone injection. The results seemed
dramatically successful and he returned home in triumph, though
uncertain enough in his walking to make it necessary to install a second
banister on the main staircase and handholds wherever there were steps.
It was a false dawn; within two years the trouble was back, and in the
second knee as well. Rupert was soon subsisting on a diet of painkillers,
eight pills a day, which made life tolerable but also 'kill my memory, my
wits and my handwriting'.[26] In 1993 he had his first heart attack which
kept him in hospital for twelve days. He made a good recovery but the
thought that it might at any moment recur was always thereafter at the
back of his mind. A few weeks after he got home he told Paul Chipchase
that, so far that year, he had suffered from arthritis in both legs, angina
and prostate trouble. '"Else fine," as the secondhand book-sellers say at
the end of their description of a battered volume,' he concluded
sardonically.[27]
    'So long as Rupert keeps (1) well and (2) happy and (3) his work goes
on – that's all that matters,' June had written to Janet Adam Smith in
1983. 'And I realise more and more that (1) and (2) are all bound up
with (3).'[28] Now the work had almost stopped and he was far from well,
but he was not unhappy. Old age mercifully anaesthetizes the emotions
so that the deaths of those near to one no longer cause the pangs they
would once have done. Janet Adam Smith herself, Peggy Ashcroft, Jock
Murray, Hamish Hamilton, one by one they died. Rupert went to none
of their funerals and greeted the news of their deaths with a perfunctory
'very sad' in his diary. Shortly after Hamilton's death his widow,
Yvonne, told Deirdre that she planned to visit Rupert 'as there were so
few people she could talk to about Jamie'. Rightly realising how

horrified Rupert would be by this prospect, Deirdre replied: 'You can't do that, Yvonne. He's a recluse nowadays and doesn't see anyone.' 'Oh!' said Yvonne. 'I'm sure he'd see me because he was a great friend of Jamie's.' 'No, he won't,' concluded Deirdre. 'He sees absolutely no one.'[29] Mercifully for Rupert's peace of mind, her view prevailed.

It was Deirdre's death that left the greatest gap. 'Alas,' Rupert had ended a letter in 1996, 'we are both too groggy to see each other again in this life, and I have little hope of another life to come. Anyway, I shall love you for ever.'[30] She had been suffering from Parkinson's Disease for many years and towards the end she depended on others to take down the weekly letters to her brother. Yet still they kept a faltering correspondence going; Rupert's last letter to her was written on 23 November 1998, the day she died. In a way it was a relief to Rupert not to have to spend his Sunday mornings scrawling the ever more illegible pages to somebody who was barely able to take them in, but it had been a duty which had to some small extent kept him in touch with the outside world. He loved and took a continuing interest in his children, followed the doings of his grandchildren, but he rarely took any initiative in suggesting that they should come to Marske. Almost all the time he and June were alone.

The last annual outing – the visit to Scarborough – had been abandoned in 1983. The following year he resigned from the Garrick Club. It was nearly twenty years since he had been there and he knew he was supremely unlikely to do so again, but its renunciation still seemed sadly final. He suggested that the Committee should make him an honorary member but 'they churlishly refused, so my membership lapsed'.[31] Deirdre had been only slightly overstating her case when she told Yvonne Hamilton that Rupert now saw absolutely nobody. A few visitors were still admitted, though with dwindling regularity and for shorter and shorter periods: Richard and Jane Garnett; Jane Gardam and her husband David, who had bought a house in the neighbourhood; his devoted helper, Ernest Mehew. Neighbours, at least those of any social pretension, were debarred. The vicar called and was rebuffed, tried twice more and still persisted, at last was let in and given a glass of sherry. 'A very nice, friendly and interesting man,' commented Rupert, 'but I hope he doesn't come too often.'[32] Even members of the family visited more rarely. Adam arrived at teatime, slept for two hours before dinner, went early to bed and left directly after breakfast the following day: 'We are both so fixed in our routine of solitude that even so brief and pleasurable a visit as this leaves us whacked,' wrote Rupert.[33]

From time to time Rupert admitted that it was he who was fixed in his routine of solitude and that June might hanker for a little more variety: 'I fear she is often bored and fed up with having no-one to talk to but dreary old me.'[34] But such scruples did not oppress him too severely. One family, particular friends of June, used to stay every year at Easter. In the end she concluded that it was becoming too much for Rupert and that they must be stopped from coming. He claimed that, when he found out, he tried 'in a purposeful way' to persuade her to change her mind. His efforts do not appear to have been long sustained. 'Junie, entirely on her own, decided to put off the Russells,' Rupert told Deirdre. 'Indeed, I tried to dissuade her, knowing how fond of them she is. She used my age and prostate etc as an excuse, but in fact the visit would have been a greater strain for her than for me.' Almost he persuaded himself that the cancellation of the visit had been entirely June's idea and for her own good; only on Easter Sunday did he have the grace to admit: 'I fear that Junie is mourning the absence of Russells, but to me it is an immense relief.'[35]

Rupert took it for granted that June would outlive him and that she would continue to sustain him, physically as well as emotionally, until he died. Then, on 23 December 1997, he came down to the kitchen to ask why supper was so late. He found June on the floor, having suffered a stroke. He had no idea how serious it was but could see that she found it impossible to get up, let alone produce the supper. Help was summoned. 'Ever since those two huge men carried your lovely little body out to the ambulance,' Rupert wrote to her in hospital a few days later, 'I have thought of nothing but YOU, past, present and future, all day and a good deal of the night. Oh darling, the thought of having you back brings tears of happiness to my eyes. I've loved you for well over 30 years but never quite as deeply and longingly as now. *Oh, I do love you so.*'[36] The thought of life without her was insupportable; even thirty years before he had found it difficult to sustain existence by himself, now it would be impossible. By the time he wrote this letter she was coming home, but she would have to return to hospital at the end of January for further tests; only after these would it be clear whether she would make a full recovery.

Rupert's children were almost as distraught as he was. What would happen to their father if June did not recover? Bridget and Adam hastened north to hold the fort but they had responsibilities of their own. A woman was found to move in and run the household but this could not be a permanent solution. It was unthinkable that Rupert should leave the Old Rectory, still more unthinkable that he should stay there alone. Mercifully the worst did not happen. The tests proved satisfactory and it was clear that June would make a full recovery. But it proved to be a slow business. 'She used to do *everything* in the house, including shopping, and now she can do *nothing*,' wrote a relieved but still desolate Rupert.[37]

For more than eighty years his principal pleasure and occupation had been reading. Gradually he became less adventurous in his choice of material. The papers were filled with rapes, murders and massacres, he told Deirdre, so he stuck to the crossword and cricket scores 'and favourite old books: the new ones reviewed in the papers sound deadly dull'.[38] Then, in 1997, his eyesight deteriorated rapidly. Although he had always enjoyed reading aloud he hated being read to; at the insistence of his family he tried Talking Books but could never master the mechanism. He would press the fast-forward button, miss several chapters, then complain that the plot of the novel he was listening to was unreasonably obscure. Large-print books were slightly more satisfactory but he found them heavy to hold and the titles available at that time tended to be confined to bad thrillers or romances. Soon, anyway, he could not see enough to read even these; the inexorable decline went on and television too became impossible. 'It's horrible not to be able to read *anything*,'[39] he told Deirdre, after struggling ineffectively with a large magnifying glass. Then an eye specialist offered a ray of hope. At the age of ninety he had two operations for cataract. He complained bitterly about the discomfort that followed but rejoiced at being able to read again. He celebrated by re-reading *The Arms of Time*.

Even after the operation he approached with caution anything that threatened to be ponderous or protracted. In 1998 I sent him a copy of my biography of Osbert Sitwell. 'A huge, heavy volume', he described it – a harsh judgment seeing that it was a hundred pages shorter than his own biography of Hugh Walpole. He told Deirdre that he was 'forcing his way through it'. Then he came across a reference to 'Rupert Hart-Davis, that paragon among publishers'. 'Now I must write a praising letter to Philip,' he told his sister. He duly did so – 'a fascinating book. I have enjoyed it immensely' – but his final word to Deirdre was that it was 'an enormously long and heavy book . . . Very well done, but Osbert wasn't a very attractive man, and I don't advise you to tackle his life.'[40]

Osbert Sitwell was an exception; presumably undertaken because he had known its subject. Much more often he concentrated on old favourites, and even among these tended to select the short and uncomplicated. He re-read Dickens certainly, and Conrad, but was as likely to find his pleasure in the adventure stories of Buchan or Sapper. 'Reading *Black Beauty*,' he noted in his diary, 'which is still as delightful in second childhood as it was in first.' More than anything else he re-read his own books. As early as 1981 he had told Deirdre that he had just finished reading *The Arms of Time*, which he had not looked at for two years: 'Damn good and very moving, I thought, with no awkward sentence! I thoroughly enjoyed my afternoon. How's that for Narcissism?'[41] He did not let so long pass before the next re-reading. As for *The Lyttelton Hart-Davis Letters*, no year went by without him working his way through the entire sequence and marvelling at the wit and wisdom which they displayed. Deirdre was constantly urged to return to the books herself and challenged for her opinions. 'Don't you think [my letters] astonishingly well written, considering that I was always whacked by the time I got back to Bromsden at the weekend?'[42]

At first his failing memory added pleasure to his reading; ensuring that he could get renewed satisfaction from old favourites whose plots he had forgotten. In his last years, however, he found that he could not even remember what he had read on the previous page; the stories became incomprehensible and every new effort to read caused fresh frustration. He nearly always had an open book in front of him but more often than not was dozing or musing over the past. He kept his commonplace book going until a few years before his death. His last entry, in a quavering hand, came from one of the poems he loved most and could recite by heart: *The Rime of the Ancient Mariner*.

> Oh Sleep! it is a gentle thing
> Beloved from pole to pole!
> To Mary Queen the praise be given!
> She sent the gentle sleep from Heaven,
> That slid into my soul.

June had hired a caterer and made elaborate plans for a ninetieth birthday party, then at the last minute Rupert decided he could not go through with it and everything was cancelled. He was still enough himself to record proudly that he had received fifty cards – one signed by everybody in the village – and six parcels; but the fire had now indeed burned low. 'I think quite a lot about death,' he had written in

1990, and after his first heart attack a few years later the thoughts took on new urgency. Most of all, it was his relationship with June and her future that preoccupied him. In the summer of 1994 he wrote her a letter which he then put away to await his death:

> I want to write you this letter to tell you how much I love and admire you.
>
> I have loved you constantly and increasingly for twenty-six years, and today I love you more than ever, however dull, deep and dotty I become. What *should* I have done without you? You have been wife, lover, companion, ace-typist, wonderful cook, house-keeper, shopper, gardener, valet, and now chauffeur, financial manager and more. You are a wonderful person and I truly love you more than ever.
>
> I am not afraid of death, which I imagine as being very like going to sleep, but I want to postpone it as long as possible. The only thing that worries me constantly is your future . . . But before that there will be an appalling tidying-up job here. In the middle drawer of my desk you'll find a little yellow notebook, in which I've made a few suggestions.
>
> Oh, my darling Junie, I do love you so.[43]

The yellow notebook contained a ragbag of instructions for his funeral and the disposal of his possessions: a Beerbohm cartoon was for Paul Chipchase, a drawing by Charles Conder for Barry Humphries. The letters to and from Ruth were to be burnt (in fact he had done the deed himself before he died). Jonathan Bailey was to be asked to conduct the funeral. 'If you put up a gravestone I suggest putting on it simply

Sir Rupert Hart-Davis
Man of Letters
And
Lover of Swaledale
1907 – ?

'I wish you could be buried in the same grave as me,' the injunctions concluded, 'but if you are still determined to be cremated, perhaps you might leave instructions for your ashes to be buried in my grave.'

It remained only to fill in the missing date on the gravestone. He wanted to postpone death as long as possible, he had told June in 1994. That was no longer true. He was tired, he was bored, he had little left to give and he felt that he was becoming more and more of a burden on those whom he loved. Occasionally he would murmur to himself: 'Poor old sod,' as he sat musing somnolently. There was a touch of self-pity, perhaps, but far more it was a quiet and apathetic resignation. Also, he knew it would make June smile

On 20 November 1999 he had another heart attack. At his age it seemed unlikely he would recover: the doctor said that 'he has one great thing going for him – his amazing stubbornness', but even that was running low. He was in a public ward, something which normally he would have hated, but now he paid little or no attention to his surroundings and drifted in and out of consciousness. After a fortnight or so things took a turn for the worse. 'We had one horrible day,' June remembers. 'Rupert was very distressed, groaning, crying out, not knowing we were there or where he was. It was almost as if his soul was having one last great battle, crying out not to go.' She and Adam went sadly back to the Old Rectory. Next morning Adam telephoned the hospital and was told that his father had passed a peaceful night. An hour later, at about 9 a.m. on 8 December 1999, Rupert died. He would not have wished to see the new millennium.

In a somewhat supercilious obituary *The Times* concluded that, though Rupert had been 'a great literary figure', his taste had been 'strikingly middle-brow'. Apart from his memoirs and his 'amusing and urbane' correspondence with George Lyttelton he had written only one proper book. He had, it was conceded, edited many more, but only of such 'clubbable figures' as Max Beerbohm or Siegfried Sassoon. As a publisher he had earned his money from writers such as Peter Fleming, Ray Bradbury and Eric Linklater rather than from 'more sophisticated literary books'. It seemed as if the shades of Leavis and Grigson had been resurrected to excoriate him. At least he was not rebuked for publishing Stanley Cullis's book about Wolverhampton Wanderers.

Even arguing from the point of view of the obituarist, there were some questionable points about this judgment. Did many publishers actually make their money from 'sophisticated literary books'? Could a man who had done so much to spread knowledge about William Blake, Henry James, Coleridge, Dickens and Henrik Ibsen really be dismissed as 'strikingly middle-brow'? Was 'clubbable figure' an apt description of Oscar Wilde? But even though all these points be admitted – and there was nothing blatantly untrue about any of them – the obituary still missed the point about Rupert.

He was neither an intellectual nor a daring innovator – but nor would be have wished to be remembered as such. He was a guardian of the flame, not one who lit the fire. In the eighteenth century he would probably have rejected *Tristram Shandy*, in the nineteenth he might have looked with scepticism on much of the poetry of Robert Browning. Yet the fact that he was unadventurous in no way impaired his passionate defence of the highest literary standards. He believed that authors must have something of interest to say and that they should say it with style and authority; a book should be worth reading because of its content and a pleasure to read because of the quality of the writing. Elegantly written nothings and clumsy worthiness were both to be eschewed; of the two the second offered the greater hope, since clumsiness could be redeemed by skilful editing while substance could not be injected into nothings. Given the right material, it was the duty of the publisher to help the author improve its presentation and to produce it in a form that would be durable and good to look at. If the material was wrong, it was equally the duty of the publisher to reject it; the fact that it might make a lot of money was an irrelevance. He had certain rigid standards to which he almost always adhered; he accepted that to some people they might seem old-fashioned but he himself did not believe that they were subject to the vagaries of fashion, they were constant. Good writing, good books, rang true, from whatever generation they might stem; they might become temporarily unfashionable, be scorned by middlebrow readers or highbrow critics, but sooner or later they would prevail. The meretricious, the cheap, the vulgar would always ring false. Rupert believed that he could tell the difference. He missed some genuine talent through his caution and his conservatism. He very rarely worshipped false gods. He was right far more often than he was wrong.

Many years before, Edward Garnett had pointed him towards the High Line, 'the path of Spiritual Rectitude'. To that path he had conscientiously adhered. He was, in a sense, the conscience of literature. A conscience can be irritating, boring, sometimes even debilitating, but woe betide the world that does not hear its voice.

Books Written or Edited by Rupert Hart-Davis

Books Written by Rupert Hart-Davis

Hugh Walpole (Macmillan, 1952)
The Arms of Time (Hamish Hamilton, 1979)
The Power of Chance (Sinclair-Stevenson, 1991)
Praise from the Past (Stone Trough Books, 1996)
Halfway to Heaven (Sutton Publishing, 1998)

Books Edited by Rupert Hart-Davis

The Essential Neville Cardus (Cape, 1949)
George Moore: Letters to Lady Cunard 1895–1933 (Rupert Hart-Davis Ltd, 1957)
The Letters of Oscar Wilde (Rupert Hart-Davis Ltd, 1962)
Max Beerbohm: Letters to Reggie Turner (Rupert Hart-Davis Ltd, 1964)
More Theatres by Max Beerbohm (Rupert Hart-Davis Ltd, 1969)
Last Theatres by Max Beerbohm (Rupert Hart-Davis Ltd, 1970)
A Peep into the Past by Max Beerbohm (Heinemann, 1972)
A Catalogue of the Caricatures of Max Beerbohm (Macmillan, 1972)
The Autobiography of Arthur Ransome (Cape, 1976)
Electric Delights by William Plomer (Cape, 1978)
The Lyttelton Hart-Davis Letters: 1955–56 (Murray, 1978)
Selected Letters of Oscar Wilde (Oxford University Press, 1979)
The Lyttelton Hart-Davis Letters: 1956–57, II (Murray, 1979)
Two Men of Letters (Michael Joseph, 1979)
The Lyttelton Hart-Davis Letters: 1958, III (Murray, 1981)
Siegfried Sassoon Diaries 1920–1922 (Faber, 1981)
The Lyttelton Hart-Davis Letters: 1959, IV (Murray, 1982)
Siegfried Sassoon Diaries 1915–1918 (Faber, 1983)
War Poems of Siegfried Sassoon (Faber, 1983)
A Beggar in Purple (Hamish Hamilton, 1983)
The Lyttelton Hart-Davis Letters: 1960, V (Murray, 1983)
The Lyttelton Hart-Davis Letters: 1961–62, VI (Murray, 1984)
Siegfried Sassoon Diaries 1923–25 (Faber, 1985)
More Letters of Oscar Wilde (Murray, 1985)
Siegfried Sassoon: Letters to Max Beerbohm (Faber, 1986)
Letters of Max Beerbohm (Murray, 1988)

Note on Manuscript Sources

Rupert's library, together with the bulk of his literary correspondence, is in the McFarlin Library at the University of Tulsa in Oklahoma. Most of the letters are catalogued under 'Hart-Davis General' but the more substantial holdings are gradually being re-entered under the names of the correspondent concerned – eg, Peter Fleming, C. V. Wedgwood. Since this process is still going on and knowledge of it is not necessary to track down a particular letter, I have used the designation 'H-D Tulsa' throughout.

Outside Tulsa, by far the most important collection is with Rupert's son, Duff Hart-Davis ('DH-D papers'). This includes the diaries which Rupert kept erratically throughout his life, the many hundreds of letters he wrote to his sister, Deirdre, and the bulk of his correspondence with his mother and his first two wives, Peggy Ashcroft and Comfort Borden-Turner.

Other members of the family have important holdings, particularly his widow, June Hart-Davis ('June H-D papers') and his nieces Annabel Rathbone and Lucy Bland. Duff Cooper's diaries and Rupert's letters to Duff and Diana Cooper are in the possession of Lord Norwich ('Norwich papers').

Rupert was an inveterate letter-writer, but three recipients were particularly favoured. His sister, Deirdre, is mentioned above. The correspondence with George Lyttelton was published in six volumes and the originals were destroyed. He also wrote regularly to Edmund Blunden while the latter was in Tokyo and Hong Kong. These letters ('EB papers') are in the Harry Ransom Humanities Research Center of the University of Texas at Austin.

Other collections particularly rich in letters from or about Rupert are those of Janet Adam Smith (National Library of Scotland or, more often, in the possession of her son, Professor Andrew Roberts);

Joyce Grenfell ('JG papers') (Lucy Cavendish College, Cambridge); Merlin Holland; Eric Linklater (National Library of Scotland); John Murray Publishers; William Plomer (University Library, University of Durham); Arthur Ransome (Brotherton Library, University of Leeds); and Siegfried Sassoon (University of Tulsa).

Only one set of minutes of a board meeting of Rupert Hart-Davis Ltd appears to survive. It is to be found in the Library of King's College, Cambridge, RCB/XL/9.

Other manuscript sources of relevance are the Allen & Unwin papers (University of Reading); Jonathan Bailey, Bishop of Derby; Balliol College, Oxford (Personal Dossier); L. Conrad Barnes (School of Oriental and African Studies); John Bell; Jonathan Cape (University of Reading); Paul Chipchase; Richard Church (John Rylands Library, University of Manchester); Winston Churchill (Churchill College, Cambridge); Nancy Cunard (Harry Ransom Humanities Center, University of Texas at Austin); Lionel Curtis (Bodleian Library); T. S. Eliot (Valerie Eliot); Peter Fleming (University of Reading); the *Guardian* (John Rylands Library); Denis Johnston (Trinity College Library, Dublin); Geoffrey Keynes (Cambridge University Library); Alan Lascelles (Churchill College, Cambridge); Rosamond Lehmann (King's College, Cambridge); Nico Llewellyn-Davies; Macmillan Publishers (University of Reading); Ernest Mehew; Walter Monckton (Bodleian Library); Robert Nye (National Library of Scotland); the Royal Society of Literature; Sidgwick & Jackson (Bodleian Library); Norah Smallwood (Brotherton Library, University of Leeds); Louis Spears (Churchill College, Cambridge); Leonard Woolf (University of Sussex).

Notes

Abbreviations Used in Notes

Comfort:	Comfort Borden-Turner, later Hart-Davis
DC:	Duff Cooper
Deirdre:	Deirdre Hart-Davis, later Balfour, Wolfers, Bland and Inman
DH-D:	Duff Hart-Davis
EB:	Edmund Blunden
H-D:	Hart-Davis
H-D Tulsa:	Hart-Davis papers, University of Tulsa
JG:	Joyce Grenfell
June:	June Clifford, later Williams and Hart-Davis
L H-D Letters:	*Lyttelton Hart-Davis Letters* (The second to sixth volumes of the *Letters* are numbered as such; the first in the series was not numbered and references to it therefore appear without a volume number.)
PA:	Peggy Ashcroft
RH-D:	Rupert Hart-Davis
Ruth:	Ruth Ware, later Simon and Hart-Davis
SH-D:	Sybil (Sibbie) Hart-Davis

Chapter 1 (pages 1–15)

1 DC diary, December 1909, Norwich papers.
2 SH-D to RH-D, 26 November 1923, DH-D papers.
3 DC diary, 13 January 1948.
4 Susan Lady Tweedsmuir to RH-D, 18 July 1975, DH-D papers.
5 SH-D diary, 30 July 1910; 11 March 1910; 21 March 1910; 29 March 1911, DH-D papers.
6 Ibid., 7 February 1910.
7 *The Arms of Time*, p76.
8 RH-D to Deirdre, 25 January 1976, DH-D papers.
9 *The Arms of Time*, p30.
10 Conversation with Sir Martyn Beckett.
11 I am indebted to Richard Garnett for drawing my attention to this.
12 *The Bulletin and Scots Pictorial*, 20 December 1929.
13 JG to Virginia Graham, 8 August 1970, JG papers.

14 RH-D to Deirdre, 10 March 1996.
15 Deirdre's 'Memories of Childhood', Lucy Bland papers.
16 *The Arms of Time*, p32.
17 Mrs Lowis to RH-D, 20 December 1928, DH-D papers.
18 DC diary, 19 August 1917.
19 *Some Sort of Genius: A Life of Wyndham Lewis*, Paul O'Keefe, London, 2000, pp200–207.
20 Richard H-D to SH-D, undated, DH-D papers.
21 DC diary, seriatim.
22 Nancy Cunard diary, 7 June 1919, DH-D papers.
23 RH-D diary, 2 January 1925, DH-D papers.
24 Deirdre's 'Memories of Childhood'.
25 SH-D to RH-D, 12 October 1919, DH-D papers.
26 *The Arms of Time*, p91.
27 DC diary, undated and 25 December 1917.
28 *The Power of Chance*, p28.
29 SH-D diary, 1 May 1916.
30 RH-D diary, 2 May 1928.
31 *The Arms of Time*, p62.
32 RH-D to Edmund Blunden, 29 December 1965, EB papers.
33 RH-D to Deirdre, 12 December 1982.
34 Deirdre to RH-D, 1 July 1992, Annabel Rathbone papers.
35 Deirdre's 'Memories of Childhood'.
36 DC diary, 25 July 1922.
37 SH-D to RH-D, 5 June 1924 and 26 March 1925; RH-D to SH-D, 27 March 1925.
38 RH-D's school reports are among the DH-D papers.

Chapter 2 (pages 16–30)

1 RH-D to Deirdre, 15 July 1990, DH-D papers.
2 Conversation with Lady Silsoe.
3 *The Arms of Time*, p78.
4 DC diary, 28 April 1921, Norwich papers.
5 *The Arms of Time*, p104.
6 RH-D to Alan Lascelles, 15 April 1974, Lascelles papers.
7 E. L. Churchill's report of July 1921, DH-D papers.
8 *L H-D Letters*, VI, p17; *The Arms of Time*, pp106–108.
9 DC diary, 10 October 1921.
10 Ibid., 13 November 1921.
11 RH-D to SH-D, 7 and 16 October 1922, DH-D papers.
12 E. L. Churchill to SH-D, Christmas 1922, DH-D papers.
13 Ibid., April and July 1923.
14 E. L. Churchill to RH-D, 1 December 1921, H-D Tulsa.
15 SH-D to RH-D, 16 October 1922, DH-D papers.
16 Ibid., undated, probably 20 September 1921.
17 RH-D to Deirdre, 6 February 1977.
18 SH-D to RH-D, 4 April 1923.
19 RH-D to SH-D, 3 April 1923.

20 Ibid., 20 May 1923.
21 Ibid., undated and 30 October 1923.
22 *The Arms of Time*, p115.
23 *To Keep the Ball Rolling*, Anthony Powell, Penguin edition, London, 1983, p410.
24 E. L. Churchill to RH-D, undated.
25 Maurice Baring to RH-D, undated, H-D Tulsa.
26 RH-D diary, 8 July 1922, DH-D papers.
27 RH-D to SH-D, 9, 16 and 21 May 1924.
28 RH-D to Deirdre, 19 August 1948.
29 E. L. Churchill to RH-D, 24 October 1921.
30 RH-D to SH-D, 8 March 1925.
31 *The Arms of Time*, p133; RH-D to SH-D, 21 July 1925.
32 RH-D to SH-D, 23 May 1926.
33 *Another Self*, James Lees-Milne, London, 1970, pp38–40.
34 RH-D diary, 7 January 1922.
35 *Eton College Chronicle*, 17 December 1925.
36 RH-D diary, 19 March 1926.
37 *Eton College Chronicle*, 25 March 1926.
38 Report for Lent Half, 1926, DH-D papers.
39 Report for Michaelmas Half, 1925.
40 *The Arms of Time*, p134.
41 RH-D to SH-D, 26 May 1926.
42 *The Arms of Time*, p129.

Chapter 3 (pages 31–42)

1 Rev. M. R. Ridley to E. L. Churchill, 14 December 1925, Balliol College Archives.
2 Churchill to Ridley, 10 December 1925, ibid.
3 Ibid., 21 December 1925.
4 *Peter Fleming*, Duff Hart-Davis, London, 1974, p52.
5 RH-D to SH-D, 8 December 1925, DH-D papers.
6 *L H-D Letters*, IV, p20.
7 Ibid., Vol. III, p30.
8 Iris Tree to SH-D, 14 March 1917, H-D Tulsa.
9 RH-D to Deirdre, 11 February 1975, DH-D papers.
10 Deirdre diary, 16 August 1927, DH-D papers.
11 RH-D to Deirdre, 22 April 1990.
12 Ibid., 5 January 1986.
13 RH-D to SH-D, 31 October 1926; SH-D to RH-D, 1, 9 and 15 November 1926.
14 RH-D to Deirdre, 10 November 1968.
15 *The Arms of Time*, p143.
16 RH-D to SH-D, 15 December 1926.
17 Dr Risien Russell to Richard H-D, 13 January 1927, DH-D papers.
18 Peter Fleming to RH-D, late 1926, H-D Tulsa.
19 Duff to Diana Cooper, 3 January 1927, *A Durable Fire: The Letters of Duff and Diana Cooper*, ed. Artemis Cooper, London, 1983, pp242–3.
20 Deirdre's 'Memories of Childhood', Lucy Bland papers.
21 *L H-D Letters*, II, p136.

22 Duff to Diana Cooper, 28 January 1927, *Durable Fire*, p248.
23 *Duff Cooper*, John Charmley, London, 1986, p59.
24 Nancy Cunard to RH-D, early 1927, H-D Tulsa.
25 RH-D to Deirdre, 14 June 1987.
26 RH-D to Comfort H-D, 11 May 1941, DH-D papers.
27 *The Power of Chance*, p3.
28 *Praise from the Past*, p9.
29 M. R. Ridley to RH-D, 28 March 1927, June H-D papers.
30 RH-D to Deirdre, 28 April 1967.
31 DH-D papers.
32 Robin Brindley to RH-D, 3 March 1983, June H-D papers.

Chapter 4 (pages 43–56)

1 Augustus John to RHD, 2 March 1927, H-D Tulsa.
2 RH-D diary, 26 August 1928, DH-D papers.
3 Ibid., 3 March 1928.
4 *Vic-Wells: The Work of Lilian Baylis*, ed. Harcourt Williams, London, 1938, p2.
5 *Lilian Baylis*, Sybil and Russell Thorndike, London, 1938, p100.
6 RH-D, 'Letter from London', *Isis*, February 1928.
7 RH-D diary, 26 February, 22 and 27 March 1928.
8 Ibid., 28 May 1928.
9 Jean Forbes-Robertson to RH-D, undated, H-D Tulsa.
10 *The Power of Chance*, p10.
11 Ibid., p8.
12 Harman Grisewood to RH-D, 2 April 1928, H-D Tulsa.
13 *L H-D Letters*, IV, pp23-4.
14 RH-D diary, 13 March 1928.
15 RH-D to Deirdre, 11 January 1976, DH-D papers.
16 RH-D diary, 11, 12, 13 and 16 April 1928.
17 *Old Vic Magazine*, May 1928.
18 RH-D diary, 10 and 24 April 1928.
19 Peter Fleming to RH-D, 4 November 1927, H-D Tulsa.
20 RH-D diary, 30 June and 17 August 1928.
21 Peter Fleming to RH-D, 6 October 1928
22 RH-D diary, 20 October 1928.
23 Peter Fleming to RH-D, 21 April 1928.
24 *Daily Chronicle*, 22 September 1927.
25 *L H-D Letters*, II, p199.
26 RH-D diary, 19 December and 15 May 1928.
27 RH-D to Deirdre, 16 April 1989.
28 *The Power of Chance*, p11.
29 *Another Self*, James Lees-Milne, London, 1970, pp75-6.
30 James Lees-Milne to RH-D, 17 May 1970, H-D Tulsa.
31 RH-D diary, 21 and 23 August 1928.
32 *Peter Fleming*, Duff Hart-Davis, London, 1974, p53.
33 *The Power of Chance*, p20.

34 RH-D diary, 28 February 1928.
35 *L H-D Letters*, III, p117.
36 *Eric Linklater*, Michael Parnell, London, 1984, p145.
37 RH-D diary, 9 and 12 March 1928.
38 RH-D to Magnus Linklater, 14 July 1997, June H-D papers.
39 RH-D diary, 31 March 1928.
40 Ibid., 12 July 1928.

Chapter 5 (pages 57–70)

1 RH-D diary, 1 March to 7 April, 1929, passim, DH-D papers.
2 RH-D to Kate Fleming, 17 November 1988, Kate Fleming papers.
3 *Peggy Ashcroft*, Michael Billington, London, 1988, p8.
4 *The Secret Woman: A Life of Peggy Ashcroft*, Garry O'Connor, London, 1977, p10.
5 RH-D diary, 29 May 1929.
6 *The Secret Woman*, p21.
7 RH-D to Kate Fleming, 17 November 1988.
8 PA to RH-D, 12 June 1929, DH-D papers.
9 Ibid., 26 June 1929.
10 Ibid., 29 June 1929.
11 Ibid., 26 June 1929.
12 RH-D's letters to PA written during this holiday are in DH-D's papers. Their counterparts do not survive.
13 Celia Johnson to RH-D, 14 August 1929, Kate Fleming papers.
14 RH-D to PA, 23 August 1929, DH-D papers.
15 Ibid., 30 August 1929.
16 *Alistair Cooke*, Nick Clarke, London, 1999, p41.
17 RH-D to PA, 5 August 1929.
18 Ibid., 31 August 1929.
19 Peter Fleming to RH-D, 23 October 1929, H-D Tulsa.
20 *Ashcroft*, Billington, p34.
21 RH-D to PA, 19 August 1929.
22 PA to RH-D, 4 September 1929.
23 *Evening Standard*, 4 November 1929; *Daily Mirror*, 21 January 1930.
24 PA to RH-D, 20 November 1931.
25 *L H-D Letters*, V, p111.
26 PA to RH-D, 12 May 1931.
27 *A Mingled Measure*, James Lees-Milne, London, 1964, p230.
28 *The Power of Chance*, p44.
29 *The Secret Woman*, pp20–21.
30 *Ashcroft*, Billington, p31.
31 *The Power of Chance*, p56.
32 *J. B. Priestley*, Vincent Brome, London, 1988, pp115–24.
33 PA to RH-D, 7 November 1931.
34 Ibid., 4 September 1929.
35 RH-D to PA, 5 September 1929.
36 PA to RH-D, 13 March 1930 and 20 November 1931.

37 RH-D to Deirdre, 10 December 1989.
38 RH-D to Hamish Hamilton, 29 October 1931, H-D Tulsa.
39 Harman Grisewood to RH-D, 23 October 1931, H-D Tulsa.
40 *The Power of Chance*, p57.
41 PA to RH-D, 20 and 29 October, 7 and 26 November 1931.

Chapter 6 (pages 71–87)

1 RH-D to PA, 14 August 1929, DH-D papers.
2 Ibid., 16 August 1929.
3 RH-D diary, 29 January 1931; RH-D to Deirdre, 24 June 1990, DH-D papers.
4 *L H-D Letters*, II, p30.
5 RH-D diary, 9 February 1931.
6 Ibid., 12 June 1931.
7 RH-D to Deirdre, 3 November 1974.
8 *Jamie: An 80th Birthday Tribute*, privately printed, p22.
9 RH-D to Deirdre, 7 August 1983.
10 *William Heinemann: A Century of Publishing*, John St John, London, 1990, p196.
11 *Bookseller*, 2 May 1946.
12 *The Power of Chance*, pp40–41.
13 *Louis MacNeice*, Jon Stallworthy, London, 1995, pp134–50.
14 Nancy Cunard to RH-D, 9 and 21 January 1930, H-D Tulsa.
15 Keith Winter to RH-D, 26 May 1930, H-D Tulsa.
16 RH-D diary, 8 January 1931.
17 Ibid., 15 and 21 January 1931.
18 *William Heinemann*, p205.
19 *In His True Centre*, Arnold Haskell, London, 1951, p77.
20 Peter Fleming to RH-D, 30 September 1931, H-D Tulsa.
21 RH-D diary, 13 January 1931.
22 Graham Greene to RH-D, 7 February 1932, H-D Tulsa.
23 *The Power of Chance*, p61.
24 RH-D diary, list of books read in July 1928.
25 *Praise from the Past*, p14.
26 *Edmund Blunden*, Barry Webb, London, 1990, pp194 and 237.
27 RH-D to EB, 8 March 1952, EB papers.
28 Clemence Dane to RH-D, undated, H-D Tulsa.
29 *Blunden*, Webb, p193.
30 PA to RH-D, 5 February 1932.
31 *The Life of Graham Greene, Vol. I*, Norman Sherry, London, 1989, p425.
32 George Gordon to RH-D, 26 September 1932, H-D Tulsa.
33 *Greene*, Sherry, pp431–2.
34 RH-D to EB, 23 May 1932.
35 Somerset Maugham to RH-D, undated, H-D Tulsa.
36 RH-D diary, 13 February 1931.
37 RH-D to Celia Johnson, undated, probably June 1932, Kate Fleming papers.
38 Peter Fleming to RH-D, 19 June and 25 July 1932.
39 Eve Fleming to RH-D, undated and 10 December 1932, H-D Tulsa.

40 *Peter Fleming*, Duff Hart-Davis, London, 1974, p187.
41 Deirdre to RH-D, 2 April 1988, Annabel Rathbone papers.
42 RH-D to DH-D, 22 May 1990, DH-D papers.
43 *The Power of Chance*, pp68–9.
44 Ibid., p64.
45 Comfort to RH-D, 24 June, 22 July, 16 August 1932; 16 February 1933, H-D Tulsa.
46 Margaret Turner to RH-D, 28 February 1933, DH-D papers.
47 Comfort to RH-D, undated, probably February 1933.
48 *The Power of Chance*, p70.
49 Comfort to RH-D, 5 March 1933.
50 PA to RH-D, undated.
51 Comfort to RH-D, 15 May 1933.
52 Ibid., 8 February 1933.

Chapter 7 (pages 88–103)

1 *The Power of Chance.*, p72.
2 *L H-D Letters*, V, p26.
3 *Jonathan Cape, Publisher*, Michael S. Howard, London, 1971, p174.
4 *William Plomer*, Peter Alexander, Oxford, 1989, p208.
5 *The Blossoming World*, H. E. Bates, London, 1971, p14.
6 *Plomer*, Alexander, p208.
7 RH-D diary, 26 May 1931, DH-D papers.
8 Jonathan Cape to RH-D, 14 January 1933, DH-D papers.
9 Eve Fleming to RH-D, undated, H-D Tulsa.
10 *Alistair Cooke*, Nick Clarke, London, 1999, p137.
11 *Nancy Cunard: Brave Poet, Indomitable Rebel*, ed. Hugh Ford, Philadelphia, 1968, p30; *Nancy Cunard*, Anne Chisholm, London, 1979, pp207–208.
12 *The Power of Chance*, pp76–77.
13 Robert Graves to RH-D, 30 April 1938 and undated, H-D Tulsa.
14 *Some Sort of Genius: A Life of Wyndham Lewis*, Paul O'Keefe, London, 2000, pp361–3.
15 *The Life of Arthur Ransome*, Hugh Brogan, London, 1984, p348; Ransome to RH-D, 6 August 1934, Arthur Ransome papers.
16 Stephen Spender to RH-D, 22 August 1934, H-D Tulsa.
17 RH-D to EB, 24 October 1934, EB papers.
18 RH-D to Deirdre, 25 September 1973, DH-D papers.
19 *Plomer*, Alexander, pp194 and 200.
20 *Blossoming World*, p80.
21 H. E. Bates to RH-D, 5 February 1935, H-D Tulsa.
22 *Blossoming World*, p148.
23 RH-D to H. E. Bates, 23 February 1939, Jonathan Cape papers.
24 RH-D to Denis Johnston, 21 February and 1 March 1935, Denis Johnston collection.
25 Malcolm Muggeridge to RH-D, 23 February 1937, H-D Tulsa.
26 *John Betjeman Letters 1926–51*, ed. Candida Lycett Green, London, 1994, p149.

27 *A Kind of Survivor*, Guy Chapman, London, 1975, p169.
28 Ibid., p173.
29 *Blossoming World*, p111.
30 *Stevie Smith*, Frances Spalding, London, 1988, pp122–3.
31 Robert Frost to RH-D, 16 January 1937, H-D Tulsa.
32 C. Day-Lewis to RH-D, 10 March 1935, H-D Tulsa.
33 *The Buried Day*, C. Day-Lewis, London, 1960.
34 *C. Day-Lewis: A Literary Life*, Sean Day-Lewis, London, 1980, p90.
35 *Eric Linklater*, Michael Parnell, London, 1984, p96.
36 Ibid., pp169 and 163.
37 *Praise from the Past*, p50; *The Gates of Memory*, Geoffrey Keynes, Oxford, 1981, p250.
38 Geoffrey Keynes to RH-D, 1 April 1940, H-D Tulsa.
39 *Vita*, Victoria Glendinning, London, 1983, p267.
40 Osbert Sitwell to RH-D, 1 February 1935, H-D Tulsa.
41 *The Power of Chance*, p74.
42 Edward Garnett to RH-D, 29 September 1934, H-D Tulsa.
43 Ibid., 18 August 1934.
44 Ibid., 22 August 1934.
45 RH-D to EB, 4 August 1936.
46 Theodora Bosanquet to RH-D, 14 May 1945, H-D Tulsa.
47 Peter Fleming to RH-D, 15 January 1937, H-D Tulsa.
48 RH-D to DC, 19 March 1946, Norwich papers.
49 *The Power of Chance*, p121.
50 *Darling Ma*, Joyce Grenfell, ed. James Roose-Evans, London, 1988, pp36 and 43.
51 *Linklater*, Parnell, p195.

Chapter 8 (pages 104–116)

1 *Under Two Flags*, Max Egremont, London, 1997, pp140–41.
2 Comfort to RH-D, 7 February 1941, DH-D papers.
3 Churchill papers, CHUR 8/624/187.
4 RH-D to EB, 28 September 1939, EB papers.
5 Comfort to RH-D, 16 January 1940.
6 Ibid., 2 January 1940.
7 Ibid., 10 July 1940.
8 RH-D to EB, 24 July 1940.
9 RH-D to Comfort, 25 August 1940, DH-D papers.
10 Ibid., 1 August 1940.
11 RH-D to EB, 7 August 1940.
12 Keynes to RH-D, 23 September 1940; Morgan to RH-D, 2 November 1940, H-D Tulsa.
13 Jonathan Cape to David Garnett, 8 October 1940, Jonathan Cape papers.
14 Hamish Hamilton to Comfort H-D, 23 October 1940, DH-D papers.
15 RH-D to Comfort, 8 December 1940.
16 Ibid., 29 September 1940.

17 Ibid., 2 October 1940.
18 Ibid., 25 September and 8 December 1940.
19 Ibid., 25 September 1940, cf. *The Power of Chance*, p109.
20 Ibid., 29 November 1940.
21 *L H-D Letters*, II, p67; *The Power of Chance*, p109.
22 *The Power of Chance*, p36.
23 RH-D to Comfort, 6 October 1940; Comfort to RH-D, 27 October 1940.
24 RH-D to Comfort, 24 November 1940.
25 David Garnett to RH-D, 10 February 1941, H-D Tulsa.
26 RH-D to Comfort, 20 April 1941; conversation with Richard Kingzett.
27 *The Power of Chance*, p138.
28 G. D. Turner to Comfort, 23 May 1941, DH-D papers.
29 RH-D to Deirdre, 14 September 1986, DH-D papers.
30 RH-D to EB, 11 December 1941.
31 Daniel George to RH-D, 22 October 1941, H-D Tulsa.
32 RH-D to EB, 29 July 1962.
33 Jonathan Cape to RH-D, 11 December 1942, DH-D papers.
34 Julian Maclaren-Ross to RH-D, 15 November 1942, H-D Tulsa.
35 Ibid., 7 February 1943.
36 Nancy Mitford to RH-D, 3 May 1944, H-D Tulsa.
37 RH-D to Deirdre, 11 April and 5 September 1943.
38 Ibid., 26 September 1943.
39 RH-D to EB, 1 March 1944.
40 Daniel George to RH-D, 24 July 1944, H-D Tulsa.
41 Lt Col. Maurice Trew to RH-D, 5 April 1945, DH-D papers.
42 RH-D to Deirdre, 16 September 1990 (quoting letter received in 1979).

Chapter 9 (pages 117–129)

1 RH-D diary, 13 February 1940; RH-D to Comfort, 15 July and 25 October 1940, DH-D papers.
2 C. V. Wedgwood to RH-D, 23 June 1943, H-D Tulsa.
3 Ibid., 8 July 1944.
4 Ibid., 10 December 1944.
5 Ibid., undated.
6 Ibid., undated.
7 Ibid., 14 April 1944.
8 J. Maclaren-Ross to RH-D, 3 June 1944, H-D Tulsa.
9 RH-D to Jonathan Cape, 9 November 1942, H-D Tulsa.
10 H. E. Bates to RH-D, 15 November 1944, H-D Tulsa.
11 DC to RH-D, 15 September 1942, *Duff Cooper*, John Charmley, London, 1986, p164.
12 Jonathan Cape to RH-D, 14 September 1942, Jonathan Cape papers.
13 DC to RH-D, 29 September 1942.
14 C. V. Wedgwood to RH-D, 27 April 1943, H-D Tulsa.
15 RH-D to Jonathan Cape, 22 April 1943, Jonathan Cape papers.

16 *Chips: The Diaries of Sir Henry Channon*, ed. Robert Rhodes-James, London, 1967, p363.
17 RH-D to Ernest Mehew, 9 May 1989, Ernest Mehew papers.
18 C. V. Wedgwood to RH-D, 27 April 1943.
19 Comfort to RH-D, 15 July 1940; RH-D to Comfort, 11 May 1941.
20 RH-D to Comfort, 13 January 1941.
21 Ibid., 8 June 1941.
22 Conversation with Diana Gamble.
23 *The Power of Chance*, p145.
24 RH-D to Comfort, 22 March 1941.
25 Comfort to RH-D, 18 April 1941.
26 RH-D to Deirdre, 22 October 1942, DH-D papers.
27 C. V. Wedgwood to RH-D, 27 August 1943.
28 Comfort to RH-D, 2 January 1942.
29 RH-D to Comfort, 28 April 1941.
30 RH-D to Deirdre, 28 April 1941.
31 *Reminiscences of Affection*, Victor Gollancz, London, 1968, p80.
32 RH-D to Deirdre, 26 September 1943.
33 Arthur Ransome to RH-D, 4 May 1945, Arthur Ransome papers.
34 David Garnett to RH-D, 10 February 1941, H-D Tulsa.
35 RH-D to Comfort, 15 February 1941.
36 David Garnett to RH-D, 28 January 1945.

Chapter 10 (pages 130–143)

1 *A Kind of Survivor*, Guy Chapman, London, 1975, p184.
2 Jonathan Cape to RH-D, 24 October 1945, June H-D papers.
3 *Halfway to Heaven*, p2.
4 *Jonathan Cape: Publisher*, Michael S. Howard, London, 1971, p197.
5 RH-D to DC, 19 March 1946, Norwich papers.
6 Jonathan Cape to RH-D, 14 November 1959, Jonathan Cape papers.
7 *L H-D Letters*, II, p165.
8 J. B. Priestley to RH-D, 20 November 1945, H-D Tulsa.
9 Charles Morgan to RH-D, 14 November 1945, H-D Tulsa.
10 RH-D to EB, 6 November 1945, EB papers.
11 RH-D to Deirdre, 3 April 1977, DH-D papers.
12 David Garnett to RH-D, 21 September 1938, H-D Tulsa.
13 'At the Sign of the Fox', Richard Garnett, talk given to the Double Crown Club on 8 April 1969.
14 Teddy Young to RH-D, 27 January 1946, June H-D papers.
15 *Eric Linklater*, Michael Parnell, London, 1984, p255.
16 RH-D to DC, 19 March 1946.
17 14 June 1947, Peter Fleming Mss, University of Reading MS1391.
18 *Signalling from Mars: The Letters of Arthur Ransome*, ed. Hugh Brogan, London, 1997, p328.
19 RH-D to Teddy Young, 22 January 1946, June H-D papers.
20 Ibid.

21 RH-D to William Plomer, 4 March 1946, William Plomer papers.
22 David Garnett to RH-D, 31 August 1946.
23 Richard Garnett, *Book Collector*, Vol. 50, No 3, Autumn 2001.
24 *L H-D Letters*, IV, p1.
25 RH-D to Deirdre, 23 September 1948.
26 RH-D to Annabel Rathbone, 23 February 1989, Annabel Rathbone papers.
27 *L H-D Letters*, p42.
28 RH-D to Paul Chipchase, 19 October 1984, Paul Chipchase papers.
29 Conversation with Robert Cross.
30 RH-D to Arthur Ransome, 3 February 1944, Arthur Ransome papers.
31 John Bayley to RH-D, 28 May 1950, H-D Tulsa.
32 *L H-D Letters*, p18.
33 RH-D to EB, 29 December 1962.
34 RH-D to William Plomer, 26 March 1969.
35 Michael Sadleir to RH-D, 9 May 1946, June H-D papers.
36 David Garnett to RH-D, 31 August 1946.
37 RH-D to Robert Nye, 5 October 1973, Robert Nye papers.
38 RH-D to DC, 19 March 1946.
39 DC to RH-D, 3 February 1947, Norwich papers.
40 RH-D to Eric Linklater, 22 May 1946, Eric Linklater papers.
41 *Linklater*, Parnell, p259.
42 *Halfway to Heaven*, p11.
43 *Linklater*, Parnell, p259.
44 RH-D to William Plomer, 4 March 1946.
45 RH-D to Louis Spears, 14 March 1951, Spears papers 2/17A.
46 RH-D to Eric Linklater, 24 April 1949.
47 *Jonathan Cape*, Howard, p206.
48 Arthur Ransome to RH-D, 22 December 1949, Ransome papers.
49 *Ian Fleming*, Andrew Lycett, London, 1995, p201.
50 David Garnett to RH-D, 21 March 1947.
51 Conversation with June Hart-Davis.
52 Undated memoranda, H-D Tulsa.
53 RH-D to Eric Linklater, 2 June 1946.
54 Leon Edel to RH-D, 9 December 1946, 2 June and 5 May 1949, H-D Tulsa.
55 RH-D to Humphry House, 6 January 1949, H-D Tulsa.
56 RH-D to Deirdre, 30 August 1948.
57 David Garnett to RH-D, late 1948.

Chapter 11 (pages 144–159)

1 Arthur Ransome to RH-D, 19 October 1948, Arthur Ransome papers.
2 RH-D to Arthur Ransome, 12 April 1949, Ransome papers.
3 RH-D to EB, 10 October 1949, EB papers.
4 RH-D to William Plomer, 18 November 1967, William Plomer papers.
5 RH-D to Arthur Ransome, 20 August and 25 October 1948.
6 David Garnett to RH-D, 26 June 1950, H-D Tulsa.

7 RH-D to Deirdre, 15 August 1950, DH-D papers.
8 RH-D to Arthur Ransome, 23 August 1949.
9 RH-D to Deirdre, 19 February 1989.
10 *The Saga of Ring of Bright Water*, Douglas Botting, London, 1993, pp150-55.
11 RH-D to Siegfried Sassoon, 30 April 1946, Siegfried Sassoon papers, Add. 8887/168.
12 Quoted in RH-D to Deirdre, 10 January 1993.
13 RH-D to EB, 18 February 1950.
14 Arthur Ransome to RH-D, 22 December 1949.
15 *Alistair Cooke*, Nick Clarke, London, 1999, pp257-60.
16 RH-D to DC, 2 February 1949, Norwich papers.
17 Arthur Ransome to RH-D, 3 March 1950.
18 RH-D to EB, 9 July 1949.
19 Ibid., 3 December 1949.
20 Ibid., 3 May 1949.
21 DC to RH-D, 16 May 1949, Norwich papers.
22 T. S. Eliot to RH-D, 17 February 1949, H-D Tulsa.
23 *Rosamond Lehmann*, Selina Hastings, London, 2002, p259.
24 RH-D to Rosamond Lehmann, 5 April 1953, Lehmann papers, RM14, Misc. 42.
25 Nancy Mitford to RH-D, 9 January 1946, H-D Tulsa.
26 RH-D to Arthur Ransome, 8 August 1949.
27 RH-D to EB, 13 March 1949.
28 *Edmund Blunden*, Barry Webb, London, 1990, p270; RH-D to EB, 11 April 1946.
29 RH-D to DC, 19 March 1946, Norwich papers.
30 RH-D to EB, 11 January 1948
31 RH-D to Deirdre, 6 February 1977.
32 RH-D to John Guest, 3 September 1982, John Guest papers.
33 *Hugh Walpole*, pp32, 84 and 149.
34 RH-D to EB, 11 January 1948.
35 *Halfway to Heaven*, p13.
36 *L H-D Letters*, III, p117.
37 RH-D to Teddy Young, undated, June H-D papers.
38 JG to Virginia Graham, 22 May 1966, JG papers.
39 RH-D to G. M. Young, 11 September 1946, H-D Tulsa.
40 *L H-D Letters*, III, p117.
41 RH-D to Deirdre, 16 July 1947; Deirdre to RH-D, 17 July 1947.
42 Joan Astley to the author, 4 July 2000.
43 *To Keep the Ball Rolling*, Anthony Powell, London, 1983, p405.
44 *Printer and Playground*, Oliver Simon, London, 1956, p31.
45 Conversation with Verily Anderson.
46 RH-D to Paul Chipchase, 12 November 1992, Chipchase papers.
47 June H-D papers.
48 Conversation with Diana Gamble.
49 JG to Virginia Graham, 25 May 1966, JG papers.
50 RH-D to EB, 20 February 1947.
51 Ibid., 11 April 1948.

Chapter 12 (pages 160–179)

1 *Million Dollar Movie*, Michael Powell, London, 1922, p369.
2 *L H-D Letters*, p9.
3 RH-D to Louis Spears, 23 April 1951, Spears papers.
4 Ibid., 10 April 1952.
5 *Under Two Flags*, Max Egremont, London, 1997, p279.
6 *L H-D Letters*, p173.
7 RH-D to EB, 17 January 1954, EB papers.
8 RH-D to Deirdre, 3 October 1982, DH-D papers.
9 *George Lyttelton's Commonplace Book*, ed. James Ramsden, York, 2002, p154.
10 RH-D to EB, 20 December 1953.
11 RH-D to G. M. Young, 28 July 1952; Young to RH-D, 13 November 1952, H-D Tulsa.
12 Minutes of board meeting of 25 June 1962, RCB/XL/9, King's College, Cambridge, RM15; letters to the author from Harry Townshend of 21 December 2001 and Richard Garnett of 20 December 2001.
13 David Garnett to RH-D, 7 June 1953, H-D Tulsa.
14 Geoffrey Keynes to RH-D, 7 June 1953, H-D Tulsa.
15 *Diaries 1939–1972*, Frances Partridge, London, 2000, p356; cf. Richard Garnett, *Book Collector*, Vol. 50, No 4, pp493–4.
16 Richard Garnett to RH-D, 14 January 1975, H-D Tulsa.
17 'Swaledale Diary', 4 May 1956, DH-D papers.
18 RH-D to William Plomer, 22 January 1955, Plomer papers.
19 Ibid., 5 March 1952.
20 RH-D to Deirdre, 19 November 1955.
21 *Gerald Durrell*, Douglas Botting, London, 1999, pp 204–64.
22 Maclaren-Ross to RH-D, 23 September 1952, H-D Tulsa.
23 RH-D to Maclaren-Ross, 23 February 1953, H-D Tulsa.
24 Ibid., 2 September 1953.
25 Maclaren-Ross to RH-D, September 1953.
26 Charles Causley to RH-D, 16 November 1955, H-D Tulsa.
27 Ibid., 6 December 1998.
28 Deirdre to RH-D, 19 September 1946, Annabel Rathbone papers.
29 RH-D to Thomas Mark, 5 July 1948, Macmillan papers.
30 RH-D to Rache Lovat Dickson, 5 June 1951, ibid.
31 *To Keep the Ball Rolling*, Anthony Powell, London, 1983, p406.
32 Anthony Burgess to RH-D, 16 April 1979, DH-D papers.
33 *Selected Letters of Philip Larkin*, ed. Anthony Thwaite, London, 1992, p529.
34 Daphne du Maurier to RH-D, 26 May 1953, H-D Tulsa.
35 *The Letters of Nancy Mitford and Evelyn Waugh*, ed. Charlotte Mosley, London, 1996, p270.
36 RH-D to William Plomer, 22 January 1955.
37 The collection was eventually published as *George Moore: Letters to Lady Cunard*, ed. Rupert Hart-Davis, London, 1957.
38 DH-D papers.
39 RH-D to Vyvyan Holland, 30 November 1950 and 5 January 1951, Merlin Holland papers.
40 *Halfway to Heaven*, p44.

41 RH-D to EB, 14 October 1956.
42 RH-D to Vyvyan Holland, 26 April 1960.
43 RH-D to EB, 30 December 1956.
44 T. S. Eliot papers, undated, H-D Tulsa.
45 Arthur Ransome to RH-D, 3 January 1952, Arthur Ransome papers.
46 RH-D to EB, 4 April 1954.
47 *The Arms of Time*, p138.
48 *L H-D Letters*, p6.
49 RH-D to EB, 13 March 1955.
50 RH-D to Deirdre, 18 September 1955.
51 Ibid., 2 October 1955.
52 RH-D diary, 8 June 1955, DH-D papers.
53 RH-D to Deirdre, 4 December 1955.
54 Ibid., 13 November 1955.
55 Ruth to Deirdre, 11 October 1955.
56 RH-D to Deirdre, 25 September and 13 November 1955.
57 Ibid., 10 December 1955.
58 RH-D to EB, 11 December 1955.

Chapter 13 (pages 180–199)

1 *Eric Linklater*, Michael Parnell, London, 1984, p295.
2 *Signalling from Mars: The Letters of Arthur Ransome*, ed. Hugh Brogan, London, 1997, p348.
3 *William Heinemann: A Century of Publishing*, John St John, London, 1990, p419.
4 RH-D to EB, 17 February 1957, EB papers.
5 Ibid., 20 April 1958.
6 *L H-D Letters*, III, p75.
7 RH-D to EB, 11 March 1956.
8 *L H-D Letters*, II, pp157 and 207.
9 RH-D to Mrs Beth Zion Abrahams, 3 July 1961, Holland papers.
10 Stanley Unwin to RH-D, 19 November 1958; RH-D to Unwin, 25 November 1958, Allen and Unwin papers.
11 *Halfway to Heaven*, p49.
12 *L H-D Letters*, II, p173.
13 E. M. Forster to RH-D, 14 July 1960, H-D Tulsa.
14 RH-D to T. S. Eliot, 7 January 1960, Valerie Eliot papers.
15 Siegfried Sassoon to EB, 17 July 1960, EB papers.
16 Sassoon to RH-D, 19 March 1960, Sassoon papers, Add. 9454.
17 *L H-D Letters*, III, p141.
18 Sassoon to EB, 24 November 1958.
19 *L H-D Letters*, VI, p73.
20 RH-D to Stephen Tumin, 25 October 1995, June H-D papers.
21 RH-D to EB, 1 November 1959.
22 RH-D to Elizabeth Beerbohm, undated, DH-D papers.
23 *L H-D Letters*, III, pp62, 103 and 130.
24 RH-D to EB, 29 September 1962.

25 *L H-D Letters*, p82.
26 Ibid., II, p138.
27 RH-D to EB, 1 June 1958.
28 *L H-D Letters*, II, p62.
29 RH-D to EB, 11 November 1961.
30 Ibid., 11 November 1956.
31 Ibid., 16 January 1960.
32 Ibid., 13 January 1957.
33 *L H-D Letters*, II, p140.
34 RH-D to EB, 30 December 1961.
35 Ibid., 4 April 1954.
36 Ibid., 5 January 1958.
37 *L H-D Letters*, V, p181.
38 RH-D to EB, 8 June 1963.
39 *L H-D Letters*, p3.
40 RH-D to Deirdre, 7 January 1967, DH-D papers.
41 RH-D to EB, 30 December 1961.
42 Ibid., 23 February 1963.
43 *L H-D Letters*, III, pp166 and 169.
44 RH-D to EB, 17 February 1957.
45 JG to Virginia Graham, 25 May 1966, JG papers.
46 *L H-D Letters*, IV, p64.
47 *The Letters of Evelyn Waugh and Diana Cooper*, ed. Artemis Cooper, London, 1992, p270.
48 Diana Cooper to RH-D, May 1959, Norwich papers.
49 T. S. Eliot to RH-D, 9 May 1959, H-D Tulsa.
50 Arthur Ransome to RH-D, 9 August 1961, Arthur Ransome papers.
51 *Halfway to Heaven*, p48.
52 *L H-D Letters*, V, p51.
53 RH-D to G. M. Young, 11 February 1952, H-D Tulsa.
54 *L H-D Letters*, VI, p136.
55 *Halfway to Heaven*, p58.
56 *L H-D Letters*, VI, p1.
57 *John Betjeman: Letters 1951–1984*, ed. Candida Lycett-Green, London, 1995, p176.
58 *Diaries 1939–1972*, Frances Partridge, London, 2000, pp356 and 360.
59 *Patrick O'Brian*, Dean King, London, 2000, p187.
60 *Diana Cooper*, Philip Ziegler, London, 1981, p298.
61 *L H-D Letters*, IV, p73.
62 *Waugh–Cooper Letters*, p280.
63 Richard Garnett, 'At the Sign of the Fox', talk given to the Double Crown Club on 8 April 1969.
64 Peter Fleming to RH-D, 3 September 1957, H-D Tulsa.
65 RH-D to Nancy Cunard, 1 November 1955, Nancy Cunard papers, University of Texas at Austin, Texas, Misc.
66 Ibid., 8 October 1956.
67 Ibid., 18 June 1956, H-D Tulsa.
68 Ibid., 8 September 1956, Nancy Cunard papers.

69 *Nancy Cunard*, Anne Chisholm, London, 1979, p307.
70 *L H-D Letters*, V, p163.
71 *William Heinemann*, St John, p422.
72 *L H-D Letters*, V, p141.
73 *William Heinemann*, St John, p424.
74 *In Pursuit of Publishing*, Alan Hill, London, 1988, pp163–5.

Chapter 14 (pages 200–212)

1 *Halfway to Heaven*, p59.
2 *William Heinemann*, John St John, London, 1990, p569.
3 RH-D to EB, 18 November 1961, EB papers.
4 RH-D to T. S. Eliot, 22 November 1961, Valerie Eliot papers.
5 Margaret Lane to RH-D, 18 November 1962, H-D Tulsa.
6 *L H-D Letters*, VI, p142.
7 *Halfway to Heaven*, p60.
8 RH-D to Deirdre, 29 June 1986, DH-D papers.
9 RH-D to EB, 6 January 1957.
10 Richard Garnett, 'Rupert Hart-Davis Limited: Part 3', *Book Collector*, Vol.51, No 1.
11 *L H-D Letters*, VI, p129.
12 *Harold Nicolson: Diaries and Letters 1945–62*, ed. Nigel Nicolson, London, 1968, p413.
13 *Eric Linklater*, Michael Parnell, London, 1984, p319; Fleming to RH-D, 22 May 1962, H-D Tulsa.
14 RH-D diary, 1 April 1977, DH-D papers.
15 *L H-D Letters*, VI, p169.
16 RH-D to EB, 10 March 1962.
17 *L H-D Letters*, p145.
18 RH-D to EB, 7 April 1962.
19 Ibid., 28 April 1962.
20 Ibid., 11 May 1962.
21 RH-D to Genia Ransome, 11 March 1964, DH-D papers.
22 Conversation with Lady Hodgkin.
23 Conversation with Brendan Lehane.
24 *Remembering my Good Friends*, George Weidenfeld, London, 1995, pp242–3.
25 RH-D to EB, 17 August 1963.
26 *Halfway to Heaven*, pp61–2.
27 RH-D to EB, 10 and 24 August 1963.
28 Ibid., 1 September 1963.
29 Ibid., 14 September 1963.
30 Ibid., 26 July 1964.
31 Conversation with Harry Townshend.
32 Conversation with Verily Anderson.
33 John Betjeman to RH-D, 28 August 1963, H-D Tulsa.
34 C. V. Wedgwood to RH-D, 30 August 1963, H-D Tulsa.
35 RH-D to EB, 17 January 1954.

Chapter 15 (pages 213–224)

1 RH-D to EB, 28 December 1963, EB papers.
2 RH-D to T. S. Eliot, 29 November 1962, Valerie Eliot papers.
3 RH-D to EB, 5 June 1960.
4 Peter Fleming to RH-D, 28 January 1964, H-D Tulsa.
5 RH-D to EB, 1 February 1964.
6 Duff Cooper diary, 14 January 1947, Norwich papers.
7 RH-D to Richard H-D, 6 January 1952, June H-D papers.
8 RH-D to EB, 8 June 1963.
9 Ibid., 15 February 1964.
10 RH-D to Janet Adam Smith, 31 August 1964, Andrew Roberts papers.
11 RH-D to Genia Ransome, 11 March 1964, DH-D papers.
12 RH-D to EB, 4 April 1964.
13 Ibid., 14 March 1964.
14 *L H-D Letters*, p78.
15 RH-D to Deirdre, 21 December 1969, DH-D papers.
16 *Hugh Walpole*, p167.
17 RH-D to Deirdre, 5 November 1970.
18 JG to Virginia Graham, 21 May 1966, JG papers.
19 Ibid., 22 May 1966.
20 RH-D to Deirdre, 5 November 1966.
21 Janet Adam Smith to RH-D, 2 March 1965, H-D Tulsa.
22 Margaret Lane to RH-D, 20 March 1965, H-D Tulsa.
23 Conversation with Robert Cross.
24 RH-D to EB, 9 November 1963.
25 Geoffrey Keynes to RH-D, 20 February 1966, H-D Tulsa.
26 Leon Edel to RH-D, 15 July 1964, H-D Tulsa.
27 Alistair Cooke to RH-D, 12 December 1966, H-D Tulsa.
28 Charles Causley to RH-D, 8 June 1967, H-D Tulsa.
29 RH-D to Deirdre, 23 February 1969.
30 Leon Edel to RH-D, 5 October 1968, H-D Tulsa.
31 Geoffrey Keynes to RH-D, 16 September 1968.
32 RH-D to Janet Adam Smith, 28 January 1970, H-D Tulsa.
33 RH-D to Sidney Bernstein, 29 January 1970, H-D Tulsa.
34 Bernstein to RH-D and to Janet Adam Smith, 6 and 11 February 1970, H-D Tulsa.
35 J. C. Reynolds to RH-D, 23 June 1972, H-D Tulsa.
36 Philip Ziegler to RH-D, 15 September 1983, H-D Tulsa.

Chapter 16 (pages 225–240)

1 RH-D diary, 23 January 1965, DH-D papers.
2 JG to Virginia Graham, 17 May 1976, JG papers.
3 RH-D to Deirdre, 23 October 1983.
4 Ibid., 20 July 1975.
5 JG to Virginia Graham, 21 May 1966.
6 *Halfway to Heaven*, p67.
7 *Praise from the Past*, p53.

8 RH-D to William Plomer, 18 May 1964, Plomer papers.
9 RH-D diary, 4 February 1965.
10 *Praise from the Past*, pp32–7.
11 RH-D to Deirdre, 5 November 1966.
12 JG to Virginia Graham, 21 May 1966.
13 *L H-D Letters*, V, p100.
14 Siegfried Sassoon to EB, 18 December 1965, EB papers.
15 Ibid., 30 December 1965, Sassoon papers.
16 RH-D to EB, 1 January 1966, EB papers.
17 Siegfried Sassoon to RH-D, 1 January 1966, Sassoon papers.
18 RH-D to Deirdre, 25 December 1966.
19 *Halfway to Heaven*, p74.
20 RH-D to Annabel Rathbone, 16 November 1988, Annabel Rathbone papers.
21 JG to Virginia Graham, 8 April 1967.
22 RH-D to Deirdre, 3 June 1996.
23 *Ena Twigg: Medium*, Ena Twigg with Ruth Hagy Brod, London 1973, pxv.
24 Record of conversation made by Deirdre, June H-D papers.
25 RH-D to Deirdre, 3 June 1996.
26 Rosamond Lehmann to RH-D, 18 July 1967, H-D Tulsa.
27 Record of conversation made by Deirdre.
28 RH-D to Rosamond Lehmann, 20 October 1967, Lehmann papers.
29 RH-D to Thelma Holland, 18 January 1968, Holland papers.
30 JG to Virginia Graham, 7 August 1970.
31 RH-D to Deirdre, 3 June 1996.
32 RH-D diary, 25 February 1967.
33 Siegfried Sassoon to RH-D, 21 February 1967.
34 Sassoon to Geoffrey Keynes, 24 February 1967, Keynes papers.
35 *L H-D Letters*, p103.
36 PA to RH-D, 11 March 1967, DH-D papers.
37 RH-D to Deirdre, 28 February and 1 March 1967.
38 PA to RH-D, 20 November 1931.
39 Dickin Moore to RH-D, 29 May 1957, DH-D papers.
40 RH-D to June, 5 February 1967, June H-D papers.
41 Conversation with Mrs Astley.
42 *Halfway to Heaven*, p77.
43 RH-D to June, 18 April 1967.
44 Ibid., 19 April 1967.
45 Ibid., 20 April 1967.
46 RH-D to Deirdre, 28 April 1967.
47 JG to Virginia Graham, 26 May 1968.

Chapter 17 (pages 241–262)

1 RH-D to Richard Church, 23 October 1967, Church papers.
2 RH-D to June, 21 May 1967, June H-D papers.
3 JG to Virginia Graham, 26 May 1968, JG papers.
4 RH-D to June, 27 June 1967.

5 RH-D to Deirdre, 4 February 1968.
6 Ibid., 1 February 1970.
7 June to Deirdre, undated, DH-D papers.
8 JG to Virginia Graham, 17 June 1968.
9 PA to RH-D, 11 June 1968, DH-D papers.
10 RH-D to Deirdre, 5 October 1969.
11 RH-D to Alan Lascelles, 20 July 1970, Lascelles papers.
12 RH-D to Deirdre, 26 July 1970.
13 Ibid., 4 April 1971.
14 RH-D to Alan Lascelles, 19 August 1971.
15 RH-D to Deirdre, 10 October 1971.
16 Ibid., 9 January 1972.
17 Ibid., 16 May 1971.
18 Ibid., 12 February 1978.
19 June to Deirdre, 13 May 1968.
20 RH-D to Deirdre, 13 May 1968.
21 Ibid., 8 March 1970.
22 Ibid., 15 and 22 March 1970.
23 Ibid., 21 December 1968.
24 JG to Virginia Graham, 10 July 1971.
25 June to Deirdre, 15 May 1968.
26 JG to Virginia Graham, 13 June 1973.
27 Ibid., 22 May 1978.
28 June to Deirdre, 25 August 1968.
29 RH-D to Deirdre, 8 December 1968.
30 RH-D to EB, 11 May 1963, EB papers.
31 RH-D to Deirdre, 30 December 1969.
32 Ibid., 4 October 1970.
33 RH-D to EB, 24 May 1963.
34 RH-D to Deirdre, 18 November 1967.
35 Ibid., 3 January 1971.
36 Ibid., 12 August 1973.
37 Ibid., 15 October 1969.
38 Peter Fleming to RH-D, 11 December 1967, H-D Tulsa.
39 RH-D to Deirdre, 13 July 1969.
40 Ibid., 1 November 1970.
41 Ibid., 2 November 1969.
42 Deirdre to Janet Adam Smith, 13 February 1967, Adam Smith papers.
43 RH-D to Richard Church, 8 August 1967, Church papers.
44 Hugh Brogan to RH-D, 17 May 1977, H-D Tulsa.
45 *Halfway to Heaven*, pp90 and 92.
46 RH-D to Deirdre, 11 January 1969.
47 Ibid., 29 June 1969.
48 Ibid., 19 September 1971.
49 *L H-D Letters*, V, p156.
50 RH-D to Deirdre, 11 July 1971.
51 June to Deirdre, 9 August 1973.

52 RH-D to Deirdre, 22 March 1969 and 17 January 1970.
53 Ibid., 27 November 1968.
54 Ibid., 8 and 15 April 1975.
55 RH-D to William Plomer, 23 August 1969, Plomer papers.
56 *L H-D Letters*, III, p134.
57 RH-D to William Plomer, 21 November 1972.
58 RH-D to Sassoon, 15 June 1967; Sassoon to RH-D, 18 June 1967, Sassoon papers.
59 *The Autobiography of Arthur Ransome*, p353.
60 *The Life of Arthur Ransome*, Hugh Brogan, London, 1984, pp9–11.
61 RH-D to Deirdre, 13 August 1972.
62 Genia Ransome to RH-D, undated, Ransome papers.
63 RH-D to Deirdre, 3 January 1974.
64 RH-D to John Bell, 20 July 1975, Bell papers.
65 *William Plomer*, Peter Alexander, Oxford, 1989, p324.
66 RH-D to Deirdre, 25 September 1973.
67 RH-D to William Plomer, 27 April 1970.
68 RH-D to Deirdre, 6 October 1973.
69 RH-D to Paul Chipchase, 15 November 1989, Chipchase papers.
70 *Through Wood and Dale*, James Lees-Milne, London, 1998, p289.
71 Anthony Powell to RH-D, 30 September 1977, H-D Tulsa.
72 Raymond Mortimer to RH-D, 20 December 1967, H-D Tulsa.
73 JG to Virginia Graham, 10 July 1971.
74 *In Pleasant Places*, Joyce Grenfell, London, 1979, p283.
75 JG to Virginia Graham, 20 May 1978.
76 RH-D to Futura Publications, 3 October 1980, Ernest Mehew papers.
77 June to Deirdre, 21 October 1973.
78 RH-D to Deirdre, 19 October 1969.
79 RH-D to William Plomer, 26 March 1969.
80 Hamish Hamilton to RH-D, 26 August 1980, H-D Tulsa.
81 RH-D to Deirdre, 7 December 1969.
82 Ibid., 1 December 1968.
83 *Halfway to Heaven*, pp102–03.

Chapter 18 (pages 263–279)

1 *L H-D Letters*, p62.
2 JG to Virginia Graham, 22 May 1978, JG papers.
3 RH-D to Deirdre, 27 January 1980, DH-D papers.
4 June to Deirdre, 10 December 1974, DH-D papers.
5 *L H-D Letters*, III, p67.
6 RH-D to Deirdre, 13 December 1970.
7 Ibid., 15 November 1970.
8 Ibid., 16 and 30 April 1972.
9 Ibid., 23 May 1976.
10 Ibid., 11 January 1976.
11 June to Deirdre, 26 January 1976.

12 RH-D to Deirdre, 2 July 1989.
13 Ibid., 9 June 1991.
14 RH-D to Peter Alexander, 5 September 1989, June H-D papers.
15 RH-D to Deirdre, 4 February 1979.
16 RH-D to Robert Nye, 30 November 1973, Nye papers.
17 RH-D to Deirdre, 5 April 1987.
18 Ibid., 6 February 1977.
19 *Augustus John, Vol. II*, Michael Holroyd, London, 1975, p53.
20 RH-D to Deirdre, 13 April 1975.
21 *Halfway to Heaven*, p119.
22 RH-D to Janet Adam Smith, 15 February 1977, Adam Smith papers.
23 RH-D to Deirdre, 3 April 1977.
24 Alan Lascelles to RH-D, 18 February 1977, John Murray papers.
25 John Murray to RH-D, 25 March 1977, John Murray papers.
26 RH-D to Hamish Hamilton, undated draft, DH-D papers.
27 RH-D to Deirdre, 27 March 1977.
28 Hamish Hamilton to RH-D, 10 August 1987, H-D Tulsa.
29 RH-D to Ernest Mehew, 7 May 1986, Mehew papers.
30 RH-D to Roger Hudson, 26 September and 29 October 1977, John Murray papers.
31 RH-D to John Murray, 17 April 1978, John Murray papers.
32 Helene Hanff to Roger Hudson, 6 October 1978, John Murray papers.
33 RH-D to Deirdre, 2 and 29 July 1978.
34 John Murray to Roger Hudson, 10 July 1978, John Murray papers.
35 *L H-D Letters*, II, p ix.
36 *Joyce and Ginnie: The Letters of Joyce Grenfell and Virginia Graham*, ed. Janie Hampton, London, 1997, p471.
37 23 June 1985.
38 Roger Hudson to John Murray, 14 July 1981, John Murray papers.
39 RH-D to John Murray, 29 July 1980 and 15 June 1981.
40 Roger Hudson to John Murray, 14 July 1981.
41 RH-D to Roger Hudson, 19 October 1983.
42 RH-D to Deirdre, 5 April 1981.
43 *Selected Letters of Philip Larkin, 1940–1985*, London, 1992, p714.
44 Alan Beadle to RH-D, 30 September 1987, DH-D papers.
45 RH-D to John Murray, 30 July 1984.
46 John Murray to RH-D, 25 January 1985.
47 *L H-D Letters*, p13.
48 RH-D to Jane Gardam, 13 August 1981, Gardam papers.
49 Alan Lascelles to RH-D, 24 September 1978; RH-D to Lascelles, 6 October 1978, Lascelles papers.
50 RH-D to Deirdre, 23 December 1979.
51 RH-D to Jane Gardam, 15 May 1982.
52 RH-D to Deirdre, 5 May 1974.
53 RH-D to Janet Adam Smith, 3 January 1983, Adam Smith papers.
54 RH-D to Ernest Mehew, 12 October 1987, Mehew papers.
55 RH-D to Deirdre, 8 March 1987.

Chapter 19 (pages 280–295)

1 *Halfway to Heaven*, p121.
2 RH-D diary, 25 October 1993, DH-D papers.
3 RH-D to Deirdre, 23 March 1977, DH-D papers.
4 RH-D to Janet Adam Smith, 8 December 1976, Adam Smith papers.
5 RH-D to Annabel Rathbone, 29 April 1979, Rathbone papers.
6 June to Janet Adam Smith, 15 September 1980, H-D Tulsa.
7 Deirdre to RH-D, 3 September 1987, Rathbone papers.
8 RH-D to June, 1 March 1981, June H-D papers.
9 RH-D to Deirdre, 5 August 1979.
10 RH-D to Paul Chipchase, 15 November 1989, Chipchase papers.
11 Deirdre to RH-D, 25 October 1989.
12 John Murray papers *passim*, 27 October 1984 to 15 April 1985.
13 John Murray to Merlin Holland, 15 August 1985, Holland papers.
14 RH-D to Ernest Mehew, 12 October 1987, Mehew papers.
15 RH-D to Deirdre, 15 January 1989.
16 Deirdre to RH-D, 21 February 1990.
17 RH-D to Deirdre, 17 November 1991.
18 Ibid., 26 August 1990.
19 RH-D to Paul Chipchase, 27 May 1992.
20 RH-D to Deirdre, 20 March 1994.
21 Ibid., 13 January 1991.
22 Ibid., 8 June 1997.
23 John Murray papers, 3 November 1987, 20 June and 1 July 1988; RH-D to Paul Chipchase, 24 February 1988.
24 RH-D to Ernest Mehew, 14 April 1994.
25 RH-D to Deirdre, 29 December 1985.
26 RH-D to Ernest Mehew, 11 February 1996.
27 RH-D to Paul Chipchase, 29 August 1996.
28 June to Janet Adam Smith, 17 June 1983, Adam Smith papers.
29 Deirdre to RH-D, 1 February 1990.
30 RH-D to Deirdre, 10 March 1996.
31 Ibid., 26 February 1984.
32 RH-D diary, 31 January 1990.
33 Ibid., 6 January 1990.
34 RH-D to Deirdre, 19 May 1991.
35 Ibid., 16 and 23 March 1986.
36 RH-D to June, 29 December 1997.
37 RH-D to Deirdre, 1 March 1998.
38 Ibid., 24 May 1992.
39 Ibid., 20 October 1997.
40 Ibid., 10 and 17 May 1998; to Philip Ziegler, 11 May 1998.
41 RH-D to Deirdre, 20 December 1981.
42 Ibid., 2 August 1992.
43 RH-D to June, 24 June 1994.

Index

To save endless single entries I have generally indexed individual books and plays (except for Rupert's own) under the name of the author. *Barnaby Rudge*, for instance, should be sought under Dickens, *Hamlet* under Shakespeare.

A Beggar in Purple 283-4
Adeane, Michael 258
Adlard Coles, Publisher 205
Agar, Herbert 165, 168, 178, 181
Alexander, Peter 266
Allen and Unwin, Publisher 134, 183
Allingham, Margaret 100
Anderson, Verily 156, 211
Arnold, Matthew 59
Arran 243, 255, 263
Ashcroft, Peggy 51; wooed by Rupert 58-62; engaged 63; married 64; marital disasters 65-70, 74, 80, 83; and Rupert's second marriage 84, 86, 101, 230, 235-6; and June 244, 247, 288
Astley, Joan 237
Atkinson, Harold 254
Auden, W. H. 96, 227, 259
Austen, Jane 72, 149
Ava, Basil 27
Ayrton, Michael 151

Baddeley, Angela 51
Bailey, Jonathan 254, 293

Baldwin, Stanley 34, 163-4
Balfour, Annabel, later Rathbone 126
Balfour, Ronald 83, 127
Balfour, Susan 126
Ballantrae, Bernard 270
Balliol College 29, 31-40, 188
Bantam Books, Publisher 280
Baring, Maurice 23, 40, 76, 101, 287
Barker, Nicolas 174, 193
Barrie, James 23
Bates H.E. 89, 93-4, 95, 99, 119-20; and R H-D Ltd 133
Bayley, John 136-7, 176
Baylis, Lilian 44-8
BBC 46, 184-5
Beardsley, Aubrey 173
Beckett, Gervase 5-6
Beckett, Martyn 5
Beckett, Samuel 135
Beerbohm, Max 186, 204, 256-8, 260, 270, 279, 283, 287, 293-4
Bell, John 226
Bell, Vanessa 74
Bennett, Arnold 78, 151

Bernstein, Sydney 210–1, 221–4
Betjeman, John 35, 95, 194, 212
Birch, Alewyn 198
Blake, Nicholas, *see* Cecil Day-
    Lewis
Bland, Antony 146, 246
Bland, Lucy 265–6
Blunden, Edmumd 76; and Book
    Society 79–81, 93, 95–6; as
    cricketer 99, 105, 137; as possible
    Poet Laureate 149–50, 160, 185;
    bibliography of 204, 228–9;
    Rupert as literary executor of
    260, 283; *letters to* 106–7, 112,
    114, 132, 148–9, 152, 158, 163,
    175–7, 179, 181–2, 188–9, 201–2,
    204, 209–14, 216–7, 222, 249–50
Bodley Head, Publisher 178, 198
Bookseller, The 75
Book Society, The 78–81, 85, 90,
    127, 147
Borden, Mary 84, 190
Bott, Alan 78, 83, 127
Bowen, Elizabeth 260
Bradbury, Ray 137, 148, 187, 294
Brighton 11, 68, 156
Brindley, Anne 40–2, 54–5
Brogan, Hugh 252, 266
Brooke, Rupert 138
Brown, Pamela 160
Browning, Robert 62, 295
Buchan, John 12, 292
Buchanan, Jack 51
Budberg, Moura 74
Bulteel, Lionel 5
Bunyan, John 38
Burgess, Anthony 172
Byam Shaw, Glen 51
Byron, George Gordon 264, 269

Callaghan, James 267
Cape, Jonathan 88–91, 94–5, 97–8,
    102, 107, 113, 117–22, 129–31,
    133, 139–40

Cape, Jonathan, Publisher 76–8, 81,
    88–99, 105, 112, 114, 117–22,
    128–31, 133–4, 138–40, 148, 162,
    211, 246, 259, 271
Cardus, Neville 177, 231
Carleton, John 231, 264
Carlyle, Thomas 23, 33, 182, 264,
    284
Casson, Lewis 45, 51
Caterham 107–10
Causley, Charles 137, 171, 222
Cave, Arthur 237, 243
Cecil, David 34–5, 190
Chamberlain, Neville 104
Chancellor, Betty 70
Channon, Henry ('Chips') 122
Chaplin, Charlie 43
Chapman, Guy 95, 130
Chatto & Windus, Publisher 92,
    179
Chekhov, Anton 35, 48
Chesterman, James 169, 192
Chipchase, Paul 157, 174, 283, 288,
    293
Christie, Agatha 100
Church, Richard 241, 252
Churchill, E. L. ('Jelly') 18–21, 23,
    26, 29, 31–2
Churchill, Winston 105, 164, 184,
    188
Clark, Kenneth 251
Clifford, Edith ('Mumsie') 242, 282
Clifford, June, *see* Hart-Davis
Coburn, Kathleen 247
Coleridge, Samuel Taylor 205, 211,
    247, 292, 294
Collins, William, Publisher 162,
    165, 168, 178, 211, 224, 261
Connolly, Cyril 74, 172, 176, 203
Conrad, Joseph 151, 292
Constable, Publisher 137, 178
Cooke, Alistair 63, 91, 148, 157,
    222

Cooper, Alfred 1
Cooper, Alfred Duff 1, 2;
  relationship with Sibbie 4, 8–9;
  befriends Rupert 10, 14, 17–9,
  26; and Sibbie's death 37–40, 66;
  biographer of Talleyrand 76,
  90–1; on Louis Spears 84, 102,
  104, 106; author of *King David*
  120; and R H-D Ltd 131, 133,
  138–9, 141, 148, 149, 151, 161;
  death 162–3, 195, 216, 260, 284
Cooper, Diana 19, 50, 66, 191;
  memoirs of 195–6
Corneille, Pierre 24
Coward, Noël 57
Craig, Maurice 36
Crathorne, Nancy 252–3
Crispin, Edmund 100
Crum, Madge 5
Cullis, Stanley 192–3, 294
Cunard, Emerald 173
Cunard, Nancy 4, 9, 17, 38–9, 76,
  91, 196–7
Curtis-Brown, Spencer 168–9, 211

Daily Chronicle, The 50
Daily Express, The 66, 209
Daily Mail, The 147
Daily Mirror, The 64
Daily Telegraph, The 188, 271, 276
Dane, Clemence 78–80
Dartington Hall 66–7
Davis-Poynter, Reginald 210
Day-Lewis, Cecil 96, 99–100,
  149–50, 259
De La Mare, Walter 81, 150, 285
Dickens, Charles 12; collected
  letters of 142, 205, 211, 247,
  292, 294
Dictionary of National Biography
  287
Djilas, Milovan 207

Donaldson, Frances 207, 261
Doubleday, Publisher 70, 72
Doughty C. M. 89
Douglas, Alfred 174, 202
Douglas-Home, William 111
Dudley Edwards, Owen 174–5, 187
Duff, Agnes 1
Du Maurier, Daphne 84, 136, 172,
  272
Durham University 259
Durrell, Gerald 168–9, 211

Eccles, John 253
Economist, The 271
Edel, Leon 137, 141–2, 163, 206,
  222–3, 266
Eden, Anthony 188
Elba 255, 259, 263, 271, 282
Eliot, T. S. 53, 149–50, 176, 184,
  191, 201, 227, 251
Elizabeth, Queen, The Queen
  Mother 253, 274
Ellis, Havelock 81
Ellman, Richard 186, 266, 287
Elmhirst, Leonard 66–7
Eton College 13–29, 31, 35, 39, 99,
  107–8, 168, 177, 184, 189, 269,
  272
Evans, Charles 71–3, 76–7
Evans, Dwye 207
Evans, Edith 248, 253
Evening Standard, The 64
Ewart, Gavin 140
Eyre and Spottiswode, Publisher
  178–9

Faber and Faber, Publisher 91, 168,
  270, 278, 286
Feuchtwanger, Leon 61
Firbank, Ronald 53
Fisher, Guy 134
Flecker, James Elroy 23
Fleming, Eve 49, 82–90

Fleming, Ian 66, 90, 140
Fleming, Peter: at Eton 27–9; at
    Oxford 32–3, 37, 48–51, 53–4,
    59; on holiday with Rupert 60–1,
    63, 66, 71, 73, 77; and Celia
    Johnson 81–4, 87; author of
    Brazilian Adventure 90, 99, 102,
    105, 120; and R H-D Ltd 133,
    140, 158, 176, 178, 189, 196,
    203, 213–4, 219; dies 246, 251–2,
    294
Forbes-Robertson, Jean 52, 63, 67
Forster E. M. 81, 184
France, Anatole 30
Fraser, Lionel 178–9, 197–8
Freedman, Richard 258
Frere A. S. 76, 181
Frost, Robert 95–6
Futura, Publisher 280

Gaitskell, Hugh 188
Galsworthy, John 72, 98, 151
Gamble, Diana 124, 157
Gardam, Jane 275, 277, 289
Garnett, Angelica 134
Garnett, Constance 72, 89
Garnett, David 94, 97, 107, 110;
    proposes partnership 128–9, 131;
    and R H-D Ltd 132–3, 137;
    disagrees with Rupert 140–1,
    142, 144, 146, 155; quarrels with
    Rupert 164–7
Garnett, Edward 89–90, 93–4,
    98–9, 128, 295
Garnett, Richard 138n, 144–5, 147,
    160–1; takes over Young's work
    164, 166, 169, 172; becomes
    director 181, 192–3, 203, 205,
    210–1, 222, 289
Garrick Club 5, 71, 83, 150, 167,
    175, 178, 190, 229, 289
George V, King 49, 193
George VI, King 193

George, Daniel 112, 114–5, 118–9,
    172
Georgian Theatre, Richmond 252–3
Gibbons, Stella 75
Gide, Andre 24
Gielgud, John 51, 59, 66, 255
Giraudoux, Jean 101
Goldsmith, Oliver 48–9, 58, 146
Gollancz, Publisher 91, 179
Gollancz, Victor 92, 193, 230, 232
Goodman, Arnold 210
Gordon, George 78, 80–1
Gosse, Edmund 276
Gould, Gerald 92
Goulden, Richard 51
Goverts, Henry 146, 164
Graham, Virginia 244, 272
Granada, Publisher 210–1, 221–5,
    249
Grant, Duncan 74
Graves, Robert 79, 91–2
Greene, Graham 66, 78, 80–1, 249
Grenfell, Joyce 6, 102; on Comfort
    and Ruth 154, 157, 190–1, 207;
    at Marske 219–20, 226–9; after
    Ruth's death 231, 243–5; and
    June 239–40, 242, 244, 248–9,
    253; edited by Rupert 261–2;
    dies 263–4, 265, 272, 282
Grenfell, Reggie 248, 264
Griffith, Hubert, 48
Grigson, Geoffrey 274, 294
Grimond, Kate (*née* Fleming) 266
Grisewood, Harman 46, 69
Gross, John 193
Guardian, The 271, 274
Gyde, Arnold 77

Haggard, Rider 24
Halcot 13–4, 24
Haldane J. B. S. 176
Halfway to Heaven 168, 286–7
Hall, Peter 58

Hall, Radclyffe 53
Hamilton, Hamish (Jamie) 52, 63,
  67, 69; and Rupert's publishing
  71–2, 77, 107, 132, 230, 252,
  262, 265; wants to publish
  Rupert 270, 275, 288
Hamilton, Yvonne 265, 288–9
Hamish Hamilton, Publisher 179,
  275, 277, 284
Hanff, Helen 271
Harcourt Brace, Publisher 199–212,
  215, 225
Hardy, Thomas 24, 127, 137, 171,
  284
Harrer, Heinrich 163, 192
Harris, Frank 174
Hart-Davis, Adam 16, 125–6, 153,
  158, 168, 189–90, 203, 216,
  245–6, 280, 289–90, 294
Hart-Davis, Bridget (later Lady
  Silsoe) 101–2, 122–3, 125–7, 159,
  188–9, 214, 216, 235, 244–5,
  249, 281, 290
Hart-Davis, Comfort (*née* Borden-
  Turner): wooed by Rupert 84–7,
  99, 101–2, 104–5; in America
  106–11, 117, 122–7, 129; failure
  of marriage 153, 155, 157–8, 168,
  190–1; agrees to divorce 213–4,
  216–7, 219, 229, 242, 244; dies
  245, 247–9
Hart-Davis, Deirdre (successively
  Mrs Balfour, Wolfers, Bland and
  Inman) 4; birth 6; personality
  6–7; relationship with Rupert 6,
  7–9, 13–4; death of mother 37–9;
  comes out 50–2; marries 83, 87;
  widowed 126–7; and Rupert's
  marriage 153, 155, 162, 171, 216,
  226; and Ruth's death 230–6;
  and June 239, 246, 252; and
  memoir of mother 256, 276,
  281–3, 288; dies 289; *letters to* 4,

21, 34, 41, 47, 52, 69, 74, 93,
  114, 125, 127, 146, 179, 210,
  218, 220, 223, 226, 228–9,
  242–4, 246–53, 255–6, 259–67,
  270, 274, 278–82, 285–6, 288,
  290–2
Hart-Davis, Duff 101, 105, 123–7,
  158, 188–9, 214, 216, 243–6,
  280–1, 286
Hart-Davis, June (*née* Clifford) 134,
  156–7, 161–2; comes to Marske
  236–42; marries Rupert 243,
  246–53, 255–6, 261–6, 280–3,
  288; suffers stroke 290, 292–3;
  and Rupert's death 294
Hart-Davis, Phyllida (*née* Barstow)
  189, 280–1
Hart-Davis, Richard: ancestry 1–2;
  youth 2; marriage 3–8; and
  Rupert's parentage 5, 8; as a
  father 8–10, 13, 14, 22, 24, 31;
  and death of wife 36–8; and
  Rupert's career 40, 42; and
  Rupert's marriage 41, 64; and
  Sibbie's inheritance 83, 127–8; in
  old age 190; dies 216, 275
Hart-Davis, Rupert: ancestry 1–2;
  parentage 3–5; born 5;
  relationship with sister 6; infancy
  7–10; at preparatory schools
  11–15; at Eton 16–29; illnesses
  18–20; avoids Roman Catholicism
  22; taught by George Lyttelton
  25; friends 26–8; early acting
  28–9, 35; at Balliol 31–42; death
  of mother 36–9; first love affair
  41–2; at Old Vic 43–8; first
  serious role 47; with Nigel
  Playfair 48–51; first car 50, 54;
  writes for *Isis* 54; loves Marjorie
  MacIntyre 55–6; and Celia
  Johnson 57–62; and Peggy
  Ashcroft 58–63; marries 64; life

with Peggy 65–8; breakdown of marriage 69–70; at Heinemann's 71–7; at Book Society 77–81; and Peter Fleming 81–3; woos Comfort 84–6; marries 87; at Cape's 88–98; nature of work 90–6; edits Arthur Ransome 92; and William Plomer 93; and H. E. Bates 94; wishes to publish poetry 95–6; and Eric Linklater 96–7; influenced by Edward Garnett 98–9; reviews crime fiction 100; and plays 100–1; births of Bridget and Duff 101–2; moves to Bromsden Farm 102; at outbreak of war 104–5; joins army 106; at Caterham 107–10; Sandhurst 110–1; Pirbright 111–2; appointed adjutant 112–3; at London district 114; Pirbright again 114–6; demobilized 115–6; wartime publishing 117–22; *Other Men's Flowers* 120–2; misses Comfort and children 122–4; visits USA 125–6; becomes Walpole's literary executor 127; resumes publishing 128–9; breaks with Cape's 130–1; opens R H-D Ltd 131–8; finances 133; accommodation 134; first year's publishing 138–41; ructions with Cape's 139–40; and David Garnett 140–1; publishing in 1948 141–3; expansion 144–7; visits USA 147–8; extra-curricular activities 149–52; social life 150; undertakes Walpole biography 151–2; failure of marriage 153; and Ruth Simon 154–7; as a father 158–9; moves to Soho Square 160–1; successes of 1953 162–3; setbacks 164; reshaping of firm 165; breach

with Garnett 165–6; in Swaledale 167–8; more publishing problems 168–71; publication of *Hugh Walpole* 171–3; work as editor 173–5; takes on Wilde letters 174–5; other activities 175–7; taken over by Heinemann's 178–9; new arrangements 180–2; at London Library 182–5; rejects book ideas 186–7; changes in family 188–90; contracts jaundice 190–1; staff changes 192–4; publishing successes 194–6; and Nancy Cunard 196–7; sold by Heinemann's 197–9; taken over by Harcourt Brace 200–2; publishes Wilde letters 202–3; attempts to increase turnover 203–7; abandoned by Harcourt Brace 208–9; taken over by Granada 210–2; leaves Bromsden 213–4; buys Old Rectory, Marske 215; moves north 216; divorce and remarriage 217–8; settling in 218–21; residual publishing 221–4; entertains at Marske 225–7; awarded D Litt at Reading 227; public appearances 227–8; knighted 229–30; and death of Ruth 230–6; with June at Marske 236–7; love for June 237–40; marriage to June 241–3; progress of family 244–6; problems over entertaining 247; and money 249–50; illnesses 250–1; abandons London 251–2; takes up Georgian Theatre 252–3; and Marrick Priory 254; adopts structured life 254–5; works on *The Arms of Time* 256, 268, 275–7; and Max Beerbohm 256–8; and Ransome's

autobiography 258–9; and other people's books 259–62: and W H Smith Prize 260, 267; withdraws from society 263–6; increasing conservatism 266–7; publishes *Lyttelton Hart-Davis Letters* 268–75; exasperation with publishers 270, 273, 284–5, 287; and Sassoon diaries 277–9; love for family 280–2; and kitten 282–3; sells library 283; publishes *The Power of Chance* 285–6; final literary work 286–7; increasing isolation 288–9; and June's stroke 290–1; cataract operation 291; failing memory 292; love for June 293; dies 294; obituaries 294–5;
Characteristics: calm 16, 112, 142, 179; charm 16, 32, 73, 97; conservatism 136, 188, 266–7; dandyism 7, 62, 111; generosity 94, 98, 113, 144, 254; indifference to money 74–5, 137, 174, 194, 225, 257; indifference to religion 22, 127, 218, 231–2; industriousness/indolence 16, 20, 112, 148, 256, 261–2; insensitivity 122, 130, 166, 248; insularity 34, 61; integrity 43, 98, 136, 295; irascibility 74, 117, 119, 121, 131, 145, 168, 182, 211, 224, 265, 270, 273, 284, 287; optimism 105, 132, 179, 190, 201, 217;perfectionism 18, 144, 173, 260; self-confidence 27, 69, 71, 183; selfishness 46, 248, 254; sentimentality 109, 282–3; sexuality 17, 65–6, 84, 124, 153–5; snobbishness/indifference to class 32–3, 107–8, 116, 227; *Love of*: being in love 41, 54–6, 58–9, 62, 154, 220, 236–40;

book-collecting 14, 24, 99, 218; cricket 11–2, 25–6, 99, 161, 209, 255; food 11, 17, 108, 226; his mother 6–10, 14, 20–2, 36–9, 68–9, 275; literature 10, 12, 23–4, 35, 53, 59, 73, 151, 171, 204, 269–70, 284; *dislike of*: dancing 30, 52, 281; his father 1, 8–10, 64, 83, 216, 275; hostile criticism 74, 272, 274, 285–6; novelty 23, 44, 72, 135, 267; politics 34, 95, 188, 267; society 30, 34, 51, 63, 150, 187, 221, 226, 252, 264–5
Hart-Davis, Ruth, formerly Simon: relationship with Rupert 154–61; 164; in Swaledale 167–8; 177, 185, 190–1; in New York 193; leaves R H-D Ltd 202, 203, 209, 213–6: marries Rupert 217–8; 225–9; dies 230–6; and Rupert's remarriage 236–44, 246–9, 252, 282, 293
Hart-Davis, Sybil (Sibbie): ancestry 1; marriage 2–6; character 3–4; promiscuity 5–6, 8–9; relationship with Rupert 7–12, 14, 17–22, 24–7, 29, 31, 33, 68–9; becomes Roman Catholic 22; final illness 36–7; death 38–40, 42, 83, 162, 216, 232, 235–6, 242; and *The Arms of Time* 256, 263, 267–8, 275–6
Haskell, Arnold 66, 75, 77
Hassall, Joan 138
Hastings, Selina 266
Hatchard's Bookshop 88, 195
Heinemann's, Publisher 71–7, 83, 85, 90, 131, 162; takes over R H-D Ltd 178–82, 191–2, 195–9; sells R H-D Ltd 200–2, 205
Heinemann, William 72
Hemingway, Ernest 89

Herbert, A. P. 66
Herbert, Sydney 8–9
Heywood-Hill, Booksellers 114
Hill, Alan 198
Hill, Geoffrey 267
Hodge, Ed 209
Hodgkin, Marni 205–6
Hogarth Press 96–7
Holland, Merlin 174, 284, 287
Holland, Vyvyan 174–5, 203, 233
Holloway, Balliol 47
Holloway, David 271
Holroyd, Michael 187, 268
Hotson, Leslie 137
House, Humphry 142
Howard, Michael (historian) 194
Howard, Michael (publisher) 131
Howard, Trevor 57
Howard, Wren 77, 88, 90–2, 94–5,
    105, 117–21, 129–31
Hudson, Roger 269, 271–3, 275,
    284, 287
Hughes, David 192–3, 206
Hughes, Ted 185
Humphries, Barry 293
Hutchinson, R. C. 228, 277
Huxley, Aldous 23, 66, 176

Ibsen, Henrik 35, 44, 205, 294
Illich, Ivan 288
Inman, William 281
Innes, Michael 100
Isis, The 54

James, Henry 80, 137–8, 141–2,
    151, 163, 206, 211, 284, 294
James, Montague 22
Jerrold, Douglas 178
John, Augustus 8, 43, 187, 268
John, Romilly 76
Johnson, Celia: wooed by Rupert
    57–60; discarded 61–2, 65; and
    Peter Fleming 81–4, 102, 124,
    133, 154–5, 246, 266

Johnson, Samuel 23, 146, 284
Johnston, Denis 94
Jones L. E. 195, 252
Jovanovich, Bill 199–200, 202,
    207–9, 211
Joyce, James 24, 53, 73, 135

Keats, John 24
Kennedy, Margaret 85
Kern, Jerome 45
Ketton-Cremer, Wyndham 13, 33,
    62
Keynes, Geoffrey 97, 107; and R
    H-D Ltd 133, 145, 166, 181,
    185, 222–3, 226–7, 234
Kipling, Rudyard 12, 59, 137, 207,
    283
Kisdon Lodge 167, 214
Koestler, Arthur 95, 118–9
Komisarjevsky, Theodore 35, 86

Lamb, Charles 30
Landor, Walter Savage 137, 284
Lane, Margaret 201, 221
Lang, Andrew 221
Larkin, Philip 172, 274
Lascelles, Alan ('Tommy') 17, 176,
    229, 245–6, 258, 269, 276
Lawrence D. H. 73, 186
Lawrence T. E. 76, 89, 110, 128
Lee, Laurie 150
Leeds University 262
Lees-Milne, James 27, 52–3, 260–1,
    266
Lehane, Brendan 206
Lehmann, John 74, 176
Lehmann, Rosamond 149–50, 167,
    232–4
Leigh-Fermor, Patrick 284
Leslie, Shane 4
Lewis, Curigwen 101
Lewis, Sinclair 89
Lewis, Wyndham 8, 92

Lillie, Bea 51
Lindsay A. D. 32–3, 39
Linklater, Eric 56, 88, 96, 103; and R H-D Ltd 133, 138–41, 159, 180, 203, 294
Listener, The 35
Literary Society, 175–6, 185, 221, 229, 251–2, 269, 272
London Library 173, 182–5, 193, 221, 227, 251
Lovat Dickson, Rache 172
Lutyens, Emily 269n
Lynd, Sylvia 78, 80
Lyttelton, George 25, 28, 31, 154; engages in correspondence with Rupert 176–7; dies 204; publication of letters 268–75, 292; *letters to* 33, 38, 65, 73, 88, 100, 154, 160, 163, 178, 182–5, 188–91, 197–8, 202–5, 218, 225, 229, 235, 257, 263–4, 294; *letters from* 193, 229
Lyttelton, Humphrey 274

Macaulay, Rose 127, 172
McCallum, John 206
MacCarthy, Desmond 194
McCarthy, Mary 207–8
MacGibbon and Kee, Publisher 210, 224
McGraw Hill, Publisher 198, 201
Machell, Roger 132
MacIntyre, Marjorie 55–6, 96
MacKenzie, Compton 81
McLaren, Christabel 74
Maclaren-Ross, Julian 113, 119, 169–70
Mac Liammoir, Michael 253
Macmillan, Harold 131, 151, 188
Macmillan's, Publisher 97, 136, 171–2, 186
Macneice, Louis 75
Mailer, Norman 135

Marford, Charlie 45–7, 69, 107, 285
Mariners Library 133, 141, 145, 205
Mark, Thomas 171
Marrick Priory 254
Marsh, Ngaio 100
Maschler, Tom 259
Masefield, John 149
Maugham, Somerset 72, 81, 261
Maxwell, Gavin 147
Maxwell, Robert 165
Mehew, Ernest 174, 278, 285, 287, 289
Meredith, George 25, 27, 74, 137
Meyer, Michael 205
Meynell, Francis 140
Meynell, Victor 40
Miles, Hamish 90
Milne, A. A. 44
Mitford, Nancy 114, 150, 172
Moore, Dickin 236
Moore, George 50, 72, 173–4, 196–7
Moore, John 139
Morgan, Charles 74, 81, 107, 131, 186
Morrell, Ottoline 34
Mortimer, Raymond 29, 203, 260, 271
Muggeridge, Malcolm 94
Murdoch, Iris 137
Murray, Diana 268
Murray, Jock 268–75, 284–5, 287–8
Murray, John, Publisher 269–75, 277, 284–7
Muspratt, Eric 79

Nabokov, Vladimir 135
Naipaul, Vidia 136
Nash, Paul 54
Nelson, Thomas, Publisher 209–10
New Statesman, The 35, 128, 149

New York 70, 126, 147–8, 193, 200, 208–9
New York Times Review of Books, The 272
New Yorker, The 146, 148
Ney, Marie 51
Nichols, Beverley 93
Nicholson, William 69, 151
Nicolson, Harold 81, 148, 172, 176, 182–3, 203
Nye, Robert 138, 266

O'Brian, Patrick 194
Observer, The 35, 46, 76, 92, 148
Old Vic 42–8, 50, 54, 218
Olivier, Laurence 48, 51, 66, 100
O'Neill, Eugene 23, 89
Oppenheim, E. Phillips 24, 73
Orwell, George 79, 176
Oxford University Press 211, 245, 271

Partridge, Frances 166, 194, 286
Peacock, Thomas Love 137, 142
Pelham, Prudence 43, 56
Penguin Books 132, 178, 186, 206, 274
Penna, Lucca di 53
Pesky, Kitten 282–3
Pinter, Harold 58
Pirbright 111–2, 114–6, 119, 122, 124–5
Playfair, Nigel 48–51
Plomer, William 89, 93, 95–6, 134, 137, 139, 150, 168, 173, 227, 257; Rupert as literary executor of 259–60
Portman, Eric 11, 45–7
Potter, Stephen 140
Powell, Anthony 22, 155, 172, 203, 219, 260, 276
Powell, E. W. 29
Priestley, J. B. 67–8, 74, 77–80, 131

Publishers' Association, The 135
Pym, Barbara 172

Quennell, Peter 172

Raine, Kathleen 226
Ransome, Arthur: Cape author 92–96, 128; and R H-D Ltd 133, 136, 140–1, 144–8, 176, 180, 191, 250; autobiography of 258–9; royalties from 283
Ransome, Evgenia ('Genia') 92, 128, 176, 217, 250, 259
Rattigan, Terence 69
Reading, Stella 207
Reading, University of 227
Reed, Douglas 95
Reichmann, Eva 257
Reinhardt, Max 178
Reynard Library 146
Rhondda, Margaret 100
Rhys, Jean 260
Richardson, Ralph 66, 100–1, 255
Ricks, Christopher 267
Riding, Laura 91–2
Ridley, M. R. 31–3, 40
Robeson, Paul 45, 66–7, 100–1
Roos, Richard 193
Rossetti, Christina 85
Routledge and Kegan Paul, Publisher 211, 287
Royal Literary Fund 185
Rutherford, Margaret 231

Sackville-West, Vita 97
Sadleir, Michael 137, 178
Sandhurst 110–1, 123
'Sapper' (H. C. McNeile) 53, 292
Sassoon, George 277–8
Sassoon, Philip 51
Sassoon, Siegfried 79, 147, 150; Rupert visits 184–5, 229, 234–5; Rupert as literary executor of

258, 260, 266, 270; diaries of 277–9, 284, 294
Savile Club 150
Sayers, Dorothy 100
Scott, Walter 12, 110, 247
Seal House School 11
Secker and Warburg, Publisher 198
Severs, Boyk 227, 230, 234, 243, 252, 255
Severs, Nell 227, 230, 243, 255
Shakespeare, William 23, 35, 44–6, 48, 50, 54, 67, 100, 137, 149
Shaw, Bernard 3, 23, 28–9, 48, 72
Shelley, Percy Bysshe 27
Sheridan, Richard Brinsley 23, 49
Sherriff, R. C. 44
Simenon, Georges 123
Simon, Oliver 154, 157, 168
Simon, Ruth *see* Hart-Davis
Sitwell, Osbert 17, 79, 97, 291–2
Skinner, Martyn 277
Slocum, Joshua 141
Smallwood, Norah 264
Smith, David 26, 30
Smith, Stevie 95, 118
Smith, W. H. and Sons 26, 170; W. H. Smith Prize 260, 267, 277, 283
Snow, C. P. 137
Soho Bibliographies 205, 211
Sparrow, John 176, 203
Spears, Louis 84, 105; and R H-D Ltd 139, 162, 245
Spectator, The 35, 74, 81; Rupert reviews for 100–1, 123
Spender, Stephen 92–3, 259
Stanmore School 11–5, 18, 33
Steegmuller, Francis 161
Stevenson, Melford 266
Stevenson, Robert Louis 174, 223–4
Stockwood, Mervyn 232
Stone, Janet 225–6, 235
Stone, Reynolds 225–6

Storey, David 192, 255
Strachey, Lytton 23
Strindberg, Johan 35
Strong, Roy 258
Sunday Telegraph, The 189, 227, 275, 278, 285
Sunday Times, The 35, 76, 140, 164, 230
Sutton Publishing 286
Synge, John 35

Tennant, Stephen 278
Thackeray, W. M. 27, 247
Thatcher, Margaret 267
The Arms of Time 41, 173, 268, 275–7, 285, 291–2
The Power of Chance 66n, 285–6
Thomas, R. S. 137, 171
Thompson, Francis 186
Thorndike, Sybil 44–5, 51
Thwaite, Anthony 285–6
Tilling, Thomas, and Co 178, 180, 197–8
Time and Tide 72, 100–1, 118, 187, 204
Times, The 35, 101, 163, 182, 184, 257–8, 267, 294
Times Literary Supplement, The 172, 193
Todd, Ann 66
Tolstoy, Leo 23, 264
Townshend, Harry 144–5, 164–5, 168, 181, 198, 202, 209, 222
Tree, Iris 33
Trevelyan, G. M. 184
Trustram-Eve, David, later Lord Silsoe 189, 249
Tulsa, University of Oklahoma at 283
Tunstall, Beatrice 75
Turner, Charles Tennyson 194, 268
Turner, Douglas 84–5, 111
Turner, Margaret 85

Turner, Reggie 186, 204, 257
Twain, Mark 147–8
Tweedsmuir, Susan 2
Twigg, Ena 232–4, 236, 246
Two Men of Letters 277

Unwin, Stanley 183
Urquhart, F. F. ('Sligger') 33

Verschoyle, Derek 81
Victor, Ed 145

Wade, Alan 170, 174, 202
Waldman, Milton 165, 168, 178
Wallace, Edgar 24, 66
Walpole, Hugh 17; and Book
    Society 78–80, 127; biography of
    151–2, 168, 171–3, 175, 186,
    219, 286, 291; benefactor of
    Rupert 190, 216–7, 249–50, 260,
    283
Warburg, Fred 198
Warner, Esmond 13
Washington Post, The 258
Waugh, Evelyn 32n, 172, 191, 195,
    266
Wavell, Archibald 120–2, 130
Webb, Mary 73, 75
Wedgwood, C.V. 89, 118–22, 126,
    212

Weidenfeld, George 207–8
Weidenfeld and Nicolson, Publisher
    207–8
Wells, H. G. 72, 74
Werfel, Paul 48
West, Rebecca 150, 260, 275
Wilde, Oscar 17, 23, 46; *Collected
    Letters* of 152, 174–5, 177, 186,
    187, 190, 202–4, 245, 266;
    Selected Letters of 277; *More
    Letters* of 284–5, 287, 294
Williams, Emlyn 253
Williams, Lt Col J. H. 146, 157
Wilson, Harold 267
Wilson, Tom 205
Windsor, Duke of (King Edward
    VIII) 164, 261, 276n, 286
Woolf, Leonard 74, 266
Woolf, Virginia 74, 80, 97, 151–2,
    266

Yeats, William Butler 3, 137, 160,
    267, 284
Young, Andrew 137, 171
Young, Edward ('Teddy') 132–4,
    140–1, 154, 161, 163–4
Young, G. M. 154, 163–4, 193

Ziegler, Philip 73n, 286, 291